Research indicates that we speak, on average, about 16,000 words a day. *Speaking Code* is a powerful primer on using our words to enhance relationships. I especially appreciate the practical section on overcoming common barriers to effective communication, as well as how skillfully Di Pasquale incorporates biblical principles and verses. If you've ever longed for an effective tool to help replace hurtful speech or deadly silence with words that give life and heal hearts, *Speaking Code* is a must-read.

—KIMBERLY MILLER, MTH, LMFT

Author of *Boundaries for Your Soul: How to Turn Your Overwhelming Thoughts and Feelings into Your Greatest Allies;* counselor, speaker (kimberlyjunemiller.com)

I wish I had this book two decades ago, not only because it would have helped me deepen my own marriage and the conversations that reveal me sooner, but also because it would have better shaped the way I listen to and assist the couples and marriages under my care for so long. Di Pasquale's insightful take on orthodoxy is committed to pinning our hopes on truth rather than the false assumptions we develop from our earliest shaping experiences, helping us all to become more familiar with how our root systems work and contribute to soul crushing conversations and relationships, but also how the power of God's soul satisfying words of grace, and the practical ways to implement them day to day, can bring a renaissance to any relationship.

—DREW DERRETH

Pastor of Hanover Valley Church, PCA

In *Speaking Code,* Diana Di Pasquale patiently helps us face our past to uncover the statements and events that have molded our thoughts and influenced our conversations. She walks us, with grace, through scripture to show us how the Gospel and our relationship with Christ is the center of our healing. Diana's penetrating questions and workbook formats helped me take an honest look at myself, my relationships, and my conversations, while showing me that my Heavenly Father is the key to changing how I hear and speak to those in my life.

—BECKY

Wife, mom, grandmother, pastor's wife, lay counselor, and horse lover.

We cannot avoid conflict or misunderstanding—not indefinitely. But Di Pasquale encourages us to see those difficult exchanges as "holy sanctuaries"—places that God uses to transform us and those we speak to. Through practical exercises, personal stories, and a solid, biblical foundation, she invites us to reorient the way we view communication in a fallen world and reminds us that even the most painful conversations can be, by God's mercy, grace-filled and redemptive.

—THÉA ROSENBURG

Writer and Editor, LittleBookBigStory.com

SPEAKING CODE

SPEAKING CODE

UNRAVELING PAST BONDS TO REDEEM BROKEN CONVERSATIONS

DIANA DI PASQUALE

SQUARE HALO BOOKS

In Christian art, the square halo identified a living person presumed to be a saint. Square Halo Books is devoted to publishing works that present contextually sensitive biblical studies, and practical instruction consistent with the Doctrines of the Reformation. The goal of Square Halo Books is to provide materials useful for encouraging and equipping the saints.

The bronze relief sculptures on the cover are from the entrance of the Basilica Santa Maria degli Angeli e dei Martiri in Rome, Italy. The bound heads and the Christ figure come from the Door of the Resurrection *(2006), by a Polish artist and sculptor, Igor Mitoraj (1944–2014)*

P.O. Box 18954
Baltimore, MD 21206
www.SquareHaloBooks.com

ISBN 978-1-941106-17-4
Library of Congress Control Number: 2021939418

Printed in the United States of America

THIS BOOK

IS DEDICATED TO

ALAN DEAN

··· ·– –· · ·– –·– ·· –· – –· –·–· – – – –·· ·

LOVER BOY-COFFEE BOY-GRANDDADA/GRANDFATHER BOY-PUN MAKING BOY-GROCERY SHOPPING BOY-CAFE SITTING BOY-TEACHER BOY-MIDDLE SEAT BOY-FETCH ANYTHING BOY-COMPETITIVE BOY-GARDENING BOY-BIBLE BOY- SMARTIE PANTS BOY-WOODS WALKING BOY-TRAVELING BOY-SQUARE HALO BOY-SPORTS CRAZY BOY-CHILL BOY- PREACHER BOY-LAKE LOVING BOY-SILLY BOY-FOODIE BOY-PARENT BOY-WINE LOVING BOY-CHAUFFEUR BOY-"AS YOU WISH" BOY-CFO BOY-BEST FRIEND BOY-FARM BOY-GOD'S BOY-MY BOY (THIS IS JUST ME, SPEAKING CODE!)

CONTENTS

FOREWORD

I often wonder why there isn't a twelve-step program, like there is for Alcoholics Anonymous, for those of us who engage in problematic communication. This is how I would introduce myself if I were in such a meeting:

> *"Hello, my name is Diana, and I wound others with my words."*

All of us would qualify to be members in this twelve-step program as we process the world of communication from two sides. Sometimes we wound others and other times, we are the ones wounded. When we are wounded, we vacillate between confusion, hurt, and rejection as we try to make sense of what someone just said. When we wound others, they are confused, hurt, and feel rejected by our attempt to communicate. Something prevents the words coming from my mouth to your ears from being understood the way I intend. And what is going on with you? Why do you say things that crush my spirit? Either perspective makes us want to give up on soul-satisfying conversation. We resign ourselves to the insanity of the mundane that can lead to shallow, unfulfilling relationships. We may resolve never to talk again unless our conversations are confined to pleasantries disguised by our own self-righteousness!

Many excellent writers have explored the topic of communication. Their work is valuable and has blessed us greatly. I am writing this book because I personally struggle to be understood by others and to have them understand me. Since you and I share in our humanness, that makes us alike. Therefore, if my heart longs for soul-satisfying conversations, your heart may long for them as well.

Over many years of engaging in meaningful conversations with my clients, I have discovered that redemptive communication *is* possible. Conversations have a beginning, a middle, and an end that can span many years and involve many different voices. The benefit of this book is that it traces these conversational threads from beginning to end. Our words come from *somewhere* and take us *someplace*. This book will help us link the *somewhere* to the *someplace* in hopes of turning soul-crushing conversations into conversations that are soul-satisfying.

Soul-satisfying communication involves both speaking redemptively and listening graciously. For us to be understood, we must speak words that authentically and graciously express what is in our hearts. For us to understand others, we must engage in active but patient listening. To achieve soul-satisfying and redemptive communication, we need the Bible; therefore, this book will include Scripture. For example, the first three chapters of Genesis are particularly useful in helping us understand righteous conversations. Together we will seek our Mighty Counselor's guidance and mercy as we journey along the path toward soul-satisfying conversation.

You may ask if this journey is for you. I believe it is, but maybe not for the reasons you might think. I invite you to read the categories below and ask, "Can I find myself in these statements?" If you can locate your heart somewhere in the words and emotions below, or if you are intrigued by these thoughts, this book is for you.

If you find that, in conversations, you become frustrated because

- you feel attacked by harsh words that seem to call into question your very humanity;
- you feel shut down by fear of what might result from a conversation;
- you feel worthless, fatigued, or isolated; or
- you feel as though your words are used as a weapon against you,

then this book is for you.

If your personal history seems to interfere with how you communicate so that

- you have no idea why you say what you do, which leads you to think that communication is pointless;
- you believe your efforts to talk about an issue are never enough for the other person; or
- your past still affects how you talk to others, which may lead you to either explode or withdraw during difficult conversations,

then this book is for you.

If your communication rarely seems to work so that

- you feel people are not listening, which makes you think you are being ignored;
- you make endless efforts to reconcile a relationship, but to no avail;
- you experience such dread, when anticipating a conversation, that you decide not to speak because you believe your words will not make a difference;
- you wonder, "If I can't speak to you, to whom can I speak?"; or
- you believe you are right, but everyone else says you are wrong,

then this book is for you.

If you are a professional or lay counselor and

- you are stumped in your counseling, or . . .
- you just want to be a better communicator and a wiser listener,

then this book is for you.

BIBLICAL COUNSELING

Biblical counseling differs from other types of counseling in that it centers itself within the Bible. Therefore, this book must be rooted in the Scriptures or else it is of little value. Remember, my attempts at communication are broken, too. Anything I offer you must come from Scripture if it is to be helpful at all. I write as a participant and not as an expert.

If this biblical approach bothers you, trust me, I get that. People who I counsel often come to me not believing that the Bible offers any solutions to their communication difficulties. As we work together, sometimes we find that the Bible offers wisdom that addresses real-life conversations. Your concerns are valid. Hang in there. This is a journey. Be brave! What do you have to lose?

FORMAT OF THIS BOOK

This book has three sections. Section One introduces terminology I use to help identify the reasons we choose either soul-crushing or soul-satisfying words in conversations. Section Two continues our discussion about communication. Section Three discusses why we can have hope. This book is designed to be used as a *workbook* so that you can learn how to get communication right. Lines in the margins have been provided for you to interact with the ideas presented. Arrows following the questions suggest where you might begin to write your answers. So get to work—grab a pen and begin the journey!

These ideas may sound similar to things you have previously read or heard, particularly if you are familiar with the Christian Counseling and Education Foundation (CCEF) and the School of Biblical Counseling. The debt I owe to CCEF professors, their lectures, and their writings can never be repaid. This book draws on their collective wisdom along with my professional and personal conversations (especially with my very own Alan Dean).

Additionally, my ideas come from excellent sermons I have heard over the years from Michael Crawford and Jeremy Dickson at Freedom Church in Baltimore, Maryland. Most importantly, my understanding of soul-satisfying conversations is based on the study of real conversations between real people who suffered real problems, as recorded in the Bible.

SPEAKING CODE OVERVIEW

Section One: Communication and Scripture

Section One will introduce central communication concepts necessary for speaking redemptively. We will discuss how these ideas find their beginnings in the Creation narrative. Central communication concepts are:

- Speaking CODE
- Earliest Childhood Memories (ECMs)
- Past Powerful Identity Forming Statements (PPIFSt)/ Past Powerful Identity Forming Experiences (PPIFEx)

In this section, I will also consider how the first three chapters of Genesis shed light on our present-day conversations. While we do not know the content of the talks Adam, the Woman, and God had, we do know that they enjoyed daily conversations where they formed powerful experiences. We will link the deep implications of our Past Powerful Statements and Experiences to understand how communication works. (Just as a note, I use *Woman* as opposed to *Eve* because the experiences we will examine take place before the Fall and before Adam named the Woman Eve.)

At the back of the book you will find a list of important words and phrases (such as *Speaking CODE* and *Past Powerful Identity Forming Experiences*) that appear throughout this book.

Section Two: Communication Concepts

The second section explains soul-satisfying communication using a workbook that helps us interact with the ideas presented. This format gives us a chance to apply these communication concepts to our own experiences. I invite you to use the workbook as a convenient way to investigate your heart by writing out your responses to probing concepts and questions. We will also explore obstacles that prevent us from speaking redemptively to one another.

Section Three: Is There Hope

The third section will lay out five principles that interfere with soul-satisfying communication and how the Bible helps us overcome them. They will help us understand the barriers we face in our conversations. This section continues to provide workbook questions to help us explore these barriers. We will discuss how communication is a gospel issue when seen at the foot of the Cross.

Use of Scripture

This book is unapologetically full of Scripture because what is written in the Bible is for our instruction. God's Word helps us persevere in the hope that we can live harmoniously with each other and enjoy soul-satisfying conversations. Let us encourage one another by speaking words that edify us and bring glory to God. Read the Word of the Lord in Romans 15:4–7:

> For whatever was written in former days was written for our instruction, that through endurance and through the encouragement of the Scriptures we might have hope. May the God of endurance and encouragement grant you to live in such harmony with one another, in accord with Christ Jesus, that together you may with one voice glorify the God and Father of our Lord Jesus Christ. Therefore welcome one another as Christ has welcomed you, for the glory of God.

My desire is for this enduring and encouraging God to meet us on every page of this book so that our conversations can be harmonious to His glory.

Peter tells us that even though we know biblical truths, we need consistent reminders to stir us up, so we are ready for life. Having an abundance of Scripture about communication will stimulate us to enjoy life-giving conversations. Read the Word of the Lord in 2 Peter 1:12–15 (*emphasis added*):

> Therefore, I intend always to *remind* you of these qualities, though you know them and are established in the truth that you have. I think it right, as long as I am in this body, to stir you up by way of reminder, since I know that the putting off of my body will be soon, as our Lord Jesus Christ made clear to me. And I will make every effort so that after my departure you may be able at any time to recall these things.

When Peter knew he was about to put off his earthly body, he thought it important to remind us of qualities that will rally us in difficult times. This is for our good.

A FEW FINAL THOUGHTS

I chose not to use my clients as examples. Instead, I created imaginary scenarios based on a synthesis of many real people in real-life situations that describe basic communication themes that are common to all of us. Additionally, a few of my clients have agreed to write their own stories regarding their struggle to communicate redemptively based on the concepts I developed. Telling their stories in their own words is brave and sacrificial. I am grateful that I was allowed to be in their lives at just the right moment.

This book will also ask many questions. You may find, in some cases, that these questions have no real answers. This is purposeful. Difficult questions get us to think deeply about heart issues and drive us to the Bible for answers.

We are embarking on a journey. We need not take much with us. We simply need to be willing to look at ourselves and ask why conversations hurt us and seem to make our relationships worse. We will make progress if we have the courage to see truth, the willingness to change, and the bravery to investigate our past. God is up to something by exposing our hearts, and His work will ultimately be for our good and His glory!

We will Speak CODE for the rest of our lives because we are "perfectly imperfect" humans. That is why this book is truly a never-ending story. Read this book as though we are friends sharing our lives over hot tea served in our favorite teacup. Come with me as we discuss the joys and sorrows of our real-life conversations.

—Diana Di Pasquale

SECTION ONE

IN THE BEGINNING

HOLY SANCTUARIES

TWO INFLUENTIAL FORCES AND BRAIN DEVELOPMENT

SPEAKING CODE

BRAIN DEVELOPMENT, COMMUNICATION, AND GENESIS 3

THE SPOKEN WORD AND OUR PATH

ADAM'S SIN AND COMMUNICATION

IN THE BEGINNING

"It's been such a hard week for us, and especially for you," Alan Dean sighed as we exited the Baltimore Beltway and finally headed for home.

I agreed. "Sure has! And I, for one, am so glad it is over."

"You know what? Instead of heading home, let's go to the movies," Alan Dean suggested. "Why don't you check your phone for a movie you want to see?"

Now you might be thinking to yourself, "What a nice husband Alan Dean is (and he is). He gets it (and he does). I wish my husband would be like Alan Dean (maybe so)." You may even think I live in a redeemed garden of Eden with a husband who anticipates my every need (let's not go overboard here).

Alan Dean and I have been married for more than 40 years. Four children, six grandkids, and one great-granddaughter later, he knows that even though we have a state-of-the-art, flat-screen TV at home, there is little I love more in this world than to escape to the movies except spending my retirement years as a professional café sitter anywhere in Europe. I crave the scent of popcorn, the taste of the semi-liquid, salted ooze they pass off for butter, the guilt-alleviating Diet Coke, the dim lights, the perfect loudness of the speakers, and the comfort of the reclining seats. I love that no one can see me and that I must turn off my cell phone. What I am watching is almost secondary to the movie experience itself.

In the early years of our marriage, we did not have much money. When Alan Dean made his offer, it was a special treat because we did not go out very often. I was delighted and felt myself submitting to a wave of calmness that already began to overtake me. "Really, honey, really? You aren't too tired?"

"No. Pick the movie and we will go," Alan Dean said with assurance.

"Let's go to that new movie I told you I wanted to see. I'll Google it and see where it is playing, and we'll head over."

SOMETHING'S HAPPENING HERE

Recall the serpent's first question in the garden of Eden: "Did God really say?" Enter Genesis 3:1, with a slight rewrite of characters. Did Alan Dean really say, "You know what? Instead of heading home, let's go to the movies. Why don't you check your phone for a movie you want to see and we will go?"

Unbeknownst to me, at that time, our budget would not allow us to afford a first run movie with popcorn, Diet Coke, and chocolate candy at the local mall's metroplex. Alan Dean knew the budget because he paid the bills. As soon as he realized I wanted to go to a first run movie and not the local second run theater we more typically frequented, something began to happen in his heart.

Alan Dean's heart had an unidentified feeling that something was wrong. The ambiguity of his inner conversation, or self-talk, could have been expressed like this: "Oh my goodness! What have I done? I just offered Diana something I know she loves to do—but we simply cannot afford it. Where will I find the money to pay for a first run movie plus snacks? Perhaps Diana will think I am bad for not thinking this through before I made my offer. How could I have been so stupid? Now I will be found out for not being smart enough to figure this out before I made the offer."

But Alan Dean didn't say any of those words to me. Based on the reasoning in his heart, this is what Alan Dean said: "Actually, Diana, I am kind of tired. Let's go home and watch one of the movies we recorded and just relax. I'll even cook dinner tonight!"

In astonishment, I replied, "Wait, what? Didn't you just ask me to pick the movie and theater? What just happened? Why did you even suggest going to the movies if you were tired in the first place? I asked you if you were tired. I would rather you not even suggest going, than to take back the offer!"

Rather than telling me his self-talk, Alan Dean only told me a snippet of his confused thoughts. In this baffling moment, when Alan Dean rescinded his offer, I embarked on a journey of thinking more deeply about how we struggle in the area of communication. Something very profound happened that day which led me to believe I was missing something crucial about human interaction—particularly about the words we humans choose. Starting with the cryptic conversation in our car where Alan Dean left out important information from his self-talk, I coined the term Speaking CODE. I capitalize CODE to emphasize that what we speak needs to be deciphered. Speaking CODE happens when we have an internal conversation but only tell the listener snippets of our thoughts. This leaves the listener confused as he tries to interpret our meaning based on limited information. We will discuss the ramifications of Speaking CODE throughout this book.

By this time, I was so incensed with my Alan Dean that I didn't want him to say another word. I had no desire even to ask him if he was okay. I was hurt and indignant, and that was all that mattered. His words reminded me of past promises made and broken, and those memories instantly flooded my heart with sadness.

I was tempted to link my Alan Dean with all the others in my life who had disappointed me with broken promises and heartbreaking experiences. In that moment, I had all I could handle. Suddenly, our conversation was headed in a very bad direction.

Much later, Alan Dean discovered that during those moments when his self-talk ruled the conversation, he experienced a series of emotions that led him to rescind his offer. Those unidentifiable emotions made Alan Dean embarrassed that he could not afford to take me to a place he suggested I choose. It turned out that Alan Dean often does not know what he is experiencing in his heart during such emotional moments. The inability to understand what we are thinking or feeling during a conversation, especially if the conversations are emotional, is one of the hallmarks of Speaking CODE.

What followed was not a soul-satisfying or redemptive conversation for either of us. In our hearts, we both felt unimportant, confused, judged, unheard, and misunderstood. Neither of us had any intention of asking the other a good question to find out what was really going on. Instead, we threw accusations around, like a child throwing mud from a mud puddle without caring where it landed or who it hit. Unfortunately, we had fought this fight many times before — and it continues to the present.

As though that wasn't enough, we defended ourselves with spiteful words, portraying an attitude of self-righteousness. Imagine that! Two lovers of Jesus and lovers of each other acting self-righteously! Our responses to each other led to the breakdown of spoken communication. As so often happens, this type of breakdown culminates in the dehumanizing kind of communication that we know as silence. We say in our hearts, "You make me so angry that, in this moment, you no longer exist to me."

In the car, our hearts influenced what we said and how we interpreted what we heard. Blurred images from our past moved from their secret places in our hearts into the words we exchanged. Past Powerful Identity Forming Statements (PPIFSt) and Past Powerful Identity Forming Experiences (PPIFEx) fueled our self-talk and led us to sabotage our conversation by Speaking CODE. Our words were soul-crushing rather than soul-satisfying. But God is always at work in unlikely places such as our car.

HOLY SANCTUARIES

Indeed, God was at work in the relationship between Alan Dean and me. He used our car to become His *holy sanctuary* where God's purpose in suffering would be revealed through this frustrating exchange. A *sanctuary* is a place of safety. We need a sanctuary when we experience fear, anxiety, or suffering. God's appointed holy sanctuary does not mean He takes us away from the suffering or pain. Rather, God's holy sanctuary is a workplace where, amid suffering, God keeps us still so we can hear Him more clearly.

GOD'S AND OURS

God's holy sanctuary becomes our holy sanctuary. In our pain, God cares for us and helps us see His meaning and purpose in our suffering. He takes us to a necessary place where we, on our own, would never go. God is the Workman who wants to make us His own within these walls. Read the Word of the Lord in Isaiah 8:13–14:

> But the Lord of hosts, him you shall honor as holy. Let him be your fear, and let him be your dread. And he will become a sanctuary and a stone of offense and a rock of stumbling to both houses of Israel, a trap and a snare to the inhabitants of Jerusalem.

Isn't God like that? He can make anything a *holy sanctuary* for His redemptive purposes: the belly of a fish, the den of a lion, the majesty of a whirlwind, the cleft of a rock, and especially the Cross that is cursed. We need to look for these ordinary, commonplace, *holy sanctuaries* in our lives, where God is purposefully and actively making us His own—especially in our conversations. It is within our holy sanctuaries that we learn to honor God as holy!

What sanctuary has God made holy for you? Where has He allowed you to find purpose in your suffering and to honor Him as holy? Maybe your *holy sanctuary* was some form of electronic communication or a face-to-face talk that cut the heart out of you. Maybe it was in the bottom of a bottle, the contents of a needle, or in a handful of pills. Perhaps it was the pain you experienced at the hands of your abuser, or the blade of a razor on the body you loathe. Your *holy sanctuary* could also be your mind's never-ending echo of self-condemnation brought about by guilt or shame.

GOD'S WORDS IN OUR MOUTHS

The work God does in His holy sanctuary can even be the hurtful words we say and hear in stinging conversations. God takes hold of us, hard-hearted and self-absorbed as we are, and graciously proclaims His intentions toward us. In our holy sanctuaries, God does something purposeful so that our conversations can be different. Read the Word of the Lord from Isaiah 51:16:

> And I have put my words in your mouth and covered you in the shadow of my hand, establishing the heavens and laying the foundations of the earth, and saying to Zion, "You are my people."

Holy sanctuaries are places of God's own choosing

where He is at work in our lives to make us His people. Some of the greatest reflections of God's goodness are seen in biblical accounts where people struggled in their own holy sanctuaries. Jonah's holy sanctuary was in the belly of a great fish. Read the Word of the Lord from Jonah 1:15–2:9:

> So they picked up Jonah and hurled him into the sea, and the sea ceased from its raging. Then the men feared the Lord exceedingly, and they offered a sacrifice to the Lord and made vows.
>
> And the Lord appointed a great fish to swallow up Jonah. And Jonah was in the belly of the fish three days and three nights.
>
> Then Jonah prayed to the Lord his God from the belly of the fish, saying, "I called out to the Lord, out of my distress, and he answered me; out of the belly of Sheol I cried, and you heard my voice. For you cast me into the deep, into the heart of the seas, and the flood surrounded me, all your waves and your billows passed over me. Then I said, 'I am driven away from your sight; yet I shall again look upon your holy temple.' The waters closed in over me to take my life; the deep surrounded me; weeds were wrapped about my head at the roots of the mountains. I went down to the land whose bars closed upon me forever; yet you brought up my life from the pit, O Lord my God. When my life was fainting away, I remembered the Lord, and my prayer came to you, into your holy temple. Those who pay regard to vain idols forsake their hope of steadfast love. But I with the voice of thanksgiving will sacrifice to you; what I have vowed I will pay. Salvation belongs to the Lord!"

In this passage, notice Jonah's different experiences. Jonah disobeyed God because he did not want to speak to the Ninevites. God then put Jonah in a holy sanctuary (a sinking boat and the belly of the fish) so that God could work on him. Jonah went from being a man who ran away from God to a man who sought after Him. Holy sanctuaries change us when God is at work making us His own, and we honor Him as holy.

God can make anything His holy sanctuary, biblically speaking. This should not surprise us. After King Nebuchadnezzar experienced great success, God used Nebuchadnezzar's own self-absorbed words to capture the king's attention. God placed Nebuchadnezzar in a holy sanctuary. Read the Word of the Lord in Daniel 4:29–37:

> At the end of twelve months he [King Nebuchadnezzar] was walking on the roof of the royal palace of Babylon, and the king answered and said, "Is not this great Babylon, which I have built by my mighty power as a royal residence and for the glory of my majesty?" While the words were still in the king's mouth, there fell a voice from heaven, "O King Nebuchadnezzar, to you it is spoken: The kingdom has departed from you, and you shall be driven from among men, and your dwelling shall be with the beasts of the field. And you shall be made to eat grass like an ox, and seven periods of time shall pass over you, until you know that the Most High rules the kingdom of men and gives it to whom he will." Immediately the word was fulfilled against Nebuchadnezzar. He was driven from among men and ate grass like an ox, and his body was wet with the dew of heaven till his hair grew as long as eagles' feathers, and his nails were like birds' claws.
>
> At the end of the days I, Nebuchadnezzar, lifted my eyes to heaven, and my reason returned to me, and I blessed the Most High,

> and praised and honored him who lives forever, for his dominion is an everlasting dominion, and his kingdom endures from generation to generation; all the inhabitants of the earth are accounted as nothing, and he does according to his will among the host of heaven and among the inhabitants of the earth; and none can stay his hand or say to him, "What have you done?"
>
> At the same time my reason returned to me, and for the glory of my kingdom, my majesty and splendor returned to me. My counselors and my lords sought me, and I was established in my kingdom, and still more greatness was added to me. Now I, Nebuchadnezzar, praise and extol and honor the King of heaven, for all his works are right and his ways are just; and those who walk in pride he is able to humble.

Nebuchadnezzar, Jonah, you, me—we must rethink the purpose of our struggles and sorrows. We must begin to see them as God-given holy sanctuaries where God quiets us as He makes us His own. Left alone, we would rarely quiet ourselves to learn the extent of God's love for us. But God shows mercy and holds us still within our holy sanctuaries. God comes to us, especially in our troubles, and in His presence we find comfort and peace.

You may say, "Diana, you do not understand. When I was abused, when I drank and drugged myself silly, when I cut myself, when I deal with this pain-ridden body, when every day is a descent into pornography, when I can't even talk to my family members, how can you say God intended this for me? The holy sanctuary you describe is actually a profane hellhole. If, as you say, Almighty God is some great Workman making me His own, then I would prefer it if He stopped the madness I endure. If He does not stop it, then He is not a Workman. Rather, God has become a huge stumbling block for me."

These are fair observations that will be addressed in more detail later in this book. For now, let's consider how Isaiah speaks of God as a sanctuary. Remember what we read in Isaiah 8:13–14:

> But the Lord of hosts, him you shall honor as holy. Let him be your fear, and let him be your dread. And he will become a sanctuary and a stone of offense and a rock of stumbling to both houses of Israel, a trap and a snare to the inhabitants of Jerusalem.

While these verses speak of God as a sanctuary, this is not necessarily a happy, comfortable, "everything is just fine" sanctuary. Do we find God to be a stone of offense? He will be our fear and our dread. God will stop at nothing to enable us to honor Him as holy. He is often a stumbling block to all of us. But at the same time, He is a sanctuary amid our fear, dread, and stumbling.

Clearly, we will be in His holy sanctuary, because there is no avoiding the Lord. In fact, we are far safer in God's appointed holy sanctuary than anywhere else. However, it is hard to see safety in our holy sanctuary when our only view is of our own suffering. For Believers, there is no place where God is not present. God is everywhere. Either He is our sanctuary or our stumbling block.

Living in holy sanctuaries makes a difference in our everyday conversations, especially in our people-talk and our self-talk. In fact, holy sanctuaries even affect our God-talk—our prayers or conversations with God.

How different would our prayers sound if we believed that God designs holy sanctuaries where He works at making us His own? Perhaps our prayers would be more authentic if we begged God to let us see His purpose in our holy sanctuary. When our broken relationships are characterized by hate-filled and contemptuous words, we can ask for tender mercy and patience. God will guide us just as He guided Jonah and Nebuchadnezzar. While in our holy sanctuaries, the Spirit will teach us how to speak more wisely.

Let's see how this works in real time, and think about a soul-crushing conversation we recently had with someone. Our self-talk causes us to rehearse what the other person said over and over again. God may be placing us in His holy sanctuary through this conversation. God may want us to be still and wait before we speak. As we become still, do we feel God prompting us to apologize for our part in the difficult exchange? He may want us to be brave before we confront. God may want us to be humble before we rebuke. This is God as a Workman, in our holy sanctuary.

Holy sanctuaries show us a side of God's character that He needs us to see. Shadrach, Meshach, and Abednego certainly experienced God's holy sanctuary when God placed them in a fiery furnace. In this furnace, they saw that God, not Nebuchadnezzar, was sovereign over their lives. The words spoken by these men are epic! Read the Word of the Lord in Daniel 3:16–18:

> Shadrach, Meshach, and Abednego answered and said to the king, "O Nebuchadnezzar, we have no need to answer you in this matter. If this be so, our God whom we serve is able to deliver us from the burning fiery furnace, and he will deliver us out of your hand, O king. But if not, be it known to you, O king, that we will not serve your gods or worship the golden image that you have set up."

For these men, a redemptive conversation had nothing to do with begging for mercy or screaming profanities at their captors. They answered the king and told him of their unfaltering faith in God, no matter what the circumstances. God puts us in our holy sanctuary and works with us in our struggles. There are sides to God's character that teach us to trust Him, just like Shadrach, Meshach, and Abednego. Our painful discussions become our holy sanctuaries, where we move away from soul-crushing speech and move toward redemptive conversations. Holy sanctuaries are places where we can see God's character and His purposeful hand in our lives. God helps us find His purpose even in painful conversations, when all we want to do is escape through denial, hide through silence, or attack through words.

INTERSECTING SANCTUARIES

Let me add one last thought on holy sanctuaries. Our holy sanctuaries may intersect other people's stories as well. Their stories often cross ours, as we learn that God is working on us together. I call these moments *intersecting holy sanctuaries*. Sometimes, in our haste, we diminish the person with whom we are speaking when we lament that only our suffering is great. God is at work in that person's life, just as He is in ours. Our holy sanctuaries intersect with other people's holy sanctuaries. Be prepared.

In light of this, let's look at another biblical conversation where we see God at work. Daniel and Darius have intersecting holy sanctuaries. In Daniel 6, we read that many officials in Darius's court were jealous that Daniel distinguished himself, which led to his pending promotion (v. 3). Unable to find fault in Daniel's work ethic, his enemies decided to use Daniel's deep faith in God to destroy him (v. 5). Their plan was to prevail on Darius's ego to sign a binding decree that would throw anyone who prayed to any god for thirty days into the lion's den (v. 7). Darius realized that what he had done all but ended Daniel's life (v. 14). At this point, Daniel and Darius's lives intersected. Darius called on Daniel's God to do for Daniel what Darius himself could not do. Read the Word of the Lord from Daniel 6:16–17:

> Then the king commanded, and Daniel was brought and cast into the den of lions. The king declared to Daniel, "May your God, whom you serve continually, deliver you!"

After a sleepless night, Darius rushed to Daniel's holy sanctuary. In anguish, Darius cried out to Daniel to see if Daniel's God was able to save him (v. 20). Daniel responded that God had sent an angel to shut up the mouth of the lions. Daniel was alive and proven to be innocent of any wrongdoing (v. 22).

Darius punished the evildoers by throwing them into the lion's den (v. 24). Then Darius's holy sanctuary that intersected with Daniel's was revealed. Read the Word of the Lord in Daniel 6:25–28:

> Then King Darius wrote to all the peoples, nations, and languages that dwell in all the earth: "Peace be multiplied to you. I make a decree, that in all my royal dominion people are to tremble and fear before the God of Daniel, for he is the living God, enduring forever; his kingdom shall never be destroyed, and his dominion shall be to the end. He delivers and rescues; he works signs and wonders in heaven and on earth, he who has saved Daniel from the power of the lions." So this Daniel prospered during the reign of Darius and the reign of Cyrus the Persian.

Daniel and Darius's lives crossed as God put them in intersecting holy sanctuaries so that they would honor God as holy and God would make them His own. A heathen king and a Jewish exile extolled Almighty God. Be encouraged! We are not alone in our conversations that cause us so much suffering. Together, we endure in the holy sanctuaries that God gives us. There is great purpose in how our holy sanctuaries intersect with the holy sanctuaries of others. Read the great biblical dialogues of people who were unexpectedly brought together by God. Learn their stories. Observe their holy sanctuaries as they honored God as holy. And in our holy sanctuaries, believe that God is at work!

TWO INFLUENTIAL FORCES AND BRAIN DEVELOPMENT

There are Two Influential Forces that shape our communication:

- Earliest Childhood Memories (ECMs)
- Past Powerful Identity Forming Statements (PPIFSt), and Past Powerful Identity Forming Experiences (PPIFEx)

These two concepts are integral to Speaking CODE. Together, the Two Influential Forces fuel the self-talk that leads us to Speak CODE. These past statements and experiences affect us by bringing up confusing emotions that may interfere with our present conversations.

Which of these statements ring true to you?

- I cringe inside every time I hear you make "helpful" suggestions that override what I am saying.
- I feel apprehensive when you ask me if we can be intimate tonight.
- I feel anxious every time I think about certain conversations or events that happened in my past.
- I want to jump out of my skin when you catch me off guard with your unexpected behavior.
- I feel nervous, tense, or sick to my stomach every time I anticipate what comes next in our conversations.
- You still cannot understand or believe what I say even though I have said the same thing a gazillion times before.
- We do not seem to understand each other when it comes to how we react to things going on in our life together.
- I seem to sabotage my relationships in how I speak or in the way I understand what is said to me.

Imagine we are sipping hot tea together, discussing your reactions to the questions above. I would ask additional questions and listen carefully to your responses. Through this process, we would gain a better understanding of what is happening in your heart. This would help us uncover the heart issues that make you hear and speak as you do.

Many times, heart issues find their roots in our ECMs, PPIFSt, and PPIFEx. Our self-talk becomes the rehearsal stage for them. Together, they influence how we feel, which affects how we express ourselves. Self-talk may convince us that we are unheard, unloved, unaccepted, uncared for, or unimportant. These feelings are typically tied to our past relationships. Additionally, some of us have suffered unspeakable abuse or trauma which seeks to become our narrative. An abuse or trauma narrative has deep and lasting affects in nearly every area of our lives—especially in how we communicate with one another.

In that moment when our car became our intersecting holy sanctuary, I was confounded by how Alan Dean and I, who were so much in love, failed miserably to speak to each other with understanding. As I tried to make sense of that incident, I was stunned by an idea that the words Alan Dean and I spoke were influenced by powerful memories, statements, and experiences from our past. These ECMs, PPIFSt, and PPIFEx predisposed us to say the very words we said in our car. This led me to find an explanation of how our past and present intersect and seem to compromise our ability to communicate soul-satisfyingly in real time conversations.

ECMs

Years ago, a godly therapist introduced my colleagues and me to the concept of Earliest Childhood Memories (ECMs) and how he used them in his counseling practice. Since then, I have incorporated and expanded his ideas into my own understanding of how ECMs affect how we communicate. While we could say that our ECMs are part of our PPIFSt/PPIFEx, our ECMs are specific and personal to us. Additionally, our ECMs set up how we take in and give out information. Essentially, our ECMs set our *communication table* in that our ECMs act as a filter to help us interpret what we hear and say.

Our ECMs are powerfully entrenched in our hearts because our earliest memories have become our *familiar*. Our familiar consists of what we accept as normal, natural, or things consistent with our upbringing. They are habit-forming memories born out of our PPIFSt and PPIFEx. Our familiar started developing in our family of origin and can be disastrous; but, at least there is a sense of comfort in the known.

Downton Abbey

Let me give you an analogy that might help you understand what I mean by setting our *communication table*. The British drama series *Downton Abbey* (I saw that smile) is set in the early 1900s and chronicles the lives of the wealthy Lord Grantham, his family, and their servants. My little analogy has nothing to do with activities of any of the people in the series, but with the opening credits that ushered in each episode. Even the most diehard fans may not remember this few second clip.

Wait for it . . . here it comes! We see the opening credits as we move from the outdoors into the Georgian mansion. The camera follows us as we walk into the dining room, as though we are one of the servants. In the dining room, the camera lingers for a few seconds on the elaborate table settings, and then we see it! The servants use a ruler-like gizmo to make sure the table is set perfectly, down to the centimeter.

Earliest Childhood Memories set our *communication table* as precisely as Lord Grantham's servants set his dinner table. ECMs also act like a measuring stick. They measure how we take information in and give information out. ECMs are measuring sticks because when we hear something said to us, we already have a measured response in place based on our early memories. ECMs are so important to communication that I ask all my new clients to describe their earliest memories during our first session. Invariably, their ECMs resurface throughout our subsequent sessions, especially when communication issues arise.

Listed below are defining statements regarding ECMs, as I have come to use them in counseling. As we read these crucial statements, begin to think about how you would describe your Earliest Childhood Memory. Keep in mind that this book is about communication; therefore, we will link our ECMs to how we communicate through thoughts, words, and deeds.

- ECMs are the first influential force that shapes the pattern of how we communicate.
- ECMs begin to define our familiar because they have been our memories since birth.
- ECMs set our communication table in that they inform us how we initially take in and give out information.
- ECMs are more than a single memory. Whether they are good, bad, or neutral, ECMs teach children what to expect from life.
- ECMs allow us to interpret or make meaning of our life or to understand what is happening to us.
- ECMs sink down deeply into our heart. Whatever rules our heart shapes our behavior, including our communication.

- ECMs are an essential tool we can use as a starting point to help discover our PPIFSt and PPIFEx.
- ECMs act as a bridge linking our past to our present, in that they help explain the connection between past events and the words we use in present conversations. This bridge also explains our thought processes.

In our intersecting holy sanctuary, Alan Dean and I confronted our ECMs. For Alan Dean, he was taught that displaying emotions was not safe. To protect himself from the consequences of emotions, Alan Dean learned how to ignore feelings when in difficult conversations. His ECMs set his communication table, which acted to suppress his emotions in the moment. My ECMs told me that my wants were unimportant in the scheme of things. I wanted to go to the movies, but Alan Dean changed his mind. My ECMs set my communication table for me by telling me if I put up a fight, I might get my way.

ECMs AND THE BIBLE

Let's examine how Earliest Childhood Memories work as we continue to build our biblical framework. Framing ECMs biblically is difficult. I do not want to fall into the pattern of depending on proof-texting to establish my point. However, there is an abundance of Scripture that talks about what happens to Israel when fathers neglect to instruct their children about God. Read the Word of the Lord from Judges 2:10–12:

> And all that generation also were gathered to their fathers. And there arose another generation after them who did not know the Lord or the work that he had done for Israel.
>
> And the people of Israel did what was evil in the sight of the Lord and served the Baals. And they abandoned the Lord, the God of their fathers, who had brought them out of the land of Egypt. They went after other gods, from among the gods of the peoples who were around them, and bowed down to them. And they provoked the Lord to anger.

This passage shows the consequences when our children's earliest memories are not filled with the great work God has done for them. In Judges, the ignorance of Israel's children led them to run after idols, forsake God, and provoke Him to anger.

Passages like Deuteronomy 4:9 and 11:19, and Ephesians 6:4, lead us to believe that if our ECMs are God-centered, life will look differently than if they are not. Therefore, I believe we love our children well by establishing early memories for them based on what the Bible says about God and His everlasting love for His creation. This gives our children the ability to seek God in difficult times even when their hearts are profoundly sad. God-centered ECMs may offer children hope amid despair.

The Bible teaches that whatever we learn as young children will set our communication table throughout our lives. For proof, re-read the lives of the Patriarchs Abraham, Isaac, Jacob, and Joseph. Even if our parents repent of their bad behavior, we as children still have been powerfully influenced by what we observed in them. For example, Jacob's sons emulated their father's past deceitful behavior, as seen in the account of Dinah's rape in Genesis 34.

Our ECMs become increasingly important in our later years. ECMs that offer good memories may result in healthier perspectives on life. For Believers, raising children with godly memories sets a righteous communication table for them.

Timothy is an example of someone who received good training early in his life by his mother and grandmother. Paul pointed out Timothy's ECMs. Read the Word of the Lord from 2 Timothy 1:3–5:

> I thank God whom I serve, as did my ancestors, with a clear conscience, as I remember you constantly in my prayers night and day. As I remember your tears, I long to see you, that I may be filled with

> joy. I am reminded of your sincere faith, a faith that dwelt first in your grandmother Lois and your mother Eunice and now, I am sure, dwells in you as well.

ECMs that foster bad memories in children make them tend to see the world as harsh, unkind, or dangerous. This unhealthy perspective sets children on a path where they feel unimportant or marginalized. These children may look for ways to self-protect, causing them to be self-absorbed in their relationships.

Not only are bad memories harmful, but failing to provide care and discipline in the Lord can affect children's thoughts, words, and deeds. Eli demonstrates the consequences of uninvolved parenting. Read the Word of the Lord from 1 Samuel 3:12–14:

> On that day I will fulfill against Eli all that I have spoken concerning his house, from beginning to end. And I declare to him that I am about to punish his house forever, for the iniquity that he knew, because his sons were blaspheming God, and he did not restrain them.

Eli's sons, Hophni and Phinehas, lived an unrestrained lifestyle. They were scoundrels with women and had no regard for the Lord. They treated the Lord's offering with contempt. And because Eli did not train them to control themselves, Samuel, and not Eli's sons, became Israel's priest before the Lord.

As we consider our own Earliest Childhood Memories, we can be aware of how our *communication table* has been set. This awareness may better equip us to understand those everyday conversations that seem confusing or unsettling.

PPIFST AND PPIFEX

The second Influential Force that shapes how we communicate consists of two components. The first component is *Past Powerful Identity Forming Statements.* Beginning in infancy, these statements are spoken to us by parents and others throughout our lives. Their words find a place in our hearts and act as triggers in everyday conversations. These triggers can evoke either good or bad memories, both of which will affect our conversations.

The second component is *Past Powerful Identity Forming Experiences.* These experiences happen soon after we are born and continue throughout our lives. These experiences also find a place in our hearts and can be triggered if we find ourselves in circumstances that remind us of our past. PPIFSt and PPIFEx influence our self-talk, our people-talk, and our God-talk, giving them a commanding influence over our ability to communicate.

How We Come By Our PPIFSt and PPIFEx

Let's review how we come by these experiences in the first place. As we develop from infancy into adulthood, we hear statements that we try to interpret. Our interpretations of our PPIFSt and PPIFEx grow as we mature and affect how we decode life. They can remain silent or go unnoticed until whatever time they are needed, especially when something is triggered in our body, soul, or mind. PPIFSt/PPIFEx try to get our attention by inserting themselves into our present conversations. Their authority is formidable, because the connection between our memories and our emotions is very strong.

PPIFSt and PPIFEx can also be as vivid today as when they first happened. For us, these statements and experiences are forever in the front of our minds, first in our hearts, or on the tip of our tongues. These powerful memories can be so intense that nearly all the decisions we make are based on their imposing and pervasive presence.

Examples of Past Powerful Identity Forming Statements we may have heard in our past, that could resurface in our present conversations, may include (please note we are only listing negative statements):

- You know girls will always try to trap you into marriage.
- You are such a cry baby.
- You are so lazy that you will never accomplish anything.
- You embarrass me.
- You will never amount to anything.
- God will never love you if you keep acting that way.
- If people really knew you, they would never like you because you are a fake.

Examples of Past Powerful Identity Forming Experiences we may have had in our past, that could resurface in our present conversations, may include (please note we are only listing negative experiences):

- The exposure of a private behavior that caused extreme embarrassment
- Sexual abuse from a trusted person
- Physical abuse from a parent or caregiver
- Someone taking credit for your work
- Past indiscretions
- Loss of close relationships
- Failure to perform
- Any other form of betrayal

In the remainder of this chapter and in Section Two, we will learn more about our PPIFSt and PPIFEx. Now let's consider brain development and the affect our Two Influential Forces have on our ability to communicate.

THE DEVELOPING BRAIN

These next few paragraphs on brain development come from Dr. Curt Thompson's insightful book, *The Soul of Shame*. I highly recommend this book to you for a broader explanation of the topic. My condensed version draws from Dr. Thompson's work, on which I overlay my idea of how our ECMs, PPIFSt, and PPIFEx affect our conversations.

Dr. Thompson says that our brain has a vertical and a horizontal domain. The vertical domain develops from the bottom to the top. There are three parts to the vertical domain: the brain stem, the limbic circuitry, and the neocortex. We will discuss the horizontal domain shortly. For now, let's explore the three parts of the vertical domain.

The Brain Stem

The brain stem develops first. This part of the brain is responsible for controlling bodily functions we hardly consider, such as breathing, heart rate, appetite, wake/sleep cycle, and blinking. Thus, the brain stem is geared toward basic functions necessary to survival, including our fight-or-flight reflex. Pause here for a minute. We have so many things that cause us to become anxious, worried, and fearful. How crushing it would be if we added the burden of controlling our breath, heart rate, digestion, or any other functions delegated to our brain stem?

The Limbic Circuitry

The limbic circuitry develops second. This system is largely responsible for the development of our emotions. Emotions, or e motions, can be understood as "that which precedes movement."[1] If we took emotions out of humans, we would tend not to move. We would get stuck. Emotions are the energy around which the brain organizes itself. The primary structures within the limbic circuitry system include the amygdala, which is the emotion center of the brain. Also included in this system is the hippocampus, which plays an essential role in the formation of new memories about past experiences. Almost all sensory information passes through the limbic circuitry.

The Neocortex

The neocortex develops last. It controls higher brain functions, such as information processing, sensation, perception, memory, association, thought, and voluntary physical action. The neocortex is also responsible for linear thinking, analysis, and order. One might see this as the ultimate information processing and control center in our brain.

The neocortex gives understanding and meaning to what life throws at us. It is not until the neocortex sufficiently develops that we can understand our mystifying emotions in a more thoughtful way. Our emotional experiences and our logical interpretation intersect every time we say, "I have always felt/thought like this, but that doesn't mean I have to think/feel this way forever."

The neocortex takes the emotions from our limbic circuitry and helps us make sense of them. We can act logically, reflectively, and decidedly, rather than purely automatically and emotionally. The neocortex is the center of the brain and is the seat of higher-level thought. There is debate as to when the neocortex is fully developed. The safest consensus would be between eighteen and twenty-five years of age.

EMOTIONS: BODY AND SOUL

The following is how I link brain development and the Two Influential Forces that affect communication. There are broader implications that are especially interesting as we consider the formation of our ECMs, PPIFSt, and PPIFEx.

The limbic circuitry engages when our younger self becomes involved in statements or experiences that are deeply emotional. Our neocortex has not developed sufficiently to allow our younger self to understand highly emotional information. Therefore, our little bodies will absorb incoming emotions like guilt, shame, disapproval, or contentment well before these emotions can be understood.

Please do not dismiss the idea that our bodies are affected by emotions. Many verses in Proverbs discuss how our bones are impacted because of emotional words spoken to us.

Read the word of the Lord in Proverbs:

> A tranquil heart gives life to the flesh,
> but envy makes the bones rot. (14:30)
>
> A glad heart makes a cheerful face, but
> by sorrow of heart the spirit is crushed.
> (15:13)
>
> The light of the eyes rejoice the heart, and
> good news refreshes the bones. (15:30)
>
> A joyful heart is good medicine, but a
> crushed spirit dries up the bones. (17:22)

The earlier we are introduced to highly emotional memories, statements, and experiences, the more deeply they become hidden in our hearts and begin to form our identity apart from logic or understanding. Our bodies store our emotions before the neocortex fully develops. Our older selves react in our present conversations when our stored emotions are awakened. This reaction causes confusion, which makes us more likely to sabotage our present conversations.

There is a disconnect between how we intellectualize our ECMs, PPIFSt/PPIFEx, and the emotions that have been awakened. Intellectualizing baffling emotions can make our words contemptuous, sarcastic, narcissistic, belittling, bitter, dismissive, or hurtful. If we do not uncover the highly emotional statements and experiences, we encountered in our younger selves, our older selves' present-day conversations will tend to be soul-crushing rather than soul-satisfying.

In our car, Alan Dean knew he felt some type of deep emotion, but he had no idea why or how his emotions led him to rescind his offer. Alan Dean's limbic circuitry is where his emotions developed. As Alan Dean's brain developed, his neocortex gave him the ability to understand the unique nature of long forgotten emotions and how to make sense out of them. However, those ancient lessons of feeling fearful when expressing emotions were still deep within him. Those old feelings broke through and whispered guilt to Alan Dean because he could not afford what he offered.

Alan Dean's PPIFSt/PPIFEx caused confusion, leading him to Speak CODE. He only spoke a snippet of his self-talk. Both of us found ourselves in intersecting holy sanctuaries. Had I realized that confusing conversations often come from Speaking CODE, I would have asked Alan Dean a good question. Instead, I focused only on my own hurt in our confusing conversation. Alan Dean's response to me was so much deeper than the words he spoke in real time. His ECMs, PPIFSt, and PPIFEx were brought forward and mingled with the conversation we had in the car.

MULTISENSORY EXPERIENCES

Our powerful experiences involve not just our memories but our other senses as well. We know these senses mainly as sight, smell, taste, sound, and touch. Our senses are inextricably tied to the memories we experience. The fullness or intensity of our sense-memories shape how we connect to people around us, including the words we say. We may hear a song and remember how hilarious it was to see our friend dancing to it on the top of a bar as though no one was watching—especially not folks from his church! We laughed until we hurt. When we are reminded of that memory, we may call our friend and talk about the different aspects of that bar top dancing fool.

Experiencing My Moon

Try this. Right now, close your eyes and think about a statement or experience that brings you joy. Note how you feel or what happened to your face as you remembered the event. You just tapped into a PPIFSt or PPIFEx that was stored in your heart. Our memories can take us to heights of joy or to the pit of despair. These memories affect every area of our lives, including how we approach communication.

My thoughts went to the fascination I felt the first time I saw the full moon rise out of the vast darkness of the Atlantic Ocean. The moon started as an unidentifiable orange speck on the dark horizon, which I interpreted as a light from a faraway ship. As this small orange speck rose out of the ocean, I began to realize it was not a light from a faraway ship at all. Ships do not grow. Rather, it was the light from my one and only moon! This golden orange speck on the horizon eventually grew into a semicircle, then finally into a full-blown orb just above the horizon. My moon left a blood orange path from the horizon to the shoreline, where my feet could stand in its path. Eventually, that mysterious speck of orange in the distance grew into our milky white moon high in the night sky, which caused a huge swath of the dark ocean to glow creamy white from the heavens to the surf. Viewing it was fantastical.

Years later I held my grandson in my arms, wrapped in a fur blanket that my daughter brought back from Greece, as we watched the January moon rise out of the ocean. These intense multisensory memories tie my grandson and me together.

Engaging Multisensory Memories

Here are a few of my favorite multisensory memories. I grew up in a neighborhood called Highlandtown, which is in southeast Baltimore City. It was the center of my known universe. We lived in a row house (not a townhome) with marble steps (not stoops). Every Saturday, we had to scrub the steps with either Comet, pumice stone, or Lava soap. Just the mention of Comet evokes memories of its distinctive smell as I sprinkled the brilliant green powder over the marble steps! If you stood on my steps looking up or down the street, you would see rows and rows of Formstone homes with marble steps, street lights, and sidewalks suitable for games such as hopscotch, blocks, colored eggs, hide-and-seek, curb ball, or tag. Missing from this scene were hillsides, clumps of trees, grass, and earth.

Each summer, my church would load up a bus full of earth-and-grass-deprived city kids and take them to Mountain View Bible Camp, deep in the country where there were no street lights, sidewalks, Formstone row houses, or marble steps. Instead of city dirt, there was country earth. Rather than city blocks lined with row houses and sidewalks, there were hillside farms tilled to look like a huge patchwork quilt. Instead of the familiar, silently crawling city wildlife, we heard the morning sounds of songbirds and the nightly sounds of crickets.

We city kids soon discovered grass and earth . . . acres of it . . . as far as the eye could see! Did you know that the smell of city earth is very different from the smell of country earth? City earth smells stale, while country earth smells fresh. My brain soon learned to love the sweet fragrance of freshly mowed grass, ancient hedges of boxwood, and the scent of country earth. Mountain View Bible Camp's unique sights and scents got locked deep down in my heart, and still make up some of my most cherished childhood memories. In my mind, I see the patchwork hillsides looking like a gigantic checkerboard. Each new morning, I hear the day announced by songbirds and each night introduced by crickets. However, my deepest memory is the smell of freshly mowed grass, ancient boxwood, and country earth. I felt invincible with each breath I took in and breathed out at Mountain View.

This very morning, as I walked around Lake Montebello's freshly mowed grounds, its scent transported me back to the invincibility of my childhood at Mountain View. This morning, the memory of those fragrances soothed the burdens of my present-day broken heart, which were brought on by soul-crushing conversations that have torn my deepest relationships asunder. With each deep breath I took in, a locked away sadness was calmed in my heart, because of my powerful, multisensory memories of Mountain View. If you and I were sharing a pot of hot tea together, I would tell you about how the smell of mowed grass, ancient boxwood, and country earth reminded me of living where distressing conversations did not pierce my broken heart. I would ask you to share your multisensory experiences with me, as we asked God to make Himself real to us in the middle of our confusion.

The Sanctified Bible Cleaner

PPIFSt and PPIFEx can go terribly wrong even in the strongest relationships. A single experience has the power to forever shape conversations between two loving and committed people—including Alan Dean and me. Read our story and lament that Alan Dean is stuck with me.

When Alan Dean and I were first married, he pastored a small church in Media, Pennsylvania. Alan Dean kept, it seemed to me, a very sloppy Bible. I do believe he had kept every church bulletin since childhood. How could anyone keep track of important theological concepts with a chaotic Bible? So, as his bride of six months, I decided to clean out his clutter. I reasoned that when he realized how I had sacrificially exercised my spiritual gift of decluttering, he would love me even more deeply than he ever had before.

So I crept into his study on Saturday night and went through all his papers. I exercised a subsidiary gift of decluttering known as Organizer of Sacred Bibles. I am sure you have heard of it. When my mission was over, I experienced a new wifely sensation never felt before in all my six months' experience as Alan Dean's wife. I felt very self-satisfied. I could hear Alan Dean exclaim, "Well done, good and faithful wife! Here is fifty dollars to spend on shoes!" Not only was I an efficient homemaker, declutterer, lover, and friend, I could now add Organizer of Sacred Bibles to my list of accomplishments.

Before I left his office, I turned my eye toward his library of books. Now organizing those shelves would earn me a star in my crown of glory. In my effort to be humble, I decided not to tell him what I had done but waited for him to praise me like the woman in Proverbs 31 was praised.

After leading worship the next day, Alan Dean prepared to deliver his sermon. I was sitting in the front row. I knew he would be delighted that I was so concerned for his well-being that I decluttered his Bible. A slight smile even came over my mouth, but I did not want to give away the kindness I had showed him. Humility was very important. The Proverbs 31 woman had nothing on me.

However, I was surprised to find that Alan Dean did not give me the quick, knowing smile I so clearly deserved. Instead, I saw Alan Dean begin to flip through his Bible as though he was looking for something. Then I saw panic on his face. Panic instead of undying love for my act of spiritual service! Not once did Alan Dean look up at me with a knowing smile of thankfulness.

Alan Dean preached his sermon, and after the last hymn, I thought confidently, "Surely now my husband will bless my name for exercising my spiritual gift as Organizer of Sacred Bibles." He walked over to greet me and said, "I looked for my sermon that I am sure I printed out last night and put in my Bible. It was not there! I had to preach the sermon from memory. Did my sermon sound okay?"

I could not bear it any longer. I confessed to exercising my spiritual gift as Organizer of Sacred Bibles. Fortunately, people were still around and Alan Dean exercised his gift of mercy by waiting until later to discuss it.

True Confessions

What makes me confess to you the poor exercise of my spiritual gift? Ever since that day nearly forty years ago, if something belonging to Alan Dean goes missing, he almost always asks me if I had anything to do with it. That powerful experience that happened so long ago still negatively affects our conversations. Alan Dean's PPIFSt and PPIFEx lead him to believe I may interfere with where he decides to store things. And rightly so!

Exercising my spiritual gift as Organizer of Sacred Bibles created PPIFSt and PPIFEx in Alan Dean's heart that still affect our conversations today. It is not that he hasn't forgiven me for not asking permission to help him be more organized—rather, it is that I did something that affected him so profoundly. This one act causes most missing objects to come under the suspicion that I moved them or put them somewhere safe. My past action may also cause Alan Dean to question his own ability to take care of his business. Alan Dean wonders if I believe he can take care of me.

Additionally, exercising my spiritual gift as Organizer of Sacred Bibles as I did has affected me as well. If Alan Dean innocently asks me if I have seen something of his that he cannot find, I begin to question myself. Did I move it in my compulsion to have things in their correct place? Was I still at fault for interfering with someone else's belongings? Has Alan Dean forgiven me? This feeling of shame and guilt is very real. Only in the past few years have we been able to stop being suspicious of each other. Sadly, it has taken us years to have soul-satisfying conversations over missing objects.

Thankfully, this incident has now become a matter for inside jokes instead of anger, guilt, and did-you-really-do-that. Still, there have been recent times where my PPIFSt and PPIFEx over this incident will come out of hiding and catch me off guard. Sometimes I hear Alan Dean's righteous disappointment rather than hearing the kind of praise the Proverbs 31 woman heard. Additionally, my conversations with Alan Dean regarding missing things tend not to be open and honest. My words tend to be evasive and suspicious.

HARMFUL MULTISENSORY MEMORIES

Blessed are the conversations that ensue from life-giving multisensory memories, like the previous examples. However, some multisensory memories are not life-giving. In fact, some of our past powerful multisensory memories are hurtful.

Many of our PPIFSt and PPIFEx can intrude in our lives and catch us off guard. These statements and experiences are ever-present and often shout at us with overwhelming emotions that ignite contentious dialogue. PPIFSt and PPIFEx are players in our lives. Perhaps they play out when the family gets together for parties. Maybe they play out at weddings or funerals, when extended family members are forced to occupy the same space. Under these circumstances, conversations can be very upsetting as PPIFSt/PPIFEx assert themselves at family gatherings.

PPIFSt and PPIFEx have the power to keep us from engaging in conversations with those who harmed us.

They may keep us from attending events where we may run into people from our past we choose to forget. These may keep us from inviting people to celebrations which they would have otherwise attended. PPIFSt and PPIFEx may make us anxious when we are forced to be in certain people's company. They will lead us to either soul-satisfying conversations, soul-crushing speech, or total silence. These experiences will affect the words we use (if we speak at all), the places we go (if we go at all), or the emotions we display (if we emote at all). Our self-talk will fuel the CODE we speak making our conversations disingenuous.

A Christmastime Example

Multisensory experiences are not viewed the same by everyone involved in the event. Remember all the years when the family got together to trim the Christmas tree, and we drank spiked eggnog as we prepared the Feast of the Seven Fishes? We laughed at the fact that we had to start the decorations about a third of the way up the tree because the two most destructive forces known to humankind, toddlers and pets, sought to undo all our hard work.

Recall the aroma coming from the kitchen? It was garlic and onions sautéing in olive oil as the Feast was prepared. The scent of cinnamon permeated every corner of the house as Aunt Mary's Ultimate Cinnamon Ball Cake baked in the oven. As soon as the vial of anise oil was opened, the fragrance lingered for days. Scents and scenes similar to these ushered in the joy of the Christmas season.

However, in the middle of that idyllic picture, those of us with dietary restrictions did not find this scene life-giving. Mom never seemed to remember or care that eating shellfish, for some, was problematic—no matter how often she was reminded. For some reason known only to Mom, she still prepared seafood that some could not eat, and she neglected to offer an alternative. While many family members formed deeply positive and nurturing PPIFSt and PPIFEx, others did not. For those family members, their PPIFSt and PPIFEx were not the Norman Rockwell picture at all. It would be understandable if their experience led them to feel like an outcast in their own family—one who was unheard, marginalized, uncared for, or unimportant.

Carrying these memories from Christmas to Christmas was not life-giving. In fact, it was isolating. Rather than past powerful Christmas experiences being soul-soothing, the experiences were soul-confusing. One child may lament, "What is wrong with me that Mom would not remember that I cannot eat shellfish?" Another child may think, "I wish my sibling would stop being so dramatic, eat the traditional food, and stop being so difficult!" The smell of cinnamon, anise, or garlic sautéing conjures up a whole host of unwanted memories that may compromise the very conversations during the celebration. We ask ourselves, "Why even show up?" And then the guilt-shame cycle rears its ugly head.

We might not relate to this specific Christmas example. And yet, many of us can connect with having these same feelings of being marginalized and isolated when we interacted with family or close friends. These negative multisensory feelings can be most powerfully awakened during weddings, funerals, and celebratory events. Our communication can be inauthentic, accusatory, aggressive, or we may just shut down.

MULTISENSORY EXPERIENCES AND ABUSE

There are multisensory memories that are shaped by horrific events that happened to us. Those ensuing conversations are characterized by self-protection, excruciating pain, suspicion, shame, and fear. People suffering from childhood sexual abuse are often haunted not just by the memory of the intolerable event, but also by their own senses.

For example, the perpetrator may have worn a particular cologne or had a specific tattoo, which became part of the victim's sensory memory. Perhaps the victim heard a certain sound in the background or the abuser spoke as the abuse took place. The abuser's hands may have been unusually calloused. Perhaps the pressure from the perpetrator's body weight made it hard for the victim to breathe. Bodily sensations associated with sexual abuse become part of these powerful and devastating multisensory memories.

Therefore, any time victims are confronted with present-day sensory reminders of their abusive past, that reminder will move the memory from their past into the present. Unfortunately, the present-day reminders themselves add another layer to the victim's past powerful experiences. These memories affect the victim's self-talk, people-talk, and God-talk. She may fly into a mode of self-protection, based on the memories and emotions tied to the sensory reminders. Control over the situation may be her method of restoring a feeling of safety.

The victim's body reacts physically to PPIFSt and PPIFEx. During abuse, the victim may have experienced any number of physical symptoms, such as pain, nausea, anxiety, or even pleasure. As a result, the victim may avoid situations where similar bodily reactions could happen, including anxiety-producing conversations. Just the thought of a painful discussion will produce bodily sensations like the physical reactions his body endured during the abuse.

It is common for sexually abused people to scan their surroundings to ensure they are safe before entering a conversation. Sometimes victims will opt out of conversations because their present multisensory memories are unwanted, just like their past multisensory body sensations were.

Victims of sexual abuse may go into a trancelike state or even faint when the memory of their PPIFSt and PPIFEx surfaces. If, during a conversation, a sensory memory invades their minds and bodies, victims may exhibit seemingly inexplicable behaviors. These memories take them to a place where they endured great danger. The Bible tells us we are both body and soul. What sickens our body will also sicken our soul. Conversely, what sickens our soul will often sicken our body as well.

Reverberations and Our PPIFSt/PPIFEx

Those of us who suffer physical or sexual abuse experience reverberations in our PPIFSt and PPIFEx. Our past often keeps us from staying present in our conversations. When our PPIFSt and PPIFEx are awakened during a difficult conversation, our heart may re-live the trauma from our past. In those moments, we may be transported back to the horrific memory. While our present conversations may arouse vivid scenes from our past, we must understand that the person to whom we are speaking may or may not be the same person who caused our feelings to resurface. If we do not distinguish between our abuser and the person to whom we are currently speaking, our conversation will be compromised. To some extent, we all experience reverberations when our conversational partner sounds like someone from our past. This causes our self-talk to fuel the CODE we speak, leaving the listener confused.

The Developing Brain and Childhood Trauma

If we suffered abuse as young children, our neocortex would not have developed enough for us to understand the reasons for the abuse. By the time our brain can function at that level, the damage to our souls has been done. As children, we had few resources to help us make sense out of the shameful things we heard or experienced. To be sure, our emotions developed. But we lacked any logical explanation for them. In other words, just because we could not understand why our early caregivers abused us, that does not mean we did not feel the emotions evoked by their abusive behavior.

Maybe our caregivers leered at our younger selves, pounded us with contemptuous words, crushed us with sarcastic comments, or scolded us in condemnatory rants. These words and deeds produced all sorts of feelings. It would make sense that our young selves felt bad, wrong, deficient, guilty, shameful, fearful, responsible, or detached. These emotions lived in us then and perhaps still do now. We heard the tone of deep, disappointed sighs. Our younger selves felt rejected then, which often allows our older self to feel rejected in the here and now. We felt the agony of the abuse against our little bodies then, and we are still haunted by confusing body sensations now. We still struggle to understand the emotional toll the abuse took on us then, as well as the toll it takes on us now. Our trauma has the potential to work its way into our present conversations, causing us to Speak CODE. Hear George's story in his own words:

> George had experienced trauma as a young boy. His caregiver had his own history of physical/psychological damage that fueled an almost manic anger that he then directed at George. George did not know how to minimize the impact of his caregiver's wrath. He tried to address the most common accusations that justified the abusive behavior of the caregiver. He cleaned the kitchen, put away his toys, and made his bed. But no matter what he did, the abusive caregiver found some other reason to throw things and hit George. As a child George did not understand why the caregiver acted to physically and emotionally terrify him.
>
> When George grew into adulthood, he was relatively successful in establishing a home. He actively participated in church activities and in the workplace. However, the impact of the early childhood abuse fueled his own overreaction to any sort of suggestion that he was not doing well enough or had failed to meet some sort of standard. He also had trust issues that came out when someone, who he knew loved him, said anything that was critical. His wife regularly had to remind him that she was on his side.
>
> George had to wrestle with the idea that he had built a cocoon around himself to protect him from harm. While some people build cocoons of withdrawal or isolation, George's cocoon was one that protected him by causing him to be more aggressive, especially in conversations. That approach had been fairly effective in childhood but was a disaster in adulthood. By understanding his ECMs, PPIFSt, and PPIFEx, George was able to begin cutting away the cocoon and to be vulnerable and more open. This gave him the opportunity to grow in a way that allowed him to not Speak CODE but rather to speak more redemptively to friends and acquaintances and to deepen his relationship with his spouse.

Just like George, we all have difficulty understanding the harsh words and actions we experience as children. Perhaps if we had possessed a fully developed brain, we would have been able to process that Mommy or Daddy were too emotionally involved in their own issues to see the damage they did to us. Instead, we made up our own stories to explain the emotional pain their behavior caused us. We surmised that maybe Mommy or Daddy behaved as they did because we somehow deserved it. Our younger selves may have felt responsible for the chaos in our dysfunctional family. We took responsibility then and we still do now.

To make matters worse, Mommy and Daddy might have used Bible words to support their abuse. God must have been on their side, especially when they repeated words like "Spare the rod and spoil the child." Rarely did they fall under the biblical conviction that their behavior exasperated their children. Our younger selves understood God based on the character and behavior of our parents or caregivers. Truth be told, our older selves still fight to separate God's character from our parent's behavior.

The results of childhood emotional, physical, or sexual abuse, if unexamined, may last our entire life. As young children, we take the feelings inextricably tied to our emotional experiences and lock them in our hearts. Without wisdom, we are unable to attach appropriate meaning to our past. These burdensome experiences become part of our repertoire of ECMs, PPIFSt, and PPIFEx, which formulate the basis on which we understand our world.

Our Two Influential Forces guide the very words we use in our conversations. If we do not have a wise understanding of our past, we will find soul-satisfying communication elusive or nonexistent, and instead we will Speak CODE. Our older selves can hardly grasp what a healthy conversation looks like when our younger selves rarely saw one. Experiencing healthy conversations are especially rare for those of us who have suffered sexual or physical abuse.

PRIMARY PPIFST AND PPIFEX

PPIFSt and PPIFEx can be broken down into two categories: primary and secondary. Since we interpret our life based on the information coming at us, there is a fluidity between primary and secondary statements and experiences. Both types are stored in our hearts and have the potential to become triggers. Additionally, both are active participants in our self-talk, people-talk, and God-talk.

Primary PPIFSt or PPIFEx are those words spoken or behaviors done to us before our brain has fully developed. In *The Soul of Shame,* Dr. Thompson writes that as soon as a baby is born, he begins to seek after the ones who have already been seeking after him. We can think of primary PPIFSt/PPIFEx as simply living life in our family of origin, as we get to know those who have been looking for us.

Our primary PPIFSt and PPIFEx teach us to trust (or not), to expect continuity (or not), to assume all is ordered (or not), to believe in dependability (or not), to pursue self-awareness (or not), to anticipate acceptance (or not), and to understand love (or not). Typically, these primary statements and experiences come through some form of communication. The communication mode can be verbal or nonverbal. Dr. Thompson says that 60–90 percent of all communication is nonverbal.

PPIFST, PPIFEX, AND THE CHARACTER OF GOD

Most importantly, these primary statements/experiences begin to teach us about God's character. Our parents and caregivers are the first reflectors of God's attributes. If our parents reflect mercy, grace, love, and forgiveness, we come to know God as a good Father who is merciful, grace-filled, loving, and forgiving.

On the other hand, our parents or caregivers may reflect a marred view of God's character. Our younger selves may not have seen mercy, grace, love, and forgiveness from our parents. The absence of these blessings defaces the character of God. This makes it hard for our older selves to see God's mercy, grace, love, and forgiveness toward us. Seeing God's character inaccurately affects how we talk to one another and to God.

For example, if parents use a tone that is harsh and critical, children will more likely hear God's tone as harsh and critical. In fact, these children will often speak harshly and critically to others even into adulthood. If parents exhibit behavior toward their children that is arbitrary and capricious, then their children will more likely see God's providential care over them as arbitrary and capricious. If parents speak sarcastically and contemptuously, then their children will more often see God as sarcastic and contemptuous. If parents are gracious and loving, then their children will more easily see God as gracious and loving. The work of the parents will affect how children see God, interpret His response, and then form the words they use in their conversations. Scripture teaches us God's character, and we bear the responsibility of communicating these attributes to our children. Read the Word of the Lord:

> But you, O Lord, are a God merciful and gracious, slow to anger and abounding in steadfast love and faithfulness. (Psalm 86:15)

> As a father shows compassion to his children, so the Lord shows compassion to those who fear him. For he knows our frame; he remembers that we are dust. (Psalm 103:13–14)

> What father among you, if his son asks for a fish, will instead of a fish give him a serpent; or if he asks for an egg, will give him a scorpion? If you then, who are evil, know how to give good gifts to your children, how much more will the heavenly Father give the Holy Spirit to those who ask him! (Luke 11:11–13)

As parents or caregivers reflect God's attributes, we should also make it our goal to parent our children as God parents us. If not, we present an obstacle that keeps our children from resting in the fact that God is their Heavenly Father. God parents us with patience and kindness. His love for His children is everlasting, steadfast, and unending. We should keep in mind that God does catch us every time we do something wrong. He sees our every bad act. Yet, He does not immediately punish us every time He catches us. His actions toward us cannot be called harsh or exasperating. He disciplines us for our good, and His treatment of us is far kinder and more merciful than we deserve. Therefore, the primary statements and experiences we develop in our children must reflect how God parents us, so that our children's ability to know God fully is unencumbered.

If we show our children the attributes of God and parent them in a way that reflects how God parents us, our children are more likely to live and speak as God's children. If we do not provide our children a picture of God's character and we parent them too harshly or too leniently, they will live and speak in a way that reflects the reality we have shown them.

Please do not think that this method is a lucky charm. It is not. Many of us parented our children following the pattern of how God parented us and our children still followed their own path. The path our children choose to follow is God's business. Our business is to parent them using the parenting model that God uses. To know God's parenting methods, we must read the Bible. The more closely we follow God's model, the more likely we will promote helpful primary PPIFSt and PPIFEx that foster soul-satisfying conversations in place of CODE Speaking. However, we get no guarantees that godly parenting will prevent our children from making sinful decisions. Some of us will be called on by God to raise and love an Esau.

These primary statements and experiences are foundational to how we self-identify, regardless of whether they are good, bad, or indifferent. For you counselors, who help carry the burdens of others, how many times have you heard from your clients that an unsatisfying or problematic behavior was normal for them in the house in which they grew up? For example, shouting at one another may have been a normal primary experience in your client's home. Your client may believe that expressing oneself in loud tones is not problematic. He blames others for their unwillingness to move beyond his communication style. And yet, your client might wonder why he cannot seem to have a soul-satisfying conversation with the people in his life.

Even more sad than a lack of satisfying conversations is the possibility that your client may believe God behaves like his parents. To your client, God may be a God of chaos. He has little to no understanding of how destructive screaming can be in a conversation. But God is not a God of chaos, and He has instructed us how to speak to one another. As burden bearers, we point him to the wisdom found in Proverbs or any of the recorded biblical conversations. Helping our client uncover primary statements and experiences can be a crucial component in achieving redemptive communication. We can help him explore how his self-talk fuels the CODE he speaks and sabotages his present conversations.

SECONDARY PPIFST AND PPIFEX

Secondary PPIFSt and PPIFEx are those words spoken or behaviors done to us after our brain has sufficiently developed. There is no hard line of demarcation between primary and secondary, because the brain develops differently in each of us. Even though primary and secondary statements and experiences develop at different times, they still impact our communication.

Secondary statements and experiences occur as we get older and begin to develop new relationships outside our family of origin. Our primary identity forming experiences were the building blocks on which we constructed our secondary statements and experiences. These secondary statements and experiences continue to shape how we self-identify. Often what seems normal to us is called into question as we encounter others with different primary and secondary experiences. Keep in mind, we use past powerful statements and experiences (primary or secondary) to interpret reality.

Our PPIFSt and PPIFEx (primary or secondary) are

also shared. We enjoy spending time with our good friends because we have many PPIFSt and PPIFEx in common. Our past provides us with endless topics for soul-satisfying conversations. We are tied to each other by our past conversations and exploits. The ties are so strong that if we ever suffer a falling-out, it is our PPIFSt and PPIFEx that often give us the strength we need to restore our relationship.

Conversely, those same shared statements and experiences (primary or secondary) can also cause us terrible grief as we find ourselves moving toward alienation in our necessary relationships. Those shared life statements and experiences, sunk deep within our hearts, are a major reason that disagreements between dear friends, cousins, and sibilings can be so devastating. In the midst of sorrow, we may be able to use the strength of our shared past to find a pathway back to these necessary relationships. This pathway links our shared history to our present situation. Talking about this pathway may awaken something in us that allows us to move toward confession, forgiveness, and reconciliation.

PPIFST, PPIFEX, AND OUR WORDS

Our PPIFSt and PPIFEx, primary or secondary, shape and form how we talk to each other. They can sabotage even a casual conversation. If a sensory memory is triggered or an experience awakened, it will be brought forward into our conversation. This memory can derail our discussion or halt it in its tracks. In contrast, if the memory evokes pleasure, people may suddenly break out in song and dance without a word being exchanged!

If the person with whom we are speaking awakens in us a fearful PPIFSt or PPIFEx, we may lose trust in the safety of the conversation. What could have been a soul-satisfying interaction now produces fear and suspicion. Where once we had no control over our past, we now can take matters into our own hands and control the present. We seek to control the outcome in order to protect our carefully-crafted personal world. We may become accusatory and distrustful of what the speaker says, leading us to twist their words into something that makes us feel safe. We make assumptions, as we assign our own meaning to the words said to us, without asking a good clarifying question.

Additionally, we can become aloof, using superficial words to hide our fears. We may choose to leave the conversation altogether, as the lack of trust sends us back to a memory that sabotages our present interaction. Communication falls victim to the past we endured. Soul-satisfying conversations cannot happen if we fear or distrust the person with whom we are speaking. This is true even if that person is actually trustworthy and safe. As a safeguard, trauma sufferers are more likely to leave what they perceive to be a fearful conversation.

If strong or even confusing emotions are involved in our communication, we may Speak CODE. In that moment when our emotions are awakened, it is hard to think clearly about our present conversation. Our past joins forces with our present, allowing unresolved hurts to sabotage our relationships. This ongoing process can create a very confusing internal battle, which could cripple communication. The person hearing our words may respond with confusion, doubt, or even anger. The hearer may make accusations or plead to change the tone of the conversation. Both parties may bail out of the conversation altogether.

In our hopelessness, we may ask ourselves if our PPIFSt and PPIFEx (primary or secondary) doom us to a life in which our past determines how we engage in conversations. After all, our past has been with us from infancy. I am not saying we should dismiss all past statements and experiences when engaged in present conversations, but I am saying we must be alert to the possibility that our past influences how we hear what is being said.

We do not want to dismiss our history, because our history is who we are and we are precious. Our history is central to how we are known by others. But we do have a choice about how we approach or evaluate what is sunk down deep within our hearts. We can choose to use our past selfishly or ambitiously and, as we wrongly interpret what we hear, to turn our conversations into soul-crushing exchanges. Or we can choose not to allow our PPIFSt and PPIFEx to dictate the direction of our conversations. We can honor ourselves and the person with whom we are speaking by having the mind of Christ. Read the Word of the Lord in Philippians 2:3–8:

> Do nothing from selfish ambition or conceit, but in humility count others more significant than yourselves. Let each of you look not only to his own interests, but also to the interests of others. Have this mind among yourselves, which is yours in Christ Jesus, who, though he was in the form of God, did not count equality with God a thing to be grasped, but emptied himself, by taking the form of a servant, being born in the likeness of men. And being found in human form, he humbled himself by becoming obedient to the point of death, even death on a cross.

We can use our PPIFSt and PPIFEx to craft words that express concern for the interest of others. This unifies us because, when we do this, we look at everyone's needs. We can speak well because we have the mind of Christ. The choice is before us.

We cannot avoid, deny, or forget our history. If we do so, our past will scream louder to get our attention. Instead, we do well to honor our ECMs, PPIFSt, and PPIFEx, because they are part of the path of righteousness upon which God has set us. These are the rooms in our holy sanctuaries, where God works to make us His own. God has not abandoned us. Rather, He has designed circumstances in our past, good and bad, that will lead us to Him. Our ECMs, PPIFSt, and PPIFEx are steps along the righteous path where God calls us to honor Him as holy. By following God's righteous path, we will minimize Speaking CODE.

In summary, we now have a basic understanding of how our brain develops. Brain development helps us understand the intricacies of communication. Our PPIFSt and PPIFEx can be either primary or secondary, which enables multisensory memories. PPIFSt and PPIFEx fuel our self-talk and can lead us to Speak CODE. Speaking CODE harms both the speaker and the listener, making communication itself vulnerable.

Let's turn our attention to a deeper analysis of Speaking CODE.

SPEAKING CODE

In our car all those years ago, Alan Dean and I discovered that what was left unspoken between us deeply affected our ability to understand each other. Additionally, the words we did speak were not words that brought meaning and clarity to our conversations. We were irritated and deeply saddened by what we said, but for vastly different reasons. Eventually our dialog became soul-crushing rather than soul-satisfying. All of us have experienced the effects of Speaking CODE to some degree.

Since that pivotal encounter, I discovered that something hampers our choice of words in our conversations. This interference also appears to control how we interpret what others say to us. I asked myself what made Alan Dean invite me to select a movie of my choice and then suddenly rescind his offer? What was I missing? Was there some sort of gatekeeper to Alan Dean's heart that would only allow me in if I knew the right password?

As I pondered this question, I realized that what prevented us from understanding each other was much more than a barricade that stood between us. There is a complex communication process, involving our past and present, that affects what we say and hear. The resulting confusion limits the ability of both speaker and hearer to have a clear verbal exchange. Even more interesting is that, in the moment, neither one recognizes that he is unable to communicate effectively.

After many discussions regarding that offer made and rescinded, we discovered that Alan Dean had a vague memory of uneasiness awakened in his heart. This illusive memory seemed to point his self-talk toward something being wrong. Alan Dean knew he loved to make me happy. However, his offer was impossible to fulfill due to our budget. Haven't we all had a similar experience where we perceived that something was wrong, but we could not identify what it was?

UNLOCKING THE CODE

Speaking CODE can be good, bad, or neutral. CODE Speaking typically happens when a memory, elusive or obvious, gets triggered and causes internal turmoil. In this confusion, the speaker may omit words that would allow the hearer to understand him better. The hearer's interpretation is based on incomplete information which forces him to make assumptions. Assumption-making is disastrous in relationships and all but kills soul-satisfying conversations.

Alan Dean Spoke CODE to me when he rescinded his offer to take me to the movies. He said he was tired (possibly true) which was CODE for "we cannot afford it" (actually true). He suggested an alternate plan which involved cooking dinner, which was CODE for "What else can I offer to appease Diana for disappointing her?" However, I had specifically asked Alan Dean if he was too tired to enjoy an evening out.

Now, there may be those who would say, "Diana, really? Can't you just be grateful that Alan Dean may have been tired but still offered to cook dinner for you before you watched a movie together?" If the answer to that question becomes our sole focus, we would miss deeper heart issues. We would never get to the bottom of the PPIFSt and PPIFEx that caused Alan

Dean to Speak CODE in the first place. Both our hearts actively heard and responded to something that was said, which linked our past to our present. If we do not identify that link, we are doomed to see our past fuel the CODE we speak.

Alan Dean learned that when he confronts conversations, like the experience we had in the car, he feels clueless as to how his emotions affect his responses. This is especially true if emotional memories of hidden wounds surface. Something was said or felt in the car that tapped into Alan Dean's PPIFSt/PPIFEx. His past interpreted our conversation as "Caution! Danger ahead." As Alan Dean rescinded his offer, he Spoke CODE which only reflected the snippets of his self-talk that he actually understood. Most of his memories were hard to grasp. The fact is, we both Spoke CODE to each other in that intersecting holy sanctuary where God was making us His own as we regarded Him as holy.

Alan Dean's self-talk informed him that we could not afford a first-run movie plus snacks. He did not know how to articulate his self-talk without hurting me. He also confronted his own PPIFSt/PPIFEx, which made him feel inadequate and embarrassed. Had Alan Dean been in touch with his past feelings, he might have had the ability to speak loving truth to me and explain our budget shortfall for the week.

Instead, the elusiveness of his emotions blocked him from accessing or understanding his true feelings. That elusiveness caused Alan Dean to Speak CODE and think that his substitute plan would override his original suggestion and prevent me from feeling bewildered. His alternative plan did not change my disenchantment no matter how sacrificial his plan sounded. At this point, Alan Dean's offerings were not acceptable to me.

SELF-TALK

Our self-talk tells us many stories based on our current situation and how it relates to our memories of past statements and experiences. In our minds, our self-talk produces a movie script destined for the silver screen where we cast who will be the winners and losers in our melodrama. We become the leading actor, with soliloquies so convincing and motivations so pure that the Self-Talk Committee for Thoughts and Behaviors exonerate us from any wrongdoing. In our internal dialogue, we win and all those who hurt us lose. But the result of our inward melodrama is that our self-talk eventually leads us to Speak CODE. Our real-life conversational partner is confused because we do not tell him all that is in our self-talk. We Speak CODE which compromises the hearer's ability to understand us.

In our internal melodrama, we sometimes manipulate the dialogue so that we are shown to be innocent and good, and everyone else is declared guilty and evil. The veracity of our dialogue does not matter because we are the only ones who count in our self-talk. We dazzle others with the righteousness of our point of view, as we internally call attention to their sophomoric understanding of the issues. Yay for us! Applause and accolades to Diana, et al. Now onto our ever-so-humble acceptance speech, because we just won the Academy Award for *People Who Suffer Well* in the category of Self-Talk.

The result of our melodrama is heartbreaking. Soul-satisfying conversations lose, as we play a warped game of hide-and-seek. Communication breaks down as the speaker mostly hides behind Speaking CODE, fueled by his self-talk. The listener tries to seek but soon becomes bewildered, as he tries to make sense out of the CODE he hears.

It does not matter if our CODE Speaking is intentional or unintentional. The result is still the same. When we leave out portions of our thoughts and only say snippets of information, the hearer is forced to make assumptions, which stifles intimacy. As we inwardly fight for authenticity but are too fearful to drop the CODE we speak, we become emotionally exhausted.

Alan Dean could not identify all his emotions in that moment or recognize the effect his words would have on our relationship. He did not see any real reason to tell me all he was thinking because he was not even sure of his own thoughts or feelings. As a result, Alan Dean set aside what he did not understand and spoke only what he thought was important and necessary, in the moment, to keep danger at bay. He left me with the difficult task of interpreting his statements about going home rather than going to the movies. I interpreted his statements based on my own PPIFSt/PPIFEx. My interpretation told me that what I want is unimportant in the scheme of things.

Self-talk can be endless and nearly impossible to stop. We say the words we said to one another repeatedly in our mind anytime day or night. We find ourselves absorbed in rehearsing the conversation, which makes it exceedingly difficult for us to think clearly or even to sleep well. Heaven help us if we wake up at three in the morning and our self-talk gets started. Our internal conversation may go on for hours.

KEY IDENTIFIER

Speaking CODE jeopardizes communication. The list below presents key identifiers to help us recognize when we Speak CODE:

- Speaking CODE comes from things we ponder in our hearts. From our hearts we reason and eventually speak.
- Speaking CODE occurs because we do not live in the facts, but in the interpretation of the facts based on what is in our hearts.
- When we Speak CODE, we may be unaware of why we are not saying what is on our mind.
- When we Speak CODE, we may know what we are thinking, but we are not willing to say it out loud.
- Speaking CODE can be nonverbal; we may physically avoid or turn aside from the person with whom we are in relationship.
- Speaking CODE can be verbal, as seen in our responses while we are engaged in conversations.
- Speaking CODE may seem like a safe way for us to hide our real thoughts and feelings.
- Speaking CODE is what we say when we are not aware of what is going on within us.
- Speaking CODE can be purposeful or unintentional.
- Speaking CODE is sometimes done to protect the hearer.
- Speaking CODE is sometimes done to protect the speaker.
- Speaking CODE is hard to detect, which often confuses both the hearer and the speaker.

BENEFITS OF SPEAKING CODE

Many arguments or hard feelings occur because we Speak CODE, either knowingly or unknowingly. If Speaking CODE leads to soul-crushing speech, why then do we Speak CODE? That is a good question, especially since Speaking CODE limits clarity. But Speaking CODE does offer some benefits.

Speaking CODE benefits our desire to . . .

- control the information that would make us vulnerable.
- organize what we can say and what we cannot say.
- justify our behavior.
- avoid being seen as a failure, wrong, or stupid.
- determine the trustworthiness of the other person.
- protect ourselves by keeping us clueless as to what we are really thinking or feeling.
- remain neutral or detached from emotional issues or highly charged discussions.
- establish roadblocks designed to test people's sincerity toward us.
- avoid entering repetitive or unproductive conversations.
- hedge our bets before taking sides.
- keep unsafe people at arm's length.

WHO SPEAKS CODE?

You do it. I do it. We all Speak CODE. Trust me, you do as well. Married couples as well as individual folks Speak CODE to each other. People who come to me for biblical counseling Speak CODE to others and hear CODE spoken to them. We humans live with conversations that are mystifying and bewildering, and we have no idea why or how to change it.

Speaking CODE can be heard nearly everywhere. Just listen to conversations from Main Street, to Wall Street, to our street. Speaking CODE can jeopardize simple interactions as well as highly-charged political discourse. It is no wonder that conversations can leave us feeling confused, angry, ambivalent, anxious, and empty. Sometimes we Speak CODE deliberately, and sometimes we are completely unaware of the CODE we speak. Why is that?

OUR HEART'S TREASURES

Someone once said, "The heart of the matter is always the matter of the heart." The sweeping narrative of our lives is written based on what we store in our hearts. Read the Word of the Lord in Matthew 6:19–21:

> Do not lay up for yourselves treasures on earth, where moth and rust destroy and where thieves break in and steal, but lay up for yourselves treasures in heaven, where neither moth nor rust destroys and where thieves do not break in and steal. For where your treasure is, there your heart will be also.

The concept of Speaking CODE goes hand in hand with the biblical theology of the heart which is seen throughout Scripture. Whatever rules our heart will eventually be shown in our thoughts, words, and deeds. As a biblical counselor and a proficient sinner, I am struck by the profundity of this concept. What we store in our hearts has a deep impact on our everyday life, including the words we choose to say to one another. The interaction between our mind and our heart produces our self-talk which fuels Speaking CODE.

Throughout our lives, our hearts store up these treasures. Our treasures can be anything from comfort, success, fame, worthiness, or pleasure, to isolation, mayhem, or nihilism. What we treasure in our hearts often comes from our Past Powerful Identity Forming Statements and Experiences. Read the Word of the Lord in Proverbs 4:20–23:

> My son, be attentive to my words; incline your ear to my sayings. Let them not escape from your sight; keep them within your heart. For they are life to those who find them, and healing to all their flesh. Keep your heart with all vigilance, for from it flow the springs of life.

The encouragement to the son suggests that the many sayings of the father are life-giving and healing. They are to be accumulated and vigilantly guarded in his heart and will form the basis of his PPIFSt/PPIFEx.

WHAT DEFILES US

Twenty-first century Americans are as confused as to what corrupts us as were the Pharisees in Jesus's day. Jesus clears up this confusion. Read the Word of the Lord from Matthew 15:17–20:

> Do you not see that whatever goes into the mouth passes into the stomach and is expelled? But what comes out of the mouth proceeds from the heart, and this defiles a person. For out of the heart come evil thoughts, murder, adultery, sexual immorality, theft, false witness, slander. These are what defile a person. But to eat with unwashed hands does not defile anyone.

The larger context shows how the Pharisees hated Jesus because He exposed their wicked hearts. Based on the Pharisees PPIFSt and PPIFEx with Jesus, they used anything they could find to defame Him, including maligning His disciples. But Jesus turned the tables on the Pharisees by exposing the hate and hypocrisy they treasured in their hearts. He called on the people to understand what defiles them. It is not what they put into their mouths. It is what comes out of their hearts.

CODE AND CONFUSION

Some of the CODE we speak, fueled by our past, can make the hearer question whether he is in the same conversation that we are. We, too, may experience those same questions, leaving both parties baffled by the conversation. Both the hearer and the speaker may find it hard to trust each other, which can lead both parties to feel unloved, judged, empty, disrespected, confused, disconnected, or lonely. The following list describes how Speaking CODE confuses our conversations:

- Speaking CODE is confusing because the words we use do not always have the effect we want, especially when feelings are involved.
- Speaking CODE gives our assumptions power which can kill relationships.
- Speaking CODE blinds us from seeing that God desires a relationship with us.
- Speaking CODE provides cover, limiting how much we expose our hearts.
- Speaking CODE makes authenticity challenging, especially in conversations where emotions are involved.
- Speaking CODE prevents us from being truly known. But past triggers are strong and erode trust, which leaves us bewildered and fearful.

As we conclude this chapter, let us be aware of the CODE we speak. Speaking CODE compromises communication. Communication that is soul-satisfying and seeks understanding is buried alive by the CODE we speak and by our resulting assumptions. We must be willing to investigate our hearts—where Speaking CODE originates. Hang in there. This is a journey with many dimly-lit paths. We need God's Word as a lamp to light it up!

BRAIN DEVELOPMENT, COMMUNICATION, AND GENESIS 3

Genesis 3 reveals a singular conversation where we can examine the effect emotions have on the words we choose. We already discussed the vertical development of the brain which begins with the brain stem, moves to limbic circuitry, and finally culminates in the neocortex. We will continue to use Dr. Thompson's material to show us how the horizontal domain develops. Understanding basic brain development will enable us to see how the Two Influential Forces and Speaking CODE affect our conversations, particularly when emotions are involved. We will apply these findings to the narrative in Genesis 3.

THE HORIZONTAL DOMAIN AND THE RIGHT HEMISPHERE

According to Dr. Thompson, the horizontal domain develops from our right hemisphere to our left hemisphere. The right hemisphere starts developing before birth and continues to develop until the age of five or six. The right hemisphere matures more quickly than the left hemisphere. The right hemisphere is responsible for nonverbal forms of communication, creativity, visual/spatial relationships, and feelings of ease. The right hemisphere also tracks the emotional parts of our mind and has a map-like quality as it helps us see what is going on inside us.

The left hemisphere is responsible mostly for the development of language, logic, and linear thinking. One easy way to understand the different functions of the two sides of our brain is to think that the left brain's job is to make sense out of what the right brain sends it. The left hemisphere begins to develop between the ages of eighteen to twenty-four months. The left hemisphere develops much more slowly than the right hemisphere.

Interpersonal Neurobiology

Dr. Thompson uses the term *interpersonal neurobiology* to describe our brain-talk. Brain-talk is brain activity that moves information back and forth, much like water flows from one side to the other in a partially-inflated water balloon. Interpersonal neurobiology regulates the free flow of energy and information. This movement never stops. Interpersonal neurobiology helped me formulate my understanding of how our ECMs, PPIFSt, and PPIFEx form a pathway, linking our past to present-day conversations. Recognizing these pathways can clarify why we choose the words we do and how we interpret what we hear. The free-flowing nature of interpersonal neurobiology also explains how we are always developing primary and secondary experiences with each new person we meet.

Emergent Brain

Dr. Thompson describes our brain as emergent. Emergent means that a brain's single tiny neuron cannot do much by itself. But grand things happen when millions of tiny neurons act together, making it possible for us to enjoy the complexity of Van Gogh's *Starry Night* or Handel's *Messiah.* The emergent nature of our brain also allows us to do small things like say "thank you" or express feelings and emotions. Our emergent brain explains how our memories can be very vivid, like the details of my experience at Mountain View Bible Camp. Our emergent brain can incorporate all our senses into our memories. Because our brain is emergent, the unique expression of our experiences will be deeply personal and specific to us.

Embodied Brain

According to Dr. Thompson, our brain is also embodied. An embodied brain means that our brain and our body interact with the world around us. The brain sends messages throughout the extensive nervous systems within our body. Therefore, what we experience is not just in our minds, but in our bodies as well. This helps explain why those who suffer from physical trauma, such as sexual abuse, experience bodily sensations long after the event happened.

SHAME ATTENDANTS

Dr. Thompson also discusses how emotions, like shame, disrupt our interpersonal neurobiology's free flow of energy. This disruption makes us feel disconnected. Dr. Thompson calls these disruptors Shame Attendants. Shame Attendants give life to our shameful feelings. Shame is exceptionally good at dragging us away from ourselves, others, and God.

Remember, our emotions develop early in the limbic circuitry. Very young children experience feelings of guilt and shame. This often leads to feelings of embarrassment or vulnerability based on their caregivers' interactions with them. Even though young children cannot verbalize their feelings intellectually, that does not mean that the effects of their feelings aren't registered in their bodies. These emotions get locked down deep in their hearts. The developing right hemisphere gives young children the ability to figure out nonverbal cues, as their emotions continue to develop in the limbic circuitry.

The Difference Between Guilt and Shame

While shame and guilt are closely related, there is a distinction between the two. We feel guilty if we do not measure up to our own standards or the standards imposed on us by others. We hide our guilt through sophisticated coping mechanisms. We alleviate our guilt by re-examining or re-evaluating the standards by which we live our lives. If we change our standards, so that they are more attainable, feelings of guilt will lessen. However, changing our standards can result in chaotic conversations.

We feel shame when we believe that everyone can see how miserably we have failed to meet our own standards or those imposed on us by others. Shame entices us to feel inadequate, wrong, naked, inferior, and dirty in our world. Shame can also be immobilizing, resulting in behaviors that lead us to hopelessness. Hearts that are shame-filled produce conversations that are painful because we are terrified at the prospect of being exposed.

Contamination of Shame

The pathway through shame is different than the pathway through guilt. Shame is a condition of our heart over which we have little control. Sure, we can appropriate coping behaviors that might mitigate the feeling that our disgusting hearts are exposed for all the world to see, but shame is a condition we cannot tolerate for any length of time. It will affect our thoughts and behaviors, which will eventually come out in our conversations.

Think of a glass of clean water to which we add a particle of contamination. It will not take long for that particle to mix in with the clear water and turn that clean water into contaminated water. We can use an immersion blender to pulverize that contaminant until it is unrecognizable. However, that particle is still in the water even if it cannot be seen.

Similarly, shame is the contaminating particle in the clear water of our soul. Shame affects us to our very core and impacts our ability to speak redemptively to ourselves and others. As a result, we hide behind a façade of superficiality that we present to others. This façade keeps us from addressing our own shame as well. We retaliate with bitter words, daring the listener to continue speaking. We deny our shame, and hope we will not be exposed. Our conversations are filled with confusion as we bounce between over-reaction and shutting down. The pathway through shame is outside of us. But how do we find this path?

An Old Hymn and the Bible

The old hymn writer Robert Lowry equates shame with sin. His hymn describes a remedy for sin and shame. Read the words of the hymn, "Nothing But the Blood," written in 1876:

> What can wash away my sin? nothing but the blood of Jesus; what can make me whole again? nothing but the blood of Jesus. O precious is the flow that makes me white as snow; no other fount I know, nothing but the blood of Jesus."[2]

David calls on God to cleanse him from sin. Read the Word of the Lord as spoken by David in Psalm 51:7:

> Purge me with hyssop, and I shall be clean; wash me, and I will be whiter than snow.

Ezekiel shows us that it is God who initiates and completes our cleansing. Read the Word of the Lord from Ezekiel 36:25–27:

> I will sprinkle clean water on you, and you shall be clean from all your uncleannesses, and from all your idols I will cleanse you. And I will give you a new heart, and a new spirit I will put within you. And I will remove the heart of stone from your flesh and give you a heart of flesh. And I will put my Spirit within you, and cause you to walk in my statutes and be careful to obey my rules.

Shame has disastrous effects on our conversations because statements we heard or experiences we had filled our hearts with disgrace and humiliation. What do we do?

The Great Exchange

The pathway through shame leads us to the Cross of Christ. On the Cross, Jesus takes our shame and exchanges it for His righteousness and holiness. Dr. Ed Welch calls this "The Great Exchange." In his comments at CCEF's National Conference in 2012 and in his book *Shame Interrupted,* Dr. Welch declares that because Jesus was crucified in weakness, we can identify with and associate with Him. Dr. Welch says that our union with Jesus, and His with us, is by faith. Hence, Jesus is the only pathway to end our shame. A pathway to redemptive conversations, where Shame Attendants cannot derail us, flows through that Great Exchange.

SHAME AND GENESIS 2

Let's look at the first time the Bible uses the word shame and see how it affects our conversations. Read the Word of the Lord from Genesis 2:25 (NIV):

> Adam and his wife were both naked, and they felt no shame.

The question that begs to be asked is, why did the writer of Genesis use the word shame? Why not use words like embarrassment, disappointment, lust, fear, ambivalence, admiration, confusion, or whatever word that describes how humans feel when they share a very intimate space?

Think about the intimate moments that Adam and the Woman shared. What would be the nature or quality of the conversations when neither one of them felt any hint of shame? Are we thinking that those conversations were heavenly, authentic, open, vulnerable, honest, and soul-satisfying? Indeed, they were!

Now think about a conversation we had where we gossiped about someone. The next time we are with that person, how would we feel? Would we feel a sense of shame? If our gossip was exposed, we might try to deflect the shame as we cover ourselves using lies, justifications, or blame shifting.

Our conversations are deeply affected by the shame we carry. We all have Shame Attendants. We feel shame over our perceived body image, our sexual experiences prior to marriage, our pornography use, any extramarital affairs involving physical contact, clandestine interactions including emotional intimacy, prior sexual abuse (either as a victim or a perpetrator), or even how we were raised. We feel shame if we are caught, called out, or if we think everyone can see our secret failures. The words we use will be affected by the shame we carry.

Feeling shame, leading to soul-crushing speech, affects all of us. Parents may feel shame based on how they raised their children, which will affect their conversations. Parents often use words to minimize the effects of their shameful behavior toward their children. They say, "I did the best I could." "Stop complaining and get over it." "I had it worse than you ever did." "Your experience wasn't that bad." "I already apologized to you." "I am not solely responsible for this." "You tempted me to do what I did." "I can't believe how disrespectful you are toward me."

We may feel shame if we have envious feelings about our friends' successes or accomplishments. We may feel such a deep sense of shame that we cannot bring ourselves to compliment them in their successes. To others, we may use words to downplay or minimize their achievements. We may feel shame in the workplace when we perceive ourselves as being inferior to our coworkers. We may remain silent as others pick apart our coworker in an attempt to tear down the excellent job he is doing. In these relationships, our shame will affect our people-talk, our self-talk, and our God-talk.

Where we worship is one of the most interesting places that we feel shame. We may feel shame because our past or present lifestyle tells us we have no business in such a gathering. We may feel shame when we tell ourselves we do not know religion as well as that person sitting next to us. We may feel shame if we believe we do not sound holy enough, sing loudly enough, or feel emotional enough during worship.

Shame comes to us the moment we realize we do not fit into any small groups, church-sanctioned organizations, or fellowship cliques. Those of us who are sophisticated churchgoers may know how to hide this shame. We may manipulate people to feel sorry for us because of our shame. We may fish for compliments or attempt to justify our failures. We may self-righteously attack others, by using prayer requests that border on gossip. We do it in the name of Jesus, of course. Our conversations will not even skip a beat as we learn how to fit into the life of our church despite our shame. On Sunday mornings, we arrive late or leave early so we can avoid the casual questions about how we are doing. While we may fool others, we cannot fool ourselves. Despite our sophistication, our self-talk is tainted by the shame we feel.

In the absence of shame, true intimacy allows for soul-satisfying communication rather than soul-crushing speech. Why would I say that? Shame is an emotion loaded with judgment and self-diminishment. Shame is void of humanness, which conflicts with how we were created. Shame is loaded with sin from without and sin from within. Shame often devastates us to the point that we are afraid to be truly known in the conversations we have. Shame leads us to a distorted love of self. Please do not misunderstand me. I am not advocating that we wear our hearts on our sleeves and say whatever intimate thoughts we have. Sharing everything about ourselves is another shame-hiding tactic that will affect our conversations.

Let's look at one small example of how shame affects our communication. Because of shame, appropriate or realistic body image is hard for many of us to achieve. Body shame may follow us throughout our lives, regardless of our weight. The PPIFSt and PPIFEx related to body image hide shame deep within our hearts. We know these statements:

- Do you really need to eat that dessert?
- Why don't you exercise more?
- Do you really like how those clothes look on you?
- Your calves look like tree trunks.
- I do not know what you will wear to hide those extra pounds.
- You are eating that? I thought you were on a diet.

- I hate myself since I have no self-control when it comes to food.
- I am ashamed of myself because of how I look. I am a failure.
- I am controlled by food, and that is shameful.

Married women often report feeling shame over their bodies. Their statements may sound like the following during intimate moments:

- Don't look at me!
- Please turn off the lights.
- How can you say you love this body when it looks like this?
- Are you blind? Look at these scars and stretch marks!
- How can I believe anything you tell me, when you say crazy things about my body looking good?
- I hate my body and so should you.
- Maybe this body is why you struggle with lust and pornography.

Shame is ruinous because it inhabits our self-talk and causes us to Speak CODE. We simply cannot handle the consequences of being truthful. Rather than speaking truth in love, we say soul-crushing or critical words to hide our shame.

Shame in the Garden

Adam and the Woman offer us invaluable insights regarding shame. After the Woman was deceived and Adam sinned, their relationship with God drastically changed. In fact, Adam and the Woman hid from God. Sinful emotions and behaviors were now part of Adam and the Woman's history together. Prior to the deceit and sin, neither of them had experienced any shame, as evidenced by the fact that they were naked and unashamed. Now, out of fear, Adam and the Woman hid from God. There can be no soul-satisfying communication when people hide due to their shame.

Hiding is a nonverbal form of communication and interferes with soul-satisfying conversations. If you do not believe me, ask anyone who tries to communicate with someone addicted to some form of self-soothing behavior. (And yes, that includes our electronic gadgetry.)

The Search

In Genesis 3, we hear God call out to Adam, "Where are you?" (v. 9). Adam declares that after discovering he was naked, he became afraid. Do not miss this. Adam hid because he was afraid. Adam's first powerful experience post-Fall is something he had never experienced before. Adam was afraid, and he spoke to God out of this experience, which was now embedded in his heart. Adam sinned and instantly he experienced shame and fear that drove him into hiding. This is the first time we see how negative emotions affect both verbal and nonverbal communication.

In addition to hiding from God, Adam and the Woman hid their shame from each other by sewing fig leaves together to serve as coverings. Shame produced fear in Adam and the Woman. Fear prohibited them from communing with God in the cool of the day. Fear drove them to cover up their intimacy. We follow in Adam and the Woman's footsteps. Our own fear drives us to hide and damages our ability to enjoy soul-satisfying communication. In the Garden, soul-satisfying communication became one of the casualties of sin.

God asked Adam and the Woman, "Who told you that you were naked?" (v. 11). It is interesting that God does not wait for Adam to answer His question. Why is that? The only way Adam could possibly have known he was naked was by eating the forbidden fruit. Judging from the next question God asks, it is obvious God knows exactly how Adam came to know he was naked. Without hesitation God asks, "Have you eaten from the tree that I commanded you not to eat from?"

When Adam and the Woman disobeyed God, their eyes were opened. Their reality was altered forever. Adam and the Woman replaced innocence with sin and shame that affected all future conversations. Eating the fruit brought grief and shame that only Jesus could rectify.

The New Normal

These new Powerful Identity Forming Statements and Experiences led Adam and the Woman to scheme and pursue self-sufficiency. Both Adam and the Woman learned blame-shifting words. They learned accusatory words, as they pointed fingers at each other, the serpent, and God. When sin opened Adam and his wife's eyes, redemptive and soul-satisfying communication was replaced with soul-crushing speech.

Our PPIFSt and PPIFEx are affected by sin, which makes our communication vulnerable. If we feel fearful or ashamed, our words will affect what is in our hearts. We may doubt the motives of others, or we may opt out of conversations. We may use grandiose words. We may lure people into rescuing us so that we feel powerful. We may entice people by manipulating their emotions with our words so that we get what we want. We may play the victim so that people feel sorry for us. Then we may harass them for not caring for us the way we want them to.

A Better Normal

We will have much to say about our better reality. For now, let us remember that Great Exchange where Jesus reverses the effects of Adam and the Woman's sin. Jesus makes it possible for us to enjoy soul-satisfying conversations, either verbal or nonverbal, once again. As He heals our brokenness, we can mend the discord between us and enjoy righteous conversations. We can be inquisitive as we seek to know and be known. We trust more freely, which allows us to see other people's words as reliable. Trust makes our words more honest.

We may still experience guilt or shame. But because of Christ, we seek understanding and forgiveness. I am not saying that soul-satisfying speech is not contentious at times. It very well may be. But in the end, our PPIFSt and PPIFEx can be uncovered, addressed, and put to death. Our past shame does not have to sabotage our conversations. We can reduce how often we Speak CODE.

Let's not lose sight of our main question in this section. We are considering the role emotions play in our communications. We look to Adam and the Woman because we see the progression of both the positive and negative emotions they experienced. We look to God so that we can see how He redeemed His children and instituted a plan of salvation.

CONFLICTING REALITIES

When we encounter emotionally laden conversations that we process through our PPIFSt and PPIFEx, we may sacrifice the reality where God turns our soul-crushing words to soul-satisfying speech. Let's look at Sintra and Gaudio as an example. Sintra is tired of Gaudio's lack of emotional awareness in important discussions. Hardly anything rises to the level where Gaudio experiences emotions that would cause him to engage at the level Sintra desires. Sintra wants Gaudio to say words that reflect her need to discuss the emotions involved in important relationships, so she feels understood rather than lonely. Sintra even tells Gaudio the exact words to say to help her feel understood. However, this is not Gaudio's reality. He has a different view and cannot satisfy Sintra's desires. In this situation, neither can live in each other's reality. This makes emotional conversations very unsatisfying.

Maybe we are living in someone else's reality where they tell us how to think and speak. In these conversations, we feel forced to accept how they understand the situation. This can create conflict as two unique people disagree in their point of view. Discussions between them will sound confusing, because their interpretations differ. Their narratives are based on how they interpret the PPIFSt and PPIFEx stored in their hearts. When we are asked to live in someone else's reality, our conversations will clash. Even in the midst of such discord, God is able to work redemptively because He is greater than our hearts.

In summary, how our brains develop affects how we communicate. Genesis 1–3 confronts us with the affect shame had on Adam and the Woman, which was evident in their conversations. While guilt and shame are similar, shame is a devastating emotion. But the Great Exchange where Jesus took our shame and gave us His righteousness makes it possible for us to enjoy soul-satisfying conversations.

THE SPOKEN WORD AND OUR PATH

In Genesis 1–3, we see how God values words. We read fascinating dialogues between God, Adam, the Woman, and the serpent. These passages describe the successes and failures of human interactions. Words show the creative power of communication when God speaks creation into existence. Out of nothing, God spoke, "Let there be," and it was so. Genesis also shows the terrible damage that takes place when we misuse God's gift of words. Adam and the Woman demonstrate that even loving people can abuse God's gift of speech. When words are motivated by sin, soul-crushing conversations occur.

CENTRALITY OF COMMUNICATION

In Genesis 1, look at how often the phrases "God said" or "God called" appears. In God's management of His world, He uses words to call forth creation. We observe a Trinitarian conversation as God reveals Himself in Scripture. God teaches us that communication is a central component in human relationships. We address each other by using spoken or written words. The words we use can bless or curse one another.

The Bible does not tell us why God chose speech to communicate with His creation. He could have used the Vulcan Mind Meld to talk to Adam and the Woman. To bring creation into being, God could have waved His magic "God wand" to do "God magic," as my daughter, Maya, loves to say about God. But He did not.

Instead, God specifically speaks to Adam and the Woman. He walks with them in the cool of the day. God spoke, and that makes communication noble. With all of its messiness, communication is a gracious gift God has given us for His glory and our good. God chose to speak, and that is a compelling reason why soul-satisfying communication is possible.

Man's Chief End

In the Larger Catechism of 1648, the Westminster Divines posed an epic question:

> *QUESTION: What is the chief and highest end of man?*
> ANSWER: Man's chief and highest end is to glorify God, and fully to enjoy Him forever.[3]

"Fully to enjoy him forever" includes communication. Enjoying Him forever encompasses this life and the next. Therefore, soul-satisfying communication is for God's glory and our enjoyment, both now and forevermore. We should treasure communication because it is a gift from God into eternity.

God was purposeful, meaningful, and wise as He spoke creation into existence. We too, must seek to be purposeful, meaningful, and wise in our communication with Him and with each other. Even though our Two Influential Forces would have us flee from difficult conversations, be encouraged. In those trying interactions, where Speaking CODE seems much easier than speaking truth, God gives us grace. Our hearts may ache from conversations based on the hurt, shame, and frustration we carry from our past. The words we choose can be redemptive because God has overcome past pain.

Biblical Purposes for God's Gift of Words

After Adam and the Woman sinned and felt shame, they became afraid. Fear sent them into hiding. Here are a few ways in which fear affects our communication:

- We may fear that the words we use will expose us.
- We may fear that our words could be used against us.
- We may fear that the words we use could be misunderstood.
- We may fear that the words we use will not be cherished.
- We may fear that the words we use will fail to accomplish our desired task.

These fears push us to seek safety in Speaking CODE. Nevertheless, even though the spoken word can produce fear, God designed communication for a purpose. The following series of Scriptures show us the importance of words.

The heavens and earth respond to God's communication:

> The heavens declare the glory of God, and the sky above proclaims his handiwork. Day-to-day pours out speech, and night to night reveals knowledge. There is no speech, nor are there words, whose voice is not heard. Their voice goes out through all the earth, and their words to the end of the world. (Psalm 19:1–4)

The living hear and respond to God's communication to them:

> Through him then let us continually offer up a sacrifice of praise to God, that is, the fruit of lips that acknowledge his name. (Hebrews 13:15)

The dead hear and respond to God's communication:

> Truly, truly, I say to you, an hour is coming, and is now here, when the dead will hear the voice of the Son of God, and those who hear will live. For as the Father has life in himself, so he has granted the Son also to have life in himself. And he has given him authority to execute judgment, because he is the Son of Man. Do not marvel at this, for an hour is coming when all who are in the tombs will hear his voice and come out, those who have done good to the resurrection of life, and those who have done evil to the resurrection of judgment. (John 5:25–29)

All creation and heavenly beings worship and glorify God:

> Ascribe to the Lord, O heavenly beings, ascribe to the Lord glory and strength. Ascribe to the Lord the glory due his name; worship the Lord in the splendor of holiness. (Psalm 29:1–2)

The voice of the Lord is power:

> The voice of the Lord is over the waters; the God of glory thunders, the Lord, over many waters. The voice of the Lord is powerful; the voice of the Lord is full of majesty.
>
> The voice of the Lord breaks the cedars; the Lord breaks the cedars of Lebanon. He makes Lebanon to skip like a calf, and Sirion like a young wild ox.
>
> The voice of the Lord flashes forth flames of fire. The voice of the Lord shakes the wilderness; the Lord shakes the wilderness of Kadesh.
>
> The voice of the Lord makes the deer give birth and strips the forests bare, and in his temple all cry, "Glory!"

The Lord sits enthroned over the flood;
the Lord sits enthroned as king forever.
May the Lord give strength to his people!
May the Lord bless his people with peace!
(Psalm 29:3–11)

Even infants and babies hear and respond to God's communication:

And the blind and the lame came to him in the temple, and he healed them. But when the chief priests and the scribes saw the wonderful things that he did, and the children crying out in the temple, "Hosanna to the Son of David!" they were indignant, and they said to him, "Do you hear what these are saying?" And Jesus said to them, "Yes; have you never read, 'Out of the mouth of infants and nursing babies you have prepared praise'? (Matthew 21:14–16)

Do we comprehend the significance of these verses? Communication is essential, and words are God's gift to us. Communication is one of the main vehicles whereby we glorify God and enjoy Him forever. For this reason, we must pursue soul-satisfying and redemptive communication.

A CHOICE OF THREE PATHS

Difficult conversations, where soul-crushing words eviscerate our hearts, can tempt us to avoid speaking to each other. In place of a dialogue, we say to ourselves, "It is too much, I just don't care." This ambivalent attitude can lead us down different paths.

First Path: Keep Out

The first path is a path of isolation. We build walls of silence around ourselves or hang out cleverly worded signs designed to keep out would-be intruders. We are tempted to live safe and self-absorbed lonely lives. We build our fortress with bricks that say, "Fool me once, shame on you; Fool me twice, shame on me," "How dare you?," or "I'll never let you hurt me again!"

Second Path: Canio The Clown

The second path is like the first in that both are self-protective. But on the second path, we act superficially cheerful. In truth, our heart is downcast due to devastating relationships and conversations. Rather than living in the moment of the pain, we utter Christian platitudes that say, "Don't worry. Be happy. God will work it out. Just work on that faith of yours!"

We take the same path as the famous character in the opera *Pagliacci,* written by Ruggero Leoncavallo. I call this the Canio Path after the main clown in *Pagliacci.* In the opera, Canio believes he is being betrayed by his wife, but he must hide his pain behind his clown's laughter. Read the words he deliriously sings in the aria, "Vesti La Giubba" (Put on the Costume):

I no longer know what I say,
or what I do!
And yet it's necessary . . . make an effort!
Bah! Are you even a man?
You are a clown!
Put on your costume, powder your face.
The people pay, and they want to laugh.
And if Harlequin steals your Columbina,
laugh, clown, and everyone will applaud!
Turn your distress and tears into jokes,
your pain and sobbing into a grimace, Ah!
Laugh, clown, at your broken love!
Laugh at the grief that poisons your heart![4]

Third Path: A Path of Righteousness

Read the Word of the Lord in Proverbs 12:28:

In the path of righteousness is life, and in its pathway there is no death.

The first two paths are unsatisfying; however, there is a third path. This is the path of righteousness. On this path, we turn toward others, despite our fears. Cautiously, we tear down our strongholds by asking good questions rather than adding additional bricks of assumptions, self-defensive words, or clownish behavior. As the rest of this book unfolds, we will see how this path of righteousness enables our communication to be soul-satisfying rather than soul-crushing.

To be sure, all three paths bring pain. We must be sober-minded. Without the assurance that God is up to something, we tend to choose the path that we believe will cause us the least amount of heartache. We are silly sheep, grazing in the pasture of our Good Shepherd, when we tell ourselves that there will be no pain or fear on our path. But the Good Shepherd will guide us with His rod and staff and go after us when we wander away from His fold.

As we conclude this chapter, let us remember that God gives us the gift of speech to enjoy in this life and the next. Fear interferes with redemptive conversations. But we can wisely set our hearts on that righteous path where we tear down our walls, brick by brick, so that we can enjoy the gift God has given us. And, by God's mercy, on that journey we will consider the words we use in our everyday conversations as gifts we give to one another.

ADAM'S SIN AND COMMUNICATION

UNDERSTANDING SINLESSNESS

Adam and the Woman's identity were shaped by the powerful statements and experiences God gave them. As sinners, we can never fully understand the uniqueness of Adam and the Woman's relationship with their Creator. We tend to view Adam and the Woman, before the Fall, as being just like us. We have always been sinful, which is why it is hard to understand Adam and the Woman's PPIFSt and PPIFEx. King David captures the very essence of our condition. Read the Word of the Lord in Psalm 51:5:

> Behold, I was brought forth in iniquity, and in sin did my mother conceive me.

While David was conceived in sin, Adam and the Woman were created good, with no speck of sin. God walked with Adam and the Woman in the cool of the day. We cannot even fathom what that was like. We can properly say we walk with God. The difference is we walk with God while living *sinful* lives. Adam and the Woman walked with God, but they were *sinless.*

In their unfallen state, conversations between Adam and the Woman would never contain any hint of misery brought about by intentional or unintentional sin. Think about the implications of this statement. No self-talk could lead Adam and his wife to Speak CODE that obscured their true feelings. Our self-talk often leads us to Speak CODE because our sin nature feeds fear, shame, and guilt. Sin is always present in our conversations and in our behavior.

I am not saying that we never experience sweet interactions that lead to deep connectedness and fellowship. I am saying that within these soul-satisfying times, sin is always present. Sin is the reason our conversations can never be like Adam and the Woman's. Our sin makes communication hurtful and baffling.

We know that Adam and the Woman enjoyed daily walks with God. We have no idea what the three of them said or did during those walks. We do know that when conversations took place, God was sinless, Adam was sinless, and the Woman was sinless. As God spoke to Adam and the Woman, they developed powerful experiences that gave them a clear understanding of God's nature and character. Fallen humans, living in a fallen creation, cannot physically walk and talk with God. Yet, we clearly see and understand God's invisible attributes sufficiently, so that we are without excuse. Read the Word of the Lord in Romans 1:18–20:

> For the wrath of God is revealed from heaven against all ungodliness and unrighteousness of men, who by their unrighteousness suppress the truth. For what can be known about God is plain to them, because God has shown it to them. For his invisible attributes, namely, his eternal power and divine nature, have been clearly perceived, ever since the creation of the world, in the things that have been made. So they are without excuse.

This text tells us that fallen humans see God clearly and understand His divine character, through nature, well enough that they are held accountable. If this is true, unfallen humans would have had an even clearer understanding of God. Adam and the Woman walked with God in an unfallen creation, spoke to Him directly, and knew Him intimately.

Let's not miss the distinct nature of these walks as we reflect on the sweet communion they shared. Since Adam and the Woman were not conceived in sin, their interpretation of God's interaction with them was, by nature, different than ours. That is hard for us to understand. To be clear, the difference is not on God's part. He is perfect and never changes. The difference comes from our sinful minds that fail to understand our good God and His relationship with our first parents. Sin distorts our comprehension of this unique relationship.

Unlike us, their unfallen minds enabled them to see God with perfect clarity as their powerful experiences with God developed. Adam and the Woman trusted God without doubt, loved God without limits, understood God without blind spots, believed God without reservations, and obeyed God without hesitation. As fallen people, we struggle to see God's specific goodness to us as His plan for our lives unfolds. Not so with Adam and the Woman.

Adam and the Woman were the best of the best. They were the champions of champions not because they were smarter or physically superior to us (although they probably were). They were the best of the best because they were not conceived in sin but were created sinless. This allowed them to be in an open, loving relationship with God without the impediment of sin. Adam and the Woman were better than we are, as they were able to stand face to face with God. In contrast, we know from biblical texts that for sinful humans to see God's face is a death sentence. Read the Word of the Lord in Exodus 33:18–20:

> Moses said, "Please show me your glory." And he said, "I will make all my goodness pass before you and will proclaim before you my name 'The Lord.' And I will be gracious to whom I will be gracious, and will show mercy on whom I will show mercy. But," he said, "you cannot see my face, for man shall not see me and live."

UNFALLEN VS. FALLEN CONVERSATIONS

Try, if you will, to imagine conversations between unfallen people. I find that thought hard to process. Unfallen people would have no need to explain the motives behind the words they said to each other. Assumptions leading to misunderstandings would not exist. If people were unfallen, any misunderstanding could never lead to hurt feelings or the breakdown of the relationship. Unfallen people would have no agendas or motives influenced by the sin hiding behind their words. There would never be hidden agendas or ulterior motives involving trickery or deceit. No one would Speak CODE because everyone would understand his own emotions as well as the emotions of others. Self-talk would not be guided by past negative statements and experiences.

Unfallen people would never involve themselves in any form of evil speech, either with one another or with God. For them, what God said would always be wise, trustworthy, loving, true, unquestionable, infallible, and kind. Their sinlessness would inform them that only good comes from God's hand. Sinless people would be extraordinarily grateful, because they would recognize how much God has given them. Sinless people would celebrate the goodness of God just because He is God. This close communion with God would be completely satisfying.

Obviously, fallen people can be noble and generally obedient. However, they will regularly express the sin in their hearts. They may either openly or secretly accuse God of not being good because they are blinded by sin. Sinful people grumble and complain, which prevents them from being grateful to God and others. Fallen people's God-talk, people-talk, and self-talk promotes soul-crushing conversations. Fallen people's hearts are characterized by ingratitude. In their speech, they express words of retaliation, greed, hurt, and bitterness.

To summarize, sinful people talk to one another, and to God, differently than Adam and the Woman did. We can never fully understand Adam and the Woman's experiences with God and with each other because we are sinful from the womb. However, a deeper understanding of their relationships will lead us toward more soul-satisfying conversations.

There are several challenging issues remaining in Genesis 3:

- What led to the Woman's deception and fall?
- How did that deception lead her to tempt Adam to sin?
- What were the consequences of Adam's willful sin?
- Why does any of this matter when it comes to our soul-satisfying communications?

We will use Adam's response to his wife's temptation to explain a unique form of communication known as *turning toward.* Turning toward happens when we have been placed in unimaginable situations but choose not to abandon the relationship. Instead, we seek reconciliation, in the hope of restoring the relationship.

WHAT ABOUT THE WOMAN?

Before we begin our analysis of the Woman, let's look at five statements we can know about her from the Creation narrative. For us to understand what redemptive communication means, we must be brave and ask the text good questions based on what Scripture tells us and not on what we think it says.

- The Woman was created sinless, which means that all her PPIFSt and PPIFEx were unaffected by sin. We do not know the timespan between her creation and her deception. We do know that before she ate the fruit, all her words, thoughts, attitudes, motives, or behaviors were sinless.
- God said it was not good for Adam to be alone, so He created the Woman.
- The Woman walked with God and Adam in the cool of the day.
- The Woman was deceived into sinning by the cunning of the serpent.
- The Woman tempted her husband by offering him the fruit.

With these statements as a backdrop, we can now look at that fateful conversation between the Woman and the serpent. In our consideration, we need to be very careful how we judge her as we attempt to make her fallen like us. We know that the Woman was deceived. Read the Word of the Lord in 1 Timothy 2:13–14:

> For Adam was formed first, then Eve; and Adam was not deceived, but the woman was deceived and became a transgressor.

And in 2 Corinthians 11:3:

> But I am afraid that as the serpent deceived Eve by his cunning, your thoughts will be led astray from a sincere and pure devotion to Christ.

This Woman, whom God created specifically to be a suitable helper for Adam, was deceived, then sinned. Adam was not deceived when his wife gave him the fruit. Adam willfully sinned. As we continue looking at the Woman as presented in the Creation narrative, let's keep this question in the back of our minds: what would ever convince sinless Adam to turn toward his now-sinful wife and eat the fruit she offered him, and how does this sin affect our conversations today?

What Deceived the Woman

Let me lay a bit of groundwork to help us understand how the Woman was deceived, so that we can better understand how our present conversations are vulnerable. Read the Word of the Lord from Genesis 3:1–7:

> Now the serpent was more crafty than any other beast of the field that the Lord God had made.
>
> He said to the woman, "Did God actually say, 'You shall not eat of any tree

> in the garden'?" And the woman said to the serpent, "We may eat of the fruit of the trees in the garden, but God said, 'You shall not eat of the fruit of the tree that is in the midst of the garden, neither shall you touch it, lest you die.'" But the serpent said to the woman, "You will not surely die. For God knows that when you eat of it your eyes will be opened, and you will be like God, knowing good and evil." So when the woman saw that the tree was good for food, and that it was a delight to the eyes, and that the tree was to be desired to make one wise, she took of its fruit and ate, and she also gave some to her husband who was with her, and he ate. Then the eyes of both were opened, and they knew that they were naked. And they sewed fig leaves together and made themselves loincloths.

We have probably read this account many times before. Maybe we have become so familiar with these verses that we forget to ask the text important questions or to allow the text to speak to us. For example, without asking the text what the phrase "more crafty" means, we may conclude that the Woman had a character flaw or a blind spot when it comes to obeying God.

How could the cunning of the serpent deceive the sinless Woman into becoming a transgressor? Let's look at the word crafty in the Hebrew text. The word "crafty" comes from the Hebrew word *arum,* which can also mean subtle, shrewd, clever, prudent, or cautious. In the Septuagint, the Greek Old Testament, arum becomes the Greek word *phronimotatos,* which translates into English as "most sensible," "most prudent," or "most wise."

Understanding this phrase helps our twenty-first century fallen minds see that this serpent had a reputation. He was the most crafty, most wise, most clever, most sensible, and most prudent of all the beasts of the field God created. Did the Woman know the serpent's characteristics? If so, how would she have known them?

Perhaps the serpent spoke to her before the events recorded in the early part of Genesis 3. There is no evidence that the Woman was surprised by the serpent's speech. We cannot know if the Woman was aware of the serpent's cleverness or sensibleness. The Woman may have had some understanding of his character because she entered a thoughtful dialogue with him. She considered the evidence presented to her, although she did add words to the prohibition that God never said. Regardless of what she knew about the serpent, once the Woman ate the fruit, she was a transgressor. In one act, the Woman moved from a position of purity and harmony with God, Adam, and all creation to sudden isolation—alienated from God, Adam, and the created order. Words always have consequences.

What We Miss as Accomplished Sinners

You will see that I use several adjectives to describe how we have accommodated sin. We all too often are accomplished, sophisticated, practiced and sadly comfortable sinners. This is not a good thing, but it accurately describes who we are.

We cannot underestimate the Woman's reaction to becoming a transgressor just because we are accomplished sinners. Her sense of guilt and shame is something to which we can finally relate—with one significant difference. This was her first sin. We understand the effects of sin all too well because we have been practicing sinners since birth. However, for the Woman, her guilt, shame, and the loss of her sinless nature would ruin her intimate relationship with both Adam and God. This loss would have affected every part of her body and her soul. The impact of this sin is almost incalculable, and we must not miss its significance because we are sinners.

Might she have wept uncontrollably in her devastation? Might she have felt physically sick and utterly unsalvageable? Might the endearing eyes of her sinless husband now see her sinful body and soul as horrific? We must not forget that we share the very image of God with this Woman. Many of us have experienced a sense of guilt and shame over sin that made us feel so wretched that our eyes became swollen from the tears we shed. However, unlike the Woman, we are experienced and sophisticated sinners! King David was a practiced sinner, and his profound reaction to his sin is extraordinary. Read the Word of the Lord in Psalm 38:3–8:

> There is no soundness in my flesh because of your indignation; there is no health in my bones because of my sin. For my iniquities have gone over my head; like a heavy burden, they are too heavy for me. My wounds stink and fester because of my foolishness, I am utterly bowed down and prostrate; all the day I go about mourning. For my sides are filled with burning, and there is no soundness in my flesh. I am feeble and crushed; I groan because of the tumult of my heart.

Most of us can easily identify with David's description of what happens to us when we sin. If we cannot identify with David, we underestimate the severity of our personal sin. But the Woman's experience was more cataclysmic in its damage to her than we or David could ever imagine. This was her first sin, and we cannot minimize that fact. We can take David's description and magnify it tenfold, and still we could never relate to the Woman's emotional and physical condition at the moment she ate the fruit and offered it to her husband. This will become a devastating PPIFEx for her.

After the Woman's fall, we must consider the question of what led to Adam's choice. Is it possible that unfallen Adam would not notice that his wife was broken, fallen, and alienated from all creation? According to David's description of sin, I think not. It seems that he must have seen the Woman's reaction to her own sin. She could not move from purity and holiness to being dead in her trespasses and sin and merely shrug her shoulders. Was Adam repulsed by her corruption? Did he see a vision of a monster in front of him, or did Adam still see his vision of loveliness? In all creation, only the Woman knew the ugliness of sin. She stood before him, broken beyond recognition and offered unfallen Adam an impossible choice: either join me in my misery or desert me. Adam, the decision is yours.

WHAT ABOUT ADAM?

What made Adam eat the fruit, knowing full well that God clearly told him if he ate it, he would die? Read the Word of the Lord in 1 Timothy 2:14:

> . . . and Adam was not deceived, but the woman was deceived and became a transgressor.

Adam's heart and mind were still sinless when his wife held out her hand and offered him the same fruit that ruined her. As he considered this choice, we know that Adam was not deceived.

The biblical text is clear. Adam could not have a desire to be greater than God or believe that God withheld good from him, for two reasons. First, had Adam believed God withheld good, he would have been deceived. Clearly, Adam was not the one deceived. Second, those evil thoughts and ideas in his heart would have been his first sin, since sin originates in the heart. We know that his first sin was eating the fruit offered to him by his wife.

Before we answer the question as to why Adam turned toward his wife, let's look at these statements about Adam. We must not assume that Adam was a sinner like us *before* he ate the fruit.

- Unlike his wife, Adam did not succumb to the serpent's deceptive words; he was not tricked into sinning.
- Because he was not deceived, Adam knew that eating the fruit would cause him harm.
- Adam understood that eating the fruit was open rebellion against the God he loved.
- From Adam's creation, his deep love and sinless communion with God provided him with powerful statements and experiences.
- Adam's PPIFSt and PPIFEx with God were unlike ours and unique to him and his wife.
- Adam's past experiences with God had demonstrated that God always solved Adam's problems.

GOD'S SPECIFIC GOODNESS

To see God's specific goodness to Adam, read the Word of the Lord from Genesis 2:18–23:

> Then the Lord God said, "It is not good that the man should be alone; I will make him a helper fit for him." Now out of the ground the Lord God had formed every beast of the field and every bird of the heavens and brought them to the man to see what he would call them. And whatever the man called every living creature, that was its name. The man gave names to all livestock and to the birds of the heavens and to every beast of the field. But for Adam there was not found a helper fit for him. So the Lord God caused a deep sleep to fall upon the man, and while he slept took one of his ribs and closed up its place with flesh. And the rib that the Lord God had taken from the man he made into a woman and brought her to the man. Then the man said, "This at last is bone of my bones and flesh of my flesh; she shall be called Woman, because she was taken out of Man."

These events built in Adam immensely Powerful Identity Forming Statements and Experiences about the God he loved. God commented that Adam's aloneness is not good. He caused all the beasts of the field and birds of the air to appear before Adam in a naming ceremony, demonstrating that Adam was, in fact, alone. According to God's declaration, no created thing fit him.

There is no hint that Adam complained to God about his aloneness. Our oh-so-sinful hearts complain when faced with issues that make our lives difficult. We often take matters into our own hands and solve our own problems, which leads to untold heartache and sadness. But we are sinful, and Adam is not.

Based on Adam's loneliness, God demonstrated specific goodness to him when He created the Woman while Adam slept. God not only identified Adam's need, but He also took care of it. This act became a significant PPIFSt/PPIFEx for Adam. In the same way, the God we love identifies and solves our deepest needs. He is the same yesterday, today, and tomorrow. Just as God cared for Adam's specific need, we can be confident God cares for ours as well, including our desire for soul-satisfying communication.

THE FIRST ADAM AND THE SECOND ADAM

We should read the entire chapter of Romans 5 to see the incredible likeness Adam shares with Jesus. But for our purposes, focus on the unique transgression of Adam. Read the Word of the Lord in Romans 5:14:

> Yet death reigned from Adam to Moses, even over those whose sinning was not like the transgression of Adam, who was a type of the one who was to come.

Adam's transgression was different from all other transgressions because his transgression came from a heart that was heretofore sinless. Because of this, I believe the strongest human temptation ever experienced (except for Christ's temptation) was in that very moment when the Woman tempted Adam with the forbidden fruit.

Adam is a type of the one to come, namely Jesus. Paul talks about Adam's importance by contrasting Adam to the Second Adam, Jesus Christ. The comparison is helpful because the paths taken by the two sinless men went in totally different directions that will help us understand Adam's decision to eat the fruit. Consider the comparison between the First Adam and the second Adam:

- Adam's transgression was unlike any other sin in human history. But Jesus's sinlessness made Him God's perfect sacrifice to take away our wrongdoings.
- We died through Adam's sin. But we live to eternal life through Jesus's free gift of salvation.
- Adam's sin brought us condemnation. But Jesus's one act of righteousness brings us

justification.

- Adam's sin of disobedience made us sinners. But Jesus's obedience makes us saints of God.

WHAT MADE ADAM TURN TOWARD HIS WIFE?

What I am about to write are my own thoughts based on many years of counseling, a careful study of the Scriptures, and by the fearless analysis of Genesis 1–3 found in *The Beginning: A Second Look at the First Sin.*[5] We read that after the Woman was deceived by the serpent and ate the fruit, she offered it to Adam. We discussed the likelihood that the Woman was physically altered based on our experience of sin and on David's description of the effect sin had on his own body. I believe Adam saw his wife as utterly broken, wounded, and sinful. Adam, who was still without sin at this point, would have recognized that his wife was completely undone and changed immeasurably.

The Final Answer

Let us now answer the question we have been working toward based on the Creation account from Genesis 1–3 and explore how it relates to our present-day conversations. We discussed God's specific goodness to all His creation. We looked at how God's goodness provided Adam and his wife with Powerful Identity Forming Statements and Experiences, which shaped their identity in God. We read how God identified the needs of His creatures and met them. Now, we consider the significance of Adam's decision to willingly sin by eating the fruit his beloved wife offered him. How does Adam's fateful choice shed light on how we speak to each other, even in impossible situations?

What were Adam's choices after his wife tempted him with the fruit?

- He could have simply turned and walked away and left her alone in her sin.
- He could have punched the lights out of the serpent or grabbed him by his lying throat and thrown him at the feet of God.
- He could have berated and cursed his wife for putting him in such a lose-lose situation.
- He could have sent the bone of his bone and flesh of his flesh away from the garden of Eden, where she would be isolated from him and God.
- He could have suggested that she curse God and end it all.
- He could have trusted that the God who provided his wife as a remedy for his aloneness would find a way out of this unbearable situation.

What could the Woman have done after she was deceived?

- She could have lived in total isolation from Adam.
- She could have killed herself.
- She could have cursed God.
- She could have shrugged it off and made a home for herself outside of Eden.
- She could have trusted that God would provide a way out as He always did.
- She could have tempted Adam to join her in her utter misery and sin.

Misplaced Sacrificial Love

Scripture says Adam was not the one deceived. Consider that carefully. Many hold theories about Adam that require him to be ignorant and deluded. Adam was aware that his wife sinned. It appears the only answer that explains why he ate the fruit is that he ate it out of misplaced sacrificial love for his wife. Based on his PPIFSt and PPIFEx, Adam joined his wife, believing that God would find a way out for them!

I can hear you screaming, "Wait. What? I thought Adam was proud and wanted to be like God. Diana, are you crazy? What folly is this you are saying?"

You will need to decide if unfallen Adam had the sin of pride in his heart before he ate the fruit. If he did, he was fallen before he ate and so could not have fallen by eating it. But if we believe Adam fell by eating the fruit, it appears more reasonable to attribute his sin of disobedience to misplaced sacrificial love for his wife. We look at what happened and think, "Adam, can't you just do the right thing? You are Adam, for heaven's sake. Just do not eat the fruit. Even we know enough not to eat that forbidden fruit! Adam, get a grip, because our lives depend on your decision."

Adam sinned when he turned toward his wife and ate the fruit she offered him. The act of turning toward is provocative because it confronts our paradigms. Nevertheless, God shows us a man-Champion, created sinless, who turned toward the bone of his bone and flesh of his flesh even after she became a transgressor. I am not saying Adam made the right choice. In my view, Adam made a compassionate choice, but a very wrong and sinful one. Was this a horrific sin? It was a sin more egregious than we could ever imagine! In fact, it was a sin that only Jesus could remedy through His sacrificial death on a blood-stained cross. Adam faced his sinful wife and willingly joined her in her misery. He turned toward her. And thank God, Jesus, the Second Adam, turns toward us.

As we think about the Second Adam, let us celebrate that Jesus turns toward the miserable sinners that we are and joins Himself to us. The Second Adam's sacrifice has the power of God to save us, as He exchanges His righteousness for our shame. The First Adam's misplaced sacrificial love for his wife had no power to save her. The First Adam could join his wife in her sin but never exchange his righteous sacrificial act for his wife's sinful act. Adam's erroneous sacrifice mirrored the Second Adam's compassion and holy sacrifice in the following ways:

- The first Adam was the first human in Creation. The Second Adam is the firstborn in many ways: he is Mary's firstborn, the firstborn of all Creation, the firstborn from the dead, and the firstborn among many brothers.
- The first Adam gave himself up for the Woman. The Second Adam gave Himself up for His people.
- The first Adam's sacrifice was of no value. The Second Adam's willing sacrifice was effective for the sins of the world.
- The Woman stood before Adam utterly undone. We stand before the Second Adam utterly undone as well.
- Adam experienced separation from God when Adam committed his first sin. The Second Adam experienced separation from God when God placed the sins of the whole world on Him as He hung on the Cross.
- The first Adam could not atone for his own sin. But the Second Adam became our atonement.

The Second Adam accomplished what the first Adam could never do. And that shows us how to turn toward others in their brokenness and gives us courage to face soul-crushing conversations.

NECESSARY RELATIONSHIPS

God places us in *necessary relationships.* These relationships may be parent to child, friend to friend, family to family, or employer to employee. Each relationship has loosely defined roles. Wherever God places us, we must show that necessary relationship honor.

Marriage is one of God's necessary relationships. The marriage relationship is unique because God makes married people one flesh. There is an exclusivity to marriage unlike any other relationship. For example, acts of sexual intimacy are reserved to married couples. Additionally, each individual's body belongs to the other. Sexual intimacy and ownership of our bodies are forms of communication which belong solely to married couples. Adam and the Woman represent the first marriage in human history. Both were sinless and enjoyed a deep connectedness that knit their bodies into one flesh. Again, read the Word of the Lord from Genesis 2:23–24:

> Then the man said, "This at last is bone of my bones and flesh of my flesh; she shall be called Woman, because she was taken out of Man." Therefore a man shall leave his father and his mother and hold fast to his wife, and they shall become one flesh.

ONE FLESHING

Even in a fallen world, married couples are one flesh, patterned on the example of Adam and his wife. Read the Word of the Lord from Ephesians 5:25–33:

> Husbands, love your wives, as Christ loved the church and gave himself up for her, that he might sanctify her, having cleansed her by the washing of water with the word, so that he might present the church to himself in splendor, without spot or wrinkle or any such thing, that she might be holy and without blemish. In the same way husbands should love their wives as their own bodies. He who loves his wife loves himself. For no one ever hated his own flesh, but nourishes and cherishes it, just as Christ does the church, because we are members of his body. "Therefore a man shall leave his father and mother and hold fast to his wife, and the two shall become one flesh." This mystery is profound, and I am saying that it refers to Christ and the church. However, let each one of you love his wife as himself, and let the wife see that she respects her husband.

As we continue to answer the question why Adam turned toward his wife, let's look at unique aspects of one fleshing. Love in a one fleshing relationship is vastly different than the love in all other relationships. In the Ephesians passage, the idea of one flesh from Genesis is expanded. Paul emphasizes that love in marriage is sacrificial, sanctifying, and cherishing, all of which leads to holy splendor. This love is exclusive in that it requires leaving all others. Additionally, this love is a mystery reflecting Christ's love for His church. Adam and the Woman experienced this pure love with no impediment of sin. This concept of one fleshing love, may have been more significant for them because the Woman was created from Adam's own flesh.

The Connectedness of One Fleshing

One fleshing unites two separate people. It is almost as though the two people have become a single entity. What hurts one—emotionally, physically, and even spiritually—hurts the other. The joys, accomplishments, and sorrows experienced by one are shared by the other. Husbands and wives go about their daily lives, but because of one fleshing, they are always tethered to each other. One fleshing is always present, even if a married couple is separated physically or emotionally. The connectedness of one fleshing is expressed in a married couple's deepest form of communication, the act of sexual intimacy. Even though one fleshing is more than sexual intimacy, one fleshing can begin with the sexual act, whether two people are married or not. Read the Word of the Lord in 1 Corinthians 6:16:

> Or do you not know that he who is joined to a prostitute becomes one body with her? For, as it is written, "The two will become one flesh."

If we violate our marriage, we desecrate God's purpose of being one flesh. Such a disobedience severs communication, creates alienation, and destroys the unique love between married couples. This also explains why adultery (including pornography) devastates marriages. Now that we have broadened our understanding of one fleshing, let's see the connection to Adam's decision to turn toward his wife.

Because Adam and his wife were one flesh and sinless, they shared a love unlike any we have known. This made Adam's temptation to join his wife in her sin and misery a uniquely difficult choice. Adam turned toward his one flesh in her utter despair. This is a choice we can barely fathom. However, we must remember that Adam's marriage shares all the characteristics found in Ephesians 5, except that Adam and his wife were sinless. Sinless Adam's action was profoundly sympathetic, deeply devoted, extremely connected, and very sacrificial. However, it was a devastating choice that led to the fall of Creation.

We should note that there is another category of relationships sometimes known as one-anothering. Husband and wives participate in one-anothering as well as one-fleshing. In one-anothering we care for neighbors, those in need, our family, our friends, and even our enemies as instructed by Scripture. We one-another, or care for each other, by incarnating the comfort of Christ as we carry each other's burdens as seen in 2 Corinthians 1:3–7. When we practice one-anothering, our conversations become part of the caring process as our words reflect humility, understanding, and compassion.

THE BENEFITS OF TURNING TOWARD

While Adam shows us that not all sacrifice is good, the Second Adam shows how His sacrifice leads to salvation. So how can we use the example of Adam's and Jesus's sacrificial love to help us redeem conversations? In those situations where we must make impossible decisions and where our words will destroy or heal, perhaps we can turn toward offenders as Adam did. After many tears, prayer, counsel, patience, and the desire to be obedient, we turn toward others "at just the right time."

God does everything "at the right time." Jesus's birth, the Cross, and God's activities in our lives are "at the right time." Read the Word of the Lord in Romans 5:6 (emphasis added):

> For while we were still weak, *at the right time* Christ died for the ungodly.

Let's look at what well-timed turning toward communicates.

At the right time, perhaps we can turn toward our spouse who committed adultery with our best friend. Turning toward may not mean taking our spouse back (although it could). Turning toward means speaking authentic words of disbelief, rebuke, and horror rather than simply turning away. Behaviors involved in turning away are nearly limitless. These behaviors are driven by revenge and could include rage, acts of retaliation, or deadly silence.

At the right time, we parents may be able to turn toward our child who chose an alternative lifestyle, speaking words of wisdom rather than turning away with words of rejection or condemnation.

At the right time, we may be able to turn toward the person who spun our life upside down because of his sinful lifestyle, regardless of whether it was intentional or unintentional. We can confront him with words full of shock, bewilderment, accountability, and truth.

At the right time, we may be able to turn toward those who falsely accuse us. We can use words expressing righteousness, strength, and power.

At the right time, we (perhaps through a designated surrogate), may be able to turn toward our abuser. We employ a surrogate in situations where facing our abuser would cause us more pain. In turning toward, we use words that will bring us healing and hold the offender accountable for his inexcusable behavior. Our objective is to point the perpetrator to God's unshakable standard rather than turning away.

At the right time, we who have been betrayed, can turn toward our betrayer. We point him to confession, repentance, and forgiveness rather than turning away.

At the right time, we who have perpetrated sinful acts on others can turn toward them and away from ourselves. Rather than deny, minimize, or ignore their words we can turn toward them in confession and repentance, leading to forgiveness and reconciliation.

THE CONSEQUENCES OF TURNING AWAY

If we cannot turn toward those who have harmed us, what is our alternative? Chances are good that every time we see or think about that person, memories will flood our thoughts which will affect the words we say or the silence we choose. If we turn away from difficult conversations, we will continue to carry the pain based on our Two Influential Forces. Our past statements and experiences will determine our present and future, leaving little hope for redemption. Thankfully, Scripture gives us the example of Adam who turned toward his wife in spite of a situation more devasting than any we might experience.

Therefore, in the depths of the sin we commit against each other and the soul-crushing conversations that ensue, we can follow Adam's model of sacrifice by turning toward each other. At just the right time, we can love one another in the chaos. Remember: . . .it must be at just the right time.

REDEMPTIVE CONVERSATIONS

Prior to the Fall, communication between Adam, the Woman, and God was without sin. That means Adam and the Woman never Spoke CODE, intentionally or unintentionally. No sin ever hindered their communication. God is sinless and trustworthy. Adam was sinless and trustworthy. The Woman was sinless and trustworthy. We cannot even comprehend the kind of communication Adam, the Woman, and God shared with each other. But it is worth the effort to at least try. Communication pre-Fall was sinless and soul-satisfying. Communication post-Fall is vulnerable. Post-Fall words can rip us apart with little hope of the split ever being repaired. We often choose Speaking CODE over speaking truth in love.

Let's try to compare Adam and the Woman's powerful experiences with each other to the powerful experiences we have with the people in our lives. For one thing, our parents, who formed many of our ECMs and PPIFSt/ PPIFEx, were sinners. I am not saying all past statements or experiences we had were bad; I am not saying all memories are terrifying. I am saying that all PPIFSt and PPIFEx, good or bad, come to us from sinful people. Not so with Adam and the Woman, who had God as their Father. Adam and the Woman before the Fall had ideal, sinless PPIFSt/ PPIFEx. They never sinned against each other. After the Fall, our Two Influential Forces make our communication vulnerable to all sorts of folly. Our ability to speak redemptively is compromised, even with the people who love us. Why? Because even loving people are sinful.

But that does not mean we cannot try to redeem our PPIFSt and PPIFEx by seeking and granting forgiveness based on the power of God to renew us. We can learn from Adam's misplaced sacrifice and, at the right time, turn toward others in a profound act of communication.

Mercy, New Every Morning

How did God show mercy to Adam and Eve after they sinned? In the remainder of Genesis 3, we see God's specific goodness in the middle of unprecedented sin that led to a cosmic mess. Re-read the conversation in Genesis 3:8–19 between God, Adam, and the Woman. We see God's mercy as He asks Adam and the Woman a series of good questions. Their answers reflect how unsophisticated and childlike they were as sinners, in that they blame-shifted and hid. To be merciful, we must ask good questions, that lead to soul-satisfying conversations. Imitating God by asking good questions honors our relationships.

God explained the curses He imposed on the serpent, the Woman, and Adam, so there was no doubt why their lives had been changed forever. Perhaps the sweetest mercy is revealed when God promises Adam and the Woman a Savior, who will restore what they destroyed. Read the Word of the Lord in Genesis 3:15:

> I will put enmity between you and the woman, and between your offspring and her offspring; he shall bruise your head, and you shall bruise his heel.

Jesus our Savior will crush the head of Satan and reclaim His kingdom. At the end of this chapter, we see how God's mercy abounds. Read the Word of the Lord in Genesis 3:20–24:

> The man called his wife's name Eve, because she was the mother of all living. And the Lord God made for Adam and for his wife garments of skins and clothed them.
>
> Then the Lord God said, "Behold, the man has become like one of us in knowing good and evil. Now, lest he reach out his hand and take also of the tree of life and eat, and live forever." Therefore the Lord God sent him out from the garden of Eden to work the ground from which he was taken. He drove out the man, and at the east of the garden of Eden he placed the cherubim and a flaming sword that turned every way to guard the way to the tree of life.

God's mercy is specific and loving. Let's look at how deeply God demonstrated His love for them, as God helped Adam and the Woman deal with the overwhelming consequences of their sin:

- God showed His children mercy by allowing Adam to name the Woman Eve, which means "mother of all living." This gave Eve a unique place in human history, even though her deception caused chaos and rebellion.
- God showed mercy by setting up a necessary hierarchy within one flesh relationships, allowing for harmony even when disagreements are substantial.
- Most disagreements require only negotiation and compromise. When a crucial decision must be made, the husband has the final authority. That authority allows him to choose his wife's approach and sacrifice his preference. However, a husband will answer to God for his decisions. He must choose what he believes is best.
- God showed mercy by killing animals to make suitable garments for His children, so they could come out of hiding.
- God showed mercy by protecting Adam and Eve from eating the fruit that would condemn them to live forever in their sinful state. God placed cherubim to guard the way to a tree that would harm them.

Almighty God, Creator of the Universe, showed His goodness to Adam and the Woman despite their rebellion. We can emulate God during those heartbreaking conversations we have with each other. As Adam turned toward the bone of his bone and flesh of his flesh, he showed us how we can turn toward the difficult people in our lives when the time is right. We can begin to take an honest look at our own Two Influential Forces, self-talk, and CODE Speaking and see how deeply they affect every part of our verbal and nonverbal communication, including our self-talk, our people-talk and our God-talk.

SHARING HUMANNESS AND BETRAYAL

People who come to me for biblical counseling start by telling me their story. Since we are all humans, I have learned that there are certain familiar themes woven into our stories. One such theme is the profound devastation that comes from betrayal.

Perhaps there are as many types of betrayal as there are humans. While betrayals share certain similarities, the consequences and the amount of harm they cause is dramatically different. These experiences fall somewhere on a continuum of the betrayals we experience as humans. The deeper the betrayal, the more desperate the pain, and the harder it is to heal as we move forward. Our spouses may commit adultery; our children may reject our guidance; our friends may disclose a confidence; our business partners may steal from our firm.

One of the deepest forms of betrayal is that of an abusive father who uses his daughter's body for his own sexual pleasure. The idea that a father would betray his child in this way is unfathomable. This father's treachery is completely different from and much weightier than the betrayal of breaking a friend's confidence.

When we feel betrayed, our conversations may be characterized by anger-filled rants, accusations, denial, or deafening silence. Our explosive emotions prevent our conversations about the betrayal from being soul-satisfying or redemptive, and they compel us to Speak CODE.

People typically come to me after they have engaged in brutal arguments about the betrayal. Sometimes, those soul-crushing conversations spill over into our counseling session as we try to find a righteous path forward. What makes it hard for us to see the path of righteousness in the middle of soul-crushing conversations? Perhaps a look back to the first betrayal in human history will help.

The Woman betrayed Adam when she was deceived by the serpent and ate the fruit. The Woman also betrayed her Maker. How Adam responded to the Woman's deception demonstrates a different approach to betrayal. Genesis tells us that Adam turned toward her and ate the fruit. What was the conversation between the two of them? We do not know. All we know is that Adam sinned the moment he ate the fruit. Before Adam sinned, he chose to turn toward his ruined wife, eat the fruit, and willingly commit a sin that affected every human being who has ever lived.

No Cheap Excuses

One last idea we need to consider. As we turn toward those who have wounded us in thought, word, or deed, that does not mean we excuse, ignore, justify, or pardon their behavior. We observe that the conversations between Adam and the Woman did not go well after they sinned. But that does not mean we do not wait for just the right time to turn toward those who harmed us. It may take many steps before we can imagine being in a conversation with people who did us great injury. Soul-satisfying communication is not cheap.

Unfortunately, turning toward broken relationships may not be possible. The person who damaged us through his evil action may have died. He may not want to accept responsibility for his abusive or destructive behavior toward us. Until he is willing, turning toward him may not be recommended or even possible. Section Three will present ways we can turn toward difficult but necessary relationships.

Genesis 1–3 is an essential tool for understanding human communication. We must confront our propensity to judge our first parents based on our own sinful nature. Instead, commit to seeing them with eyes that truly believe that Adam and the Woman were created sinless.

As we end this section and begin our journey toward soul-satisfying conversations, may we recognize how Speaking CODE based on our Two Influential Forces affect the words we say to one another. May we use God's Word as a lamp to our feet and a light to our path as we find ourselves in our holy sanctuaries where we honor God as holy as He makes us His own. Let's prepare ourselves to turn toward one another at just the right time to the glory of God.

Section Two features a workbook that deals specifically with how our Two Influential Forces, self-talk, and Speaking CODE affect how we communicate with ourselves, others, and God. God, help us to be courageous as we open ourselves up to surprising findings.

SECTION TWO

THE COMPLEXITIES OF COMMUNICATION

HOW OUR OBJECTIVES INFORM OUR WORDS

OUR TWO INFLUENTIAL FORCES

PPIFST + PPIFEX

SPEAKING CODE AND BEING KNOWN

IT'S THEOLOGICAL AND IT'S PERSONAL

GOD'S SPECIFIC GOODNESS TO US

HUMANS IN *IMAGO DEI*

PALM TO PALM

THE COMPLEXITIES OF COMMUNICATION

Let's begin a deeper analysis of how Speaking CODE, fueled by our ECMs, PPIFSt and PPIFEx, influences our self-talk, people-talk, and God-talk. Using this section as a workbook, we can interact with these concepts in the hope that our conversations will be soul-satisfying rather than soul-crushing.

Below is the general outline we will use (the last two bullet points will be discussed in Section Three).

- Present a unique approach to communication that moves us toward soul-satisfying (life-giving) and away from soul-crushing (life-taking) speech.
- Examine how our Earliest Childhood Memories, Past Powerful Identity Forming Statements, and Past Powerful Identity Forming Experiences (Two Influential Forces) shape our communication.
- Explore Speaking CODE, in the light of how our PPIFSt and PPIFEx (primary or secondary) influence our hearts and affect our communication.
- Introduce the five elements on our path of righteousness.
- Find hope for redemptive communication.

ANATOMY OF COMMUNICATION

Communication is the process of getting an idea or thought from me to you. In that complicated process, I reveal to you my experiences—good and bad, past and present. In turn, you reveal to me your experiences—good and bad, past and present. Because our ECMs, PPIFSt, and PPIFEx are different, the idea I express may not necessarily be received by you as I intend. That may or may not be a problem.

How would you define communication?

OUR UNIQUE APPROACH TO COMMUNICATION

Communication includes nonverbal cues such as facial expressions, gestures, sighs, or guttural sounds. A smile communicates a job well done, while a frown communicates failure or dissatisfaction. A thumbs-up signals encouragement to carry on, while a vulgar hand gesture communicates loathing. A sigh/guttural sound may communicate complete exasperation, while a squeal may communicate utter delight. Eye rolling, finger wagging, slaps, blows, pushes, punches, embraces, and high-fives are nonverbal ways in which we communicate.

Which nonverbal methods do you typically use in your approach to communication?

Additionally, communication may include silence. Silence communicates many things. In our silence, we may communicate that we have gone far enough for now or that we are dead to each other. Silence can also communicate connectedness, as we sit silently by the side of our friend who just suffered loss. However, sitting in withdrawn silence by the side of our loved one during or after an argument can be soul-crushing.

How have you used silence as a form of communication? What were you communicating?

How has someone else used silence on you as their form of communication? What were they communicating?

How did that person's silence affect you?

HOW WE APPROACH COMMUNICATION

How would you describe your ability to communicate? Read the statements below and see if any of them sound like something you have said to someone or have heard said to you. This will help clarify if your words are soul-satisfying or soul-crushing. You can fill in the underlined spaces as appropriate. Do you find yourself saying . . .

"Why can't you see I am giving you the best of me? What stops you from hearing what I am saying? How is it that you do not understand me? Can't you just listen to me?"

☐ YES, I DO. *With whom?* ______________________

☐ NO, I DO NOT. ☐ OTHERS HAVE SAID THIS TO ME.

"How do our conversations get turned around so that, somehow, what I have against you becomes my fault?"

☐ YES, I DO. *With whom?* ______________________

☐ NO, I DO NOT. ☐ OTHERS HAVE SAID THIS TO ME.

"What is the point of talking when we end up like this? I can't understand why I continually put myself through this."

☐ YES, I DO. *With whom?* ______________________

☐ NO, I DO NOT. ☐ OTHERS HAVE SAID THIS TO ME.

"When we talk, I feel as though I get trapped in your web. After you accuse me of hurting you, I try to comfort you. But then you attack me for not caring for you well enough. When I try to defend myself, you play the victim and start the whole process over again! This is exhausting."

☐ YES, I DO. *With whom?* ______________________

☐ NO, I DO NOT. ☐ OTHERS HAVE SAID THIS TO ME.

"I am through talking to you, and I don't care if we ever talk about anything significant again."

☐ YES, I DO. *With whom?* ______________________

☐ NO, I DO NOT. ☐ OTHERS HAVE SAID THIS TO ME.

"I need to find some way to protect myself from your words, so I can feel safe. You force me to shut myself off. But then you exasperate me so much that I jump into the madness all over again!"

☐ YES, I DO. *With whom?* ______________________

☐ NO, I DO NOT. ☐ OTHERS HAVE SAID THIS TO ME.

"As far as I am concerned, our conversations are hopelessly confusing. Either you do not acknowledge how badly your words hurt me or you do acknowledge them and change how you talk to me. Just pick one or the other!"

☐ YES, I DO. *With whom?* ____________________

☐ NO, I DO NOT. ☐ OTHERS HAVE SAID THIS TO ME.

"When we talk, why do the words you choose have to be so painful?"

☐ YES, I DO. *With whom?* ____________________

☐ NO, I DO NOT. ☐ OTHERS HAVE SAID THIS TO ME.

"I hate it when you use words to hijack my pain and turn it into your pain. Can't I just tell you how hurt I am?"

☐ YES, I DO. *With whom?* ____________________

☐ NO, I DO NOT. ☐ OTHERS HAVE SAID THIS TO ME.

"I don't think I can handle one more disappointment from you. It would be better if you did not promise me anything rather than not following through."

☐ YES, I DO. *With whom?* ____________________

☐ NO, I DO NOT. ☐ OTHERS HAVE SAID THIS TO ME.

"I hate that you do not believe me."

☐ YES, I DO. *With whom?* ____________________

☐ NO, I DO NOT. ☐ OTHERS HAVE SAID THIS TO ME.

"Why do our conversations always end up with us doing what you want?"

☐ YES, I DO. *With whom?* ____________________

☐ NO, I DO NOT. ☐ OTHERS HAVE SAID THIS TO ME.

"Are you kidding me? We are not talking about this again. Will you ever cut me a break?"

☐ YES, I DO. *With whom?* ____________________

☐ NO, I DO NOT. ☐ OTHERS HAVE SAID THIS TO ME.

"You are never satisfied. No matter what I say, it's never going to be enough to make you happy."

☐ YES, I DO. *With whom?* ____________________

☐ NO, I DO NOT. ☐ OTHERS HAVE SAID THIS TO ME.

"You talk to me just like everyone in my past has talked to me."

☐ YES, I DO. *With whom?* ____________________

☐ NO, I DO NOT. ☐ OTHERS HAVE SAID THIS TO ME.

"I am sick of arguing with you because nothing ever gets resolved."

☐ YES, I DO. *With whom?* ______________________

☐ NO, I DO NOT. ☐ OTHERS HAVE SAID THIS TO ME.

"Why should I tell you how I really feel? Either you don't believe me, or you refuse to understand me."

☐ YES, I DO. *With whom?* ______________________

☐ NO, I DO NOT. ☐ OTHERS HAVE SAID THIS TO ME.

"You have a way of saying things that makes me feel unimportant and worthless."

☐ YES, I DO. *With whom?* ______________________

☐ NO, I DO NOT. ☐ OTHERS HAVE SAID THIS TO ME.

"You are saying the same old thing again. Get over it!"

☐ YES, I DO. *With whom?* ______________________

☐ NO, I DO NOT. ☐ OTHERS HAVE SAID THIS TO ME.

"You can't even hear how the words you speak make me feel so rejected."

☐ YES, I DO. *With whom?* ______________________

☐ NO, I DO NOT. ☐ OTHERS HAVE SAID THIS TO ME.

"Don't tell me how to feel."

☐ YES, I DO. *With whom?* ______________________

☐ NO, I DO NOT. ☐ OTHERS HAVE SAID THIS TO ME.

"Our conversations are so confusing that I have no idea what to say back to you. I feel like I am always walking on eggshells around you."

☐ YES, I DO. *With whom?* ______________________

☐ NO, I DO NOT. ☐ OTHERS HAVE SAID THIS TO ME.

"The words you hear me say to you are all your fault. If you do not want me to talk to you like this, then stop behaving the way you always do."

☐ YES, I DO. *With whom?* ______________________

☐ NO, I DO NOT. ☐ OTHERS HAVE SAID THIS TO ME.

"Did anyone ever tell you that you talk too much without saying anything of substance? No wonder I cannot understand what you are trying to say."

☐ YES, I DO. *With whom?* ______________________

☐ NO, I DO NOT. ☐ OTHERS HAVE SAID THIS TO ME.

"Must you get so stuck in your routine that talking to you depends on your availability and not my needs?"

☐ YES, I DO. *With whom?* ______________________

☐ NO, I DO NOT. ☐ OTHERS HAVE SAID THIS TO ME.

"Why try to change things? Stop worrying and forget about it."

☐ YES, I DO. *With whom?* ______________________

☐ NO, I DO NOT. ☐ OTHERS HAVE SAID THIS TO ME.

As you wrote out your answers, did the same person keep popping up? If so, list the reasons why you believe this person is problematic.

List one or two statements from the above list that capture the essence of how you feel when in difficult conversations.

Deeply connected and necessary relationships are an eye-opening place to observe how people approach communication. In my counseling, I seek to honor these relationships even if they appear to be broken beyond repair. As we noted in Section One, these relationships can be parent to child, employer to employee, roommate to roommate, best friend to best friend, sibling to sibling, or especially between husband to wife (one-fleshing).

MEN ARE FROM . . . *WHO KNOWS WHERE?* AND WOMEN ARE SOMEWHERE DOWN THE STREET FROM THEM

While you read the statements above, did you notice a tendency to hear men and women making specific statements, as though each had their own point of view? Typically, men approach communication differently than women. I am not making a universal statement, but generally speaking most men seem to want to fix problems quickly, so they can stop the barrage of words and get on with their comfortable lives. For the most part, women crave emotionally-laden, satisfying connective words that facilitate deeper intimacy and understanding.

I remember with great fondness John Lowe, my General Manager at a hotel in Baltimore. John hired me as the hotel's Experience Specialist; I was the Magic Maker for the guests who stayed with us. John and I communicated routinely throughout the day. I would email him a lengthy, carefully composed laundry list of concerns. His response would typically be fifteen words or less that completely addressed all my issues! What is up with that? Not all men are succinct like John. However, for the most part, men and women approach communication differently.

Emotions and the Sexes

Men do not always know how they feel about the words they hear during a conversation, especially if the words evoke emotions. Emotional words can become obstacles to communication for men. Women typically seem to have a better understanding of how to navigate emotionally loaded dialogue. There is no judgment here. In fact, both tendencies can cause problems for soul-satisfying communication. These roles can also reverse.

Living in Our Heads

Men would mostly say that they evaluate conversations in their heads. Men seem to do this because it is safe and controllable. Living in one's head means that a person tends to process feelings and thoughts internally, rather than processing their feelings and thoughts out loud. As an aside, women have lamented to me that their significant other finds it easier to talk to a complete stranger than to them. This confuses women because they wish their partners would talk to them like they do to strangers. For men, talking to strangers is like processing information in their heads because strangers have no skin in the game. The difficulty with living in our heads is that it can paralyze our ability to participate in discussions. The benefit of living in our heads is that we have much more time to process information without the intrusion of the other person's words, thoughts, and emotions.

Additionally, living in our heads allows us to compartmentalize information more easily. Recalling and sorting similar issues allows communication to be less stressful. However, if we are faced with a more interactive conversation, we lose the luxury of time, safety, and control. Living in our heads makes it harder to understand our emotions as well as the emotions of the person with whom we are speaking. Speaking CODE thrives when we live in our heads and makes our responses confusing. Speaking snippets of information is rarely soul-satisfying.

LIVING IN A POOL OF THOUGHTS AND IDEAS

If men live in their heads, most women live in an overflowing pool of thoughts and ideas. This translates into an abundance of emotional words. Women can become lonely and confused as they wonder if they are in a different conversation than men. How can women use all these words, while men are satisfied with grunts, followed by a few catchphrases that seem to have worked in the past? In a conversation, the clash between many words on one side and few words on the other leaves both people feeling alone. In the absence of verbal parity, Speaking CODE will fill the communication gap and force the participants to make assumptions.

Women's self-talk is an unseen participant in the conversation. The overflow of their thoughts and ideas intrudes into their discussions. The hearer may become confused, which often leads to misunderstanding and bewilderment. Women's self-talk may sound like the following:

- I'll stand in front of the TV or wait for a commercial. Then I will have his undivided attention.
- Maybe I will just turn off the electronics.
- I know! I'll overwhelm him with lots of words so he sees my point.
- Hmm . . . maybe I need to ignore him for a bit.
- Why doesn't he want deeper emotional intimacy with me?
- Can't he understand that going to work every day is not enough to make me satisfied in this relationship? I need his undivided attention as I talk out all these ideas I have been thinking about today.
- I realize he needs time with his friends, but how often?
- I know he is trying, but his ideas are so inefficient. Why can't he see my way is really the best way?
- What does he think I do all day?
- Why can't he just take the lead and plan something instead of leaving me to do all the work? I would be happy if he just started a conversation!
- I'll cry. That always gets his attention.
- Well, maybe I will try pouting. Slamming doors? Heavy sighs?
- Maybe now is the time to ask for that pair of shoes I want, so at least I get something out of his silence.

Men's self-talk is much more pragmatic. They believe they understand what they say to themselves. Men are more perplexed by what they hear. This bewilderment will be reflected in how they communicate. Men's self-talk might sound more like the following:

- Why does she get so upset?
- What does she expect me to say?
- I don't need to hang on her every word or understand her completely in order to fix the problem.
- What is the big deal? Why is this so important to her?
- I was just offering suggestions that could solve the problem.
- Chances are she won't listen to my advice or do what I say anyway, so why even suggest it?
- She wants me to plan something, but I know whatever I do will not satisfy her. Why try?
- How did what I just said communicate to her that I was minimizing her concerns? I cannot connect those dots. Who thinks like that?
- Truth be told, we have gone over the same issues until I am sick of them. I know if I engage her in a conversation, I will be up all night talking in circles! Worse still, she will ultimately turn this around, so it is my fault.
- Now it is time to tell her to go buy that pair of shoes she wants. At least I will get some peace and quiet while she is gone.

NOTE TO MEN

It may be more difficult for many men to answer the workbook questions. When I ask you to answer questions, you may find this a pointless exercise. Perhaps you could think about a particular exchange that fits a pattern of unsatisfying or even soul-crushing communication. Focus on a conversation where you end up feeling insufficient, insignificant, unappreciated, angry, frustrated, or confused because your efforts fell short. In that conversation, look for the words you used as you attempted to solve the problem.

Write out what words you most often say to solve problems presented to you.

In what ways did your partner tell you that, in offering a solution, you failed to fully understand that issue?

NOTE TO WOMEN

Women, write out how an important man in your life attempted to solve your problems. Note that this important man can be your boyfriend, husband, father, brother, grandfather, pastor, or any man who has played a significant role in your life.

How would you say that this person understood the problem as you expressed it?

We know that self-talk, Speaking CODE, and past experiences play a role in conversations. How do you communicate your expectations to that important man in your life when you do not believe he understands how you perceive the problem?

GRAVITATIONAL PULL

Both men and women tend to gravitate toward a particular communication strategy. Either we process conversations in our heads, or we present our conversations using a flood of words. The former creates a secret echo chamber where the listener is excluded from our actual thoughts. This is a recipe for Speaking CODE. The latter creates an emotional soapbox that can easily overwhelm the listener. Wherever we hold our conversations, internally or externally, our conversations may sound like we are talking to someone who lives on a different planet.

Describe a difficult conversation where you processed the information mostly in your head. Which words did you actually speak and why?

Describe a difficult conversation where you said nearly everything you were thinking. Which words did you use and why?

GOOD PROVIDER VS. GOOD COMMUNICATOR

Men may assume that the things they do, such as providing for their wives, can serve as a substitute for the ability to communicate satisfactorily. I hear married men lament, "Don't I do enough around here? It seems like nothing satisfies you. I get up every day and go to work. Can't you see from my actions that I care about you? I am still here, aren't I? What else do you want?"

Single men in relationships may say, "What makes you think spending every waking minute together is good for us? Spending time with my guy friends does not mean I don't want to spend time with you. For heaven's sake, we aren't breaking up over this. I need competitive sports and my gym time to stay healthy. This is suffocating. Why is that a problem?"

Aha! Here is the rub. Men offer up their role as a good provider to offset a woman's demand for deeper conversations filled with emotional intimacy. Usually, men feel disconnected from, or fearful of, emotions that may pull them out of their pragmatic comfort zone and into a world of nuanced definitions that stir up unpredictable feelings. This holds true in dating relationships or in relationships where people are dependent upon each other.

His manly ideals of being a good provider sometimes crumble under the weight of her womanly demands for deeper emotional intimacy. As a result, he may conclude that nothing he can do will ever be good enough. He does not share his wife's sense of urgency, and he certainly does not believe their relationship is on the rocks. Hence, men put on their best stoic face, mount their armored BarcaLounger chair as they arm themselves with the TV remote, and rally under the battle cry, "Discretion is the better form of valor." Or they will just agree with whatever is being said until the woman stops saying it!

PRESSING IN VERSUS DEATHLY SILENCE

Women react to this conflict in their own way. They might keep pressing in by asking questions. If they are not satisfied with the answer, women press in even harder. Men might say, "I just told you what I thought about that. See? You don't pay attention to what I say." Alan Dean and I call this the-every-third-sentence rule. Alan Dean believes I only listen to every third sentence he says.

If pressing in does not get the job done, women may revert into deadly silence, punctuated by moans, huffs, and door slamming. Both men and women may tell themselves, "This too shall pass." Well, maybe so. But what would make us want to settle for that? This conflict may turn into secondary PPIFSt and PPIFEx that will fuel the CODE we speak.

DIFFERENT VESSELS

Is there a biblical reason why men experience emotions and express these emotions differently than women? The differences between men and women often lead to soul-crushing conversations rather than soul-satisfying talks. Men take in and give out information much differently than women. The differences between men and women's responses are typically related to the degree men want to take on the emotions surrounding the discussion.

That is not to say all men respond differently to emotions than women. But I am comfortable saying that most men and women have enough differences in how they evaluate emotions that eventually this will affect how they talk to one another. Many men normally have a much harder time identifying how they feel in the moment emotions confront them. Emotions can produce fear, which causes men to look for a way out of the discussion. Therefore, the inability to identify emotions during a conversation affects what a man says or does not say. Men may be able to identify their emotions but simply do not know how to express them. This was what Alan Dean experienced on that fateful day when our car became our holy sanctuary where God was making us His own.

Women may be very skilled at identifying their emotions in the moment. Sometimes, women weaponize their emotions rather than using them to help the hearer understand what is happening. This cat and mouse game is not exclusive to married couples. We all play this game.

Write out the reasons why it is hard to identify your feelings while you are in an emotional conversation. Ask yourself, what does this conversation remind me of? This may be difficult, so look for the feelings that surround your fears.

Write out the reasons why it is hard for you to identify the emotions of the listener/hearer in a conversation.

Write out how you may weaponize your emotions. Ask yourself why you seek to punish the person by using emotions.

TUGGING TOWARD HARSHNESS

Sometimes, men are tugged toward harshness as they struggle to put words to their confusing feelings. Peter notes the dilemma in his epistle. Read the Word of the Lord in 1 Peter 3:7:

> Likewise, husbands, live with your wives in an understanding way, showing honor to the woman as the weaker vessel, since they are heirs with you of the grace of life, so that your prayers may not be hindered.

Paul also comments on this. Read the Word of the Lord from Colossians 3:19:

> Husbands, love your wives, and do not be harsh with them.

No matter how you exegete these passages, it is clear that men and women are *different vessels.* Their approach to communication is different based partially on their genders. They are then further impacted by their Two Influential Forces and the CODE they speak.

Both Peter and Paul comment on men's need to care for their wives by being understanding rather than harsh. Harshness or misunderstanding influences communication, both for the speaker and the hearer, and can affect their prayer life. How all this plays out in words or deeds depends upon the individual couple. Harshness and misunderstanding separate spouses and should be addressed so the concept of one flesh is upheld.

How has your spouse told you that you speak or behave harshly?

What makes you act harshly?

How has your spouse acted harshly toward you?

BUILDING UP OR TEARING DOWN

As we have seen, men are tugged toward harshness, which impacts both their wives and children. But men are not the only ones to be warned regarding their words. Women are also responsible for the words they choose in conversations. Read the Word of the Lord in Proverbs 14:1:

> The wisest of women builds her house,
> but folly with her own hands tears it down.

This verse warns women that they can singlehandedly tear down their homes with their own two hands. This Scripture paints a devastating picture of ruin and chaos. To gain a more complete understanding of this passage, let's broaden the concept of home to include other industries in which women are involved. "Home" could refer to a physical place, but it also could be her workplace, civic organizations, church groups, circle of friends, apartment, family of origin, or nuclear family. But how does a woman destroy her home? If wisdom builds and folly tears down, how do we understand the biblical concepts of wisdom and folly? Read the Word of the Lord in Proverbs 1:7:

> The fear of the Lord is the beginning of knowledge;
> fools despise wisdom and instruction.

Wisdom does not reside in us at birth, but folly certainly is our birthright. But fearing the Lord is where wisdom begins. Therefore, as a wise woman fears God, she builds her home. For women who fear God, the Two Influential Forces do not control their conversations. Self-talk becomes God-talk which minimizes Speaking CODE. Fearing God leads to gracious words and a spirit of forgiveness. Conversations stemming from foolish hearts are more likely to tear down than to build up.

Using the traditional definition of home, in what ways have you spoken words that led to the tearing down of your home?

Using the definition of home more broadly, list ways in which you have spoken words that tore down your life in community.

COMMUNICATION IS A BATTLEGROUND

Communication can become a battleground in a relationship—anytime and anywhere. Words spoken and even unspoken obstruct redemptive conversations. No one feels heard or understood, but for different reasons. Everyone feels bewildered and confused, but for different reasons. These misperceptions are particularly noticeable in relationships where people are confined in the same living space.

For married couples, husbands begin to resent the all-out assault on their comfort allegedly perpetrated by their wives. Wives may stew in a contemptuous simmer. They believe their spouse is not listening to them because they do not see their husbands implementing their womanly ideas. Eventually, both want to be left alone, because each one experiences soul-crushing conversations rather than soul-satisfying interactions. This stifles one fleshing!

While the patterns are especially striking in marriages, these observations also fit roommates or family members who live together. All of us—husbands and wives, parents and children, friends and acquaintances, male or female, rich or poor, black or white, gay or straight—experience frustrating conversations because all of us are human. Therefore, these frustrations can apply to everyone, not just to married couples.

People from the same family are especially interesting. Siblings can experience soul-crushing communication as they interact with each other. I am often astounded at how two parents can have children who take information in and give information out so very differently from each other. Mothers and daughters can struggle with communication, as can fathers and sons. In those unsatisfying and perplexing moments, we wonder how we can ever achieve soul-satisfying conversations.

TWO AGENDAS

As a biblical counselor and a sophisticated sinner, I see two agendas at work when we are in the middle of conversations that are confusing and messy. Both agendas awaken in us an elusive frustration. Each of us express these agendas in subtly different ways.

First Agenda: Sanctified Backseat Drivers

The first agenda that affects our communication comes from that moment when we see issues with uncanny clarity (or so we believe). We courageously begin to identify the stumbling blocks that cause our communication to be hurtful and soul-crushing. However, we still have no real solution that will allow us to keep those stumbling blocks out of our conversations. We have identified them, but we cannot control our response to them.

We may fall back into the same old habits or become discouraged as we cycle through upsetting feelings and failures. A good example is the truly sanctified backseat driver. You know who you are. The way we inject ourselves into fixing problems in conversations is like how some of us drive from the back seat. We have been told numerous times to please let the driver drive!

Meet Sally and Sam. Sally believes she is a consummate backseat driver and often appears to communicate that Sam is an incompetent driver. For some reason, Sam does not acknowledge her backseat driving skills. Even though Sally and Sam agree on driving etiquette, Sam takes a turn that Sally would never take. Sally tells herself, this route is not efficient, especially with the price of gas. Doesn't Sam see his route is inefficient? Sally certainly does because she is a sanctified backseat driver and Sam . . . well, let's not go there.

Sam has had years of hearing which route should be taken and why Sally alone knows the best route. Sally and Sam have previously identified this communication problem. They agreed to let whoever is in the driver's seat drive the car. But then that old familiar lump creeps up in Sally's throat, filled with words of godly efficiency that she needs to express. Sally sanctimoniously tells herself that it is for the Sam's sake that, in the name of Jesus, she calls him out on his inefficient route. Sally must speak up, if not for herself, then for all of humanity who depends on her to save the planet from inefficient and gas-wasting drivers like Sam.

This semi-autobiographical example is tongue in cheek, but it clarifies the first agenda. We sometimes see the problem with communication very clearly. However, we simply cannot keep ourselves from speaking words of wisdom in that moment when the conversation seems to take an inefficient turn. Indeed, those of us who see the issues clearly find it difficult to shut our mouths. We simply cannot remain silent because our ECMs, PPIFSt, and PPIFEx with the person to whom we are speaking drive us crazy (no pun intended)! We know we are whip-smart, which makes it easy for us to see their communication breakdown with uncanny clarity. But seeing our agenda clearly? That is a vastly different issue. We use words like, "I told you this would happen. Why don't you ever listen to me? Here we go again." Soul-satisfying communication just took a back seat.

Second Agenda: Hurry Up and Wait

The second agenda is like the first. Here we clearly see which issues crush soul-satisfying communication. However, we soon become discouraged because the other person's behavior does not change based on our timeline. Change is way too slow. We huff and puff and mutter random words we tell ourselves came from somewhere in the Bible like, "Snap to it," "Time is wasting," "Time is money," or "Time and tide wait for no one." We justify ourselves by spouting off all these gems from somewhere in the Bible, where sanctification is linked to snappiness. We look so spiritual in our haste to solve the problem that one can almost see us levitating.

Our agenda makes us sound like an overbearing boss. We become impatient with our partner. We demand to know why he does not see and implement the solutions we have proposed. How much more time will we lose while we wait for him to do what we believe is right?

Secretly, we might condemn ourselves as fools for wasting one more ounce of breath on the same subject and on the same person. He says he understands, but the moment the same situation arises, he behaves as though this is the first time we brought it to his attention. He reverts to the same wrong response that we have already agreed is disastrous. Our frustration rockets up into the stratosphere.

In fact, after tasting the sweet possibility of soul-satisfying speech, we are almost tempted to despair. Why is our partner taking so long to catch hold of what we already said? This desperation can turn into bitterness and resentment as we say, "Here it is. Here is the answer, so now why are you dragging your feet? You say you see the issue. Why can't you change?"

Write out which of the two agendas you adopt most often: Sanctified Backseat Driver or Hurry Up and Wait.

AGENDAS AT WORK

As a biblical counselor, I have been privileged to hear the heartbreaking emotions in these kinds of conversations. Here is an example of communication agendas at work.

Two close friends co-own a business together. One partner is the visionary person. The other is a practical, nuts-and-bolts person. Often the visionary partner would offer interesting scenarios on how to grow the business to the practical partner. Time after time, the practically-minded owner would almost immediately shoot down the thoughts of the visionary owner. The outcome led to hard feelings and heated arguments. When the visionary owner reached his limit, he begged the practical owner to hear him out before rejecting his proposal. Both partners agreed this was wise.

After a restless night, the visionary partner had an excellent thought. But before expressing his thought to the practical partner, the visionary person told his partner exactly what to say after he expressed his excellent idea. The script was this: "That is an interesting proposal. I was thinking of going in a different direction. But let's talk it over." The practical partner agreed to the script.

As soon as the visionary partner introduced his thoughts, the practical partner said, "No. That will not work." The visionary partner was furious and flew into a rage. Both partners saw the issue very clearly but neither one could control their PPIFSt or PPIFEx long enough to keep the promise they made to each other.

Write out an experience where you and your friend agreed how you would speak to each other but when confronted with the same issue, communication broke down.

Take heart. Identifying these two agendas becomes part of the path of righteousness that God has set us upon. Let's look at an example of how differently two people approach communication.

JOE AND JACK'S APPROACH TO COMMUNICATION

Joe was brought up in a home where emotional conversations were not allowed. As with all of us, his Two Influential Forces, self-talk, and CODE Speaking shaped how he interpreted life. His past taught Joe how to shut down when emotionally charged conversations confronted him.

Jack was raised very differently than Joe. Jack's ECMs, PPIFSt, and PPIFEx informed him that you must state your thoughts aggressively or you may not be heard. It mirrored the competitive eating that went on during family dinners. You grabbed your food before someone else beat you to it. This aggressiveness was a way of life for Jack. Just as with Joe, Jack's past shaped how Jack saw his world, especially in the area of communication. Communication between Joe and Jack was strongly influenced by their ECMs, PPIFSt, and PPIFEx. The more strongly Jack expressed himself, the more quickly Joe shut down. Self-talk and Speaking CODE ruled the day.

In this example, we see how communication styles derived from the Two Influential Forces turned soul-satisfying speech into soul-crushing words as each struggled to be heard. It is important to understand that not only were Joe and Jack speaking to each other, but they were also speaking to those people in their past who formed and shaped their identity. This confused Joe, who wondered why Jack talked like a bully. Jack pushed Joe for answers rather than allowing him to process what Jack said. It was hard for Joe, in the moment, to respond to the emotionally-charged ideas Jack presented. Joe needed to thoroughly process what Jack said. Only then could they have a constructive conversation.

On the other hand, Jack wanted to grab Joe by the throat and tell him to man up! He wondered what stopped Joe from answering direct questions. Jack thought Joe should keep up with him and stop stalling.

Write out if you are a Jack or a Joe and why.

COMMUNICATION IS VARIED AND COMPLICATED

Given the many ways we communicate, it is hard to focus on one specific communication method without touching on the many other ways we interact with each other. Therefore, we will include as many different methods as possible as we work to turn soul-crushing communication into soul-satisfying and redemptive speech.

The way we approach communication is as varied and complicated as our ECMs, PPIFSt, and PPIFEx. Both the speaker and the hearer interpret communication based on the voices from their past that influence their present conversations. Therefore, we must ask good questions to understand the person to whom we are speaking. In Section Three we will consider in depth how to ask good questions.

If our approach to communication is negative, our discussions may be soul-crushing. Negative techniques may include deception, manipulation, brutal honesty, deadly silence, schoolyard bullying, childlike pouting, incessant nagging, explosive rage, or unsubstantiated accusations. Sometimes, a negative approach may be used to get attention or to elicit a response.

Write out how someone's approach to communication has affected you. Include which method you think he may have used.

Write out how your approach to communication has affected someone with whom conversations are difficult. Which method did you use?

Hitting a Moving Target

Often, conversations feel like we are speaking to a moving target, which makes it hard for us to identify our specific communication approach. One way to stop this moving target is to ask good questions when we feel confused. In fact, the person may be speaking to someone in their past and not realize it. This places us in a conversation that does not really exist. A sign that this is happening is that we hear someone say something about our words or behavior that makes no sense. They may be Speaking CODE based on self-talk to which we are not privy. Our immediate reaction may be to defend ourselves by responding to the confusing words we hear. Defending ourselves makes the moving target even more elusive.

Write out the outcome of a conversation where you felt like you were talking to a moving target. If you get stuck, try starting with this: "When I said this, your response felt as though you were not in the same conversation with me."

Two-Way Street

Communication is a two-way street, with the speaker and the hearer equally affected by their Two Influential Forces. In a conversation, we may hear the following response, "You think what you are saying to me is new? Well, it isn't. I heard this same old crap from my parents long before you came along. Go ahead and dump on me just like they did."

The problem with the Two Influential Forces is they keep us tied to our past. They make our conversations sound like we are locked in mortal combat, but not necessarily with the person to whom we are speaking. We unknowingly weaponize our PPIFSt and PPIFEx and make our present conversation soul-crushing and confusing. Our past forces us to look in two directions. We face the person with whom we are speaking, and at the same time, we face the person in our past who wounded us so deeply. Upon realizing this, we feel remorse, but we also feel unable to change. Unfortunately, the hearer may be completely unaware that there is another voice in the conversation.

When we are in a contentious conversation, is there a second person to whom we are actually speaking? It is possible that the two people we are addressing may both be the same person (past and present). Or we may be addressing someone totally different, such as our parents, our abusers, our ex-spouses, our siblings, our friends, or those in authority over us. The idea of speaking to people from both our past and present may sound odd, so I am asking you to dig deep.

In your difficult conversations, name the person from your past that you actually want to address.

What do you want to say to that person from your past?

The Power of Words

Whatever our approach to communication, our words, past and present, are powerful. Words can preserve or devastate. Words have weight and direction: they take us back to our past, speak to our present conversations, or reach into our future. The words we speak to others take them in different directions as well. We would be wise to pay attention to the response we get and see if it matches the words we spoke. This will tell us if our words have awakened another's Two Influential Forces. A certain word or phrase, a tone of voice, a smell, or a gesture can transport us back to a particular memory. This memory may cause a reaction, leading us to shut down or go ballistic.

Write about a conversation where you were surprised by where your words took the person with whom you were speaking.

Write about a time when words said to you took you back to a past statement or an experience you had.

COMMUNICATION EVENT

It is time for you to pick out some type of communication event, current or from your past, that made you feel bewildered or exasperated. Your memory of this communication event should feel confusing and unsatisfying. This event should be something you've rehearsed repeatedly in your heart. It has become your mind's self-talk and fueled your CODE Speaking. When that happens, we write a secret script which sets up our inner theater, where everyone plays a role and where we are both the star and the director. We say our lines, then they say their lines, and eventually we become either the saint or the sinner of this internal play. Because we are created body and soul, this event should also be something that makes us experience a feeling of dread or doom somewhere in our bodies.

Write out a communication event that fits the above description.

Typically, which words do you use to address this experience?

Please note that what we say will vary from time to time or person to person. Feel free to keep adding information to the event you selected so that you can better understand how you approach communication. Or feel free to change the event if, upon reading further, some other incident works better for you.

THE EMOTION AND BODY BOX ACTIVITY

If you and I were sitting down together over a pot of hot tea, I would ask you to participate in an assignment I was asked to do during one of my classes at CCEF. In fact, I use this assignment with every person I counsel.

Below is a slightly modified version of the exercise I use. Before we start, I inform my clients that I cannot explain the instructions, but I can repeat them as often as they need. After giving them a paper with a simplified drawing of a person, I give a series of four instructions and allow time for them to complete each direction.

- Write your name over your person.
- Select the six emotions you currently feel (or frequently felt within the past year or so), and write them in the boxes next to your person.
- Select a color that best expresses the selected emotion, and color the box that color.
- Put the emotions in the part of your body where you most often feel them.

Let's get started! It is important to include why you selected the emotions you did, the colors you chose, where in your body you felt the emotions, and what effect these emotions had on your selected body part.

> *For example, I might select the emotion "Sadness." I would color the box blue because it reminds me of the 1968 song "Love is Blue," and connect it to my eyes (since everything I see is sad).*

This exercise accomplishes two things. First, it gets us to engage our emotions. Second, this exercise helps us link our soul to our body. If our soul feels sad, our body may experience tiredness. If our body experiences pain, our soul may feel emotional distress. If we were talking about this exercise over tea, we would discuss your answers, allowing me to ask better questions. I hope this exercise helps you clarify the emotions you most often experience. Understanding emotions is foundational to soul-satisfying communication.

As we conclude this chapter, it would be wise to acknowledge our unique approach to communication. Men and women communicate differently. Despite these differences, we all share in our humanness which means we share many similarities in how we communicate. Our ECMs, PPIFSt, and PPIFEx are varied and unique, but we all have them.

As we saw in the example of Joe and Jack, communication is complicated. Remember, our PPIFSt and PPIFEx cause us to speak to people in our past and present. The next chapter will discuss our objectives in communication.

HOW OUR OBJECTIVES INFORM OUR WORDS

Now that we have discussed the two agendas for communication, let's look at the motives behind our agendas. When we enter a conversation with someone who does not share our ideas, we would be wise to examine our Personal Communication Objectives. Our Personal Communication Objectives will influence the words we choose and the tone we use in our conversations. Communication is broad and varied, making it hard to describe all the ways we personally converse. Discussing the various extremes of the spectrum helps us find where we are in the process. As we discuss the PCOs below, I will focus on three possible objectives: the Animator, the Wallflower, and the Provocateur.

THE ANIMATOR

Animators believe that if they speak a little louder or act in a more animated way, the listener will acquiesce to their point of view. Their PCOs lead them to escalate their words and tone so that their ideas will prevail in a discussion. Animators believe that their personal objectives for winning the conversation are the best objectives because those objectives make sense to them.

In a conversation, the Animator's ECMs, PPIFSt, and PPIFEx may awaken when his PCOs are thwarted. Perhaps memories of not being heard surface. Perhaps he remembers being told to shut up and obey. An Animator may remember feeling a sense of power when he realized that raising his voice resulted in getting his own way. No matter which memories are brought forward, our recollections will fuel our self-talk. Our self-talk leads to Speaking CODE, resulting in us sharing a snippet of our thoughts. This process rarely leads to redemptive conversations because our self-talk and CODE Speaking is one-sided. The hearer is left to make assumptions.

For Animators, the objective is to persuade the hearer to change his mind, and to force him to set aside his own thoughts. We may be an Animator if we say "no" after someone expresses an opinion. We may raise our voice to correct the idea and offer many reasons why the speaker's thoughts are insufficient. By saying "no", we give the impression that the speaker is not entitled to his own thoughts. We read about an Animator's tactic in Chapter 8, which described the visionary partner and the practical partner. This response often leads to soul-crushing conversations.

Animators have many good ideas, but that is not the point. They use an abundance of words to get some type of buy-in. These words are often coercive or manipulative. The Animator's wish becomes their hearer's command . . . or perhaps the Animator's demand becomes their hearer's command! The resulting conversations become soul-crushing and unproductive.

An Animator would be wise to acknowledge what was said. He fears that affirming others would undermine his position. It would be better if Animators began a conversation with "I hear what you are saying." Or, "That's interesting," followed by, "Here is what I am thinking." These kinds of responses lead to a more soul-satisfying dialogue, rather than beginning the conversation with "no."

As you begin to understand your PCOs, write out how you may see yourself as an Animator.

◀ ··· ·— —· · ·— —·— ·· —· — —· —·—· — — — —·· ·

What behaviors do you exhibit as an Animator?

◀ ··· ·— —· · ·— —·— ·· —· — —· —·—· — — — —·· ·

What do you gain by being an Animator?

◀ ··· ·— —· · ·— —·— ·· —· — —· —·—· — — — —·· ·

What do you lose by being an Animator?

◀ ··· ·— —· · ·— —·— ·· —· — —· —·—· — — — —·· ·

Identify the Animator in your life. In what ways do his PCOs affect you?

◀ ··· ·— —· · ·— —·— ·· —· — —· —·—· — — — —·· ·

Becoming an Animator

How does one become an Animator? Because humans are so different, it is hard to provide a list of experiences that explain why one chooses this form of Personal Communication Objectives. We can say that our ECMs, PPIFSt, and PPIFEx (primary or secondary) eventually play out in the CODE we speak, leading us to choose an Animator's style as our Personal Communication Objectives. Perhaps we learned that to be heard we needed to raise our voice, which caused us to speak over others. We may have learned not to trust others, leading us to insist on doing things our way. Perhaps we are fearful of losing control, which causes us to demand our way.

As an Animator, write out experiences that led you to develop strategies to achieve your Personal Communication Objectives.

How does being an Animator cause you to Speak CODE?

THE WALLFLOWER

The Wallflower's experience is just the opposite. Maybe he cannot find his voice in difficult conversations, and his Personal Communication Objectives are to remain silent. Rather than speaking in an animated way, he nods passively in agreement when he really believes the other person is wrong. His PCOs appear to be compliant or silent because his ECMs, PPIFSt, and PPIFEx scream at him that he is in danger. He has fought this type of battle countless times before and lost. He learned that it is useless to engage in pointless or even aggressive discussions. These conversations are fear-producing and exhausting.

Oddly enough, a Wallflower desperately wants to achieve his PCOs but often feels unimportant or intimidated. A Wallflower realizes that an escalating conversation is futile and costly. Memories from PPIFEx map onto the very conversation in which he is engaged. Affirmation seems impossible, as a Wallflower believes talking is too risky. Painful words from the past, coupled with the feeling of being unheard in the present, act like wallpaper paste that glues him silently to the wall. As strange as it seems, a Wallflower finds comfort fading into the background.

A Wallflower's tactics might temporarily meet his Personal Communication Objectives by stopping the anxiety-producing discussion. If he's speaking with an Animator, both get their way: the Animator by overwhelming others, and the Wallflower by withdrawing. For both, communication unravels, leaving only threads of a conversation that could have been soul-satisfying. A Wallflower may want to test the safety of a conversation by saying, "I am confused by this discussion. Would it be possible for you to tell me how you define this word and explain how you mean it in the context of this discussion?"

As you begin to understand your PCOs, write out how you may see yourself as a Wallflower.

What behaviors do you exhibit as a Wallflower?

What do you gain by being a Wallflower?

What do you lose by being a Wallflower?

Identify the Wallflower in your life. In what ways do his PCOs affect you?

Becoming a Wallflower

How does one become a Wallflower? It is hard to provide a list of experiences that explains why we choose this form of Personal Communication Objectives. As with the Animator, our ECMs, PPIFSt, and PPIFEx (primary or secondary) eventually play out in the CODE we speak, leading us to choose a Wallflower style as our Personal Communication Objectives. Perhaps we did not want people to notice us because attention always involved disappointment. When we experience disillusionment on top of failure, fading into the background seems much safer. Perhaps fear and mistrust of others produces a desire to go unnoticed. We find solace in being an ornament hanging on a wall. It is easier for Wallflowers to suppress their thoughts and feelings, especially when interacting with an Animator who has no feelings for the well-being of others. Wallflowers can become deeply resentful of Animators because of their bullying tactics. However, Animators are unaffected by a Wallflower's behavior, because the Animators get their way.

Write out experiences that led you to employ Wallflower as a strategy to achieve your Personal Communication Objectives.

How does being a Wallflower cause you to Speak CODE?

THE PROVOCATEUR

Unlike an Animator or a Wallflower, Provocateurs launch hand grenades into conversations. They hope that the resulting shrapnel elicits provocative responses. They do this for several reasons. Perhaps they want to shock listeners out of their complacent state of well-being. Another reason to launch a grenade is that it helps Provocateurs explore their self-talk in order to test their thoughts against the beliefs of others. Provocateurs may think that a sudden jolt is more likely to get an unfiltered response.

Using their PCOs, Provocateurs need to be right. But, unlike the Animator, they do not talk over others or tell them "no." The Wallflower does not care who is right or wrong, he only cares about his safety. Provocateurs want to initiate arguments through bombastic statements. Their highly-charged discussions are personally challenging. Provocateurs desire truth in a world that marginalizes the have-nots. They lob grenades as public service announcements. Rehearsed answers do not satisfy them, especially from important people in their lives. Grenade attacks force people to speak truthfully as they dig down to a place of honesty. Shocking statements strip off the false outer layer, hoping to get a reaction that is more open and vulnerable. But often the Provocateur get a response that is defensive, argumentative, and hostile.

A Provocateur's tactics might temporarily meet their PCOs as they cut through the superficiality of meaningless exchanges. However, just as the Animator gets his way by overwhelming others and the Wallflower get his way by withdrawing, the Provocateur uses the hearer's incredulity to accomplish his goals. The explosive opening to the conversation destroys any hope that what is said can be soul-satisfying.

A Provocateur may want to reduce the shock of what he is about to say by prefacing his statement with, "I know what I am about to say might deeply offend you, but I need to think this through." This statement prepares the listener for the coming chaos.

As you begin to understand your PCOs, write out how you may see yourself as a Provocateur.

What behaviors do you exhibit as a Provocateur?

What do you gain by being a Provocateur?

What do you lose by being a Provocateur?

◀ ... .--. . .- -.- .. -. --. -.-. --- -.. .

Identify the Provocateur in your life. In what ways do his PCOs affect you?

◀ ... .--. . .- -.- .. -. --. -.-. --- -.. .

Becoming a Provocateur

How does one become a Provocateur? It is hard to provide a list of experiences that explains why one chooses this form of PCOs. As with the Animator and Wallflower, a Provocateur's ECMs, PPIFSt, and PPIFEx (primary or secondary) eventually play out in the CODE he speaks, leading him to choose a Provocateur style as his PCOs.

If we are Provocateurs, our self-talk tells us that we need to blow things up. Our goal is to break through whatever obstacles exist that block us from understanding ourselves and others. Whatever drives our Two Influential Forces, leads us to different perspectives that reinforce our PCOs. We may become a social justice warrior who offers public service announcements that sound accusatory. Memories from our past shape our demands that others stop hiding behind their virtue signaling.

Perhaps as Provocateurs, we experienced unfairness in life that we were powerless to address. This perceived unfairness can be cultural, such as discrimination based on race, gender bias, or sexual orientation. We may believe that we need to fight passionately against religious bigotry or socio-economic disparities. Because we have observed that nothing significant has been done to address these issues, our PCOs lead us to drop "talking bombs" to wake people up to the inconsistencies around them. As we draw attention to ourselves, we draw attention to our cause.

We have no concern for fear or failure as long as our important issues are addressed. Our self-talk tells us that the world is inequitable, and it fuels the CODE we speak. The hearer is gob-smacked and has no idea that the Provocateur desires to enlighten people on society's ills. The Wallflower sinks deeper into his wall as the Animator screams, "No. No. No!"

Write out the experiences that led you to develop Provocateur as a strategy to achieve your Personal Communication Objectives.

◀ ... .--. . .- -.- .. -. --. -.-. --- -.. .

How does being a Provocateur cause you to Speak CODE?

◀ ... .--. . .- -.- .. -. --. -.-. --- -.. .

SELF-TALK, SPEAKING CODE, AND PCOs

Self-talk continues no matter what Personal Communication Objectives we use. Our internal conversations feed the CODE we speak, affecting our PCOs. Our self-condemnation, self-accusations, or self-importance provide justification for executing our PCOs. Speaking CODE plays a significant role in controlling the words we say or do not say out loud. Our Two Influential Forces, self-talk, and CODE Speaking set us on a course that determines our PCOs.

Write out how your self-talk, which fuels the CODE you Speak, affects your PCOs.

During counseling sessions, as people's PCOs become apparent, I have witnessed changes in posture. The Animator may stand up and walk around the room to own the physical space. The Wallflower begins to lower his head as he slumps in his chair. His shoulders begin to cave in. Finally, he appears to have given up. The Provocateur stares you down with wild eyes as he makes outrageous statement that make him sound like he is on a soapbox calling everyone to repent. Redemptive conversation suffers. The Animator, Wallflower, and Provocateur achieve their PCOs, but in quite different ways.

How do we represent our Personal Communication Objectives without hindering others? We need to identify the objectives in our conversations. These objectives reflect heart issues. This is harder than it sounds. The confusion arises because our PPIFSt and PPIFEx are our reality but not necessarily the hearer's reality. The hearer cannot read our mind, nor can we read his. Each of us has our own self-talk which leads to Speaking CODE. This confusion leaves communication vulnerable.

The internal war between our PCOs and our PPIFSt and PPIFEx leaves us mystified. Sometimes, we deny or hide the pain brought about by our past, which complicates our conversations. This complication interferes with developing PCOs that are righteous and lead to soul-satisfying communication.

How has your past shaped your PCOs?

People who suffer from complex trauma often hear their abusers during present conversations, which threatens their ability to communicate authentically. Typically, their Personal Communication Objectives are overpowered by the horror of their past abuse. For them, PCOs are lost in difficult conversations, which ramps up their need for control.

Identify to Whom We Are Speaking

It helps our present conversations if we can identify to whom we are speaking. If we had an overbearing father, we may recognize his words, actions or tones while in conversations that remind us of his authoritarian objectives. Our father may have said, "The Bible says that the rebellion in you needs to be driven out. The more you cry over this spanking, the harder I will spank you. I am doing what God wants me to do to get obedience from you for your own good." In our present conversations, anything that sounds authoritarian may confuse our PCOs. Those of us who have these PPIFSt/PPIFEx may find an Animator's approach to communication compelling. In present conversations, we must ask ourselves: whose voice do we hear?

List what your father, or a similar caretaker, said to you in the past that affects how you evaluate/understand your current PCOs.

Perhaps our mother was manipulative. She may have said, "Can't you see you are making me sicker than I already am? Why can't you do this like your brother does? If you want me to love you the way I love him, then make me proud and treat me like he does. Otherwise, you will put me in an early grave." Maybe our mom was physically present but emotionally unavailable. She never showed affection or treated us like we were her very own child.

In a present conversation, if we hear words that sound like our mom's manipulation, it becomes harder for us to maintain righteous PCOs. We may gravitate to a Wallflower's PCOs because the pain of not being good enough evokes the feelings of guilt and shame which plastered us to our walls then and still does today. In present conversations, we must ask ourselves: whose voice do we hear?

List what your mother or a similar caretaker said to you in the past that affects how you evaluate/understand your current PCOs.

Perhaps we grew up in a privileged—or diminished—lifestyle. We may have heard our parents or caregivers tell us to work hard so that we would be successful. We may have heard that we have little hope to ever rise above our circumstances. Perhaps we chose an alternative lifestyle or had friends who were marginalized, and we got frustrated that our family seemed unconcerned for the welfare of others. We may decide that communicating like a Provocateur brings attention to our crusade. In present conversations, we must ask ourselves: whose voice do we hear?

List how your family of origin's unconcern for the welfare of others affects how you evaluate/understand your current PCOs.

FOUR WAYS TO CHANGE THIS CYCLE

Because we do what we think is best for us, we need new PCOs that will promote soul-satisfying people-talk and self-talk. First, in our new PCOs, we must *want* to change our motives. This want is a heart issue. Changing the want happens when what we are currently doing no longer works for us. In fact, we begin to feel disgusted by our Animator, Wallflower, or Provocateur tactics.

In what ways are your PCOs unsatisfying, so that you want to change?

Second, we can begin to adopt new PCOs that reflect biblical values. We replace selfish motivations with those that recognize the person to whom we are speaking is a human image bearer.

Describe how the words you use to achieve your PCOs can honor the person to whom you are speaking.

Third, our new PCOs do not motivate us to try to convince the hearers that they ought to do our will. Our new objectives cause us to use words that honestly reflect our view and why it makes sense to us. We will not change the hearer's minds by uttering words of flattery or dropping public service bombs, or by using manipulation, accusation, intimidation, shaming, belittling, bullying, or silence.

These new objectives create a unique way to communicate. They eliminate the pressure to make the person change his point of view. That frees us to hear one another without the fear that harsh and damaging words may be spoken to try and change our hearts. We can finally tear ourselves away from being that Animator, Wallflower, or Provocateur. We can talk honestly and authentically as we employ our new PCOs. Additionally, the person to whom we are speaking can add his wisdom to our ideas.

Write out how our new Personal Communication Objectives will affect the words you use in a conversation where the objective is not to change the hearer's mind.

Fourth, at the center of our new PCOs is the sure belief that God is at work in everyone's heart. We may remember the idea of intersecting holy sanctuaries. We want God's will to be done on Earth as it is in Heaven. Read the Word of the Lord from Proverbs 16:

> The plans of the heart belong to man,
> but the answer of the tongue is from the Lord. (16:1)
>
> The lot is cast into the lap,
> but its every decision is from the Lord. (16:33)

Write out the benefits you expect to receive if you believe and act as though only God can change a person's heart and not your words or lack thereof.

What prevents us from adopting these new objectives for communication? I believe that Speaking CODE, fueled by our Two Influential Forces, interferes with or sabotages our ability to hear what is being said. PPIFSt and PPIFEx are stubborn. They are deeply embedded in our hearts, giving us an excuse to change the hearer's mind. This justification makes it harder to esteem the hearer as a human image bearer. Plus, the other person could be woefully wrong, ignorant on the topic, or unable/unwilling to see different points of view. Our observations might be true, but only God can change the human heart.

To be sure, there are some conversations where we need to change the mind of the other person, either immediately or soon. Any sinful activity or self-harming behavior to which we are privy must be addressed with confidence, boldness, and sternness. Still, we must not bully, cajole, trick, bribe, ignore, or manipulate the person. Our admonishments must be specific to the danger at hand. If we speak words of admonishment or state our case honestly, we do it knowing that God has the final say. Our job is to be faithful to the Scriptures and speak true things with love and respect.

HEART CHECK

Understanding that only God can change the human heart to hear or speak redemptively poses another question for soul-satisfying communication. We must ask ourselves what is going on in our hearts that our objective is to persuade the listener to agree with us. Isn't being heard enough to satisfy us? If being heard is insufficient, then what would be enough? Agreeing with us? If so, we may become consumed with winning the discussion. In fact, some might describe us as being that type of person who believes it is our way or the highway.

Archangel Michael and the Devil

I find the confrontation between the archangel Michael and the devil relevant here. Read the Word of the Lord from Jude 1:9:

> But when the archangel Michael, contending with the devil, was disputing about the body of Moses, he did not presume to pronounce a blasphemous judgment, but said, "The Lord rebuke you."

Good gracious! Michael is an archangel who understands his place in this argument. Michael knows that God will settle it. How differently would our conversations turn out if we presented our case, then gave the settlement to God? I do not want to build a whole theology around this verse. I do want to say that Michael certainly has credibility to press an argument with the devil. But Michael does not rebuke the devil. He leaves those words to God. We can find this communication objective personally encouraging if we get stuck wanting to win an argument.

In this workbook, we cannot analyze how *all* the ECMs, PPIFSt, and PPIFEx hidden in our hearts affect our PCOs. That job is better accomplished face to face. The intricacies of our past are nuanced and complicated because we are human. But this we can say with certainty: if we are brave and look deeply into how our communication has been unsatisfying, we will see the impact of our Two Influential Forces. To uncover our past, we must pay attention to our self-talk. Typically, our self-talk, which leads to the CODE we speak, is the first place our Two Influential Forces appear.

Understanding and changing our PCOs is in God's plan for redemptive and soul-satisfying speech. This plan involves using language that respects people as bearers of God's image. God calls on us to fulfill the Law and the Prophets by loving Him, others, and ourselves. God alone applies the words we use to the hearer's heart. God alone uses our words to work for our good and His glory. Through God's good work, we are able to speak redemptively, knowing that God will bless our efforts. Gone are the fears and anxieties tied to our ECMs, PPIFSt, and PPIFEx.

The power behind the words we choose is enormous. That is why we need to expose the Two Influential Forces that lead us to Speak CODE. While our self-talk and our PPIFSt and PPIFEx inform our words, these are not what ultimately matter. What matters is who rules our heart. Read what Jesus tells the Pharisees in Matthew 12:33–37:

> Either make the tree good and its fruit good, or make the tree bad and its fruit bad, for the tree is known by its fruit. You brood of vipers! How can you speak good, when you are evil? For out of the abundance of the heart the mouth speaks. The good person out of his good treasure brings forth good, and the evil person out of his evil treasure brings forth evil. I tell you, on the day of judgment people will give account for every careless word they speak, for by your words you will be justified, and by your words you will be condemned.

Good words come from a good heart. Evil words come from an evil heart. Our words have consequences. It is important that we identify our PCOs so we are not condemned by our words. Change comes when we recognize that our conversations are unsatisfying and no longer work for us. We rest in the fact that God alone changes the human heart. Our objective is to enter a conversation where we lovingly use the best and most honest words we can find to express what we believe to be true, rather than Speaking CODE.

Finally, let us remember that God is at work in everyone's heart, even during our most difficult conversations. Trust God while we are in intersecting holy sanctuaries.

> Write a prayer asking God to help you see that only He can change the human heart.

In summary, identifying our Personal Communication Objectives help us to understand the words we use when in conversations. We must be aware to whom we are speaking when we talk to one another. Let us glorify God as we choose righteous PCOs knowing that God alone can change the human heart.

OUR TWO INFLUENTIAL FORCES

We know that our Two Influential Forces shape how we communicate with each other. As we continue our journey toward redemptive conversations, we ask why our people-talk can be soul-crushing. Let's look deeper into the components that make up our Two Influential Forces.

EARLIEST CHILDHOOD MEMORY

Allow me to share my ECM so that you can get an idea of what an ECM looks like and what role ECMs play in our lives before you write yours. I was about three or four years old. I know I was not any younger than three because I was three when we moved into the house where the event took place. My baby brother is three years younger than I am, and I remember him in the house. That is how I can determine my age when my ECM occurred.

Our washer and dryer were in our kitchen on the first floor. I was on the second floor when my mom asked me to throw my dress down the stairs so she could wash it. I remember standing at the top of the steps and swinging my little arm back. Problem was, I did not let go of the dress and I threw myself down the steps along with it.

I remember the feeling of tumbling and spinning. I don't remember getting hurt as much as the experience of being out of control. I guess my mom heard the thumping because she appeared at the bottom of the stairs. She was hysterical and, judging by her reaction, she thought I was dead. Tumbling down the steps set my communication table for me and my memory of it offers clues as to how I process life.

Anyone who knows me will tell you that my life can be characterized as chaotic, like tumbling and spinning down steps. I have stumbled down dark pathways in my life. The link between my ECM and how I experience life has played itself out repeatedly, especially in my behavior and how I talk. I repeat myself and sort of spin communication in my self-talk to a place where my thoughts become disorganized. I even write like I am spinning out of control.

As for my tumultuous life and my mom's reaction to it, well, that may be the topic for my next book. My mom was no different from many Italian moms when it came to the safety of their children. Some of my antics were laughable and others were miserable. My dad was not at home when this memory occurred. He probably would have been at work. I have no memory of him even knowing it happened.

Throughout my life, my dad was a hardworking man with a blue-collar job. In those days, dads rarely had much to do with the day-to-day activities in the household. In my younger years, I hardly ever went to my dad with questions about life. Only much later did my dad take an active role in my life, and I thank God he did. He rescued me from several tumbles and spins. While my dad loved me dearly, it was my mom who made the most noise in my life—much as she did . . . when I fell down the steps. This has been problematic in my personal relationship with Alan Dean: it has been hard for me to hear him, and this plays itself out in our conversations. My communication table was set precisely for me based on my ECM.

CONSTRUCTING ECMs

Now it is time to describe your Earliest Childhood Memory. Below are a series of questions to help guide you through this assignment. Answer the questions before you write your ECM as a narrative or a story. If you begin writing and change your mind because you remembered something even earlier, that is fine. Just start over. Take notes in the spaces provided.

What is the Earliest Childhood Memory you can remember?

How old might you have been? Sometimes remembering where you lived or what school you were in helps to determine your age. Recalling siblings present or not yet born may help as well.

List everyone who was present or involved in your memory.

What did each person do or how did they react in your ECM?

How did they affect you in your memory?

Who was not present in your ECM that you believe should have been?

How did you feel in your memory?

Was the memory good, bad, neutral, or something you cannot determine?

Try hard to remember as much as you can as you write out the story of your ECM. Use your notes above as guidelines.

MY EARLIEST CHILDHOOD MEMORY

Describe the link or links between your ECM and how you evaluate the words or actions that characterize your life. This is very subjective, but as you begin to get into the spirit of this you will find the links. Remember, this exercise is to get you to see how you take in information (interpretation) and give information out (communication) as your ECM sets your communication table for you.

THE SECRET HIDING PLACE FOR ECMs

We might ask ourselves, where have our ECMs been hiding all these years? We have discussed how Scripture says we treasure things in our hearts. We know that out of the abundance of our hearts our mouth speaks. Perhaps our ECMs really haven't been hiding that far from us. Perhaps if we listen well enough, we will hear our ECMs play out in our everyday dialogue. For me, that meant realizing that fathers really do have a say in the rearing of their children despite my ECMs and the experiences with my parents.

Our hearts often disguise our ECMs due to years of confusing events in our lives. Perhaps some of us use the phrase, "I've always talked like this. It is just who I was growing up." Unfortunately, our familiar does not mean our interpretation is correct or even good for us. My Alan Dean could tell you stories about how I tried to interfere with his parenting because my familiar informed me that dads did not involve themselves in childrearing.

Sherita Wants This and Not That

Let's explore how our ECMs set our communication table for us by reading Sherita's story. Sherita came to me because her life was just not working for her. In fact, Sherita never thought her life would turn out as it did.

During our first session, I asked Sherita to tell me about her Earliest Childhood Memory. She said she remembered sitting in her high chair in the kitchen. Sherita distinctly remembered her mom opening a jar of baby food for her to eat. As was her pattern, Sherita pointed to something else she wanted more than what her mom offered her. Her mom complied. But once her mom tried to feed her what she wanted, Sherita decided she wanted the food her mom offered her initially. Even as her mom complied, Sherita went back to the other jar. No matter what she told her mom, Sherita could never make up her mind what she actually wanted. Sherita told me she remembered not being able to decide between the two options. Sherita told me, "I want this and not that."

As we dug deeper into Sherita's story, she told me that it was hard for her to make life-defining decisions. She came to me because she was being forced to choose between two decisions that were opposites. She could not decide if she wanted "this and not that." After several sessions, Sherita did make the agonizing decision for one option. However, she found it utterly impossible to be satisfied. Therefore, Sherita sabotaged her original decision by not being truthful with herself or with those in her life who were directly affected by her decision. When that path became unmanageable, Sherita abandoned the first decision and went for the competing one. Regardless of her decision, her life became lonely, obligatory, secretive, disingenuous, unsatisfying, and desperate. Life for Sherita felt paralyzing. Everyone involved in Sherita's vacillation was completely bewildered and exasperated. Conversations with those who loved her were mystifying and unfulfilling. At that point, all they wanted was for her to commit to a decision.

For Sherita, her ECM informed her that there was always something better than what she decided she wanted. Even though the "grass is always greener" rang true, she knew that while it may have looked greener, it still did not satisfy. From the beginning of her self-awareness, satisfying decision-making had been nearly impossible for Sherita. Sherita anguished over the choices she had to make in the here and now. Her conversations with those who loved her could not be truthful, because Sherita could not choose between two opposite decisions.

List ways in which your ECM sets your present-day communication table much like Sherita's ECM set her communication table with indecisiveness.

ECMs AND COPING MECHANISMS

Our coping mechanisms develop out of our Earliest Childhood Memories and our PPIFSt/PPIFEx. God gives us coping mechanisms as young children so that we can make sense out of the statements we hear and the experiences we have.

Remember our discussion on brain development. Our neocortex is not fully developed when we are young, which means we cannot reason why Mommy screams at us all the time. We have no idea how to logically determine why Daddy drinks beverages we are not allowed to drink, which make him look sleepy or act angry most of the time. We do not have the fully developed brain that would tell us Daddy is depressed because there isn't enough money to pay the bills and feed our tummies, so he drinks. While we cannot connect those dots between our parents' fear and their thoughtless behavior toward us, we still experience the icky feelings related to this mess. Remember, our limbic circuitry system functions very well, which is why we feel emotions long before we can intellectualize them.

In fact, we often interpret our caregivers' harmful behavior as actually being our fault. Therefore, we grab onto whatever helps us cope in those fearful moments. These coping mechanisms are rooted in our ECMs which establish our PPIFSt/PPIFEx. Coping mechanisms help us survive the emotional roller coasters that often characterize our lives. This accounts for our lack of emotional awareness. We know we are flooded with body sensations that accompany our confusing emotions. But how to intellectually interpret those emotions eludes us.

Coping Mechanisms

As our brains begin to develop, we can find coping mechanisms that help us soothe or defend ourselves against what comes at us, including abuse. We may:

- suck our thumb.
- rock back and forth.
- hit ourselves.
- pull out our hair.
- pick at our skin.
- hold fast to our stuffed animal.
- rub a silky cloth between our fingers.
- fade into the background.
- try to appease the abuser.
- run away.
- stop eating or overeat.
- lie.
- tell stories or draw pictures.
- escape into electronics.
- be the peacemaker.
- be the disruptor.
- regress in our physical or emotional development.
- act out by using our method of choice.

This list is not exhaustive by any means. Whatever coping mechanism seemed best for us, please understand that we will carry some form of it into adulthood. Adult self-soothing behaviors very often mimic our childhood coping mechanisms. Also, our adult coping mechanisms rarely take us too far from our ECMs or what was familiar in our family of origin.

REDEMPTIVE COMMUNICATION AND OUR ECMs

Our ECMs influence our ability to communicate redemptively. We get bogged down in hearing what we have always heard rather than hearing what is actually being said. We also get bogged down in accepting bad or abusive behavior from others because abusive behavior is in our past. Our ECMs interpret the confusing words said or perplexing actions done to us by people in our past. This affects our response to others in real time situations. Our ECMs can even inform us who is reliable and who is not.

Coping mechanisms mitigate fearful situations. They provide ways by which we self-soothe and self-protect. We try to soothe and protect our vulnerability so that the fearful words and actions coming at us will not be as devastating. Coping mechanisms help quiet and soothe our confusing emotions brought about by our experiences.

Make a list of your childhood coping mechanisms.

There is a link between your ECMs and your coping mechanisms. Write how your ECMs influenced the coping mechanisms you chose.

While these coping mechanisms helped us survive our childhood, they will never work for us as adults. In fact, childhood coping mechanisms fail us in our adult life. If we try to use the same coping skills we used as children in our adult life, our communication will not be soul-satisfying. The reason that our communication will not be soul-satisfying is because a childlike attempt to cope in a grown-up world will not allow us to deal effectively with our present-day situations. Childlike coping skills also deny the power of God in our lives. Because of the work of God's Holy Spirit in our hearts, Jesus calls us to trust Him and not our coping mechanisms. As His dear little children, He gave us ways to survive some very devastating childhood situations. Our grown-up biblical view of God tells us that God is now our ever-present help in times of trouble. He is our shield and defender. Nothing can pluck us from His hand, and nothing can separate us from His love.

Because of our God, we are not to be anxious or fearful. Instead, God calls us to set aside the coping mechanisms we needed to survive as children and cling to Him, the only true Lover of our souls. Read the Word of the Lord from Proverbs 3:5–8:

> Trust in the Lord with all your heart,
> and do not lean on your own understanding.
> In all your ways acknowledge him,
> and he will make straight your paths.
> Be not wise in your own eyes;
> fear the Lord, and turn away from evil.
> It will be healing to your flesh
> and refreshment to your bones.

God upholds us. Read the Word of the Lord from Isaiah 41:10:

> Fear not, for I am with you; be not dismayed, for I am your God; I will strengthen you, I will help you, I will uphold you with my righteous right hand.

God carries us from the womb to death. Read the Word of the Lord from Isaiah 46:3–4:

> Listen to me, O house of Jacob, all the remnant of the house of Israel, who have been borne by me from before your birth, carried from the womb; even to your old age I am he, and to gray hairs I will carry you. I have made, and I will bear; I will carry and will save.

We are called to shed our childlike coping mechanisms and replace them with knowledge of the Lord. This is very theological and deeply personal. As children, our ECMs allowed us to lean on our own understanding of our world. We developed coping mechanisms to help us make sense out of the senselessness around us. As adults, we have God to make our paths straight, heal our flesh, and refresh our bones as we acknowledge God's everlasting love for us. We must trust that God will uphold us with His righteous arm, from womb to tomb.

Paul reflects on this as well. Read the Word of the Lord from 1 Corinthians 13:11–12:

> When I was a child, I spoke like a child, I thought like a child, I reasoned like a child. When I became a man, I gave up childish ways. For now we see in a mirror dimly, but then face to face. Now I know in part; then I shall know fully, even as I have been fully known.

Giving up our childish self-soothing behaviors means we give up the coping mechanisms that kept us safe in our great big scary world. Giving up childish ways may also involve a deeper analysis of our Earliest Childhood Memories and a look at how our memories keep us from maturing. Our ECMs may alert us to how our communication table is set for us, but our ECMs do not need to sabotage our conversations. Our childlike coping mechanisms and our ECMs obscure clear thinking. Paul tells us that when we become adults, we must give up childish ways. On this earth, we only see in part. However, when we die, we will fully know as we have already been fully known by God while on this earth.

With the theology stated in the Scriptures above, we can begin to change how we react to the hurt we have experienced, past and present, and find new biblical ways to respond to that pain. As children, we are limited in how well we know God. Becoming adult men and women who strive to be fully known enables us to know God more deeply than we could ever know Him when we were children. A good way to see if we are clinging to our childhood coping mechanisms in our grown-up world would be to listen to the first words we utter when we are in a contentious conversation. If we launch into a defense, we may be relying on childhood coping mechanisms to protect us.

PAST POWERFUL STATEMENTS

Think about past statements made to you when you were young. These statements may or may not be positive. They should have meaning and be significant to you and will have had a substantial impact on how you communicate with others. If you are stuck, use words like this as a guide: "My parents told me they disciplined me this way because they said I was . . ." or "I'll never forget the time I was told . . .".

List how these statements still shape your heart today.

Identify who made the statement to you.

In what ways did the person who made those statements affect how you currently communicate with others?

Write out any statements you make today that sound similar to what you heard in your past.

The converse may also be true. We heard Past Powerful Identity Forming Statements spoken to us and determined that we would never use such words in our conversations.

Write out the word or phrase that was said to you that you will not say to someone else.

... .— —. . .— —.— .. —. — —.   —.—. — — — —.. .

PAST POWERFUL EXPERIENCES

Think about past experiences you had when you were young. These experiences may or may not be positive. They should have meaning and be significant to you and will have had a substantial impact on how you communicate with others. If you are stuck, use words like this as a guide: "I remember the incident where I thought I was going to . . ." or "I'll never forget the time when . . .".

List how these experiences still affect your behavior today.

... .— —. . .— —.— .. —. — —.   —.—. — — — —.. .

Identify who was involved in this experience.

... .— —. . .— —.— .. —. — —.   —.—. — — — —.. .

In what ways did this person's actions affect how you currently communicate with others?

... .— —. . .— —.— .. —. — —.   —.—. — — — —.. .

Write out the experiences today that remind you of what happened in your past.

... .— —. . .— —.— .. —. — —.   —.—. — — — —.. .

The converse may also be true. We had Past Powerful Identity Forming Experiences and determined that we would never do the same thing to others.

Write out what was done to you that you will never do to anyone else.

... .— —. . .— —.— .. —. — —.   —.—. — — — —.. .

FLIP SIDE OF THE SAME COIN

Our familiar is not a wise reason for us to treat others either the same way or differently than how we were treated. I am sure we all have heard the saying, "It is the flip side of the same coin." Because we have been badly treated in both words and deeds (one side of the coin), we determine we will behave in an opposite way (the other side of the same coin). Treating others in the exact opposite way of how we were treated is not the answer.

Parents use the flip side of the same coin as a parenting tool. We say we will not do or say to our kids what was done or said to us. For example, if our parent's behavior was restrictive with us, we may determine we will be permissive with our children. We resolve to behave the opposite of our parents because we hated the restrictiveness we endured. But we are still using the same coin. Just because we agree to behave the opposite of our parents does not mean the opposite is better. We need a new coin!

Conversations also tend to play out as the flip side of the same coin. If we heard judgmental words growing up (one side of the coin), we may decide to speak words that are approving (the other side of the coin). However, the flip side may be just as injurious as the first side. Being too approving of our children's poor decisions may be just as harmful as being too judgmental. Both may lead our children to making unwise decisions. Using the flip side of the same coin is selfish because we rely on our own familiar rather than looking at how we can love more wisely.

A better way is not to use the same familiar coin at all. Our new coin is the wisdom found in the Scriptures. Our new coin is loving others and ourselves as Jesus loves us. If our parents were restrictive, we are wise to go to the Scriptures and see how the Bible balances restrictiveness. A biblical balance to restrictiveness is not permissiveness. If we heard judgment, we are wise to go to the Scriptures to see how the Bible balances judgment. A biblical balance to judgment is not leniency. A biblical balance is more nuanced and merciful than just the flip side of the same coin. We cannot sacrifice truth for a coin toss.

INFORMATIVE VERSUS DETERMINATIVE

We can see how the Two Influential Forces that shape our lives affect how we speak to one another. In Section Three we will see how a path of righteousness leads us through these powerful forces. We would be wise to remember that the Two Influential Forces are informative, which means they serve to notify or inform our hearts. They are not determinative, which means they have no power to govern our words or behavior unless we give them power. God alone determines the outcome of our lives, not our Two Influential Forces.

Write out what prevents you from making your Two Influential Forces *informative* rather than *determinative*.

Write out how you can control your Two Influential Forces so that they inform but do not determine your present conversations.

INTEGRATING OUR TWO INFLUENTIAL FORCES

Now that we have examined our ECMs, PPIFSt, and PPIFEx separately, let's discuss how they together shape how we communicate.

These Two Influential Forces:

- shape the identity we embrace, leading to self-talk that fuels our Speaking CODE.
- lead to coping mechanisms that worked for us as children but tend to fail us as adult coping mechanisms.
- were directed at us when we were young and informed our pondering hearts.
- feel very familiar, which makes it hard to root them out and reject them.
- can be hard to identify because they start to happen to us at a young age and become deeply embedded in our hearts.
- can sometimes be recognized as body memories.
- can confuse present conversations because what we are hearing in the present resonates with something we heard in our past.
- are common to all humans.
- work as pathways to identify how we reason based on what our hearts treasure.
- affect how we take in information and how we give it out.
- determine how we see the world around us.
- are ever-present either as a reliable memory or as an impression that something is not right.

From the above list, which description of your Two Influential Forces most resonates with you and why?

GOD'S WAYS ARE NOT OUR WAYS

Life is full of harsh statements and scary experiences that are hard to understand. I have no idea why God allows people's behavior toward us to play such a powerful role in our lives, especially in the area of communication, but He does. I have no idea why we interpret the behavior of others in ways that can lead us to have soul-crushing conversations, but we do. Therefore, it is wise to give our hearts over to Jesus, because it is in our hearts that we hide our PPIFSt/PPIFEx.

But this I do know. Our PPIFSt and PPIFEx are powerless in light of Jesus's words of eternal life. David tells us that God's goodness and mercy will follow us all the days of our lives until He either takes us home or comes out of the clouds to retrieve us. Throughout the remainder of this book I will refer to David's words in Psalm 23. That means that God is still God, and He alone reigns supreme, even over the horrific things said and done to us, for our good and His glory.

Later we will look at how we can understand and manage the impact of our ECMs and PPIFSt/PPIFEx. Much of what we have read may have resonated with us and sets us upon our path of righteousness. My prayer is that God will light up this righteous path as we press on toward soul-satisfying communication.

Lord, have mercy on us as we journey on together.

PPIFST + PPIFEX

Based on PPIFSt and PPIFEx I have encountered both personally and professionally, I have developed a list that may help us identify statements and experiences that affect how we communicate. See which statements resonate in your heart.

The following statements are written in a specific format. The bullets begin with an opening phrase, "When I heard from you . . .". They then move to a statement of reaction, "I wondered how . . .". They conclude with, "In present conversations . . .". This gives us the opportunity to write out our own experience, based on the options that connect with us.

As you read the following statements, please keep these things in mind: These statements are not relationship-specific, which means they may have been said by parents, spouses, friends, acquaintances, siblings, or children. These statements are not time-specific, which means they could have been spoken last week, last year, or last decade. Some of these statements may seem to differ only slightly from one another. You may find that a slight rewrite of these statements may better fit your situation. Interact with the statements that best describe your heart.

OUR PPIFST AND PPIFEX IN ACTION

When I heard from you that I was your everything, I wondered how I could avoid feeling choked or suffocated at the mere thought of letting you down. In present conversations, your words make it hard for me to . . .

When I heard from you that all your happiness depended on me, I wondered how to live with the overwhelming feelings of anxiety as I frantically sought ways to make you happy. In present conversations, your words make it hard for me to . . .

When I heard from you that I selfishly wanted more than you could give, I wondered what was wrong with me for just wanting to be with you. I felt disturbed by the thought that you did not want to see me. My sense of deficiency made me either try harder to be good or not try at all. In present conversations, your words make it hard for me to . . .

When I heard from you that my behavior ruined everyone's happiness, I wondered how I would withstand my failures. I told myself I would do whatever it took to always be liked, even if that behavior was not in my own best interest. My goal became meeting other's desires. In present conversations, your words make it hard for me to . . .

When I heard from you that I was an idiot because only idiots do what I just did, I wondered why I felt uncared for and less than human. No matter what good I did, I always felt like a failure and sensed the judgmental stares of those around me. My guilt became crushing. In present conversations, your words make it hard for me to . . .

When I heard from you that I was just a girl and girls don't do that, I wondered what was so intrinsically wrong with females. Was I relegated to second-class citizenship because I was a girl? Is there a girl box into which I must fit? In present conversations, your words make it hard for me to . . .

(Let's digress, as friends often do when life's issues surface. This is one of my PPIFSt/PPIFEx. Growing up in my Italian family, girls didn't do many things except "stay-at-home" stuff. This powerful statement makes it hard to write a book, because I have no credentials other than what my culture dictated: cook, clean, and nurture. You may be tempted to say, "Diana, please don't feel that way. Your book will do just fine." I appreciate your sincerity. However, when you diminish my Two Influential Forces, where can our conversation go? We live life based on our deeply held PPIFSt and PPIFEx.

So, you may want to check your self-talk that leads to the CODE you speak. Telling me how to think makes me feel uncared for. A better response might be to say, "Diana, what is it like for you, trying to justify writing a book, when that seems inconsistent with your upbringing?" That response allows us to get to heart issues produced by my Two Influential Forces. Now we are in the struggle together as we talk about the consequences of our PPIFSt and PPIFEx.)

When I heard from you that I was a boy, so suck it up and stop crying, I wondered if it was possible for boys to experience emotions and cry. What was I supposed to do with emotions? Ignore them? Put them in a locked box? Compartmentalize them? My relationships became a game of emotional hide and seek. In present conversations, your words make it hard for me to . . .

When I heard from you that Jesus would not love me if I continue behaving that way, I wondered if my behavior was bigger than Jesus. Worse still, I wondered how I could be perfect enough so Jesus would always love me. My desire to love Jesus became a checklist of daily rules I needed to follow to be accepted by Jesus. In present conversations, your words make it hard for me to . . .

When I heard from you that I shouldn't feel that way, but rather I should feel the way you wanted me to feel, I wondered how I could ever sort out whose feelings were whose. My conversations changed in order to fit the emotional needs of others. In present conversations, your words make it hard for me to . . .

When I heard from you that if people really knew me the way you knew me, they would see the "fake" I really am, I wondered how and where I could hide, so people would never find out that I am a fraud. I find myself questioning the motivations of my own heart. In present conversations, your words make it hard for me to . . .

When I heard from you that I was a nuisance, I wondered how I might disappear so that you would be better off. Maybe you are right. It is better for me to bail on emotional or physical relationships first, rather than suffer rejection. Based on what you said, maybe I am not good, so leaving is the best thing I can do for everyone. If I cannot leave physically, I will check out emotionally. My heart struggles to stay connected in relationships and especially in my conversations. In present conversations, your words make it hard for me to . . .

◀ ... .— —. . .— —.— .. —. — —.   —.—. — — — —.. .

When I heard you say "Get away from me," I wondered about my value. Your words make me want to physically leave, emotionally remove myself from our relationship, or become so needy that I cannot untangle myself from you. My value is uncertain, which makes me feel trapped. Even if I could get away from you, I can never get away from myself. In present conversations, your words make it hard for me to . . .

◀ ... .— —. . .— —.— .. —. — —.   —.—. — — — —.. .

When I heard from you that you need "me" time, I wondered what it is about me that makes you want to escape from me. If I could just figure out why you don't want to spend time with me, I could fix it and make myself acceptable. My heart jumps into overdrive as I run scenarios that might make me worthy of acceptance. In present conversations, your words make it hard for me to . . .

◀ ... .— —. . .— —.— .. —. — —.   —.—. — — — —.. .

When I heard from you that your abusive behavior was my fault, I wondered if I made people hurt or abuse me. Am I really to blame for their mistreatment of me? My heart often condemns me and accuses me of causing the problem. In present conversations, your words make it hard for me to . . .

When I heard from you that you could not bear to disappoint me, I wondered how I could ever carry the burden of your expectations. Disappointing you makes me feel inadequate, guilty, conflicted, and shameful. My heart seeks ways to be either acceptable or to just not care. In present conversations, your words make it hard for me to . . .

◀ ... .— —. . .— —.— .. —. — —.   —.—. — — — —.. .

When I heard from you that you wanted me to be like you, I wondered if I would ever measure up. In my striving, my heart often felt hopelessly inadequate, and detached. In present conversations, your words make it hard for me to . . .

When I heard from you that my behavior makes it difficult for people to like me, I wondered how I could ever behave in a way where I was not rejected. Maybe I am a social leper and associating with me will spread my disease to others. My heart seeks isolation and insulation so that my disease will not rub off on those around me. Sometimes I want to live up to their expectations by exploding all over people with my words or behaviors. In present conversations, your words make it hard for me to . . .

When I heard from you that you wished I was never born because I am ruining your life, I wondered if there is just one thing I could do that would make your life better. Perhaps this world is better off without me. My heart desires peace but the path is clouded by the pain. In present conversations, your words make it hard for me to . . .

When I heard from you that you needed me to be successful so that you could brag about me, I wondered what it meant to be successful. What happens to us if I fail? Can't you find success on your own? My heart felt fearful that I would let you down. In present conversations, your words make it hard for me to . . .

When I heard from you that I embarrassed you, I wondered if I could ever figure out what I actually did wrong. My heart is broken because I do not want to embarrass you. In present conversations, your words make it hard for me to . . .

When I heard from you that I will never amount to anything, just like the worthless piece of crap that spawned me, I wondered what I needed to do to prove, even to myself, that I am not that person who wants nothing to do with me! My heart despaired that I would ever escape that parent's reputation or be like those people I most admire. I doubt that I will ever be successful at detaching from them. There really isn't anything I can do. In present conversations, your words make it hard for me to . . .

When I heard from you that you wanted me to behave like you, I wondered why I often feel numb, unappreciated, rage-filled, or empty. My heart struggles with authenticity in my relationships because I seek to be like the person in front of me. In present conversations, your words make it hard for me to . . .

When you said that my efforts weren't acceptable to you, I wondered why I should even try to please anyone. Putting forth any effort is not worth it. My heart struggles with the intimacy necessary for most relationships. In present conversations, your words make it hard for me to . . .

When your behavior terrified me, I wondered how not to be afraid in relationships. Fear makes me doubt that anyone can be on my side. In my heart I feel life is too scary for me to enjoy. In present conversations, your words make it hard for me to . . .

These kinds of statements and experiences are critical to unlocking the reasons why it is difficult to communicate redemptively. Words we heard in our past, or actions done to us, sabotage our ability to communicate in the present. Our PPIFSt and PPIFEx will always affect the words we use in our people-talk, our self-talk, and our God-talk.

The earlier we are exposed to powerful statements and experiences like those listed above, the deeper they sink into our hearts. Our past infiltrates our conversations and these ideas become harder to root out. As we have said, our Two Influential Forces are responsible for how we understand the world around us. Speaking CODE finds its power in our past.

A well-loved teacher in an inner-city school once observed:

> Today I found a deeper meaning to "remember not against us the offenses of our forefathers" from the litany.[6] I see it in myself, I see it in my students. The weight of generations past, their struggle, their sins, their achievements, their habits. Today I taught a class that was so clearly burdened by needs that reach far back into their past. A need to be heard. A need to stand up for right. A need to obtain justice. But all backwards in application, caught up in hurt, anger, frustration, misunderstanding, and expectation. We can't meet anyone as though they are a completely blank slate. They have generations of writing on their hearts and every word matters.

This teacher's comment is relevant and instructive. The weight of past generations is not simply an accusation against parents or caregivers. The aftermath of cultural and relational events leaves many feeling like victims who are unheard and burdened. These weights lead to the unsatisfying, confusing conversations that we presently experience.

The Patriarchs of our faith experienced this same type of generational sin. If we trace out the sinful conversations and behavior of the Patriarchs, starting with Abraham and ending with Joseph, we see a trail of favoritism, lies, deceit, and jealousy. This led to soul-crushing communication and unsatisfying relationships that were passed down from parents to children. Abraham favored Isaac over Ishmael. Isaac favored Esau over Jacob. Jacob favored Joseph over all his other sons. The Patriarchs' wives participated in deceit and intrigue based on their favoritism as well. These broken family relationships could rival those of any Jerry Springer guest.

And yet, despite the Patriarchs' utter failures, God traces out His plan of redemption. God graciously shows us generational sin and the chaos it brings to families. In the Bible, we read soul-crushing conversation after soul-crushing conversation, where generational sin is on full display. Still, God uses unredeemed speech to eventually reconcile us to Himself. This frees us from remaining stuck in our past with ghosts that haunt us. We cannot allow our self-absorbed caretakers to determine our present and future.

List ways your ability to communicate has been affected by your self-absorbed caretakers.

We are not victims. The tendency is for our self-talk, based on our Two Influential Forces, to affect our Speaking CODE. However, the Patriarchs of our faith show us how God uses even sinful behavior to demonstrate His goodness. The way we understand our past can shape our present communication approach for God's glory and our good. Because of God's sovereign plan, we can begin to embrace our history, cutting the past ties that strangle our present and future conversations.

SPEAKING CODE AND BEING KNOWN

In Section One, we began our discussion of Speaking CODE by examining the moment that Alan Dean and I experienced intersecting holy sanctuaries in our car years ago. Sadly, Alan Dean and I sacrificed trust on our altar of fear. In this chapter, we will explore how Speaking CODE prevents you and me from truly knowing each other.

One of our deepest desires is to be known. Being truly known comforts us as we experience the relentlessness of what life throws at us. Being truly known soothes our souls because we see each other as valuable and important regardless of our circumstances. Being truly known gives us deep connection because another human knows us intimately.

HUMANS AND BEING KNOWN

Let's consider how Speaking CODE keeps us from being truly known by looking at people pleasers. People pleasers are consumed with the idea of being liked. They pour so much of themselves into accomplishing this goal. All of us share people pleaser characteristics. People pleasing tactics assume that acceptability is the same thing as being known. In conversations, people pleasers use words that are typically based on self-talk. Our self-talk says that we have done something wrong or unacceptable in necessary relationships. This self-evaluation leaves people pleasers feeling unloved, left out, forgotten, or undeserving. People pleasers' internal emotional companions are loneliness, unworthiness, disappointment, dissatisfaction, ungratefulness, exasperation, and confusion.

People pleasers find it easier to please others than it is to please God. In the process we compromise biblical values, pleasing people in place of pleasing God. We view our people-pleasing behavior as loving our neighbor, which makes it appear we are obeying God. People pleasers feel as though this is an offering that makes us acceptable to God. The problem is that our agenda is self-serving. We receive several benefits, including the praise of others, the feeling of acceptance, the illusion of being known, and the thought that we are appeasing God. However, our acts are not truly sacrificial. This agenda makes pleasing God a secondary goal.

People pleasers are conflicted. We desire to be known and loved. However, we fear that if we are truly known, we will be exposed. We do not know how to enter relationships where authentic conversations require truth and love. To avoid being found out, people pleasers Speak CODE. Speaking CODE mitigates the weight that our self-identification presses on us. Speaking CODE also helps people pleasers feel more accepted, as we speak only the snippets of our self-talk designed to make others happy. Speaking CODE is isolating and helps us avoid stepping out of our self-imposed fears. The CODE words we use may be deferential and dripping with flattery. However, when we are called on to take sides, the CODE words we use can also be hostile, controlling, and filled with criticism. People pleasers live in a world of unpredictability which forces us to be hyper aware of every word spoken in a conversation.

In what ways are you a people pleaser?

What do you do to be acceptable to others?

How do your people pleasing behaviors lead you to Speak CODE?

In what ways do you use people pleasing tactics to try to please God?

HEBREWS AND SPEAKING CODE

We were created to live in community where we can know others and be known by them. But something interferes with the process of intimacy just as it did in the garden of Eden. The writer to the Hebrews talks about what prevents us from achieving true and lasting intimacy. He says that we are burdened down with every weight and sin that clings so closely to us. I believe these weights and sin become part of our self-talk that leads to our Speaking CODE. We must do something with these burdens so that we can run our race and enjoy true companionship. Read the Word of the Lord in Hebrews 12:1–2:

> Therefore, since we are surrounded by so great a cloud of witnesses, let us also lay aside every weight, and sin which clings so closely, and let us run with endurance the race that is set before us, looking to Jesus, the founder and perfecter of our faith, who for the joy that was set before him endured the cross, despising the shame, and is seated at the right hand of the throne of God.

We need endurance to run our race, which is why having a great cloud of witnesses surrounding us is so encouraging. As we emulate Christ who endured even the Cross, we are called to persevere in the difficulties of our race. We prevail as we continue on the path of righteousness God has set before us. Our Two Influential Forces tempt us to give in to soul-crushing conversations, caused by the CODE we speak. Yet our desire to be known can only be accomplished if we overcome our burdens and run our race faithfully as we look to Jesus who is the founder and perfecter of our faith.

List what you think the writer means in your life by the words "every weight and sin" that cause you to Speak CODE.

How do these "weights and sins" keep you from being known and knowing others?

In what ways can you endure by laying aside what easily entangles you and enriching your God-talk, your people-talk, and your self-talk?

THE PREDICATE NOMINATIVE GAME

Our weights and sins are mischief-makers that motivate us to hide and prevent us from being truly known. They seek to separate us from each other. To cover up these weights and sin, we Speak CODE, which it hard for us to be truly known.

The way we self-identify is expressed in the CODE we speak. I use a simple game that helps us determine how we self-identify. This game is designed to help us understand how our Two Influential Forces impact the way we see ourselves. This game also shines a light in the areas where we tend to Speak CODE that prevents us from being truly known. This game is called the Predicate Nominative Game. Let's refresh our understanding of grammar before we get started.

A predicate nominative is a word or group of words that complete a linking verb and rename the subject. Therefore, the noun (subject of the sentence) is equal to whatever comes after the linking verb. Here is an example: God is good. God is the subject. In this sentence, "is" functions as the linking verb. "Good" is the word that renames, identifies, or defines the subject; therefore, God and good are interchangeable and equal.

Here is an example of Chaz and Merri playing the Predicate Nominative Game. As Chaz and I begin the game, I ask Chaz to fill in the blank: Chaz is ________. Chaz answers, "faithful." According to Chaz, he and faithful are equal. In his self-talk, Chaz identifies as dependable. His CODE Speaking will use words to show he is available to help. Chaz welcomes opportunities to help people, knowing he can be counted on in a pinch.

When Merri and I begin the game, I ask Merri to complete this sentence: Merri is ____________. Merri answers, "fake." For Merri, she and fake are equal. In her self-talk, Merri wonders if her friends see her fakeness. Merri's CODE Speaking may cause her to use people-pleasing words so she can hide how she self-identifies. Merri lives her life in fear of being truly known.

Both Chaz and Merri reveal their hearts in this exercise. We talk about how their self-identification affects their conversations and behaviors. This game is not designed to assign blame or determine good versus bad. The game's purpose is to bring self-awareness so that we can determine how our self-talk fuels the CODE we speak. Speaking CODE affects the hearer and will determine how deeply we are known. As Counselors/Helpers, we can use the answers to the Predicate Nominative game as an entry point into our client's heart.

Now, let's play the game. In the space below, write your name, followed by the verb "is" (or some form of the verb "to be"). After you write these two words (your name and "is") put the very next word that comes to your mind. Try to come up with five examples. This list will help you see how you self-identify. This simple game exposes some of the reasons why you Speak CODE. It also may show you how you hide certain things about yourself which will prevent you from being truly known. Please be honest. No one sees this but you.

If we were sitting across from one another sharing a pot of tea, we would look at your answers to the Predicate Nominative game. We would engage in a meaningful conversation about the words you chose. We would also find the link between your ECMs, PPIFSt, and PPIFEx and the words you placed after your name and the linking verb. We would figure out how these words have settled into your heart and determined the CODE you speak. We would look to see if these words sabotage your ability to engage in soul-satisfying conversations. We would discover how your self-identification affects your self-talk and prevents you from being truly known. Additionally, we would uncover how you allow others to identify you. But more importantly, we would seek God in order to learn how He identifies you, which would bring meaning, purpose, and healing into your life. Healing will be discussed in Section Three.

List how the results of the Predicate Nominative game fuel your CODE Speaking.

List ways in which your self-descriptive words affect how you speak to others and prevent you from being known.

Recall your Earliest Childhood Memories. Write out how your ECMs influenced the words you selected in the game.

List the ways in which your PPIFSt and PPIFEx influenced the words you selected in the game.

Share your results with a trusted friend and ask him to help you see what you are missing in your evaluation.

THE UNKEMPT HOUSE

Imagine if you will, the following scenario. We have worked a long day. We come home to find dirty dishes in the sink and clean clothes still in the laundry basket. Our self-talk tells us that no one in the house cares about us. If they did, the clean clothes would be folded and neatly placed in the drawers, and the dirty dishes would be properly loaded in the dishwasher. Oh, the humanity of it all when we discover that the dishwasher still has clean dishes in it! What on God's green earth keeps people from unloading clean dishes from the dishwasher? This is not rocket science, folks. If the clean dishes are unloaded, you can easily put your dirty dishes where they belong—geesh!

Our self-talk even tells us that our family is obviously ungrateful for the blessings of modern technology. We wonder if it would be sanctifying to them if we pulled the plug on all such blessings. Based on their behavior, we tell ourselves we could be dead in a ditch somewhere and not one of them would even care. Do not laugh. This could be the self-talk of any of us reading this.

But listen to the CODE that actually comes out of our mouth when we enter the house: nothing! Speaking CODE can be as silent as the grave. We sacrificially unload then reload the dishwasher properly and neatly fold the clean laundry. While performing these sacrificial duties, we feel angry that not one of these ungrateful people living under our roof offers to help us. Our self-talk interprets their laziness to mean they will not even care enough to attend our funeral. Maybe we slam the cupboard doors extra hard as we put away the clean dishes from the dishwasher before reloading. We perfectly time our heavy sigh as we carry the laundry basket through the TV room to the second floor. Where is the family in the midst of our internal dialogue? Our family is transfixed while watching the latest episode of their favorite television series. Behold the power of Speaking CODE even in our silence.

List ways in which your silence is a form of Speaking CODE and prevents you from being truly known. What makes you use silence?

In your silence, what don't you want your family to know about you in that moment when you slam doors or huff and puff your way through the family room? What is your fear?

The Hearer

The hearer is placed in the confusing position of trying to untangle or interpret the seeming nonsense of our words, our behaviors, or our silence. They cannot read our self-talk, which fuels our CODE Speaking. Their interpretation may be based on a good understanding of who we are, but the interpretation is still predicated on assumptions. When we make assumptions, we contribute to the demise of the relationship. Keep in mind that the hearers have their own ECMs, PPIFSt, and PPIFEx that tell them what their life looks like. These statements and experiences will influence how they process the CODE we speak. Authentic, soul-satisfying communication loses. Assumptions reign. Speaking CODE wins. And truly being known breaks down.

Going Deeper into the Hearer's Experience

Let's take a deeper look at our example. We know we are tired. We came home to a mess. We have previously communicated our expectations. As we have said, our family members have their own Two Influential Forces to confront when we silently Speak CODE. Perhaps for them, our slamming the cupboard door may signal that chaos or even violence is about to break out. This silent form of communication could evoke feelings of doom or desperation for them.

It may be that hearing our heavy sighs triggered someone's experience of guilt and shame. They may be reminded that they feel inadequate to competently complete a given task, like loading the dishwasher *properly* or folding the clothes *neatly*. Our reaction to the perceived mess will contribute to secondary PPIFSt and PPIFEx of those who observe our behavior when we returned home from work.

What internal reaction do you think the hearer may have to your silent form of Speaking CODE in this scenario?

OUR ACTIVE HEARTS AND ROADBLOCKS

Speaking CODE rarely allows us to be truly known. In our people-talk, everyone's heart is actively trying to fit what they hear into their worldview. The term *active hearts* describe how we diligently search for meaning. To one degree or another, we are taking in the information we receive and running the data through our perceived filters. I believe we do this because deep down in our hearts we all have a real desire to be known as good or worthy.

Based on how you Speak CODE, list what your self-talk tells you about your active heart and your desire to be known.

Sometimes we want the hearer to look into our hearts and recognize that we are worth the difficult task of knowing us intimately. Interestingly, we put roadblocks in people's way to make knowing us even more difficult. Roadblocks can be verbal or non-verbal behaviors meant to test people's trustworthiness and commitment. Roadblocks are a form of Speaking CODE because part of Speaking CODE is to prevent us from being truly known. Therefore, when people break through our roadblocks, we can trust that they are willing to do what is necessary to get to know us. It is in their perseverance, despite our roadblocks, that we can open up just a bit more to allow others to know our darkest secrets.

In your conversations, list some of the roadblocks you set up to test other's tenacity in getting to know you well.

Speaking CODE controls what we say so that we are seen as acceptable. Speaking CODE is our way of seeking assurance. Assurance makes us feel safe. However, Speaking CODE gives us a false sense of security in that we only reveal snippets of our self-talk. We cannot be truly known if the hearer is not privy to our thoughts. Additionally, we may be confused, which prevents us from knowing our own hearts.

What criteria do you use to determine how much of your self-talk is revealed to the person in front of you?

Speaking CODE could also mean that we spill our guts and tell absolutely everything that our self-talk says. We may believe that if we are completely honest, we will be acceptable. Discretion may be lost in our efforts to be liked by those around us. As we tell all that is in our heart, we leave out the important fact that this behavior is a way to gain acceptance which is part of Speaking CODE.

List what you think you get out of spilling your guts, if that is what you do.

Speaking CODE helps us play the unwitting (or fully aware) victim, so that the person to whom we are speaking sees only our point of view or our deep hurts. We need to ask ourselves how this tactic could move us closer to knowing each other well.

List how you play the victim and only Speak CODE words that put your words and deeds in the best light possible and highlight your hurts.

Speaking CODE motivates us to play off each other in a curious verbal dance comprised of sophisticated moves that would dazzle even Fred Astaire and Ginger Rogers. To make the dance work, the speaker and the listener are depending on each other to do something neither of them was created to do. We were never created to fully satisfy each other's needs even though we have a deep desire to be truly known. Our Two Influential Forces make us fearful of vulnerability. The CODE we speak forces the hearer to interpret our meaning. We speak, but not clearly. We want to be heard, but not really.

We do the same with God. Our self-talk, based on our past, keeps us from being honest in our prayers. We Speak CODE to God with the same fear of vulnerability we experience with others. We hold God at a distance. Sadly, we allow our Two Influential Forces to affect our self-talk and Speaking CODE, leading us to push God away. We rarely remember that God deeply knows us, and that He is good to us even when all others fail us.

List how you use Speaking CODE as a protection from being deeply known.

Speaking CODE eventually leads to soul-crushing communication or a type of silent apathy that is murderous to a relationship. Remember my example of coming home from a hard day at work only to find the house in an unacceptable condition? Before long, our self-talk accused our family members of not caring enough to attend our funeral! This is extreme language, but there are those of us reading this whose heart goes to that place.

In our example, we employed a form of Speaking CODE which is deathly silence. Our desire and expectation for a clean house went unmet, which led our self-talk into assuming the very worst. And we chose silence as our form of Speaking CODE. We missed the opportunity to explore how our desire to be valued and known went deeper than seeing a cleared kitchen sink or neatly folded laundry.

WHY AM I BOTHERED?

We cannot Speak CODE indefinitely. Be assured, eventually words will be exchanged, and these words may even sound cordial or pleasant. But the subtext underneath the obligatory politeness will shout in the loudest of voices, "I just don't care if we ever speak again about what is in my heart. You should know me by now and know that I want to come home to a clean house after a long day at work. Your actions show you disrespect me and do not value me. I feel abandoned by you." Although irritating, the unkempt house is not the real issue. Being truly known is.

Write out instances where you have substituted the obligatory politeness of CODE Speaking for conversations characterized by truth spoken in love.

Married men, a clean house may not resonate with you—but perhaps sex does?" In that case it would sound like, "Saying you love me means you care about what is important to me. Coming home to a sexually engaged wife means you understand and value me."

God puts us in necessary relationships. Therefore, we must honor all the different people with whom we are connected. We evaluate statements or behaviors that do not meet our expectations of what demonstrates love and acceptance. We then use our assessment to justify our need to Speak CODE. This does not lead to soul-satisfying communication and keeps us from being truly known.

List the ways in which your heart has not been valued in relationships where God has placed you and how that has promoted Speaking CODE.

The Desire to Be Known

Let's shift gears and discuss how our desire for God and being known affects the CODE we speak. This book is rooted in the Scriptures because my good ideas are worthless. Where do the Scriptures take us when looking at the nature of desires, especially the desire to be known? When we sabotage our conversations by Speaking CODE based on our self-talk, how does God's Word speak into our loneliness? Read the Word of the Lord from Psalm 73:25–26:

> Whom have I in heaven but you?
> And there is nothing on earth that I desire besides you.
> My flesh and my heart may fail,
> but God is the strength of my heart and my portion forever.

What else do we have in heaven or on earth except God? We desire many good things, but what one thing would we desire more than a deep and intimate relationship with God? Do we desire good communication, where we do not let our past fuel our self-talk or lead to Speaking CODE? Do we desire good Personal Communication Objectives, so we are not the Animator, Wallflower, or Provocateur? Do we desire good health so we can be fully invested in necessary relationships? Do we desire to serve in the church so that we feel useful? Do we desire to be a good person so we are acceptable? We will be completely dissatisfied with whatever we offer up other than knowing and desiring God. Desiring God is the key that unlocks our hearts so that we can be truly known.

In John 6, Jesus talks about the cost of following Him. He makes a gruesome statement about eating His flesh and drinking His blood, which confuses and offends His listeners. Many disciples walk away from Jesus. Jesus turns to the Twelve and says, "Do you want to go as well?" Peter's response is breathtaking. Read the Word of the Lord in John 6:68–69:

> Simon Peter answered him, "Lord, to whom shall we go? You have the words of eternal life, and we have believed, and have come to know, that you are the Holy One of God."

Where would we go with our desires? There is no desire for anything in heaven or on earth that satisfies us like God. Therefore, if we think people are supposed to fulfill our heart's desire for redemptive communication, we will be left seriously dissatisfied. People cannot give us what only God can. We are helpless to achieve redemptive communication if soul-satisfying conversations become a desire greater than God. When desiring God becomes our highest purpose, God will fulfill all that is in our hearts, and we will be satisfied.

So, what do we desire more than God? "Diana," I say to myself, "did you actually ask that question?" We know full well that this is the kind of question that most churchgoing people can answer without thinking. We are Believers and we know the answer: we desire nothing but God. We who were raised in the church were told this from our infancy.

While we say we desire God above all else, in truth, we only wish we desired God as much as we say. Why is this? Let me offer two reasons.

Unbelief Robs Us of Desire for God

Jesus was still on the mountain when a father brought his demon-possessed son to be healed. The disciples could not heal his son, which made it necessary for Jesus to intervene. By the time Jesus arrived on the chaotic scene, an argument had broken out that prompted Jesus to inquire about the situation. Out of the crowd, the boy's father answered Jesus, telling Him of his son's condition and the disciples' inability to heal his boy. Jesus took matters into His own hands, rebuked His disciples, and demanded the boy be brought to Him. Read the Word of the Lord in Mark 9:21–24; 28–29:

> And Jesus asked his father, "How long has this been happening to him?" And he said, "From childhood. And it has often cast him into fire and into water, to destroy him. But if you can do anything, have compassion on us and help us." And Jesus said to him, "'If you can'! All things are possible for one who believes." Immediately the father of the child cried out and said, "I believe; help my unbelief!"... And when he had entered the house, his disciples asked him privately, "Why could we not cast it out?" And he said to them, "This kind cannot be driven out by anything but prayer."

We have areas of unbelief in our lives, just like this father and the disciples. We get comfort from the traditions, thoughts, and ideas that we prioritize above God. As proof, just think what we prioritize over reading Scripture and praying. Jesus tells His disciples that driving out the unclean spirit in this possessed boy can only happen through prayer. This passage exposes my own unbelief: God is not always my priority. If He were, I would pray more.
How about your unbelief?

> Be brave and answer this question: What do you desire above God? How does this desire affect your devotion to God?

◀ ··· ·— —· · ·— —·— ·· —· — —·   —·—· — — — —·· ·

Desiring God above all else means that we love him as He has revealed Himself to us through Scripture. While some offer daily words of affirmation trying to make us believe that today I'm okay and you're okay, we must avoid taking passages out of context that make us feel affirmed and happy. Rather, we meet God on His terms, through His Word.

Being truly known is linked to a sure belief that there is nothing on earth or under heaven that we desire more than God. Sometimes, we can be codependent, fearful, anxious, and self-loathing people who Speak CODE driven by our self-talk. That is who we are. If we allow these characteristics to dominate our lives, they will affect our desire to know God well. Anything in our lives that displaces God will undermine our ability to achieve soul-satisfying conversations.

Which obstacles do you face that get in the way of desiring God and lead you to Speak CODE?

... .— —. . .— —.— .. —. — —. —.—. — — — —.. . ▶

Write a specific incident where your self-talk did not match up with your desire for God.

... .— —. . .— —.— .. —. — —. —.—. — — — —.. . ▶

Desiring God lays a foundation for soul-satisfying conversations. Why? When we desire God, we purge from our minds any self-seeking agendas about our self-worth, our need for affirmation, or our longing for the good opinion of others. Desiring God above all else puts us in a much better position to enjoy soul-satisfying conversation. Additionally, desiring God above all else means we will be truly known by our Creator, which frees us from frantically seeking approval from others.

Desiring God allows us to live under God's agenda rather than our own agenda, which is characterized by Speaking CODE based on our self-talk. What is God's agenda? God's agenda is summed up in the first and second greatest commandments: Love God with all your heart, soul, and mind. Love your neighbor as yourself (Matthew 22:37–39). God's agenda also demands that if we love Him, we will keep His commandments. In doing this, we throw off the weights and sin that entangle us, and so have less need to Speak CODE.

How does promoting God's agenda counteract unbelief in your self-talk, people-talk, and God-talk?

... .— —. . .— —.— .. —. — —. —.—. — — — —.. . ▶

Using Others

Our failure to desire God as our highest good puts us in a position to use others in a way that makes us feel good about ourselves. Acting to feel needed, to impress others, or to control people and situations pushes us away from God and makes our desires preeminent.

Our hope comes from God, who sees us through the work of Christ, and not through validation from friends, acquaintances, enemies, family members, or even from our own works. When we no longer seek validation from others but rather seek after God, we stop using people for our personal gain. Therefore, we are less likely to manipulate and victimize each other.

A word of warning to married people reading this. Dr. Paul Tripp has repeatedly reminded us that our spouse is not our messiah.[7] If we expect our spouse to meet all our needs, our spouse will fail us miserably. The only one who can meet all our needs is Jesus.

Write out how you use words to manipulate others to validate you and cause you to feel acceptable.

Desiring our own way and desiring God are mutually exclusive. Therefore, when we are engaged in that soul-crushing, agenda-driven conversation, we need to use words that reflect our desire for God and not our desire to promote ourselves at the expense of others. This idea will be fleshed out more deeply in the last section of this book.

Write out which benefits you expect to receive from desiring God alone.

A Trick Question

Practically speaking, how does desiring God work itself out in our everyday conversations? Let's go back to our example. When we walk into a messy house after a long day at work, we have a choice of how we evaluate and respond to what we see. What is in our hearts will determine how we respond to the messiness.

Here is a test for you. Even though we haven't discussed how our conversations can be different when we desire God, outline a "desiring God" conversation you could have when you come home only to find a mess, as in the example previously given. Be careful, because the answer can be tricky.

The answer to this question is tricky because the answer is based on our own hearts. Here are some possible conversations we could have had with our family members after we came home from work to our messy house.

THE WELL-LOVED HOUSE

If our family rarely cleans up after themselves, and we have previously made our expectations for a clean house known, we may need to admonish them in the moment. We could press the pause button on the remote while they picked up the house. God's desire and ours would have lined up, in that the Bible shows us that rebukes and admonitions are beneficial.

Perhaps our family usually tidies up the house. However, when we saw they were so engrossed in the latest episode of their favorite television series, we might have popped some popcorn and joined them. Picking up the house could have been done as a family after the show was over. God's desire and ours would have lined up, as the Bible teaches us to be kind toward one another.

When we arrived home and saw the family gathered around the television, maybe we wanted to serve them by quietly folding the clothes and cleaning the kitchen. We would have no need to slam doors or huff our way through the family room because our desire was to bless them. God's desire and ours would have lined up, as we practiced serving our family.

Our desires were exposed the moment we entered the messy house. In the original scenario, our self-talk led us to believe no one would care enough even to come to our funeral after we were found dead in a ditch. In this example, we Spoke CODE, which was only a part of our self-talk. The CODE we spoke showed itself as a form of deafening silence. Even in our silence, we made our desires known by way of door-slamming and heavy sighs. Our desires canceled out our desire for God. We gave up an opportunity to be truly known because we chose to Speak CODE.

Think about an example in your own life that is like the messy house scenario. What was in your heart that caused your self-talk to lead you to Speak CODE?

Write out how your words or deeds did or did not reflect your desire for God above all else.

Desiring God changes our focus. We desire God and love Him with all our heart, soul, and mind. Desiring God means we keep His commandments, written for us in the Bible. Now we can communicate with people based on God's desires and not self-talk that determines the CODE we speak.

Following God's desire for soul-satisfying communication is not easy, but it is clearly found in His word. Soul-satisfying conversations may contain admonishments or rebukes; they may move us to a place where we can know others and be truly known by them. The more we believe that God owns us, body and soul, the more deeply we understand that there is nothing on earth we desire more than God. Even if we lose everything, like a perfectly clean house, desiring God will always be the strength of our hearts and our portion forever.

May we pause here for a minute? I need to wonder out loud. All of Psalm 73 gives us reason to desire God. Look up the chapter and find verses that reflect your self-talk, your people-talk, and your God-talk.

What verses in Psalm 73 express your heart in this moment?

CONTRASTING DESIRES

Our goal is to achieve soul-satisfying and redemptive communication rather than soul-crushing speech. We undermine our goal when the words we use elevate our desire for acceptance above our desire for God. Words that conflict with God's desires sound like this: "How dare you talk to me like you just did? Who do you think you are to treat me that way?" These words of desire place us in a position over people. We look down on them from our lofty, self-righteous perch as we denounce those semi-humans beneath us. Even when our position is correct, if we diminish others and elevate our own desires, our conversations will not be soul-satisfying.

Anything we do that conflicts with God's desires stands as an obstacle to our satisfaction in Him alone. God will not have anything above Him or beside Him. God is our portion forever and allows us to rest as we sing, "It is well with my soul!"

Do not confuse my meaning here. I am not saying we achieve soul-satisfying communication by ignoring the harmful words we hear (although that may be a possibility). Neither am I saying that desiring God will shield our hearts against pain (although it could). Absorbing harmful words is a choice, and it is not stoicism. We need clarity in each situation. The last section of this book will outline righteous ways to achieve soul-satisfying conversation without elevating ourselves above others.

But what if we cannot desire God above all else, or we have tried to do so and failed, or we just do not believe this is true, or we do not know what desiring God really means? These are fair and honest questions. All I can give you is the Bible. My words cannot get to the level of pain and frustration in your experience. Maybe there are those of us reading this who will never have these questions fully answered. I can only offer what I know to be true. Study the God of the Bible so that you can know Him for yourself. Read the Word of the Lord in Psalm 34:8. In fact, read all of Psalm 34!

> Oh, taste and see that the Lord is good!
> Blessed is the man that takes refuge in him!

The Word of God is bursting with Scriptures that point us to knowing God and delighting in Him. Use Google or get a concordance to look up Scriptures that speak of desiring God. Let the Bible's theology become personal and sink down deep into our ever-wondering hearts. Let us find rest in Jesus, the only true Lover of our souls.

Let us desire God above all else. We must not allow our self-talk and CODE Speaking to keep us from being truly known. While we want to be accepted, practicing such diversions will keep us from knowing and being known. There is no biblical logic to that thinking. Let's not put ourselves above others. We may be lonely and terribly afraid to come down from that self-righteous perch. Our PPIFSt and PPIFEx will certainly be revealed, but God is the strength of our hearts and our portion forever.

IT'S THEOLOGICAL AND IT'S PERSONAL

I have lived long enough to know that all of us have a theology—a knowledge of God that guides our practice. We live out our theology for good or for ill; therefore, it makes sense to place communication within a theological framework. All of us worship something. We build our personal theology around what we worship. Theology is not just an intellectual pursuit. In this chapter, we will place our personal communication challenges in a theological framework. We need a reference point for our soul-satisfying or soul-crushing words. That reference point is our theology. If you are not in a relationship with Jesus, or if you do not see yourself as theologically-minded, please keep reading. Your theology may be revealed to you. In fact, you may come to believe that Jesus is the only true Lover of your soul. Remember, even atheism is based on theology because the atheist's belief that God does not exist is still a belief about God.

Write out what you believe about God (your theology), and how you live out your life based on those beliefs (personal).

PRACTICE AND PERFECTION

Read the Word of the Lord in Hebrews 5:11–6:3:

About this we have much to say, and it is hard to explain, since you have become dull of hearing. For though by this time you ought to be teachers, you need someone to teach you again the basic principles of the oracles of God. You need milk, not solid food, for everyone who lives on milk is unskilled in the word of righteousness, since he is a child. But solid food is for the mature, for those who have their powers of discernment

> trained by constant practice to distinguish good from evil.
> Therefore let us leave the elementary doctrine of Christ and go on to maturity, not laying again a foundation of repentance from dead works and of faith toward God, and of instruction about washings, the laying on of hands, the resurrection of the dead, and eternal judgment. And this we will do if God permits.

According to this passage, understanding the basic principles of God's oracles, requires deep insight. Deep insight happens by continuous practice that allows us to distinguish the difference between good and evil. This can explain why life seems relentless for many of us who need repetition to learn essential lessons in godliness. One benefit from constant training is that our everyday conversations are shaped by God's principles and not our Two Influential Forces and self-talk that leads to Speaking CODE. If practice makes perfect, then perhaps we may want to embrace the painful opportunities to become mature on God's solid food as God trains us to be skilled in righteousness. Our paradigm shifts away from our standards to God's.

If we do not practice discernment, we run the risk of being dull of hearing, and preferring milk to solid food. Milk alone cannot prepare us for righteousness just as milk without solid food cannot grow a baby into an adult. But solid food enhances our powers of discernment as we grow in maturity. It's all about theology and it's always personal.

Redemptive Power of the Cross

If we were meeting face-to-face, discussing the details of your communication breakdown, eventually we would turn our thoughts toward the redemptive power of the Cross. After all, our Two Influential Forces merely inform or explain the situation. The explanation does not offer any hope for living differently. Acknowledging that the Two Influential Forces affect our ability to speak redemptively is not enough. Our only hope is in the Scriptures, where our practical theology is formed and personalized. The Bible records heroic conversations where we can see theology lived out personally.

The challenge in harmful conversations is to look beyond the words, which may be harsh, to consider how our heart interprets what was said. Our Two Influential Forces impact how we interpret what we hear and form many of our presuppositions and responses. The issue is how our hearts engage with what we heard. Ultimately, our heart's reaction is more important than the specific words spoken.

Our words cannot change the human heart, no matter how powerful or persuasive they may be. Only God can do that. However, by God's grace we can reorient our hearts and focus not on the hurtful words said to us but on how we will respond to them. The means by which we do this is theological, and personal.

JESUS LOVES ME, THIS I KNOW

Theology is not reserved for seminary professors, pastors, students, or zealots. Theology simply means the study of God. How we define study plays an important role in how we define God.

Karl Barth was a twentieth-century Swiss theologian and pastor who lectured all over the world. During his 1962 lecture tour in the United States, Barth was asked a question by a student during a Q&A session after his lecture. The student reportedly asked Barth if he could summarize his whole life's work in theology with a single sentence. Barth allegedly said something like this, *"Yes, I can. In the words of a song I learned at my mother's knee: Jesus loves me, this I know, for the Bible tells me so."*[8] Based on Barth's answer, even our grandbabies have a good understanding of theology.

THEOLOGICALLY-BASED GOSPEL ISSUES

I define theologically-based gospel issues as those issues where the truths of Christ contained in the Scriptures speak directly and authoritatively into our lives. Biblical language is theological language. Think of any issues you may be experiencing in your life, including problematic communication. These issues are theologically-based gospel issues. The good news is this: if we can take our issues, including soul-crushing communication, and see them as theologically-based gospel issues, the Bible will speak directly to them. This gives us a pathway to healing and redemption. Read the Word of the Lord from 2 Peter 1:3:

> His divine power has granted to us all things that pertain to life and godliness, through the knowledge of him who called us to his own glory and excellence.

Theologically speaking, our conversations fall into the category of "life and godliness," where we become part of God's glory and excellence. Now you are talking theology! The Scriptures are full of encouraging words that help us speak redemptively to one another. They enable us to live out our theology as we begin to build a theological framework around our conversations, including those that devastate us.

As we have noted, Jesus commands us to fully love God, love our neighbor, and love ourselves. This love is the hook upon which we hang all that the Law and the Prophets teach us. That is just plain good theology. If we love God, who is the initiator of love, love self, and love neighbor, our conversations will be redemptive. Why? Because the Bible defines what love looks like, down to the very words we choose. A broader discussion of this will be presented in Section Three.

We would do well to thank God that we can frame our communication problems as theologically-based gospel issues. Theologically-based gospel issues provide us with a beginning, a middle, and an end. For example, in Genesis we see the life of Joseph from beginning to end. The Bible records the conversations Joseph had with his family. In this sweeping narrative, we can read about revealing dreams, secret plans, self-talk, deceptive cover-ups, and a final great reveal. We can follow everyone's Personal Communication Objectives from beginning to end. We observe PPIFSt interpreted. We see how PPIFEx are unfolding. Earliest Childhood Memories surface. We watch as God's people Speak CODE and, finally, reveal the theological underpinnings of their words.

Consider the words to the song "In Christ Alone," written by Keith Getty and Stuart Townend. The theology revealed in this song is often better than the words we hear preached in sermons. The two lines below express the Gospel's utter command over our lives. Even the frozen chosen among us can raise our hands in praise to God. Sing with me:

> From life's first cry to final breath,
> Jesus commands my destiny. . . .
> Till He returns or calls me home,
> Here in the power of Christ I stand.[9]

However we evaluate conflict-filled interactions, our conversations are theologically-based gospel issues. Identifying our communication struggles as gospel issues does not mean the answers are easy. Just read the Psalms or the book of Job for proof. Sometimes, we gloss over the rich biblical texts discussing the effects of the Gospel in our lives. As we consider our communication problems, let's begin to frame our communication difficulties as theologically-based gospel issues.

IDENTIFYING THE PROBLEM

We may ask ourselves: What makes this ungrateful person talk to us the way he does when we do everything for him? Why do we repeatedly allow ourselves to be spoken to so unkindly? We seem torn between needing to be in relationship with him and knowing full well that most of his words and behaviors will cripple us. We need a cosmic shield to protect us from conversations that send us into the pit of despair. We tell ourselves that just one kind word would erase the fifty harsh ones said to us. We tell ourselves that if he would only speak more tenderly, we would experience true happiness and fulfillment in our relationship. We try to reveal our true heart as we respond kindly, but somehow our words are never interpreted the way we intended. In fact, our words are often misinterpreted and used against us.

We believe that if we can just find the right series of words to string together, we will be understood, our hearts will be truly known, and we will be loved. In our desperation to stop the onslaught of hurtful words, we finally resort to uttering Christian platitudes to combat the manipulative and narcissistic words we hear. This new weapon in our arsenal gives us a feeling of satisfaction as we claim Jesus for our side. Finally, we enjoy a secret sense of self-righteousness as we take the relationship into our own hands. Maybe now, after hearing our new Christian words, he will finally understand how his words have affected us and admit we were right! Funny thing is, he claims Jesus for his side as well.

Identify a person in your life whose words sound manipulative, harsh, cruel, or graceless. Write out how these words have affected you.

What makes you accept the unkind words from him?

List what you really want or need from the person who speaks harshly.

Write out how this person prevents you from getting what you desperately want or need from him.

What would you say are some of that person's ECMs, PPIFSt, and PPIFEx, which may cause him to speak to you the way he does?

Identify ways in which you resort to Christian platitudes to combat the harmful words you hear.

What PPIFSt/PPIFEx has that person awakened in you?

PARADIGM SHIFT

Soul-satisfying communication is at the mercy of many forces. I believe that what we need is a paradigm shift. A paradigm shift happens when our foundational beliefs, which lead to how we live life, are challenged, reconsidered, and changed.

We shift our paradigm by trusting that God leads and directs our lives and determines our worth. The events in our lives are part of His sovereign plan. In the new paradigm, we look for how God works through circumstances for our good rather than allowing those things that caused us sorrow to be our focus. Recognizing that it is God in the center of what we experience changes how we react to our circumstances.

Before our paradigm shift, our self-talk reflected what was in our hearts. It fueled the CODE we spoke in difficult conversations. Our focus was on the horrific pain we experienced at the hands of others as well as from ourselves. When our paradigm was driven by our Two Influential Forces, we self-identified as those unfortunates who rarely experienced soul-satisfying conversations. We told ourselves that it was others who made us believe we were losers who were unloved, forsaken, fools, forgotten, marginalized, misunderstood, helpless, hopeless, despairing, or unheard. Or we became arrogant, self-enlightened, superior, self-righteous, indignant, self-absorbed, doubting, grandiose in our thinking, contemptuous, self-reliant, or victimized.

How has your communication with the people in your life influenced how you see yourself?

Without a paradigm shift, we may be lured into living in our past. This can cause us to experience self-inflicted wounds. When we respond to the cruelty of others, we are tempted to internalize the pain they inflict on us. These inward wounds may lead into a downward spiral of shame and guilt that is terrifying and dark. Our theology becomes a study of self rather than a study of God. We inflict our souls with self-imposed wounds that separate us from the land of the living.

If we live in the past, we will hear the echoes of our past in our present conversations. Someone says something to us today, but we answer them out of the pain from the echoes of our past. Both conversations (past and present) contribute to the weariness we experience, the interpretation we assign, and the turmoil we feel. This is what happens when we remain in existing patterns rather than making a paradigm shift.

How do the echoes from your past impact present conversations?

When we shift our paradigm, we can re-evaluate years of harmful interactions that held us captive. Our paradigm moves from a reaction prompted by our Two Influential Forces to a God-centered response. In our new paradigm we are no longer at the mercy of others or ourselves, but at the mercy of God. This makes our paradigm shift theological and personal.

The contrast is striking. In our former paradigm, we lived out of our self-based theology. In our new paradigm, our gospel-based theology directs how we personally live our lives to the glory of God.

Shifting our paradigm to a gospel-focused theology unties the cords which seek to keep our identity based on past pain. We no longer pay homage to the ghosts of our past. Instead, we bow to the Savior of our soul. We have a choice of how we respond. We no longer respond to the pain we hear but rather to the Gospel that gives us hope.

Write out how your theology needs a paradigm shift from one where you react based on how others treat you to one where you respond based on the theology of the Scriptures.

How can you speak redemptively as your paradigm shifts from focusing on the painful words you hear, to concentrating on how your heart responds?

Shifting from Old to New

Oh, the heart revealing entity known as Facebook! Many of us who use Facebook to express our views on the latest political issues will find my idea of a paradigm shift intriguing. We either comment on or initiate a post that before long bears no resemblance to the first remark. Why is that? We, who contribute to the thread, respond based on our existing paradigm rather than what was posted. What we think we read is muddled with our PPIFSt/PPIFEx and clouds what was actually posted! How do we shift our paradigm from focusing on our pre-existing paradigms to considering how we respond biblically? That is a good question.

We must begin by acknowledging that the present painful words we hear or say are linked to the pain from our past. This acknowledgment is especially important because our history is part of who we are today. Denying truths about our past can be dangerous. Our new paradigm moves our response away from focusing on how the words we hear tap into these past hurts. Instead, we pay attention to how we respond to the pain we experience.

This new paradigm shift is theologically-based, and gospel-centered. It is the constant training in righteousness so we can discern between good and evil. It stops our painful past from interpreting our present conversations and dictating the words we use. God's principles and oracles become our theology that we live out personally. Please keep in mind that, even with a paradigm shift, we will still feel the awful pain of soul-crushing conversations.

Our new paradigm allows us to put our trust in Jesus so we can respond with words that are soul-satisfying rather than soul-crushing, despite our past. Shifting our paradigm is hard work because our Two Influential Forces shape how we interpret life. However, the Gospel speaks louder than the sorrow from our past. It is theological and it is personal.

Write out how you can shift your paradigm by replacing the impact of your Two Influential Forces with biblical theology to guide your reactions.

The effect of our Two Influential Forces on our present conversations is profound and can corrupt our theology. It is disastrous if our theology of God is derived from our interpretation of our past. The only way to understand the purpose and meaning behind our PPIFSt and PPIFEx is to immerse ourselves in the best theological book ever written, the Bible. God so deeply loves us that everything He does is for our good. He guides our circumstances, gives insights into how the events in our lives are to be interpreted, and gives us hope for the future. He made us and sent His Son to rescue us, and the life and death of Jesus inspires us with gospel hope. Gospel hope means God's promises, presented in the Scriptures, that call forth a response of belief in the God who works out His plan in our lives. Let's see how the hope of the Gospel plays out in an incredible theological conversation two men had on the road to Emmaus.

THE MEN FROM EMMAUS

The account of the two men on the road to Emmaus speaks to the utter importance of God's Word. These men show how their Two Influential Forces informed their theological conversation, which interpreted their world.

You may remember this account. After the death and resurrection of Jesus, two men were on their way to Emmaus. Confused by the crucifixion of Jesus, they grappled with what they had witnessed. Eventually, Jesus Himself joined them on the road. But Jesus kept them from recognizing Him (Luke 24:13–14).

Jesus gives us a good example here of what it means to hitch a ride with hurting people, rather than hijack their pain. Later, we will discuss hitching a ride with peoples' conversations, rather than hijacking them. After listening to them, Jesus asked why they were so downcast (vv. 15–17). Astonished at this stranger's complete ignorance of current events, the men related all the shocking things that recently transpired. The men's concern focused on their dashed hopes and fears that the man in the center of the news might not be the one to redeem Israel (vv. 19–24).

Let's prepare to be dazzled as we investigate further. Read the Word of the Lord from Luke 24:25–35 (emphasis added):

> And he said to them, "O foolish ones, and slow of heart to believe all that the prophets have spoken! Was it not necessary that the Christ should suffer these things and enter into his glory?" And beginning with Moses and all the Prophets, he interpreted to them in all the Scriptures the things concerning himself.
>
> So they drew near to the village to which they were going. He acted as if he were going farther, but they urged him strongly, saying, "Stay with us, for it is toward evening and the day is now far spent." So he went in to stay with them. When he was at table with them, he took the bread and blessed and broke it and gave it to them. And their eyes were opened, and they recognized him. And he vanished from their sight. They said to each other, *"Did not our hearts burn within us while he talked to us on the road, while he opened to us the Scriptures?"* And they rose that same hour and returned to Jerusalem. And they found the eleven and those who were with them gathered together, saying, "The Lord has risen indeed, and has appeared to Simon!" Then they told what had happened on the road, and how he was known to them in the breaking of the bread.

This passage is an exceptional example of how our ECMs, PPIFSt, and PPIFEx form and shape our personal theology. This passage also exposes the effects of our self-talk and people-talk. The extensive theology lesson Jesus gives is very personal to these men and to us as well. Jesus leads these men through an epic, soul-satisfying conversation. We even have an admonishment or rebuke from Jesus, as He laments that these men are foolish and slow of heart! Let's examine the theology behind this account as we personally apply it to our daily conversations.

First, our hearts can burn within us when we read and understand the Scriptures. Our theology tells us that the Holy Spirit will interpret and apply Jesus's words to every area of our lives, including how we talk to one another. Therefore, theology is personal. Jesus interprets the available Scriptures (theology) about Himself so that these two men can make sense of the very confusing moments in their lives (personal).

Second, by talking to the men from Emmaus, Jesus integrated their PPIFSt and PPIFEx, helping them see that the Crucified One was their long-awaited Messiah. As Jewish children, they would have known about the coming of the Anointed One. The day of the crucifixion brought these powerful statements and experiences forward. Their PPIFSt and PPIFEx confused their interpretation of the day's events. Past statements we heard and events we experienced often baffle us, too, and make our conversations vulnerable.

As young boys, these men would have read Scriptures proclaiming that the Messiah would come as a conquering king. Rome occupied Jerusalem, and many of the Jews thought the Messiah would expel the Romans from their country. The Jews expected that the Messiah would establish an empire. They had hoped that Jesus of Nazareth, a mighty prophet in deed and word, was the one who would redeem Israel. They were confused because Jesus had been killed, but some of Jesus's followers reported they had seen Him after His death.

Jesus used the Scriptures to transform the two men's expectations that came out of their Two Influential Forces. Their past led to their assumptions that Jesus would be their conquering king. This recorded conversation is perhaps one of the most soul-satisfying dialogues in all of Scripture because Jesus is the Expositor! Our conversations will be more soul-satisfying if our interpretation is based on Scripture and not on our bewildering past.

These men lamented that it did not appear that Jesus would be the one who would redeem Israel. Their hopes had been dashed as they faced the consequences of this idea. Jesus patiently and compassionately opened the Scriptures and altered how they saw the day's events. For these men, this was a shocking paradigm shift. Allow this to sink deeply into your soul. It is all about theology and it is very personal.

Write out ways in which this biblical account (theology) helps you shift your paradigm (personal) and allows you to interpret what you hear based on Scripture and not your past.

BEING ROOTED IN BIBLICAL THEOLOGY

There are misconceptions regarding biblical theology and how the Bible is perceived. Biblical theology is not merely an intellectual pursuit, reserved for scholars. Nor is it a collection of moralistic stories. It is a factual account of actual people doing life together so that you and I can see God working in time and space.

We must apply biblical theology to our lives as we allow Scripture to interpret Scripture and in context. Our difficult conversations are no longer interpreted by our past experiences. Shifting our paradigm points us to the Bible as our guide that helps us navigate our everyday conversations. This requires work. It requires commitment to believe the Bible really does give us all we need for life and godliness, including how we talk to one another.

Proverbs shows us how to use Scripture to guide our words. We learn to whom we should speak, why it is beneficial to speak, when the time is right to speak, and how to select words that are appropriate. Study Jesus's teachings to His disciples in Matthew 5–7. Read Ecclesiastes. God is at work redeeming our conversations. It is not up to us to assign our own meaning based on our past.

Choose a biblical account that contains theological statements that connect you to your personal conversations so that you can shift your paradigm.

We must find out how our PPIFSt and PPIFEx can be rooted in the theology of the Scriptures. We will benefit from this rooting by seeing how God planned paths of righteousness for Old and New Testament saints for their good and His glory. For us, this look-back helps connect God's providential care to us despite our PPIFSt/PPIFEx. God often permits others to use crushing words that become deeply embedded in our hearts in order to light up our path of righteousness that leads to Him. These crushing words can become the doorway into our holy sanctuaries, where God is about the business of making us His own.

What are some of your PPIFSt and PPIFEx that have shaped how you understand life? How can you interpret them theologically to shift your paradigm?

TEMPTATION TO ACT

One aspect of our paradigm shift is that we turn away from the hurtful words said to us and turn toward understanding how these words tempt us to act. The paradigm shift leads us to esteem the other person's humanity and moves our focus away from the temptation to respond harshly. Esteeming their humanity means we understand that our persuasive words cannot change their hearts. Only God can do that. But we can change the temptation we feel to react ungodly toward them despite the harm they have done.

However, our paradigm shift does call for a response, just as the two men from Emmaus responded to Jesus's words. They implored Jesus to stay with them (v. 29). The men recognized Jesus as He broke bread with them (v. 30). They believed Him (v. 32). The two men immediately walked back to Jerusalem so that they could confirm to the grieving apostles that their Lord had indeed risen (vv. 33–35).

God's Word offers many examples of how biblical truths call us to action. Let us open our hearts to God's oracles so that our response is not retaliatory because of our pain. Instead, let's allow sound biblical theology to guide our personal responses. This is our paradigm shift. It is theological and it is personal.

Think about a difficult conversation you have had and write out a sentence where you can speak redemptively based on your paradigm shift.

PRESSING INTO THE PAIN

Pressing into the pain is the act of staying committed to a necessary person in our lives whose words and deeds remain hurtful no matter our response. We press into the pain when we stand by important relationships that can be soul-crushing. Let's imagine that we are in a painful conversation with a person who has a deep desire to harm us, either as an Animator, a Wallflower, or a Provocateur. He seems to demonstrate an insatiable desire to be right, which leads us to explode, check out emotionally, or remain silent. We may interpret his need to be right as an accusation that we are wrong. We conclude that any ongoing conversations are worthless and too painful for us to maintain. But this relationship is necessary.

His PCOs limit our interactions with him. No matter how hard we try to press into this pain, no matter how many gifts we give, no matter how many words of praise or encouragement or godly rebukes we utter, his response puts us in our place. This is not the place we would choose for ourselves. For us, we feel as though we are in a new level of hell described in Dante's *Inferno.* We are only allowed out of this purgatorial state if or when we are needed, or when we capitulate to his demands. Our only action is prayer, and sometimes we hear no answers. How will a paradigm shift help us?

ESTEEMING OUR HUMANITY

Read the Word of the Lord from John 3:16:

> For God so loved the world, that he gave his only Son, that whoever believes in him should not perish but have eternal life.

There is something so valuable about our humanity that God would incarnate Himself in the form of the Man, Jesus. Jesus esteemed our humanity in that He humbled Himself to live life in our filthy skin. He experienced all the sinful temptations our human bodies suffer but He never gave in. He even tasted death for us. Jesus did this willingly, because it was the good pleasure of His Father, and He set an example for us to follow. When we are called to righteous action based on the theology found in the Scripture, even if the person in that necessary relationship acts in a beastly way toward us, we follow Jesus's love for humans. This theological statement is personal in application and honors our humanity.

How does Jesus's view of humanity help you speak righteously when you must talk to a necessary relationship in your life?

A GLORIOUS WEIGHT

Consider this excerpt from C. S. Lewis's *The Weight of Glory:*

> It is in light of these overwhelming possibilities, it is with the awe and the circumspection proper to them, that we should conduct all our dealings with one another, all friendships, all loves, all play, all politics. There are no ordinary people. You have never talked to a mere mortal. Nations, cultures, arts, civilizations—these are mortal, and their life is to ours as the life of a gnat. But it is immortals whom we joke with, work with, marry, snub and exploit. Next to the Blessed Sacrament itself, your neighbor is the holiest object presented to your senses.[10]

Lewis is right, and his statement will help us shift our paradigms. As we contemplate the elements in Holy Communion, Lewis asks us to see our neighbor with the same reverence we see the bread and wine. If we associate the holiness of the elements with the holiness intrinsic in the human with whom we speak, we will see there are no ordinary people. This begs a question: Why do we talk to each other as we do if we are immortals?

Write out how Lewis's assertion affects your conversations, even those with humans who purpose to do you harm.

◀ ··· ·— —· · ·— —·— ·· —· — —·   —·—· — — — —·· ·

Think about your favorite biblical account where Jesus esteems someone's humanity. Write out how Jesus's example encourages you. If you need help, read John 4.

◀ ··· ·— —· · ·— —·— ·· —· — —·   —·—· — — — —·· ·

I love how Jesus spoke both redemptively and personally to Simon, after Simon called out the sinful woman who anointed Jesus with costly perfume. This conversation serves as a model for us. Simon did not understand or esteem the humanity of this woman. He only saw her sinfulness. This made him unable to see the good she had done to Jesus. Jesus also saw her sinfulness, but He memorialized her for her humble devotion toward Him. The conversation that took place over dinner was both theological and personal. Read the Word of the Lord from Luke 7:36–50:

> One of the Pharisees asked him to eat with him, and he went into the Pharisee's house and reclined at table. And behold, a woman of the city, who was a sinner, when she learned that he was reclining at table in the Pharisee's house, brought an alabaster flask of ointment, and standing behind him at his feet, weeping, she began to wet his feet with her tears and wiped them with the hair of her head and kissed his feet and anointed them with the ointment. Now when the Pharisee who had invited him saw this, he said to himself, "If this man were a prophet, he would have known who and what sort of woman this is who is touching him, for she is a sinner." And Jesus answering said to him, "Simon, I have something to say to you." And he answered, "Say it, Teacher."
>
> "A certain moneylender had two debtors. One owed five hundred denarii, and the other fifty. When they could not pay, he cancelled the debt of both. Now which of them will love him more?" Simon answered, "The one, I suppose, for whom he cancelled the larger debt." And he said to him, "You have judged rightly." Then turning toward the woman he said to Simon, "Do you see this woman? I entered your house; you gave me no water for my feet, but she has wet my feet with her tears and wiped them with her hair. You gave me no kiss, but from the time I came in she has not ceased to kiss my feet. You did not anoint my head with oil, but she has anointed my feet with ointment. Therefore I tell you, her sins, which are many, are forgiven—for she loved much. But he who is forgiven little, loves little." And he said to her, "Your sins are forgiven." Then those who were at table with him began to say among themselves, "Who is this, who even forgives sins?" And he said to the woman, "Your faith has saved you; go in peace."

Jesus attempts to shift Simon's paradigm by showing him how Jesus values this sinful woman. Jesus challenges his claim to self-importance as Simon debases the sinful woman's humanity. He points out several ways Simon failed to act hospitably toward his guest even while condemning the sins of this woman. Simon did not give Jesus water to wash His feet and failed to anoint Jesus's head with oil. Simon showed little regard for Jesus's humanity as he condemned the sinful woman's actions.

On the other hand, this seemingly worthless woman wet Jesus's feet with her own tears and wiped them dry with her hair. She poured expensive perfume on His feet. But that is not the most challenging example of how Jesus forces Simon to shift his paradigm. Jesus tells the supposedly less-than-human woman that her sins are forgiven. Jesus uses His words to esteem her humanity, while respecting Simon's humanity by rebuking his self-importance. For this woman and for Simon, Jesus made their experience theological and personal.

Write out how you see Jesus esteeming both Simon and the woman in His conversation with them

Write out a time when a person sinned against you? Were you able to look past the personal sin against you and see the person's humanity and respond from a theological perspective? Please write out your answer.

Think about a soul-crushing conversation you have had. Write out how you might choose to shift your paradigm away from defending yourself (personal) and toward embracing God's purpose as you lean into the pain (theological).

In my self-righteousness, I would have blasted Simon for being a misogynist pig. I would never have thought to esteem Simon's humanity by telling a story to help him think differently about this woman. Jesus does not shy away from admonitions. He uses redemptive words even when He points out our sinfulness. That tells us that admonitions are part of redemptive conversations.

To help you shift your paradigm, write out your favorite account of how Jesus spoke redemptively and esteemed a perpetrator's humanity.

As we look at the conversation Jesus had with Simon and the woman, we see how redemptive communication has a life-giving quality to it. We acknowledge how theology impacts our treatment of the humans with whom we interact. We encourage them to acknowledge our humanity as well. Redemptive communication seeks to truly understand others, and to be truly understood.

PPIFSt and PPIFEx are responsible for clouding our ability to act biblically in personal conversations. They also drive the CODE we speak. Our PPIFSt and PPIFEx rob us of our theological underpinnings, making it difficult to esteem human image bearers. Without a strong biblical theology, we fight harder to enact our own personal agendas in our conversations.

List ways you believe your PPIFSt and PPIFEx get in the way of shifting your paradigm to allow you to see both your humanity and the humanity of the person with whom you are speaking.

PPIFSt and PPIFEx can trigger our self-talk, forcing us into a loop that focuses on the past. When you get caught in this loop, how does your self-talk fuel the CODE you speak and trap you in your old paradigm?

Through the example of the Emmaus Road, Jesus teaches us that our conversations are theological and personal. Biblical theology allows us to shift our paradigm from reacting to the words we hear to confronting how our heart responds. We must include words in our people-talk that are both kind and truthful. These words are based on good biblical theology. It allows us to shift our paradigm from a focus on self to a focus on God. The personal application of our biblical theology will always esteem our humanness and the humanness of others. The words we choose to say may include rebukes, admonishments, or encouragements. But they must be said in truth and love, reflecting a profound respect for the human we are addressing.

GOD'S SPECIFIC GOODNESS TO US

THE FIVE SPARROWS/TWO PENNIES PRINCIPLE

Now that we understand how redemptive and soul-satisfying communication is possible despite our Two Influential Forces and Speaking CODE, let's look at how God's goodness reaches into the specifics of our lives. This look will be theological and personal. We have an idea of what we think we need most of the time, but God's goodness is precisely what we need all the time.

There are those of us who would agree that God is good, but we think that somehow the specifics of our situation escape His notice. This is a dangerous and a tragic misconception. God is not a casual bystander in our lives. In fact, God is intimately involved in every area of our lives including our soul-crushing communication. I call this the Five Sparrows for Two Pennies principle. This principle comes from Jesus's words. Read the Word of the Lord in Luke 12:6–7:

> Are not five sparrows sold for two pennies? And not one of them is forgotten before God. Why, even the hairs of your head are all numbered. Fear not; you are of more value than many sparrows.

If we were constructing an analogy to show worth or value, I wonder if we would reference sparrows and pennies. How often do we ignore the penny on the sidewalk as we pass by or the sweet chirping of tiny sparrows? While ignoring the penny, we would eagerly pick up a ten dollar bill lying in a muddy rain puddle. We may drive thirty miles to the nesting place of bald eagles just to get a glimpse of their grandeur but would hardly look up to see a sparrow.

To further our analogy showing value or worth, we often compare what is valuable to what is majestic. The zoo is a wonderful place to see this in action. Upon seeing the regal lion, we may say to our grandchildren, "Do you want to know how much I value you? See that mighty lion roaring at us? His roars are a constant reminder of his greatness. Look at his mane. It is a crown for his majestic head. His worth, in the animal kingdom, is peerless. I value you like I do this fearsome creature." It is reasonable that the lion communicates value and worth in the animal kingdom.

Children do not tug on their mamma's arm and say, "Mamma, Mamma … can we go to the sparrow exhibit?" Rather, our dear little children drag us to the lion's enclosure so that they can experience the stateliness of the lions sunning themselves in the cool summer grass. Isn't it rather odd that Jesus would compare our value and worth to tiny sparrows rather than fierce lions?

However, in Jesus's example of the five sparrows sold for two pennies, He asks us to consider how specifically He cares for us. Jesus uses objects that mostly go unnoticed to teach us lessons. The lesson in this case is that we should not fear that He would forget us. If Jesus is concerned about sparrows, how much more does He care about humans made in God's image? Jesus assures us that we are of more value than the five sparrows which are sold for two pennies. We who often feel marginalized or lowly find solace in Jesus's choice of comparisons. To further prove the specificity of His love, Jesus tells us He knows the precise number of hairs on our heads.

Based on this passage, we should marvel at how much God treasures us in the particulars of our lives including not only the words we say, but the punctuation and inflection we use! The specifics of redemptive and soul-satisfying conversation are important to God.

And still, amid our fears, we doubt the specificity of God's love in the details of our lives. Fear paralyzes the eyes of our heart, rendering us almost blind to God's specific goodness to us. We weep over the devastating conversations in which we are engaged and search for the God we cannot find. We ask God where He was when that person said and did unimaginable things to us. If God is good, then why did He allow that?

We berate ourselves over the careless words we said to others. We hate ourselves for not standing up to the aggressor's words that cowed us into silence. We ask ourselves why God calls us to engage in further conversations with necessary relationships. Doesn't God know that previous communication has nearly broken our relationship? The stress is unbearable. In these situations, we may accept that God is good in general without believing that He is good to us in the specifics. And yet, it is in these very disastrous details of our conversations that God is specifically good to us—Five Sparrows for Two Pennies kind of good.

Write out your definition of the goodness of God.

◀ ... .— —. . .— —.— .. —. — —.   —.—. — — — —.. .

TEMPTED TO QUESTION

Here are some questions we may be tempted to ask God when we wonder if God is paying attention to the heartbreaking details in our lives. Write out the specific circumstances you are facing that lead you to ask these questions. Preface each question with this phrase: *God, if you are specifically good in the details of my life, then . . .*

- why am I lonely?
- why was I abused?
- why was I abandoned?
- what possible reason could there be for the death of my loved one?
- why do I experience life altering guilt and shame over the things I did or were done to me?
- what made my spouse cheat on me?
- why don't you hear me and answer my questions?
- why is there such great suffering in this world?
- why does my body hurt all the time without relief or hope for healing?
- why don't you act like you are in charge?
- why does it feel like the circumstances of my life fell through the cracks?
- why do you skip over me when it comes to having good things in my life?
- why do I feel like I am being punished for my past sins?
- why am I treated like an outcast?

These are honest questions based on our human reasoning. We will answer these questions in the remainder of this chapter as we discuss the conversations of two well-loved biblical characters: Ruth and Lazarus. These narratives show us how God is good to His people in the very specifics of their lives.

But before we proceed, let us find comfort in the Scriptures by reading King David's words of despair as he called out to God to show up in the details of his life.

Read Psalm 88 and write out the verse or verses that resonate with you.

RUTH

Ruth is a love story that starts out sad, gets sadder, and ends in an unlikely genealogy. We read in the first chapter of Ruth that there is a severe famine in Bethlehem. Naomi and Elimelech take their two sons, Mahlon and Chilion, to Moab (vv. 1–2). Within about a decade, their sons marry two Moabite women, Ruth and Orpah; then Elimelech dies, as do Mahlon and Chilion. Sometime after their death, while in the fields, Naomi hears that God has visited Israel and given them food (v. 6).

Empty-handed and with a bitter soul, Naomi decides to leave Moab and return to Bethlehem. Naomi's daughters-in-law beg to return with her. However, during a tear-filled, heart-wrenching goodbye, Naomi reveals her heart when she says, "No, my daughters, for it is exceedingly bitter to me for your sake that the hand of the Lord has gone out against me" (v. 13). Orpah relents, but Ruth refuses to leave Naomi (vv. 16–18). Together, Naomi and Ruth travel back to Bethlehem just at the time the barley harvest begins.

We are looking at the details in Naomi and Ruth's lives to see how God was specifically good to them and, by extension, good to us. As a Jew who knew the Scriptures, Naomi would have been taught that God is good. In this first chapter, however, we see Naomi questioning God's specific goodness to her. She says God's hand has gone out against her. Have we been where Naomi has been? As fine Christian folks, do we say, "God is good," but secretly believe God's hand has gone out against us because of the specific details of our lives?

In Chapter 1, how do you see evidence that the Lord's hand has gone out against Naomi?

◀ ··· ·— —· · ·— —·— ·· —· — —· —·—· — — — —·· ·

Write out what you think Naomi's self-talk would have sounded like.

◀ ··· ·— —· · ·— —·— ·· —· — —· —·—· — — — —·· ·

In Ruth 1, what evidence do you see regarding God's specific goodness to Naomi and Ruth?

◀ ··· ·— —· · ·— —·— ·· —· — —· —·—· — — — —·· ·

Read the Word of the Lord from Ruth 1:19–21:

> So the two of them went on until they came to Bethlehem. And when they came to Bethlehem, the whole town was stirred because of them. And the women said, "Is this Naomi?" She said to them, "Do not call me Naomi; call me Mara, for the Almighty has dealt very bitterly with me. I went away full, and the Lord has brought me back empty. Why call me Naomi, when the Lord has testified against me and the Almighty has brought calamity upon me?"

During their journey from Moab to Bethlehem, we can conclude that Naomi still struggled with a bitter heart brought about by God's calamity against her. When Naomi's friends recognized her, Naomi rejected her given name. In fact, Naomi changed her name from Naomi, which means "pleasant," to a prophetic name, Mara, which means "bitter." Even though Naomi had Ruth with her, she found little comfort from Ruth's loving devotion or from the prospect of being home.

Stay here for a moment. Consider the deep distress and profound bitterness of Naomi's soul, brought about by her circumstances. Consider your soul's condition as well.

List what you see about Naomi's circumstances that left her soul bitter.

Describe specific conversations that have left your soul bitter.

Does Naomi's experience resonate with you? Explain your answer.

At the right time, what advice would you give Naomi based on where her life is at this very moment?

What would you tell her about God's goodness? What words would you give Naomi that would point her to God's specific goodness?

She leaves Bethlehem with her family because of a famine. Her family seems to integrate into life in Moab. Her sons marry women who seem to be very loyal. There is no doubt that God is good. Then everything falls apart. Naomi says it well: she went to Moab full and returned to Bethlehem empty. The question for Naomi is the same question for us. God is good as I see Him working in the lives of others, but is God good to me in the specifics of my life?

In the details of your past or present conversations, list the circumstances where you find it hard to see how God is specifically good to you.

When you cannot see God's specific goodness, what are you tempted to do or say?

How do you understand God's goodness in general?

How do you understand God's goodness to you specifically?

Ruth and Naomi return to Israel in time for the barley harvest. We remember that Naomi heard that God ended the famine in Bethlehem while she was in the fields of Moab. The barley harvest, of course, takes place in the barley fields.

What do you make of this specific detail that the two women return just in time for the barley harvest to commence?

If we had never read Ruth, we might get to the end of Chapter 1 and wonder how we could make verse 22 interesting enough to entice Disney to make it into a feature film. We could make millions. We could title it, *The Foreign Princess.* The plot has ingredients that would appeal to people of all ages. We might be tempted to embellish Ruth's story. But the book of Ruth is not a fairy tale. It is an historical account that only God could write and direct.

Still, let's momentarily indulge ourselves as we look at ways to embellish what God has written. We might determine that the closing sentences in Ruth 1 lack purpose or intrigue. We might compose a more captivating sentence in order to make the end of this chapter a cliff-hanger. We might change that last sentence to say, "And they came to Bethlehem in order to seek their fortune by defying what the hand of God gave them."

But God had another closing sentence. God ends Ruth 1 by stating that while in the fields of Moab, Naomi hears that the barley harvest in Bethlehem is about to begin. Keep that specific detail in mind as we read further.

The God of the Specifics

As the book of Ruth unfolds, we are told that Ruth went to a specific barley field that just happened to be owned by a specific man who came down from Bethlehem at the start of this specific barley season in this specific field. As it turned out, the field in which Ruth happened to glean belonged to Boaz, who is her dead father-in-law's relative. Boaz showed particular kindness and protection to Ruth and asked her to glean only in his barley fields. Read the Word of the Lord from Ruth 2:19–20:

> And her mother-in-law said to her, "Where did you glean today? And where have you worked? Blessed be the man who took notice of you." So she told her mother-in-law with whom she had worked and said, "The man's name with whom I worked today is Boaz." And Naomi said to her daughter-in-law, "May he be blessed by the Lord, whose kindness has not forsaken the living or the dead!" Naomi also said to her, "The man is a close relative of ours, one of our redeemers."

We know this account. We know how Ruth listened to Naomi's wise instructions. Ruth was from Moab. She would have had limited exposure to ancient Jewish laws and customs. Boaz responded to Ruth's invitation to be her redeemer but told her that there was a redeemer even closer than he. Boaz praised Ruth for her kindness and assured her that he would not rest until she was redeemed. Boaz specifically searched out Elimelech's nearest relative and asked if he wanted to redeem Elimelech's property—which included Ruth. The nearest relative declined because he did not want to jeopardize his own inheritance. Boaz was then free to redeem all that belonged to Elimelech.

God enabled Ruth to conceive, and a baby boy was born to her. The village women blessed the Lord and prophesied that this specific baby would be a redeemer, a restorer of life, and a nourisher to Naomi in her old age.

But wait. Not only is God's specific goodness shown to Naomi and Ruth by leading them from Moab to Bethlehem at the beginning of a specific harvest season, but God also shows His specific goodness to us! Read the Word of the Lord from Ruth 4:16–22:

> Then Naomi took the child and laid him on her lap and became his nurse. And the women of the neighborhood gave him a name, saying, "A son has been born to Naomi." They named him Obed. He was the father of Jesse, the father of David.

> Now these are the generations of Perez: Perez fathered Hezron, Hezron fathered Ram, Ram fathered Amminadab, Amminadab fathered Nahshon, Nahshon fathered Salmon, Salmon fathered Boaz, Boaz fathered Obed, Obed fathered Jesse, and Jesse fathered David.

And I will add, "From whose line comes Jesus Christ, the Son of God, and our Redeemer!"

The beginning of Ruth recounts conversations filled with bitterness and sadness, crying and embracing. Further in, we read conversations between Boaz and Ruth that must have been soul-satisfying to both Ruth and Naomi. Finally, we see the results of a specific plan that makes Boaz a kinsman-redeemer. The book of Ruth ties up all the ways in which God was good to Naomi in the specifics of her entire life, including the bitterness she experienced in Moab. God's specific goodness included the village women blessing God for a loving daughter-in-law who was better to Naomi than seven sons! How full would Naomi say she is now?

How are we to interpret the specific words and experiences seen in the recorded conversations in Ruth? I would say the statements made and the experiences had demonstrated God's specific goodness as seen in the principle of the Five Sparrows and Two Pennies. The recorded conversations in this book are some of the most soul-satisfying conversations in Scripture. We may die before we see how God establishes His specific goodness to us as He did with Naomi and Ruth. If that is the case, we will be in glory and we will not care one whit.

Therefore, that last painful conversation or interaction we had is not the end of the matter. Our self-talk and CODE Speaking are not the end of the matter. Our PPIFSt and our PPIFEx, which tell us how to interpret life, are not the end of the matter. The end of the matter may be in what appeared to be a randomly chosen barley field. However, God will reveal His specific goodness to us in what we discover is His particular barley field. Or God's specific goodness will be His outstretched arms waiting for us as He welcomes us home!

Be honest: do you believe that God is good in general but not good to you in the specifics of your life? Give an example.

◀ ··· ·— —· · ·— —·— ·· —· — —·   —·—· — — — —·· ·

Using the account of Ruth, list ways where you can begin to see God's specific goodness to you even when you are empty-handed and embittered in your heart over conversations or events.

◀ ··· ·— —· · ·— —·— ·· —· — —·   —·—· — — — —·· ·

LAZARUS

The book of Ruth demonstrates the specificity of God's goodness toward Naomi, Ruth, and Boaz in bringing together a family into which our Savior was born. What began as a tragic series of events was used by God to show His specific goodness to those who suffered.

In the account of Lazarus's death, we see another example of how groups of real people, who suffer real grief, find God's specific goodness as He demonstrates His glory through theological statements. We will start prior to the funeral so we can see how a shared grief becomes the vehicle for God to demonstrate His specific goodness to everyone involved.

Do we view God's interaction in our lives as an either-or situation? If God is happy with us, we receive good, pleasant, happy, or even joyful circumstances. But if things go badly, we interpret God's actions as hostile or uncaring. Our human-centric view of goodness is rather simplistic. In contrast, God's intention to show goodness is on display throughout this narrative and is more than simply happy circumstances and good feelings. Jesus makes a surprising theological statement about Lazarus's illness. Read the Word of the Lord in John 11:4:

> But when Jesus heard it he said, "This illness does not lead to death. It is for the glory of God, so that the Son of God may be glorified through it."

In this account, we must never lose sight of this verse as we consider the work of God in each participant's life. God is specifically good to us through our difficult circumstances. His good has as its objective not just our joy or satisfaction but that God will be glorified by all that occurs in the lives of those involved.

Disciples

The biblical account begins with Jesus receiving the news of Lazarus's illness. From their limited understanding, the disciples believed that healing Lazarus would have been good for Mary and Martha. But Jesus understood how to provide abundantly for everyone involved, even beyond their expectations. Merely raising Lazarus from the dead would be good, but not as good as what Jesus had planned. There was a higher good that only Jesus could have known, because it displayed the character of God and would lead many to belief. We who doubt God's specific goodness to us should prepare to be astonished by what Jesus is about to do. Read the Word of the Lord in John 11:7–8:

> Then after this he [Jesus] said to the disciples, "Let us go to Judea again." The disciples said to him, "Rabbi, the Jews were just now seeking to stone you, and are you going there again?"

Many of the disciples were dismayed that Jesus would travel to Judea despite threats of the religious leaders. Jesus spoke about Lazarus's condition in a way that completely confused them. Read the Word of the Lord in John 11:11–13:

> After saying these things, he said to them, "Our friend Lazarus has fallen asleep, but I go to awaken him." The disciples said to him, "Lord, if he has fallen asleep, he will recover." Now Jesus had spoken of his death, but they thought that he meant taking rest in sleep.

Finally, Jesus told His disciples about Lazarus's physical condition and why it was important that He delay His departure to Bethany. Read the Word of the Lord in John 11:14–15:

> Then Jesus told them plainly, "Lazarus has died, and for your sake I am glad that I was not there, so that you may believe. But let us go to him."

Remember these words: "so that you may believe." Jesus hints of a specific good that is even better than healing Lazarus—one which would benefit his grieving family, and everyone else involved in the unfolding drama.

Martha

Let's consider the conversations Martha and Jesus had after Lazarus died. Martha remained consistent in how she spoke to Jesus and in her level of trust, based on her PPIFSt and PPIFEx. Earlier, Jesus had visited her home where she was anxious about serving a large crowd while her sister sat at Jesus's feet to hear Him teach. Her prior experience with Jesus allowed her to freely speak what was in her heart when Jesus finally arrived at Lazarus's funeral. Read the Word of the Lord in John 11:21–22:

> Lord, if you had been here, my brother would not have died. But even now I know that whatever you ask from God, God will give you.

What do we make of this? Let's imagine Martha's self-talk. It may have sounded like this: "Why did Jesus take so long to come here? Now my brother is dead. He healed others, so why wouldn't He heal Lazarus? This would have ended differently if only He arrived sooner. Jesus, your delay confuses me, but I know You can still fix this."

The Jewish tradition held that a soul remained with a dead body for three days after death. On the fourth day the soul left, apparently making a resurrection impossible. Whatever Martha's self-talk was on this issue, we know that she told Jesus plainly that had He arrived on time, He could have healed Lazarus. Nevertheless, Martha acknowledged that God would still do whatever Jesus asked of Him. She left the door open for Jesus to make this right.

This is a good lesson for us. When we pray to God in the name of Jesus, our seemingly hopeless words never go unheard, in spite of how it feels to us. Jesus answered Martha's question based on theology which may not be what she (or us) expected. Read the Word of the Lord in John 11:23–27:

> Jesus said to her, "Your brother will rise again." Martha said to him, "I know that he will rise again in the resurrection on the last day." Jesus said to her, "I am the resurrection and the life. Whoever believes in me, though he die, yet shall he live, and everyone who lives and believes in me shall never die. Do you believe this?" She said to him, "Yes, Lord; I believe that you are the Christ, the Son of God, who is coming into the world."

This passage is very theological and extremely personal to Martha. We should observe that Martha's confession occurs before Lazarus is raised. Jesus is taking Martha from a resigned acceptance of her brother's death to a place where she will have a clearer idea of what it means for Jesus to be Messiah. So for Martha, God's goodness includes showing her God's glory in providing a Messiah who is the resurrection and the life. God's goodness to Martha makes limited knowledge complete which will help her see that there is a good, more specific to her needs than just healing or raising Lazarus from the dead. This answer requires belief. Of course, in this situation there is the added goodness of turning grief to unexpected joy.

Mary

We know that Jesus delayed His trip to Bethany. If the account of Lazarus's death ended here, we would wonder how Jesus was specifically good to Mary. But this account continues to show us that God is always working, despite our Two Influential Forces, self-talk, and CODE Speaking.

Martha told Mary that Jesus wanted to see her. When Mary met Jesus, she expressed her heart. We see a poignant exchange between the two of them. Read the Word of the Lord in John 11:32:

> Now when Mary came to where Jesus was and saw him, she fell at his feet, saying to him, "Lord, if you had been here, my brother would not have died."

Once again, we see Mary's devotion to Jesus as she falls at His feet. In John 12, we read that six days prior to Passover, Mary took a pound of pure nard and anointed Jesus's feet using her hair as a towel. Mary's past statements and experiences led her to believe that Lazarus would still be alive if Jesus had arrived in Bethany on time. Maybe we are like Mary and question Jesus's timing in our lives.

In your sorrowful conversations, where words were used to harm and not heal, do you say, "Jesus, if only You had been here . . .". Write out what you would say.

◀ ··· ·— —· · ·— —·— ·· —· — —·   —·—· — — — —·· ·

The Bystanders

Those attending the funeral were baffled that Jesus delayed His arrival at Bethany. Why didn't Jesus rush to heal a man He loved? Jesus was a healer and a prophet, sent by God. Read the Word of the Lord in John 11:37:

> But some of them said, "Could not he who opened the eyes of the blind man also have kept this man from dying?"

Jesus had a specific good in mind for those He loved that only His delay would achieve. Had Jesus healed Lazarus, that act would have been good, but mostly for Lazarus's family. Healing Lazarus would simply affirm what everyone already knew. By raising Lazarus after four days in the tomb, Jesus showed a side of Himself that far exceeded their expectations. The bystanders would have the joy of seeing life come from death, leading many to believe in Jesus. However, God meant for a more specific good. All those present would have experienced the glory of God. For those who believed in Jesus the miracle would bolster their faith prior to Jesus's pending death. This example is as helpful for us today as it was for everyone involved in this unfolding drama.

Back to the Disciples

Raising Lazarus also clearly benefited the disciples. Jesus knew the disciples would soon face the trauma of His capture, trial, crucifixion, and resurrection. One benefit of Jesus resurrecting Lazarus was that it bolstered His disciples' faith. There is a bigger, more faith-producing difference between healing the sick and raising someone who was dead four days! Calling Lazarus forth from the grave could help the disciples as they waited three days before Jesus fulfilled His promise to rise again. Raising Lazarus displayed God's specific goodness to all involved and far exceeded the good of merely healing him.

If our analysis of God's goodness to us ends here, our expectations would certainly be met. But there is more specific goodness yet to be revealed than raising Lazarus from the tomb. This greater good is two-fold and closely related to God's specific provision. First, Jesus Christ is the resurrection and the life. Second, Jesus and His Father would be glorified through Lazarus's death. This two-fold goodness helps us when our dreadful conversations and resulting behavior render us hopeless.

I Am the Resurrection and the Life

Jesus identifies as the One who will resurrect Himself. He also identifies as Life itself. These theological concepts belong to us as much as they did to Lazarus's family, bystanders, and disciples. Jesus declared this to Martha when He arrived in Bethany four days after Lazarus died. Biblical conversations have consequences for our twenty-first century lives. We must be driven to these recorded dialogues to help us in our time of need and to instruct us in how to choose our words. We have already read Jesus's words to Martha where He told her He was the resurrection and the life. Jesus being the resurrection and the life was shown to be more than an illustration when He actually raised the dead.

When Jesus raised Lazarus from the dead, He demonstrated that He is the final authority over life and death. God always has a more specific good in mind for our suffering that we, like Mary and Martha, cannot see. The CODE we speak, fueled by our self-talk and our Two Influential Forces, makes it difficult for us to see God's specific goodness.

We may think that our grief will not be changed to joy through a resurrection. The lost relationships, physical ailments, or financial hardships may appear to be hopeless. Amid these difficult circumstances the challenge for all of us is to look for how God is going to be glorified through these events.

Jesus is the resurrection and the life. He confronted Martha with this theological fact and called on her to personally accept it. In life or in death, those who believe in Jesus will never die. In the big picture, our greatest specific good is the assurance of eternal life in Jesus Christ our Lord. In the account of Lazarus's death, Jesus demonstrated that His specific goodness goes far beyond what we see with our eyes, hear with our ears, taste with our mouths, smell with our noses, or touch with our hands. In the circumstances of our lives, His specific goodness will always bring God glory, be for our good, and help us believe.

How does believing that Jesus Christ is the resurrection and life change your view on God's specific goodness to you?

How does that belief make a difference in your conversations?

As I was considering this account, something revelatory occurred to me regarding the nature of Jesus's steadfast love. *His love never leaves us.* But when we are at the bottom of a deep pit, it is hard to remember how persistent His love for us is! This is where we must read and re-read how Jesus leads Mary, Martha, and Lazarus, through heartbreaking circumstances, all the while professing His deep love for them. Knowing that Jesus affectionately led them through sickness, death, and grief helps us trust that Jesus will lovingly lead us through incredible hardships for our good and the glory of God.

To God Be the Glory

A great and specific good seen in this biblical account is how it proclaims the glory of God through Jesus His Son. Remember we took special note that Mary and Martha sent word to Jesus about Lazarus's illness. Jesus's response explains the second part of His greatest and most specific good for us. Recall the Word of the Lord in John 11:4:

> But when Jesus heard it he said, "This illness does not lead to death. It is for the glory of God, so that the Son of God may be glorified through it."

Nothing will stop God from receiving glory and glorifying His Son. In fact, it is through our trials that God brings glory to Himself through Jesus. God's glory is as essential to us as the air we breathe. His glory speaks into every area of our lives where He demonstrates not only that He is good, but that He is specifically good to us. The outcome of our conversations pales in comparison to God receiving the glory that is due Him. Our chief end is to glorify God and enjoy Him forever in this life and the next. Our very lives, including our soul-crushing conversations, should always have in mind that God will be glorified.

> Write out how you can compose your responses to soul-crushing conversations to bring God glory.

Sadly, the details of suffering obscure this specific goodness. We lament that God takes too long to answer our prayers. He does not give us the answer we desire. We cannot see the faith-strengthening purpose of God's delay in our lives just as Lazarus's friends and family could not see the faith-strengthening purpose of Jesus's delay in theirs.

This makes our conversations vulnerable and causes us to deny that God is good specifically to us. Our Two Influential Forces, self-talk, and CODE Speaking stop us from seeing that Jesus will be glorified as He acts for our specific good. We allow our anxieties and troubles to obscure God's glory and His specific goodness. As we live out the circumstances of our lives, we need to rest in the certainty that God is for us.

CAREGIVERS AND COUNSELORS

If you are a caregiver or a counselor and you feel as though your client is stuck, then chances are you need to help him see that God is good to him in the specifics of his broken life. Help him see that his definition of goodness lacks substance. Most people view goodness as a marshmallow or cotton candy treat; they think goodness tastes sweet and is never bitter. But God's palate is much more sophisticated. The Cross is the ultimate standard that God holds up to show us goodness.

To help your client, love him in his story as you connect him to the biblical narratives which enliven faith. These narratives highlight God's specific goodness to His creatures. This process cannot be rushed because we cannot change a human heart. Only God does that. Our job is to have meaningful conversations, ask good questions, and pray. Never forget, our clients will benefit from seeing God glorified in heaven and on earth as He works for their good in the specific details of their lives.

ONE LAST PRACTICAL THOUGHT

A niece I dearly love asked me the question to end all questions: "Why does the aunt we dearly love suffer so much in her life?" This question was thoughtful and heartfelt given the circumstances under which it was said. As I pondered her question, the book of Hebrews put my sweet niece's question into perspective. Read the Word of the Lord from Hebrews 2:8–9 (emphasis added):

> Now in putting everything in subjection to him, he left nothing outside his control. *At present, we do not yet see everything in subjection to him.* But we see him who for a little while was made lower than the angels, namely Jesus, crowned with glory and honor because of the suffering of death, so that by the grace of God he might taste death for everyone.

To my beloved niece: we need to add this to our conversation. Presently, we can only see the effects of this sad and evil world, such as watching the aunt we love suffer tremendously. But we must believe in Jesus who is at work and has not given up His authority over our sufferings to help our unbelief. God put everything under Jesus's control, even our suffering.

Our dimly lit eyes cannot see the specificity of God's goodness in all the situations of our lives, or in that of our beloved aunt. May God allow my dearest niece, and us, to rest there. To God be the glory, for He is the resurrection and the life!

HUMANS IN *IMAGO DEI*

God's image imprinted on us gives us innumerable blessings. One such blessing is that our life has value. God's image inscribed on us is an indication of our worth and significance. All humans bear the image of God.

Years ago, my pastor, Michael Crawford, preached a sermon series on hard topics. One of those hard topics was racism.Pastor Crawford said that we are all members of one race—the human race.[11] Acknowledging that we all belong to one race stands as an indictment against those who try to separate humanness based on any manmade prejudice or distortion. Our conversations must start with the fact that we all share in our humanness and are made in God's image. Conversely, we reject conversations that makes us want to make man into an image of our own imagination.

As members of one race, we share certain things in common. We are embodied beings who experience life sandwiched between our birth and death. Throughout our lives, we may experience strength or weakness, health or sickness, differences or similarities, riches or poverty. After the Fall, we continue to bear the image of God. Bearing God's image is so important that if we harm ourselves or others, there will be consequences. Read the Word of the Lord from Genesis 9:6:

> Whoever sheds the blood of man, by man shall his blood be shed,
> for God made man in his own image.

As members of one race, we share God's common grace. We have been made by God to reflect His communicable attributes that help us interpret the world around us. Together, we delight in our joys and grieve in our sorrows. However, we sin against God, ourselves, and others when we make man into what we imagine he should be. This imaginary man will take on flesh and bones when we open our mouths!

With that in mind, we would be wise to acknowledge the link between redemptive communication and the humanity of the person with whom we are speaking. All persons are human. Imagine that. The person to whom we are speaking is a living breathing human, just like us. Humanity is the great equalizer. The Bible describes our shared humanity unequivocally. Read the Word of the Lord in Galatians 3:28:

There is neither Jew nor Greek, there is neither slave nor free, there is no male and female, for you are all one in Christ Jesus.

Go back to what you wrote regarding your Personal Communication Objectives. Perhaps you adopted an approach—like that of the Animator, the Wallflower, or the Provocateur—that does not esteem the other person's humanity. Your Personal Communication Objectives were to have the hearer adopt your view even if your aggressive words, silence, or provocation wounded them.

How would you revise your PCOs now that you recognize the God-given humanity of others, rather than making people out to be how you imagine them to be?

What might you fear if you changed your PCOs and treated the other person with a newfound respect for his humanness?

Do we only respond with redemptive words to our human conversational partner if he speaks redemptive words first? Perhaps we should rethink that tactic. In the nobility of being created in God's image, we can begin our conversations by taking the lead, speaking words filled with truth and love. This approach ensures that the listener is esteemed in his humanity, and it may change the trajectory of a difficult conversation.

As image bearers, we choose language reflecting what we read in the Bible when speaking to those who bear the imprint of God. The presupposition is that we are reading the Bible. We already mentioned good books within the Scriptures that would help contour our conversations. Biblical words are life-giving, both to the speaker and the listener, in that they connect us to Jesus. In contrast, life-taking words are words that obscure the work of Jesus in our lives. In Section Three, we will see how we put this into practice.

As we esteem the humanity of the listener, we relinquish our right to change their minds so that they believe what we believe. We are human. They are human. We have our perspective. They have their perspective. God will speak deeply into both our hearts and use everyone's words to His glory and for our good. The question is, are we willing to relinquish our need to control difficult conversations? Or will we insist on directing the outcome, even if it means disrespecting the image bearer with whom we are speaking?

Sometimes we esteem the humanity of certain people over others. Whom do you struggle to esteem and why?

SHARING LIFE EXPERIENCES

But we may ask, what do we do with our life experiences that may help a person choose a wiser path? If it is a matter of life or death or safety issues, we must intervene. If not, we must consider our motives for sharing our experiences. These are heart issues. If our purpose is in any way manipulative or self-promoting, we may wish to refrain from offering advice. Instead, we can ask good questions to determine why the person has chosen a specific course of action. Asking good questions will expose motives. At this point, we are better able to determine if our life experiences will be beneficial. We can ask permission to share our thoughts, or if we are close friends, we can offer our suggestions.

We do not need to use coercive words that bully, dissemble, strong-arm, trick, or confuse the listener. God alone will change the human heart, not the profuseness of our words, the sharpness of our tone, the shaming of our gestures, the fearfulness of our emotional outbursts, or the deafening sound of our silence.

When you are in an emotional conversation, how do you determine if it is appropriate to share your life experiences?

Write out ways you struggle to avoid manipulation as you try to keep someone from making the same mistakes you have made.

It bears repeating that there are conversations in which we must take a hard stand to protect or preserve life. I am not referring to those types of conversations. Even so, please do not miss that God is still sovereign over the words we select in conversations where rebukes and admonishments are necessary and appropriate. We must still esteem that person's humanity as we protect the defenseless, believing that only God can change the human heart. Paul gave Timothy useful categories to identify people's needs. Read the Word of the Lord in 1 Thessalonians 5:14–15:

> And we urge you, brothers, admonish the idle, encourage the fainthearted, help the weak, be patient with them all. See that no one repays anyone evil for evil, but always seek to do good to one another and to everyone.

Notice that we are called to speak to those who need admonishment, encouragement, help, and patience. Also, notice that we cannot repay anyone evil for evil but must always seek to do good. These are good guardrails that help us determine when sharing our life experiences may be beneficial to the listener.

How do these categories help you choose the appropriate words in your conversations?

Sometimes we use our painful life experience as an excuse for returning evil for evil. List ways in which you have done this.

In what ways can you "seek to do good to one another" through your conversations?

INJURIOUS CONVERSATIONS

Additionally, if a person consistently talks in ways that are injurious to us, we should not subject ourselves to such wounds. If we allow this practice to continue, I wonder what is going on in our hearts, that we believe this kind of communication is redemptive for anyone involved, including us. We are not called to cast our pearls before pigs.

Write out why you stay in a relationship where the other person consistently hurts you and does not esteem you as an image bearer.

Necessary relationships can be painful and must be handled biblically. The pain is often reflected in our conversations. In handling distressing but necessary relationships biblically, we take no revenge in our thoughts, words, or deeds. Even the vilest among us is created in the image of God. For that reason, vengeance belongs to God, whose actions are perfectly holy, wise, and loving.

Unfortunately, some relationships can never be severed no matter how grievous the sin. Grievous sins include physical, emotional, and sexual abuse. For example, if a daughter was molested by her father, the parental relationship may remain an ongoing, oppressive presence. The daughter can choose to prosecute him, not out of revenge but in a pursuit of justice. She can also establish boundaries by physically separating herself from her abusive father. This needed boundary protects the daughter even though that necessary relationship cannot be severed. God has the last say and will avenge her. Read the Word of the Lord in 1 Corinthians 3:16–17:

> Do you not know that you are God's temple and that God's Spirit dwells in you? If anyone destroys God's temple, God will destroy him. For God's temple is holy, and you are that temple.

To all of us who have suffered beyond human understanding: our body is still the holy temple of God. One day God will destroy what has tried to destroy us because God's Spirit abides in us.

Setting Boundaries

Let's look at setting boundaries that are not related to the grievous sins of sexual, physical, and emotional abuse. Conversations that legitimately require boundaries often revolve around politics, religion, or lifestyle choices.

We often set boundaries that we believe are necessary to keep us safe from conflict. It is wise to set boundaries so that we protect ourselves, others, and the necessary relationships in which God has placed us. Necessary relationships could be our parents, children, in-laws, church family, professional colleagues, acquaintances, dear friends, and adversaries.

Proverbs offers many passages that help us recognize godly limits not only on our speech but also to those we address. But what if God determines that these problematic relationships are vital to sanctify our communication, especially if we are stuck doing life together? It is the implementation or the setting of these boundaries that can be problematic. Some boundaries are inappropriately self-protective. We could prioritize comfort over the need to discuss those long-standing issues which prevent us from reconciling our relationships. Setting boundaries establishes limits on the level of pain we are willing to tolerate in conversations. However, boundaries may stifle difficult conversations and give us cover to abandon necessary relationships. In some Christian circles, we cleverly do this in the name of Jesus.

We tend to set up boundaries if our feelings are hurt based on how someone interacts with us. Confrontation can trigger our Two Influential Forces. Our self-talk flies into a frenzy that fuels Speaking CODE. We find ourselves speaking inauthentic words, causing the image bearer to make assumptions. The process causes each of us to construct boundaries where we decide what behavior is acceptable to us. We tell ourselves that it is time to set limits rather than telling ourselves it is time to speak biblical truths. We proclaim that their toxicity requires boundaries. In the turmoil, we forget about the humanity of the image bearer and believe that some type of fence will protect us. What is our alternative? Read the Word of the Lord in Proverbs 27:17:

> Iron sharpens iron,
> and one man sharpens another.

Instead of setting boundaries in or exiting necessary relationships that are not grievous, we need to embrace the conflict that comes with them. As we bump up against one another, we sharpen each other. Part of sharpening is to ask God why this image bearer is even in our life. We will find that as we are sharpened, we connect more deeply to each other and Jesus. Sometimes when we create boundaries, we frustrate the work of God in our lives and keep ourselves from being sharpened. Read the Word of the Lord in Proverbs 27:5–6:

> "Better is open rebuke
> than hidden love.
> Faithful are the wounds of a friend;
> profuse are the kisses of an enemy."

In necessary relationships, we can see individuals as faithful even in the middle of wounding conversations. Rather than establishing boundaries, we embrace the demanding relationship between image bearers. Even an open rebuke that we can see is better than hidden love that we cannot see. Embracing relationships provides an alternative to the self-protection that causes us to set up boundaries.

In what necessary relationship, that has not involved a grievous offense, have you set boundaries to protect yourself from pain?

Give reasons why you think God may have placed that necessary relationship in your life.

List ways you can see that setting boundaries has interfered with God's purpose for your growth and His glory.

Fake Peace Versus Real Peace

Our underlying fears, based on the influence of our ECMs, PPIFSt, PPIFEx, may cause us to choose words that are not exactly the truth but that will advance our agenda and calm our fearfulness toward this person. This will diminish the humanness of both of us. When we fail to recognize God's image in others, our words will never reflect how God values His creatures. We become the primary focus in the relationship. We may cleverly say pleasing words as we manipulate people to do our bidding. But our words will not lead to soul-satisfying conversations. The words we choose will certainly express our agenda, but do our words esteem the image bearer with whom we are speaking? We are called to be peacemakers, not peace-fakers (as described so aptly by Peacemaker Ministries).[12] The last section in this book will provide solutions to resolve such damaging conversations.

Think of a difficult conversation you had. Write out how you sacrificed truth to promote your agenda and please the hearer during a conversation.

What kept you from telling the truth? Write out your answer.

Describe your self-talk that reflected your true agenda.

What CODE did you speak that was not the actual truth?

Evolving Agendas

Our agenda may be to get the person off our back. We may hope to trick the person into changing his mind so that our agenda is implemented. On closer examination, our goal may be to keep us from experiencing the painful effects of our own fear, self-isolation, self-absorption, or self-denial. This pathway or agenda will not lead us to esteem the humanity of our communication partner, mainly because we want to change their thoughts into our thoughts. Sadly, we promote our own image *Imago Homo,* for God's image, *Imago Dei.*

If our hearts prevent us from speaking the truth in love, we are hopelessly locked in conversations that are not soul-satisfying. Speaking CODE will have a strong hold on us because the hearer is not privy to our thinking. Therefore, our conversations will be agenda-driven and not driven by the humanness of the listener. What do we do when our own agenda drives our speech? Remember, God may have us in intersecting holy sanctuaries.

> Describe an ongoing conversation when both you and the listener are committed to your own agendas.

◀ ··· ·— —· · ·— —·— ·· —· — —· —·—· — — — —·· ·

We must ask ourselves what makes us use words that do not esteem the image bearer to whom we are speaking? I believe we only do things that seem best for us, even if we are confused by our own words and actions. See how Paul confronts this dilemma in Romans. Read the Word of the Lord in Romans 7:15–20:

> For I do not understand my own actions. For I do not do what I want, but I do the very thing I hate. Now if I do what I do not want, I agree with the law, that it is good. So now it is no longer I who do it, but sin that dwells within me. For I know that nothing good dwells in me, that is, in my flesh. For I have the desire to do what is right, but not the ability to carry it out. For I do not do the good I want, but the evil I do not want is what I keep on doing. Now if I do what I do not want, it is no longer I who do it, but sin that dwells within me.

Paul's confusion over his actions is like our confusion. The sin that lives in us ruins everything, including our ability to speak redemptively to the human image bearers in front of us. What do we do with this mess?

HIJACKERS, HITCHHIKERS, AND BEING HUMAN

Asking good questions is one way of affirming the value of the person in front of us. Another way to esteem humanness is to resist the urge to hijack the speaker's issues. Instead, we need to hitch a ride, or stay with the person who is speaking, rather than putting forth our own agenda. Here is an example of hijacking an issue:

Tre tells us how his serious medical problems make him feel heartbroken and fearful about his future. He confesses that his faith is shaky, especially when he thinks about his wife and kids. Tre tells us about endless medical bills, fading dreams for his kids' future education, and the awful thought that his wife may have to work in order to keep the family afloat. Tre laments that he feels like a failure because he did not adequately prepare for a life-changing event like this. We are seeing Tre in his holy sanctuary.

After saying we are sorry for his illness and that we, too, had a cancer scare last year, we launch into a litany about how the awful pain in our back keeps us from going to the gym. The pain prevents us from doing squats or lifting weights. We lament that what we do not use, we will lose. We worry about gaining weight and we confess that we have body dysmorphia. Oh, we also add, somewhere amid these words, that God will work out Tre's problems if he just has enough faith.

Congratulations! We just hijacked Tre's suffering. As Dr. Ed Welch says, "Not every day is our birthday!"[13] As a result, we did not esteem Tre's humanity as an image bearer.

Our experience may be true. In fact, we may have lung cancer that is causing our back pain. Truth be told, we have always suffered from body image issues. But these words to Tre are utterly myopic and do not esteem his humanness.

Instead of hijacking Tre's pain, why not *hitch a ride* along with him? In doing so, Tre's holy sanctuary and ours intersect! Let Tre be the driver as we travel along his path of fear and despair. It is an affirmation and a tribute to Tre's humanity to ask him questions about his illness. In our conversation, ask him what this illness tempts him to do as he sinks deeper into hopelessness and anguish. Ask simple questions about his kids and wife. How do their reactions affect him? Ask Tre if he can pray. Assure him that we will pray for him, and then we can pray with Tre on the spot! Simply allowing Tre to talk about his problems—without trying to solve or minimize them, or without attempting to console him with Christian platitudes—is soul-satisfying for him. Let us resist the urge to hijack Tre's story. In doing so, our conversations will fulfill the 1 Thessalonians 5 passage where we demonstrate patience, not repaying evil for evil, and practice doing good.

It is good for Tre's soul if we make a date to speak with him again. Hitch that ride as we stick out our thumb and join him in his soul-baring suffering. Assure Tre that we are in this with him as we press into his story. Listen intently as we hear with our two ears and talk less with our one mouth. Look for body language or expressions as we see with both eyes. Resist the tendency to make someone else's pain an opportunity for us to express our own. In these sacred moments, we have an opportunity to practice one-anothering. Be assured, our experiences will be heard, especially when the person sees how interested we are in his condition. Asking good questions forms the basis of soul-satisfying conversations.

Write about your own experience when you did not esteem the humanness of your friend's story by hijacking his pain and talking about your pain instead. Include reasons why you did this.

Write out how your situation has been hijacked by another person. Include how the hijacking made you feel.

List some ways you can hitch a ride or stay with your friend as he tells you his story. If you have done this, include the results of your effort.

Remember, we regularly experience the desire to hijack a conversation as we participate in discussions where people pour out their hearts to us. Engaging in these types of dialogues can be very sacrificial. Listening sacrificially is time consuming and tests our patience. We want to share our own hurt so that we can be comforted. Who knows? Our experiences might be helpful. What we hear from them sometimes corresponds to our own sufferings. This can be an opportunity to use our PPIFSt/PPIFEx to link us to the sufferer because we share humanness as image bearers. However, resist the initial temptation to be a *conversation hijacker*. Let's hitch that ride and see where God takes us.

SCENE-STEALING THIEVES

Having a conversation stolen from us looks remarkably like having one hijacked from us. We finally got the courage to begin a very delicate conversation with a person who has harmed us. We start by saying how we specifically feel because of his behavior toward us. We express how much we are saddened by his words and actions. We share the biblical mandate with him regarding how we approach God's altar with our gifts if we know someone holds something against us.

As we anticipate having a confrontational conversation, we may break out into a cold sweat, feel the anxiety in our gut, or swallow hard to clear the lump out of our throat. We may stammer. Sometimes we start by apologizing. Maybe we vomit out our emotions, spewing words all over ourselves and the person listening to us.

Nevertheless, after we allow ourselves to be vulnerable by pouring out our heart, the person says something like this: "Are you crazy? You do the same thing to me! I cannot believe you just accused me of doing what you do all the time!" Or he says, "I have nothing against you, so this is really your problem. Go in peace and be happy. I have nothing more to say." This is an example of having the conversation stolen by a *scene-stealing thief.*

To some extent, we are all scene-stealing thieves. Here is a helpful hint to those of us who have a very strong urge to become a scene-stealing thief or a hijacker: Just stop it! The alternative to stealing the scene is to, once again, hitch a ride with the person who tells us about his concerns about our behavior. Even though we may be angry or in total disbelief, we stay with the person who is talking. We acknowledge his feelings in the moment. We ask good questions for clarification. We do not use this as a springboard to launch a counterattack on him or ignore his concerns altogether. That would be evil and will not put us on a path to do good or speak redemptively. Remember, not every day is our birthday. Focus on the image bearer before focusing on ourselves.

To avoid being a hijacker or a scene-stealing thief, we must develop good listening skills. If God blesses you with a seven-year-old grandson who believes he must tell you every single detail about his home on Jupiter, or that he really is a Transformer, God particularly wants you to develop into a patient and wise listener. This means that the person in your life who repeatedly tells you how depressed he is also represents a blessed opportunity to increase your ability to be a good and patient listener. This is an occasion for us to imitate the God we adore as we esteem the human He has created. One last thing we need to keep in mind: keen listening involves mercy and could have radical implications because through it we get the opportunity to become unselfish.

BECOMING A KEEN LISTENER

Listening well is part of redemptive and soul-satisfying communication. Keen listening helps us to focus on the other person's humanity as we celebrate him as an image bearer. However, listening for understanding is challenging, especially when we have our own problems to solve. Here are some examples of why it is difficult for us to be a keen listener. Read through these statements and check what applies to you.

- I hear what that person is saying, so I begin to formulate my response. But the person keeps prattling on and on. Before long I am lost, because he just keeps on talking and I cannot get a word in edgewise. Sometimes, I must interrupt him, or I will get lost in all the details. Interrupting the person does not go over well at all.

☐ ALWAYS ☐ SOMETIMES ☐ NEVER
☐ *With whom?* ______________________

- I know exactly where this conversation is going because I have heard it all before. It always goes there, and it is so frustrating to hear the same thing over and over again. I find myself mentally checking out.

☐ ALWAYS ☐ SOMETIMES ☐ NEVER
☐ *With whom?* ______________________

- I feel that it is just not safe to say anything at all because I always get hurt. Somehow, he turns a problem I have with him around and accuses me of being the problem! Nothing changes with him. What is going on?

☐ ALWAYS ☐ SOMETIMES ☐ NEVER
☐ *With whom?* ______________________

- Somehow, I keep hearing that critical voice from my past nearly every time he opens his mouth. I wish he did not sound so much like what I heard in my past.

☐ ALWAYS ☐ SOMETIMES ☐ NEVER
☐ *With whom?* ______________________

- I am way too busy with my own problems to concentrate on what this person is saying. I am sure this is difficult for him, but I am overwhelmed.

☐ ALWAYS ☐ SOMETIMES ☐ NEVER
☐ *With whom?* ______________________

- Oh, my goodness! Is he for real? Doesn't this person realize how good he has it? He needs to hear about some real people or third world problems.

☐ ALWAYS ☐ SOMETIMES ☐ NEVER
☐ *With whom?* ______________________

Experiences like the above, plus others we have encountered, hinder us from being good listeners. Also notice the process that goes on inside our heads before we speak. Our PPIFSt and PPIFEx are awakened. We participate in self-talk as we process what we hear. Self-talk leads to Speaking CODE. Speaking CODE only allows a snippet of what we think to come out of our mouths. Speaking CODE leads to poor people-talk, which confuses the listener. Our ECMs resurface as our communication table is set once again. Read the Word of the Lord from James 1:19:

> Know this my beloved brothers: let every person be quick to hear, slow to speak, and slow to anger.

> List ways in which this verse can help you become a keen listener instead of becoming a *conversation hijacker* or a *scene-stealing thief.*

HUMANNESS AND RADICAL MERCY

The Bible gives examples of how radical mercy trumps truth, as seen in the account of the Hebrew midwives, Shiphrah and Puah. Notice that in these conversations, the women were not truthful to the authorities. Shiphrah and Puah exercised radical mercy that saved lives and prevailed over evil.

In Exodus 1, Pharaoh told the Hebrew midwives to kill all the male Hebrew babies. But Shiphrah and Puah disobeyed Pharaoh and had mercy on those sweet baby boys. When Pharaoh confronted the midwives, Shiphrah and Puah did not tell Pharaoh the truth. They concocted a story about the vigorousness of the Hebrew moms. God dealt well with the midwives for their act of mercy and gave them families of their own. Read the Word of the Lord in Exodus 1:15–21:

> Then the king of Egypt said to the Hebrew midwives, one of whom was named Shiphrah and the other Puah, "When you serve as midwife to the Hebrew women and see them on the birthstool, if it is a son, you shall kill him, but if it is a daughter, she shall live." But the midwives feared God and did not do as the king of Egypt commanded them, but let the male children live. So the king of Egypt called the midwives and said to them, "Why have you done this, and let the male children live?" The midwives said to Pharaoh, "Because the Hebrew women are not like the Egyptian women, for they are vigorous and give birth before the midwife comes to them." So God dealt well with the midwives. And the people multiplied and grew very strong. And because the midwives feared God, he gave them families.

God rewarded Shiphrah and Puah because they showed radical mercy in saving the lives of these little image bearing boys. In our redemptive conversations we may be called upon to emulate these midwives by showing a radical type of mercy. Perhaps we will not be called upon to lie, but our act of mercy will be very sacrificial.

THE FIRST AND GREATEST COMMANDMENT

Jesus tells us what makes it possible for us to love humanity. Matthew 22 describes an ongoing conversation between Jesus and Israel's powerful ruling groups. Jesus demonstrates, in real conversations, how obeying the Law allows us to love while establishing the intrinsic value of every living soul. Read the Word of the Lord from Matthew 22:34–40:

> But when the Pharisees heard that he had silenced the Sadducees, they gathered together. And one of them, a lawyer, asked him a question to test him. "Teacher, which is the great commandment in the Law?" And he said to him, "You shall love the Lord your God with all your heart and with all your soul and with all your mind. This is the great and first commandment. And a second is like it: You shall love your neighbor as yourself. On these two commandments depend all the Law and the Prophets."

Redemptive communication begins with loving our Creator God, who gives meaning and life to all humanity. We are called to love God with all our heart, soul, and mind. Notice that loving God with all our being is the first and greatest commandment. God alone gives us dignity in our humanity which is why our words to each other mean more than just the air they push into the atmosphere. We cannot speak redemptively without first loving the Lord our God with every inch of our sinful, but redeemed, being. Do we see the majesty of this commandment, or is it just another familiar verse that has lost its impact?

Write out how loving God well allows you to speak redemptively to the image bearers in your life

THE SECOND (LIKE THE FIRST)

Read the Word of the Lord from Matthew 22:39–40:

And a second is like it: You shall love your neighbor as yourself. On these two commandments depend all the Law and the Prophets.

I do not think I have ever heard a pastor exegete this passage fully or adequately, especially in how we can love our own selves. Let's look at the second commandment. There is a link between esteeming our own humanity properly and esteeming the humanity of others. If we do not love God, how will we ever love others or ourselves? Since all other laws depend on these two commandments, all the other scriptural passages that inform redemptive speech will also rest on them. We cannot have redemptive speech without living out the reality these two commandments express.

To truly esteem each other as image bearers, we must give ourselves over to loving ourselves and others. However, neither love is possible without the first commandment, which tells us to love God completely. The second commandment is fully dependent on the first. How does loving God, self, and others shape and inform redemptive conversations? I cannot possibly speak redemptively to you without loving God first and speaking redemptively to myself as well. I will make you a prisoner of my expectations unless I free myself first of my own slavish, unrealistic, self-imposed standards, or selfish ambitions.

When my self-talk is critical of my own humanity it makes it hard to see myself as an image bearer. My people-talk will reflect my confused understanding of myself. When I love myself selfishly, I will also love you selfishly. We will miss each other in our conversations.

Love of self begins and ends with God's *initiating* love, which revives our dead hearts. Godly self-love acknowledges that we deserved God's righteous anger and Jesus took our place and bore that anger. His sacrifice shows us divine love and affirms our worth. Jesus's act inspires gratitude in us and provides an example of how we can love well. This is where love of God, love of others, and love of self begins. Only through God's initiating love can we ever love Him, ourselves, and others. This is how we esteem the humanness of mankind.

Do you love yourself? If so, how?

Write out how you personally see the link between loving God first so that you can love yourself and others well.

Write out how your lack of love for others hinders your love for God or for yourself.

What does "love yourself as you love others" mean to you?

Write out how you make others the prisoner of your own expectations if you cannot love God or love yourself.

If your self-talk is condemning, write out how you find clever ways to condemn the person with whom you are speaking.

THE COMMAND TO LOVE

We may actively practice spiritual blindness when it comes to loving our brothers. But God deals with the eyes of our hearts. Read the Word of the Lord from 1 John 4:19–21:

> We love because he first loved us. If anyone says, "I love God," and hates his brother, he is a liar; for he who does not love his brother whom he has seen cannot love God whom he has not seen. And this commandment we have from him: whoever loves God must also love his brother.

God, whom we cannot see, initiates love toward us, making it possible to love our brother whom we can see. Additionally, if we say we love God and hate our brother, we are liars and God's love is not in us.

Loving God requires that we love others. How does this affect soul-satisfying communication? The way we talk to God is the way we talk to others and ourselves. There is no room for speaking one way to God and another way to our brother. Our words reflect both our professed love for God and our obligated love for others. Only then can we esteem the humanness of our brother and speak redemptively to him.

LOVE IN PRACTICE

Paul gives us instructions on how we are to esteem the image of others through our treatment of them. Read the Word of the Lord in Romans 12:9–21:

> Let love be genuine. Abhor what is evil; hold fast to what is good. Love one another with brotherly affection. Outdo one another in showing honor. Do not be slothful in zeal, be fervent in spirit, serve the Lord. Rejoice in hope, be patient in tribulation, be constant in prayer. Contribute to the needs of the saints and seek to show hospitality.
>
> Bless those who persecute you; bless and do not curse them. Rejoice with those who rejoice, weep with those who weep. Live in harmony with one another. Do not be haughty, but associate with the lowly. Never be wise in your own sight. Repay no one evil for evil, but give thought to do what is honorable in the sight of all. If possible, so far as it depends on you, live peaceably with all. Beloved, never avenge yourselves, but leave it to the wrath of God, for it is written, "Vengeance is mine, I will repay, says the Lord." To the contrary, "if your enemy is hungry, feed him; if he is thirsty, give him something to drink; for by so doing you will heap burning coals on his head." Do not be overcome by evil, but overcome evil with good.

This passage shows us how we put love into practice. It is interesting that everything Paul exhorts us to do in this passage, Jesus did during His earthly ministry. We love genuinely and with brotherly affection. We care for others with words of comfort, honor them with words of appreciation, and provide for them with words of encouragement. We suffer patiently while eschewing vengeance. We empathize with others in our unspoken words and gestures. Even though we hate evil, we care for our enemies by showing them that good triumphs over it. Go back and underline all the sentences or phrases that shape how we talk to one another.

If redemptive communication is based on esteeming the humanity of our conversational partner, we must believe that their humanity is given and imprinted on them by God. Our desire to know and love God is our lifelong quest. If we do not know God well, we cannot fully esteem the humanity of others or ourselves. Our external and internal conversations are a reflection of our knowledge of God.

WE DO NOT KNOW GOD WELL

Take a moment and write out your confession, based on how you do not know the God you love as well as you should. Here are some helpful questions to get you thinking more clearly about your confession. This exercise is to help you see that the reason why your conversations are soul-crushing is that you may not know God as well as you should, therefore preventing you from seeing the value of the people in your life.

- What scriptural truths about God do you find hard to believe?
- What prevents you from loving God in heart, soul, and mind?
- What lies do you inwardly whisper that deny God's truths, and why do you hold on to them?
- Who told you that you are not God's beloved?
- How do your misguided beliefs about God prevent you from seeing His deep love for you even in horrific conversations?

Use the questions above to guide you in your written confession.

In summary, we demonstrate, with every breath we take, that we are humans who bear the image of God. As such, we do not need to Speak CODE to one another; let us instead speak words that demonstrate patience, utter no evil, and reflect goodness. When we speak, we can allow our words to honor each other's humanity, rather than trying to change each other's minds (unless, of course, we are speaking to someone who may be a danger to self or others). Sometimes we honor God and others by presenting necessary admonitions or rebukes. Rather than hijacking or stealing another's scene we can hitch a ride as we engage with others in their holy sanctuaries. Instead of making humans into what we imagine them to be, we reverence them as being made in the image of God.

PALM TO PALM

Dr. Paul Tripp—pastor, author, and my former CCEF instructor—calls us "Meaning Makers."[14] We see this vividly as we struggle to make sense of the words we hear and say. How we choose to make sense of our life is specific to our situation. We are free to grant grace (or not), to understand (or not), to retaliate (or not), and to shut down (or not) when we are in difficult conversations.

Just as the Woman had to make meaning out of the serpent's question, we too, must interpret the world around us. The words coming at us eventually hit our heart. They call us to action, and lead to acceptance, rage, denial, or silence. Our responses are based on our Two Influential Forces, self-talk, and Speaking CODE.

When you must make meaning out of your conversations (past or present), how do your Two Influential Forces inform your thought processes?

... .— —. . .— —.— .. —. — —.   —.—. — — — —.. . ▶

Describe how you communicate with others based on your thought processes.

... .— —. . .— —.— .. —. — —.   —.—. — — — —.. . ▶

Being made in God's image should enable us to respond to other image bearers in a way that reflects our respect for humanity and the Creator. However, our Two Influential Forces and Speaking CODE often compete for priority in how we respond to others. There is a battle between two possible ways we can be meaning makers. If we communicate with others based on a self-absorbed view of our past, we will tend to Speak CODE leading to frustrating conversations. If we understand that the Spirit of God directs our past, our communication has a far better chance of being soul-satisfying.

It is God who puts us on our path of righteousness which leads us to Him. Remember my view that life is theological and always personal. Many times, the way we talk to one another reflects the way we talk to God. When we find ourselves in a life-altering crisis that makes it hard for us to communicate with the people involved, we may find divine communication difficult as well. This difficulty can play itself out in our worship, our prayers, our personal Bible study, or our meditation.

We know this. We lament that while we love God, it is hard to experience His presence, especially when we are in contentious relationships or feel the weight of life. God knows this and He is still for us.

List feeling words you experience when you evaluate how you communicate with God as you press on through difficult conversations or life situations.

A word of caution: in our holy sanctuaries we may need to express internally or externally how utterly disappointed and lost we are in our lives. We may feel so unworthy that our shame prevents us from drawing near to God. We cannot talk to God, even though we know that talking to Him is exactly what we should be doing! In the depth of our despair, we assume that God feels about us the same way we feel about ourselves, as if the God of the Bible suddenly disavowed His own nature. We allow our feelings to remake God in our image. But God is not like us. We cannot impose our feelings on God. So, if our lives are unraveling, we miss who God is if we say He cannot love us in our unworthiness.

In what ways does your self-talk cause you to impose your feelings on God?

INTERCESSORY PRAYER

It helps to understand how we struggle to make meaning in our lives and especially in our conversations. But we need to go further to consider how we handle situations where we are alienated in necessary relationships. Imagine that you and I are talking as we sipped hot tea together. We lament over the sadness you experience because it is almost impossible to talk to a necessary person in your life. This person could be your spouse, your parent, your adult child, your best friend, your sibling, your neighbor, your coworker, or even your opponent.

We would talk through all the issues you encounter and how those issues produce soul-crushing rather than soul-satisfying conversations. Sadly, this person has rebuffed your efforts to work out your differences as the Bible requires. We would talk about what these conversations have tempted you to do. Are you tempted to gossip? Take revenge? Become bitter? Appease him?

After getting to know you and your situation as well as I am able, I agree that you and this person are at an impasse. When you are in each other's presence, you may explode in rage, exchange pleasantries, engage in conversations that feel disingenuous, or you may completely ignore each other. Nothing has worked, which makes you feel awkward when you share the same space. You confess that even if you never run into this person again, you are still heartbroken because this person has shut down any path toward biblical reconciliation. My next questions to you would be about how you pray for this person. Read what Corrie ten Boom says about intercessory prayer in *The Hiding Place:*

> I prayed to dispel my fear, until suddenly, and I do not know how the idea came to me, I began to pray for others. I prayed for everyone who came into my thoughts—people with whom I had traveled, those who had been in prison with me, my school friends of years ago. I do not know how long I continued my prayer, but this I do know—my fear was gone! Interceding for others had released me![15]

Intercessory prayers have extravagant repercussions.

If your communication is reduced to exchanging pleasantries or disingenuous conversations, how can you pray for that person? List some specifics.

If all communication comes to a screeching halt and you hear only silence, tell me what your prayers for him sound like?

As you affirm his humanity, what actions could you take to acknowledge that even though you are in conflict or estranged, this difficult person remains an image bearer?

Why are these questions important? They draw our attention to the fact that Scripture has much to say about helping us in our weakness. For example, if we are alienated from our spouse, relatives, friends, or enemies, that emotional or physical distance weakens the bonds of our common humanity. God provided a way back to each other because He forgave our debts, so we can forgive our debtors. Even if we are unable to forgive, or decide not to communicate with that person, we are still able to pray for him as we esteem him in his humanity as an image bearer.

When all other means of communication fail, the ultimate point is this: our prayers for this person are a powerful form of communication. And sometimes our prayers for him are the only communication we may have with him at this time. If we cannot utter a prayer for this person, we may need to enlist someone who will pray for him on our behalf.

List how the last resort of prayer can be more soul-satisfying than your current situation.

Please do not misunderstand me when I say prayer may be our only link to this difficult person. Often, communication shutdown is necessary because God needs to teach us something specific. This may be our holy sanctuary where God must work. This person's holy sanctuary may be intersecting ours, which is why we are in this difficult situation in the first place. God may be telling us to practice forbearance. Perhaps the hour for communicating in real time has not yet come or has long since ceased to exist. God is always taking us somewhere in our relationships, and part of our job is to identify where He is leading. Difficult people and difficult conversations are no exception.

FORBEARANCE

Redemptive communication may lead us to forbear with a difficult person and detach from him carefully. Forbearance means that, for whatever reason, neither party initiates communication except when necessary. For victims of abuse, always remember that God will severely punish those who harmed you. In the meantime, you may need a surrogate (someone other than you who cannot be influenced by the abuser) to represent your interests in the bullets below. In most other relationships, forbearance means we remain in a position to talk if spoken to. That means we respond if someone addresses us because that person is an image bearer.

- ANSWER, IF ASKED. That means we use truthful and loving words to provide the information requested. Remember, mercy trumps truth.
- FORGIVE, IF GRIEVED. That means forgiving the person is for everyone's benefit.
- SET AN AGENDA OF CLEARLY UNDERSTOOD MOTIVES. That means we must communicate our choice to forbear as we limit our interactions with each other.
- SPEAK IN ORDER TO EDIFY. That means all our forms of communication must be righteous no matter how satisfying unedifying speech feels in the moment.
- TAKE NO REVENGE. That means every form of communication with any other person should do no harm, intentionally or unintentionally, as much as it is within our power.
- NOT BE OVERCOME BY EVIL BUT RATHER OVERCOME EVIL WITH GOOD. That means whatever opposition comes our way, whether in thought, word, or deed, we do not retaliate. In fact, we actively work for that person's good, for by so doing we will "heap burning coals on his head" (Proverbs 25:22).
- BE AT PEACE IF POSSIBLE. That means we need to examine all pathways available to us so we can seek peace.
- EMBRACE BIBLICAL WAYS TO REMAIN PRESENT IN THE RELATIONSHIP. That means we study and implement what Scripture teaches to maintain appropriate connections with others.
- PRAY WITHOUT CEASING, ESPECIALLY UNDER PERSECUTION. That means we recognize that we are sufferers in constant need of prayer. What we say to God influences what we say to others and ourselves.
- HUMBLY LOOK FOR WAYS TO OWN OUR PART IN THE BREAKDOWN OF THE RELATIONSHIP. That means we must be willing to be wrong and own the consequences that may bring.

Write out which of these forbearing positions most helps you as you communicate with someone when God seems to have halted nearly all verbal communication.

One of my favorite biblical examples of forbearance is seen in the father's actions in the parable of the Prodigal Son. The father did not run after his son or send anyone to fetch him home. We are sad when we read how foolishly the son behaved in that far away country. We feel our anticipation rise when the son finally comes to his senses, recognizing the character of his father. Read the Word of the Lord in Luke 15:20:

> And he arose and came to his father. But while he was still a long way off, his father saw him and felt compassion, and ran and embraced him and kissed him.

This is forbearance. We do not run after people, but neither do we turn our backs on those from whom we are estranged.

Using this biblical example, write out how you can forebear in a current relationship that is badly broken.

◀ ... .— —. . .— —.— .. —. — —.   —.—. — — — —.. .

PALM TO PALM: OUR HANDS TELL THE STORY

Let me introduce you to a series of hand exercises, I call Palm to Palm, that a wise counselor once taught me. These Palm to Palm gestures help us understand the concept of forbearance. In this exercise, please imagine that your hands represent you and another person.

Detaching and Moving Away

Put your two hands in front of you with your palms facing each other, about six inches apart. Take your left-hand palm and turn it 180 degrees so the back of your left hand now faces your right palm. Now without moving your right hand, move your left hand away from your right palm.

This simple exercise demonstrates what it looks like when someone detaches and turns away from our relationship. As the left hand detaches and moves away, the relationship suffers, especially our conversations. There may be many reasons why the left hand turned and moved away from the right hand. Some reasons may have been trivial, and some may have come after many soul-crushing discussions. Nevertheless, detachment has happened: the person has turned and walked away, the relationship is severed, and communication is strained or non-existent.

Notice the right hand. It does not move. The right hand remains in place as it seeks out an advantageous posture to wait for the left hand to return to the relationship. The right hand's position resembles the father's behavior in the parable of the Prodigal Son. This represents forbearance.

Think about the people with whom you are in relationship. List some reasons why they detached and walked away from you.

◀ ... .— —. . .— —.— .. —. — —.   —.—. — — — —.. .

How has turning away affected the communication between the two of you?

You may be the one who detached and left the relationship. List the reasons why you decided to turn and walk away.

Detaching with Care

The previous exercise described what it looks like when someone disengages and walks away from our relationship. Let's use our palms to demonstrate what it looks like when we have no choice but to detach with care from someone. Again, put both your hands up with palms facing each other. Now move your right hand away from your left hand, but this time do not turn your right-hand palm away from your left-hand palm.

In this case, the right hand represents us, detaching with care. We do not move toward or go after the other person. We detach with care by facing the other person as we back up for a few necessary steps and catch our breath. Backing up shows our continued commitment to the relationship, by not turning and walking away from the person with whom we are in conflict. To detach with care may give us room to wisely process the other person's words and behaviors. We do not walk away or go after the person because God may want us to be ready if His desire is for us to reconcile. We are in a position to practice forbearance.

We face the person, Palm to Palm, as we continue to pray for him and seek to actively bless him. We face him because he is made in God's image. These actions esteem the person with whom communication is all but over.

Write out how detaching with care will help your relationships.

As we detach with care, we hold back our righteous anger. Detaching with care allows us to be ready if called upon to restore that person gently by pointing out his error in order to redeem the relationship. We may be called to admonish difficult people as we speak true words in love. Finally, as we detach with care, we get an opportunity to search our own hearts to see if there are any hurtful ways in us.

As you detach with care, list ways where you can search yourself to see if you have contributed to the demise of the relationship.

··· ·– –· · ·– –·– ·· –· – –·   –·–· – – – –·· ·

List the details of that hard conversation with a particular person where you had to withhold your righteous anger, gently point out error, or speak words of admonition to him.

··· ·– –· · ·– –·– ·· –· – –·   –·–· – – – –·· ·

Detaching Carelessly

Put both hands up with palms facing each other. Make your left-hand thumb and four fingertips open and close, so as to demonstrate a biting or chopping effect. Keep your right-hand palm facing toward your left hand. Continue to open and close your left thumb and fingers as your left hand moves back and forth toward your right-hand palm.

Sometimes, we detach carelessly from another person. We may need to detach but do not go about it wisely. Our conversations may be harsh, defensive, and self-serving. We may participate in backbiting or self-righteous gossip (which we may rationalize by saying we were merely sharing prayer concerns). We move in and out of the relationship as we use careless words designed to hurt the other person. Our growing anger feeds our carelessness, and allows a root of bitterness to grow within us which could possibly defile everyone. The erratic hand movements in our demonstration show our confusion. We become fearful of that person, which makes us fake a relationship. Sometimes when our hearts are full of fear or pain, our conversations may be filled with flattery or deceit.

If you have detached carelessly from someone in your life, describe the words and behavior you used. How did your actions disregard the other person's humanity?

··· ·– –· · ·– –·– ·· –· – –·   –·–· – – – –·· ·

Give examples of how someone has carelessly detached from you based on the words he said to you.

··· ·– –· · ·– –·– ·· –· – –·   –·–· – – – –·· ·

Codependent Detaching

Put your hands up with your palms facing each other as before. Turn the left-hand palm away from the right-hand palm and move the left hand away from the right-hand palm. Now have the right hand move toward the turned away left hand.

When we detach codependently, we follow the example of the right hand and pursue the one who spurned our love, demeaned us with his words, rejected our advances, and detached from the relationship. We codependents pursue the one who left the relationship, especially if we believe the person turned his back on us. Still, we will pursue toxic or harmful relationships because we need something from that person to live life.

As codependents, we rarely act in our own best interests and would rather accept other people's bad words/behaviors directed at us than think we are unacceptable or unlovable. We run after careless people who deliberately turn their backs on us, because we desperately crave any type of words or actions that will make us feel worthy, loved, or affirmed.

The guilt and shame of not being good enough overwhelms us, forcing us to remain in soul-crushing conversations or accept bad behavior. We wrongly believe that had it not been for our relational mistakes or poor choice of words in conversations, we would not have been so badly treated. We tend to be the rescuers in relationships so that we do not have to face life alone.

As codependents, we attract poor relationship partners, believing that this time we will find just the right words to fix what is broken. If left unchecked, we will move from one relationship to another, seeking acceptance even if it is disastrous. We seem to do nearly all the relational work. We repeat the same behaviors that have characterized all our previous relationships, resulting in jumping from one chaotic relationship into another.

If you have detached codependently from someone in your life, list ways in which you chased after the other person even though the relationship was toxic and chaotic.

Freely Attaching

The last little exercise is simple. Put both hands in front of you. Have both palms facing each other. Imagine energy and tension flowing back and forth between the two palms. Think of this energy as authentic conversations between two people in a relationship. These people are living their belief in God out loud. Their conversation is robust, honest, and soul-satisfying, though often very difficult. This energy is rooted in the belief that both people know they are equals as image-bearing humans. Below are two Scriptures that flesh out Palm to Palm communication. Read the Word of the Lord from Proverbs 27:9:

> Oil and perfume make the heart glad,
> and the sweetness of a friend comes from his earnest counsel.

Read the Word of the Lord in 2 Corinthians 13:11:

> Finally, brothers rejoice. Aim for restoration, comfort one another, agree with one another, live in peace; and the God of love and peace will be with you.

I desire this kind of relationship with my adult granddaughters, Lyric, Lexei, and Isabella. We have experienced enough hurt and sadness to make us turn away from each other. But God has grown us enough to face each other Palm to Palm as we experience the energy that goes along with the tension of our conversations. I cry over this work in progress and thank God for the journey we are on. My love ever deepens with each passionate disagreement we express or joyful conversation we share. I rest easier in the love we have for each other, regardless of the disappointments and mistrust. Besides, these beautiful granddaughters are mine. They are loved because they breathe.

The Palm to Palm illustrations are simplistic, but nevertheless, they allow you to visualize how you communicate. Which illustration(s) best describes you?

◀ ··· ·——· · ·— —·— ·· —· ——· —·—· ——— —·· ·

How does your understanding of these illustrations help you change the way you communicate?

◀ ··· ·——· · ·— —·— ·· —· ——· —·—· ——— —·· ·

Which of the Palm to Palm relationships do you most often use in your conversations? Write out what your dialogue looks like.

◀ ··· ·——· · ·— —·— ·· —· ——· —·—· ——— —·· ·

These visual illustrations help us understand what redemptive communication looks like, as we esteem the image bearer we face. If redemptive conversations are not possible, we still have the highest form of communication available to us. We pray and we pray earnestly.

Write out an earnest prayer of forbearance for someone from whom you have detached with care because nearly all conversations have ceased.

THOU ART THE MAN

We may have the opportunity to live out the proverbs above, or we may be called to live out the role of the prophet as Nathan did with King David. In 2 Samuel 12:1–15, we read how Nathan told David a story about two men: one wealthy and one poor. The conversation between the two of them was rich in symbolism. The poor man had a precious lamb that the wealthy man coveted and ultimately killed for his own selfish pleasure. After David declared that the wealthy man acted wickedly, Nathan told David, "You are the man!" (v. 7), because David took Bathsheba for himself even though she was the wife of Uriah the Hittite.

Write about a time where you were called to use admonishments, rebukes, or confrontation in a conversation. What was your approach?

Regardless of the types of conversations into which we enter, we must remain present by standing Palm to Palm. We must resist the desire to detach, turn our backs on one another, or codependently run after those people who have not acted in our best interest. We certainly must refrain from backbiting and gossip. If not, we are doomed to soul-crushing words rather than soul-satisfying and redemptive conversations. Standing Palm to Palm enables us to put to death the power behind our Two Influential Forces, self-talk, and Speaking CODE.

It is important to remember that the game changes when we are called to forebear with abusive people. In this context, detaching with care may mean we stop all forms of communication. This form of detaching with care is most often seen when sexual or physical abuse has taken place. Detaching with care may mean we, or someone else, inform the abuser that communication cannot happen until the perpetrator admits the sin, repents, and is restored to the satisfaction of the victim. Throughout this process we are still called to pray as we forgive our abuser to God. The ultimate goal is for the victim to receive justice and the perpetrator to truly repent, leading to whatever forgiveness and reconciliation looks like in that situation.

In a formerly abusive relationship, we may agree to speak only when it is absolutely necessary or not at all. Everyone involved in such an agreement must understand the parameters of the decision, because all humans are made in God's image. Thanks be to God for His blessings as we remain present, even in the most difficult relationships that require conversations.

If you have been abused, write out how you can detach with care using the parameters above. Who would act as your ambassador to tell the abuser the parameters of future contact?

As we end this section, let us be grateful that God made us meaning makers. Prayer may be the only way we can find peace in our difficult conversations. The visual illustrations of the Palm to Palm exercises help us see forbearance and how to detach with care. Let us resolve to stand Palm to Palm as we enter soul-satisfying conversations.

As we end Section Two, let us be encouraged as we grapple with the complexities of communications as seen in our PCOs, our Two Influential Forces, self-talk, and Speaking CODE. We are made in God's image which is why we are known in the specificity of God's goodness to us. It is theological and it is personal.

SECTION THREE

SOUL-SATISFYING
COMMUNICATION

MOVING AWAY:
ASSUMPTIONS

MOVING AWAY:
REFUSING TO FORGIVE

MOVING AWAY:
NOT SEPARATING PAST
FROM PRESENT

MOVING AWAY:
IDENTITY IN ANYTHING
EXCEPT CHRIST

MOVING AWAY:
A THEOLOGY OF SUFFERING

IS THERE HOPE?

THE GOSPEL OF THE CROSS

SOUL-SATISFYING COMMUNICATION

What would life be like if we were truly heard and understood? How would we evaluate our lives differently if our Earliest Childhood Memories provided helpful information about how we take in the world around us, rather than sabotaging our conversations? What would it be like if our Two Influential Forces no longer defined us, did not cause us to Speak CODE, and did not hijack our conversations? Our conversations would be more deeply satisfying and redemptive. Why is this true?

If we believed the powerful forces in our lives that lead us to Speak CODE were informative but not determinative, and were thus unable to predict our future, we might be more trusting of each other. It is crucial to understand that our Two Influential Forces are still just statements, experiences, and memories. They hold a powerful grip on us and leave indelible marks because of their long history with us. Our Two Influential Forces, self-talk, and Speaking CODE do not determine our present or forecast our future. That means our conversations do not have to be fueled by the memories of the horrors done to us or the wicked words shouted at us so long ago.

THE REDEEMING POWER OF GOD

While our Two Influential Forces, self-talk, and CODE Speaking can speak louder than our present conversations, they are no match for the redeeming power of God in our lives. Nothing can stand before God's power. As we have noted, God has designed our specific path of righteousness using these very things to bring us to Himself.

But along this path do we question God's specific purpose for our pain? Does our questioning lead us to theorize that this pain catches God by surprise? If we believe that God is surprised in any situation, then we believe in a superhero and not in Almighty God. A superhero god is a god created out of our imagination who seemingly bows to our demands, until we ultimately bow to our imaginary god's unrelenting control over us.

In contrast, the powerful forces we have been discussing crumble at the voice of the Great I am. Even our controlling self-talk, that leads us to Speak CODE, is no match for our matchless Savior, the only true Lover of our souls.

If we believed that the powerful forces in our lives were rendered powerless before the living God, our conversations would reflect God's power and not the power imposed by the statements we heard or the experiences we endured. Our conversations would reflect His glory over our own past. We are often fearful of being truly known, but we would hide less if we lived out our trust in the Living God.

Often, the confusion surrounding our ECMs or the guilt/shame from our PPIFSt and PPIFEx force us to hide from God, ourselves, and others. This hiding can prevent us from having authentic conversations. If we understood the isolating effects these powerful forces have on us, we would begin to resent the authority these influences exercise over us. We can be confident that God specifically designs our path of righteousness that leads us to Him. In our hearts we may not want the pain and struggle required for this path; nevertheless, there is hope in our final destination. That means our entire past has meaning and purpose. That meaning and purpose culminates in God's glory, both in this life and the next.

SPEAKING FEARLESSLY

Believing that God has given meaning to those powerful forces will give us the ability to speak fearlessly rather than fearfully in our difficult conversations. Speaking fearlessly means we can be appropriately vulnerable and wise as we trust others in the middle of soul-crushing conversations. Speaking fearlessly allows us to be unfettered from the echoes of those past conversations and the experiences that did us great harm. We can speak fearlessly because the person with whom we are conversing is not that same terrifying individual who hurt us so long ago. The meaning we assign to the words we say and hear will be understood in that moment rather than shrouded in the emotions we may have felt in our past conversations. This gives us the opportunity to enjoy the gift of dialogue.

Therefore, if we understood our ECMs, PPIFSt, and PPIFEx in light of God's path of righteousness for us, we would love God, ourselves, and others differently than has been our pattern. This kind of love means we have the ability to speak words, in the middle of our soul-crushing conversations, that can honor God's purpose, the human in front of us, and the emotions we experience from our past.

This allows us to fulfill the two great commandments, loving God with all our heart, all our soul, all our strength, and all our mind, while we love our neighbors as we love ourselves. Finding meaning and purpose in our past will allow us to break the strong bonds that keep us from moving toward others, particularly in our conversations.

Formerly, we spoke defensive words based on our familiar, leaving little room for soul-satisfying conversations to flourish. Our PPIFSt and PPIFEx spoke more loudly than the words said to us in the here and now. Presently, we are more able to speak fearlessly to others in love and honesty.

COMMUNICATION SABOTEURS

I have developed a list of five components that I believe sabotage communication. These five components contribute to the death of our relationships and turn soul-satisfying exchanges into soul-crushing speech:

- We make assumptions rather than asking good questions.
- We do not practice forgiveness.
- We do not separate our past from our present.
- We find our identity in anything except Christ alone.
- We fail to find meaning and purpose in our suffering.

Understanding these components will provide a pathway toward soul-satisfying conversations. The first three components that kill our relationships move us away from others. Moving away from people sabotages soul-satisfying conversations. The fourth component moves us not only away from ourselves but also from Jesus. Finally, the fifth component speaks to the hopelessness we experience if we do not find meaning and purpose in our suffering.

MOVING AWAY: ASSUMPTIONS

Moving away is the process of denying the truth of God's Word as it impacts our conversations. One way we move away from ourselves and others is by making assumptions. Assumptions act like assassins in that they kill relationships. Any time we assume we know what the other person is thinking, or we assume we understand what they mean without considering their interpretation, we move away from ourselves and put a nail into the coffin of that relationship. Our assumptions rob others of their perspective on their truth. We treat others as though we know them better than they know themselves. Assumptions also strip them of their humanity. To be sure, their perspective could be wrong. But without asking good questions, how would we know? To avoid assumptions, we need to ask ourselves this essential question: "How can I really know what is true in this conversation?"

> In your difficult conversations, when you do not have all the evidence you need to form your assessment, how do you gain the knowledge you need to speak righteously?

As I have stated, the only way to prevent making assumptions is to ask good questions. Read the word of the Lord from Proverbs 25:7–10:

> What your eyes have seen
> do not hastily bring into court,
> or what will you do in the end,
> when your neighbor puts you to shame?
> Argue your case with your neighbor himself,
> and do not reveal another's secret,
> lest he who hears you bring shame upon you,
> and your ill repute have no end.

This passage makes a very good case against assumptions. The person in this proverb has obviously seen something, but the writer warns this person that there is more to what he sees than meets the eye. In fact, his neighbor may have additional information that could cause him great shame if he acted on his assumption. Ask good questions and refrain from making assumptions.

In the verses above, underline the word or words that address assumption making.

> Think back to the person in your life with whom communication is problematic. List the assumptions you could be making that might sabotage communication with him.

> List the assumptions the other person may have made about you.

> Did either of you ask a good question about the confusion you experience? What was the good question?

Making assumptions (verbal or nonverbal) can easily become a way of life. Perhaps that is why many of the wise sayings in Proverbs have to do with how we communicate. Like all other thoughts, assumptions are formed in our hearts as we try to make sense of the information we glean from our conversations. Proverbs points out how dangerous it is to make assumptions. Read the Word of the Lord from Proverbs 18:13:

> If one gives an answer before he hears,
> it is his folly and shame.

We must ask good questions if we hope to fully understand the situation in which we find ourselves. Read the Word of the Lord from Proverbs 18:17:

> The one who states his case first seems right,
> until the other comes and examines him.

In the same way, a fool assumes things that lead to a poorly informed opinion. Read the Word of the Lord from Proverbs 18:2:

> A fool takes no pleasure in understanding,
> but only in expressing his opinion.

Assumptions run wild when we give an answer before we hear, fall into the trap of believe the first account of a situation, or foolishly give our own opinion without understanding. In these cases, authentic communication suffers because we failed to ask a good question.

Assumptions and Truth

Assumptions become our lifestyle, our reality, and our predictions about the future. They get in the way of how we perceive the meaning of conversations. Assumptions can quickly become the narrative of our understanding of truth. We say to ourselves, "He always responds that way, so I will just assume that this time he will do the same thing again. If I heard him say this once, I heard him say it a thousand times before. I am in no mood for the pain brought about by this folly. And he wonders why I assume what comes next? It is better to ignore him and believe what I want until he shuts up." Soul-satisfying communication comes to a screeching halt.

Assumptions and Predictability

Assumptions also present problems because assumptions can be predictive. We tell ourselves that we know how a person will answer our question, because the last hundred times we asked it, his answer has always been the same. That may be true. But what if the 101st time you asked that same question, the person responded differently? People can change. If we engage in conversations based on our assumptions, we may miss an opportunity to see change happening in a person's life. Maybe you and your beloved know exactly what each of you is thinking at any given time. However, has your beloved ever said, "Why can't you just let me finish what I was going to say before you answer me?"

Assumptions and Generalizations

Additionally, we tend to take our assumptions about that predictable person and apply the same approach to conversations with other people. This predictability makes us feel safe, because our assumptions help us control the conversations. Unpredictable conversations make us anxious and fearful that we will end up engaging in chaotic exchanges, which is why we defaulted to assumptions in the first place. This is unfortunate. Who is to say that conversations with other people will have the same disastrous outcome that our problematic conversations have had? Therefore, when we assume nearly every conversation will turn out badly because some have, we are in jeopardy of having unfulfilling communication with those around us.

Assumptions and Comfort

We also find comfort in the assumptions we make. They save us from the uncomfortable task of getting to the truth, the whole truth, and nothing but the truth. There is comfort leading to a sense of personal power or security in directing the conversation's outcome. Comfort means we do not need to dig deep or ask good questions to find the truth. We can easily slip into hiding who we are. If we are comfortable, who needs truth?

Assumptions and Air-Breathing Humans

Our assumptions tend to override the other person's ability to think and speak as they see fit. They keep us from seeking the distressing truth of the other person's real thoughts. Our assumptions often become the reality we want the hearer to accept rather than the hearer's own story. More importantly, the necessary heart issues in the conversation become obscured. Assumptions hijack the real issues from being discussed because those issues are hard, unsafe, painful, and chaotic. Assumptions relegate the true issues to secondary problems and tend to prevent soul-satisfying and redemptive interactions.

HENNIE AND THE POWER OF ASSUMPTIONS

Let's consider how the power of assumptions sabotages communication in Hennie's story. Hennie and his love interest came to me because they felt as though neither one was understood or heard.

During our first session, Hennie and his love interest told me their story. As we dug deeper into how they processed their communication, I began to see a pattern of assumptions each were making. I engaged Hennie about his assumptions and how they were influenced by his PPIFSt/PPIFEx, ECMs, and his self-talk, leading him to Speak CODE. Hennie said he saw it and told me that those influences made him desperately unhappy in his current love relationship. Hennie told me that the person he cared about the most could not see how much he wanted to be deeply loved and give love in return.

When Hennie and his love interest have substantial misunderstandings, he spins her statements out of control until his assumptions about her words and deeds become his truth. Their conversations are filled with suspicion, disbelief, inaccurate statements, wild accusations, passionate pleas, and assumptions. However, nearly all their conversations lack truth. Hennie remembers feeling trapped in the same box in which others have placed him in his past. For Hennie, this experience is both familiar and frustrating, and leaves him exhausted. He felt rejection back then, and he feels equally rejected now. His current relationship is falling apart because Hennie is unable to see that the assumptions he makes, based on his past, are sabotaging him in the present.

Hennie believes those past boxes in which he was placed mimic what he currently experiences. In other words, he assumes that his current love interest is treating him the same way others have in the past. He has no idea how to throw off the lid of his assumption box and climb out. When you ask Hennie how he knows his assumptions are true about his current relationship, he climbs back into his box and answers from that familiar place. He cannot see the power his assumptions have over him. Hennie's truth tells him that she does not see the goodness of his sacrificial actions or the purity of his undying devotion.

The power behind Hennie's assumptions are not clear to him. He is hopelessly lost in his fortress where truth is locked in a gilded box, guarded by his assumptions. No wonder Hennie's words and deeds appear frantic as he seeks desperately to share his soul with his love interest. Seeking truth, guided by good questions, does not exist in his fortress. Hennie refuses to ask good, clarifying questions to test the accuracy of his assumptions.

In the moment when he most needs to clear up his assumptions, Hennie lacks the skills needed to communicate his own desires and ask good questions. As a result, both he and his love interest are held prisoners in his jail—but in different cells. He is locked in the cell that loops the re-runs of his PPIFSt/PPIFEx. She is held prisoner in her own cell. She continuously tells herself that if only she can find the key to Hennie's heart, he will stop making crazy accusations based on his assumptions and truly love her.

For Believers, assumptions are a roadblock to the work of the Spirit in our lives. Our hearts carry the assumptions we make wherever we go, including into our relationship with Jesus. Assumptions relieve us of our responsibility to get at the root of our own sin, while convincing us that we see the other person's sin with unparalleled accuracy.

Write out an assumption you have made about a person that keeps you from soul-satisfying communication.

How have your assumptions become evident in these conversations?

Write out how this prevents you from having an authentic conversation with that person.

Assumptions and Confrontations

When we make assumptions, we avoid confrontation. Most of us prefer not to be the one who cries out, "Thou art the man!" Nor do we want to be the one who is accused of being the man! When we make assumptions, we feel free from confrontation. Assumptions allow us to sit comfortably on the sidelines and say, "Yeah, there is no point in asking him questions about his crazy remarks. He is just a know-it-all, so why bother even talking to him?" Maybe we are correct, and he is a know-it-all. But that should not stop us from asking a good question, which prevents assumptions.

Please keep in mind we are discussing reasonable people with whom discussions have become problematic. While we do not want to disregard unreasonable people, we may want to seek professional mediation if a situation cannot be resolved.

Describe how your assumptions keep you from speaking confrontational words to that difficult person in your life.

◀ ... .— —. . .— —.— .. —. — —. —.—. — — — —.. .

Assumptions and the Status Quo

We also find relief in making assumptions because our hearts are more at peace with the status quo. The status quo can easily shut down real communication, where uncomfortable or even painful dialogue might require us to go through suffering. The status quo often says, "I will believe my assumptions about you, and you can believe whatever assumptions you have about me. Let's just live in the formalities of our superficial relationship and never get to the bottom of what is going on."

List how assumptions regarding the status quo provide you with cover, so that you can live a superficial life.

◀ ... .— —. . .— —.— .. —. — —. —.—. — — — —.. .

Whatever the reason we choose to justify assumptions, know this: as long as we rely on assumptions, we will eventually cut the heart out of our relationships. This happens because assumptions allow only our side of the issue to be valid. This lopsided belief shuts down soul-satisfying communication.

Write out how your assumptions could be cutting the heart out of your conversations with others.

◀ ... .— —. . .— —.— .. —. — —. —.—. — — — —.. .

By their very nature, assumptions protect and defend us. Making assumptions connects our PPIFSt/PPIFEx to our present conversations, which are often unpredictable or chaotic. Making assumptions protects and defends us from hurtful memories, simply because assumptions keep us from addressing the memories we want to forget. Couple that with our ECMs and Speaking CODE, and our conversations will be inauthentic at best or destructive at worst.

Write out how assumptions help you avoid bringing up powerful memories.

List ways where your assumptions lead to Speaking CODE and keep you from speaking authentically.

Ultimately, we loathe the frustration and loneliness of our assumption-filled conversations. We are stuck in the same confusing maze. We lose any hope that we can find our way out. As a result, our relationships are dying because our conversations are based on assumptions and not actuality. As assumption makers, we live in a painful reality of self-denial, self-delusion, and self-absorption.

State how your assumptions create a confusing maze for you and interfere with soul-satisfying communication.

Assumptions, Moving Away, and Mini-Messiahs

Assumptions move us away from our relationships. Assumptions have a unique ability to keep us either stuck in a past conversation or lost somewhere in the future. They prevent us from living wisely in the unpredictable present moments of our daily conversations.

One last thought on how making assumptions can turn redemptive speech into soul-crushing conversations: assumptions turn us into mini-messiahs,[16] a term coined by Dr. Paul Tripp. Mini-messiahs attempt to venture into areas where only our omnipotent God can go. We who find comfort in making assumptions mistakenly believe we can read the hearts and minds of those with whom we are speaking. And that is a huge contributing factor in soul-crushing conversation.

List how you have become a mini-messiah by making assumptions in your present conversations.

Assumptions Versus Really Knowing

How do we know we are making assumptions, as opposed to really knowing the person in front of us? Surely spouse to spouse, parent to child, good friend to good friend, or opponent to opponent can know enough about the other that we can anticipate what the other is thinking or will say at any given time.

But to know for sure? That privilege belongs to God alone, who searches the hearts and minds of His creatures. How do we know we are making assumptions? We are probably making assumptions if we find ourselves speaking over or stopping the person who is speaking to us. We are probably making assumptions if we answer our own questions before the hearer has an opportunity to do so. We might also say, "Let me guess what you were about to say," or "Please don't tell me what you always say when we talk about this." Additionally, we may hear the other person tell us, "That is not what I meant at all. Why do you talk for me or not believe me when I clearly state what I want?"

Perhaps the saddest impact of assumption making happens when we are in a contentious relationship and we simply make up a script, composed of our self-talk, that attributes all kinds of questionable motives to the other person. Our thoughts can go unchallenged for years. Because our self-talk fuels the CODE we speak, chances are, we will only tell him a snippet of our thoughts. If, by God's grace, we ever have a meaningful conversation, we may feel ashamed of our assumptions rooted in our self-talk.

How do we stop making assumptions? Before we answer this question, we need to ask ourselves something more basic. What motivates our hearts to make assumptions in the first place?

Write out what motivates your heart to make assumptions.

COMFORT IDOLS

Conversations that are based on assumptions start in the heart when we feel unexplained emotions welling up—particularly fear. Fear drives us to our comfort idols (any created thing that replaces God in our lives). When we feel frightened, we are tempted to shut down or scream over the person with whom we are speaking. We seek the comfort found in making assumptions, rather than entering the unpredictable world of questions asked and answered. If the answers to our questions do not fit the assumptions we made, we might need to rethink our conclusions, which may throw us into confusion. Asking good questions begins the process of dismantling our comfort idols. Soul-satisfying conversations happen when the good questions we ask outnumber the assumptions we make, especially in the initial stages of our interactions.

How do your emotions drive you to idols that promote assumption making rather than asking good questions?

Fear typically tops the list of why we make assumptions rather than ask good questions. Think about Adam and the Woman hiding in the garden after they sinned. Even though they knew God better than any of us could ever have known Him, their fear caused them to hide. We have no way to know what assumptions they made or what the conversation between Adam and the Woman sounded like when they heard God's voice calling out to them. But we do know that fear caused them to hide themselves when they heard God's call.

START ASKING GOOD QUESTIONS

We need to learn how to stop making assumptions when we are in the middle of a confusing conversation. The righteous path is to ask helpful questions in the early moments of our exchanges. Please don't be confused by the simplicity of this statement. Remember, our hearts are loaded down with our Two Influential Forces, self-talk, and CODE Speaking. These forces are hard at work shaping how we interpret the words we hear in our everyday conversations for good or for ill.

Let's suppose we are in the middle of a conversation, and the person makes a statement that does not quite fit with our thinking. We have experienced the emotions that go along with hearing ideas that sound uninformed. It is common to hear provocative statements when discussing politics or religion. At this point we can allow our Two Influential Forces, assumptions, and self-talk to drive the CODE we speak in response. We might tell ourselves that we need to set this person straight or our own views will be called into question. Without asking a single good question, we launch into a defensive diatribe driven by our assumptions.

A wiser approach would be to ask the person a profitable question. We may ask him to define his terms. There is a high likelihood that a simple clarification of terms would stop the assumptions we make and prevent a potential argument. If the person defines his terms, and we still feel the person is grossly uninformed, more questions may be necessary. At some point we may need to assert that even with terms defined, we still disagree.

NOW WHAT?

We honor another person's humanity when we engage in conversations as equals. Both of us have a right to our own evaluation of the issue. In these early moments, we must decide if we want to stay in the conversation. Continuing the conversation depends on many things. However, the most important issue centers on how the person is connected to us. We must ask ourselves if continuing the conversation would do irreparable damage to this necessary relationship. Or we might want to change the subject. We also must consider if God will receive glory if we continue.

We can insert our own personalities into the good questions we ask. As we practice listening well, we may soon learn what the person wants from us. Knowing the person better will lessen the need to ask additional questions. As a dear friend once said to me, "When I really know someone well, I can short-cut what is on my heart and speak my mind. It may come out rough, but I know my friend will not misunderstand or else he will ask what I mean."

When we ask good questions, we begin to enter a soul-satisfying conversation. At first, the conversation may not appear so, simply because assumptions need to be eliminated by asking clarifying questions. The participants may need to demonstrate humility and sacrifice, which is especially difficult in today's culture. But in the end, we emulate Jesus because He asked good questions that got to the root of what was in peoples' hearts. Read the Word of the Lord in Mark 8:14–21:

> Now they had forgotten to bring bread, and they had only one loaf with them in the boat. And he cautioned them, saying, "Watch out; beware of the leaven of the Pharisees and the leaven of Herod." And they began discussing with one another the fact that they had no bread. And Jesus, aware of this, said to them, "Why are you discussing the fact that you have no bread? Do you not yet perceive or understand? Are your hearts hardened? Having eyes do you not see, and having ears do you not hear? And do you not remember? When I broke the five loaves for the five thousand, how many baskets full of broken pieces did you take up?" They said to him, "Twelve." "And the seven for the four thousand, how many baskets full of broken pieces did you take up?" And they said to him, "Seven." And he said to them, "Do you not yet understand?"

Throughout this chapter we see Jesus as the Master Questioner. He starts with the feeding of the four thousand and ends with a call to commitment. This chapter also includes Peter's inspired confession—given after he was asked worthy questions—that Jesus is the Christ. But verses 14–21 show Jesus as Teacher, asking His students a series of eight questions designed to get His disciples to think. These questions will prevent their hearts from hardening. Mark shows us how good questions are essential if we are going to understand each other. Good questions reduce assumptions, decrease misunderstandings, and allow us to stay connected to others in our conversations.

Asking sound questions puts our conversations on a path that eventually may come to a life-giving conclusion. It may take one conversation or one million. We may see the edifying conclusions in our lifetime or maybe they will come later, in someone else's. The timeframe is not nearly as important as the guts of the words we say to one another. We ask good questions to achieve mercy, reveal agendas, uncover heart motives, prevent personal attacks, make information clear, be life-giving, thwart ambushes, define terms, set the direction of the conversation, and point people to Jesus. No matter who the participants are, experts or novices, we are wise to follow Jesus. Ask good questions!

Based on the examples of Jesus' eight questions in Mark 8, list reasons why you should ask good questions. Explain why.

We know that our self-talk fuels the CODE we speak. Assumptions thrive on our self-talk as we tap into our Two Influential Forces. Reliving our past often assigns motivations to our conversational partner that may or may not be true. As we ruminate on these experiences, we run the risk of Speaking CODE. Speaking CODE makes the conversation more about us and less about the other person. The only way out of this mess is to ask good questions that lead to active listening.

Write about a time where CODE Speaking got in the way of asking good questions and facilitated your assumptions.

Asking trustworthy questions is the key to opening the door of our heart. Noble questions uncover the motives behind thoughts and words. We identify motives when we ask questions starting with phrases like, "Would it be possible for you to tell me what you meant," or "Help me to understand why you said this," or "Can you tell me your definition of this word?" These types of questions help expose motives. Be sure to phrase your follow-up questions based on the information you just heard. We must know motives before we can speak wisely. We cannot speak righteously into what we do not know. Therefore, to achieve soul-satisfying conversations, we must ask good questions.

COUNT THE RISKS

Asking good questions, while necessary, may not be received as well as we would wish. We may be ridiculed when we ask them. The person to whom we are speaking is a living breathing image bearer, just like us. His PPIFSt and PPIFEx may sabotage his responses. This person may Speak CODE for reasons unknown to us or to him. This is the nature of Speaking CODE. Because of his ECMs, his communication table is set just as neatly for him as ours is set for us. He may hear our questions as intrusive or abusive, depending upon his past experiences. Also, he may feel attacked when we ask questions in the first place.

Sometimes, the answers to our good questions are unexpected, and the other person may accuse us of hurting him. This may cause us to feel defensive, because their answer made us want to respond with self-protective words. Think hard and be honest. What other responses may we have to their accusatory response so that our own hearts will not be hardened? We may shut down because we were not prepared for the response we heard. We may backtrack and withdraw the question. Or we may follow up with another question based on the answer we received.

Write out your typical response to an unexpected answer.

Perhaps we may say something like this: "Actually, my question was not designed to hurt you at all but to help you. I am surprised you can't see that. Talk about feeling hurt!" That may seem like a righteous response. However, we just defended ourselves again.

A better response may be, "I'm confused. Would it be possible for you to tell me what I said that makes you say I hurt you with my question? It would be helpful to hear how you feel so that I do not make your pain any worse." These questions bring clarity. If you are going to have a fight (and you will), it might as well be a fight over the right issues and not assumptions. Remember, assumptions hijack true issues.

Write out a good response to the unexpected answer your friend might give you.

In Our Defense

What makes us defend ourselves in a conversation? I believe we defend ourselves simply because we are human, and we desire to be seen in the best light possible. It hurts to be misunderstood, which makes it natural to defend ourselves from unjust accusations. Therefore, we defend our words or actions. In a conversation where we feel like we have been unjustly maligned, we use words that we believe will justify our behavior. Eventually, we may have to defend what we said or did; however, let's start by asking good questions. The fight is certainly coming. Asking good questions makes the fight righteous.

What are some examples of good questions we may ask when we are engaged in a hard discussion? We need to ask questions that bring clarity to the conversation rather than confusion. We can ask questions that will put us on a path toward peacemaking rather than peace-faking.

Questions that move us toward peace will not necessarily be easy to ask. In fact, the questions may be difficult or provocative. Jesus asked these types of questions during His ministry. If the questions lead to answers that are hard to hear, we need to frame them up properly before asking them. The last thing we want is to add another layer of hurt. How do we frame up a question?

BASIC FORMULA FOR COMMUNICATION

Let's suppose the person responding to our good question says, "What you asked reminds me of my past when I felt pressured into answering questions that I did not want to answer. It hurt me then and it hurts me now. You say we are friends, but I see no difference between you and those who did me wrong. What is wrong with you?"

If we believe the person would become defensive at a good question, there is a way to make our response easier for the person to hear. It is important to understand that our good questions are designed not just to provide clarity but to avoid assumptions on their part. Here is an example of how we might frame up our response: "I'm feeling the need to ask you something before I answer you. My question might upset you. But I want to be truthful with you because I care a lot about our relationship. I want to follow your lead." Try to wait for the answer, and then ask your good question.

This approach may sound artificial or contrived. True enough. It is especially artificial if our questions are meant to trap the other person. We cannot forget that even our good questions are subject to our own assumptions, based on our Two Influential Forces, self-talk, and Speaking CODE. We must examine even seemingly good questions before we ask them.

Framing up confusing conversational issues may be as simple as following a basic formula for communication. This formula may be familiar to many of us.

- "**I feel** [name or state your feelings]."
- "**When you say or do** [name or state the person's problematic behavior]..."
- "**. . . it makes me** [name what this behavior tempts you to think or do]."
- "**Would it be possible for you to help me out by telling me what you mean?**" (Asking for help invites the person into the conversation.)

Good Questions Versus Interrogation

We must not confuse asking good questions with interrogation. Interrogation is designed to apply pressure to get the answers we want. Interrogation generally only benefits us. Asking good questions helps others as well as us. Interrogation tends to feel persistent or pressing, as it forces our timetable on the hearer. Asking good questions gives the hearer time and space to respond. Always remember the two great commandments: love God fully and love our neighbor as we love ourselves.

Write out a question you have used to interrogate another person.

Write out a question someone asked you that sounded like an interrogation.

You may feel as though this process is too much work. That may be valid. But what is the alternative if we do not ask good questions? We are likely to fight the wrong battle. We would allow our self-talk to have full control over our conversations, rather than seeing conversations as a two-way street. Our self-talk often makes winners out of us and losers out of them, without regard for truth. In contrast, good questions promote truth, honesty, and openness in our dialogues. That stops Speaking CODE in its tracks.

Facing Consequences

Failure to ask good questions has consequences. One consequence is that our conversation may follow a path that is self-righteous, rather than God-righteous. The conversation is no longer about that difficult person who may, in fact, be difficult. It is about us.

Assumptions put our conversations in danger of being superficial, inauthentic, and disingenuous. Asking good questions promotes honesty and integrity in our words. Soul-satisfying conversations always have us checking our own hearts.

What consequences have you experienced when you failed to ask good questions?

Benefits of Asking Good Questions

Let's look at what happens when we ask good questions rather than making assumptions. Asking good questions may defuse the situation so that the person who made the original statement rethinks his words. He may have been expecting a fight. Therefore, asking good questions may stop an argumentative conversation in its tracks.

The person may be irritated because he was asked a question, and is now—especially if the person is a Christian—obligated to answer it. The Bible clearly instructs us to engage each other when conflict exists. Read the Word of the Lord from Matthew 5:23–24:

> So if you are offering your gift at the altar and there remember that your brother has something against you, leave your gift there before the altar and go. First be reconciled to your brother, and then come and offer your gift.

In this passage, we go and seek out our brother so that we can be reconciled. Good questions facilitate reconciliation. This is still a risk, because the person who made the statement may feel threatened by having to look at his words honestly. However, the good question may lead to redemptive conversations rather than soul-crushing speech. We are not responsible for the other person's answer to our good question. Our responsibility is to leave our gift at the altar and go.

Using the Matthew 5 passage, write out how asking a good question can promote reconciliation.

Unfortunately, we get no guarantees that asking good questions, rather than making assumptions, will lead us into redemptive conversations. Why is that the case? The answer is that the person involved in the conversation is a sinner, just like us. He is human, just like us. He is made in the very image of God, just like us. Therefore, good questions are directed to a human who struggles, just like us.

God asks us good questions because God is loving and merciful to us, not because He needs answers. He already knows our heart motives.

Examples of Good Questions

Let's look at a list of good questions and see if we can incorporate them into our conversations.

- "Before we continue here, let me ask you a question: do you just need me to listen so you can get out whatever bothers you, or do you want me to tell you what I think?"

Asking this question clarifies the speaker's and the listener's agenda before any assumptions or misinterpretations happen.

- "What did you just hear me say? Please help me out because I want to be as clear as I can."

This keeps the listener in the moment and short-circuits the heart's desire to grab hold of those PPIFSt and PPIFEx, which can easily drag our conversations down a path of hurt and despair.

- "Did I hear you correctly when you said [restate or rephrase what you heard]? I just want to be sure I heard you correctly."

The speaker and the hearer need to pay close attention to the words they use. This prevents assumptions. Those Two Influential Forces can sabotage us at any point in our conversations. This keeps both hearer and speaker honest because they will be called upon to accurately repeat the statements they heard.

- "Your body language doesn't seem to match what you just said. Can you tell me why you [describe the behavior in question]?"

This keeps every part of us engaged in the conversation. Remember, communication is much more than the words we say. Our hearts and our bodies are equally engaged. Soul-satisfying communications can be reflected in our body language.

- "Would it be possible to restate what I just said? Your answer does not reflect what I said, and it isn't what I meant to communicate."

If the hearer cannot restate what the speaker said, then communication got derailed, most likely because ECMs or PPIFSt/PPIFEx spoke more loudly to the hearer than the words we spoke.

- "Do you feel like you are speaking to me right now? I have to be honest: what you said does not sit right with me because your response sounds like it is directed to someone else. Help me out here."

In this situation the speaker said something that awakened past memories in the hearer. The hearer's response did not match the speaker's words. The speaker asked a good question to identify where the hearer was in the conversation. This fights against assumptions. It also helps to identify our PPIFSt and PPIFEx.

- "Would it be possible to say that again? I am sorry. I think I misunderstood you."

Always be willing to own your sin or mistakes in the conversation. Humility is contagious.

At this point, does asking good questions seem a bit sophomoric? It may seem that way, but it is still necessary. There are broken people in our lives with whom we must hold conversations. Their brokenness may cause them to say things to us that are not true but are very destructive. We, too, are broken. That means we also do destructive things to others and ourselves. We may take what is said and filter it through our destructive CODE Speaking, driven by our Two Influential Forces. Or, in our brokenness, we may speak words that malign the person with whom we are speaking. Good questions help prevent destructive elements from entering our conversations.

God, give us the ability to enter a righteous argument by setting aside our assumptions and asking good questions so that we can see with clarity and respond with truth and love.

MOVING AWAY: REFUSING TO FORGIVE

I am about to make a crucial statement. If we don't believe this statement down to our core, we will live in a world of soul-crushing speech rather than redemptive communication. Are you ready? *If we do not forgive a person deeply and from our heart, we will never experience soul-satisfying communication.* Refusing to forgive others allows secret hopelessness or open hostility to occupy our head and our heart. In fact, neglecting to forgive deeply and from the heart promotes self-talk. This leads to Speaking CODE that could make our conversations bitter, destructive, vengeful, contemptuous, and unfulfilling. Soul-satisfying conversations cannot flourish with these emotions living in our hearts.

When we do not confront/confess, repent, and grant forgiveness, whatever requires confession and repentance becomes our new or secondary PPIFSt and PPIFEx. These new statements and experiences will link to our existing PPIFSt and PPIFEx. Together they will form an unsound basis for our communication. Do not doubt this. Failing to forgive one another deeply and from the heart suffocates authentic and redemptive communication.

PRISON GUARDS

Our PPIFSt and PPIFEx seek to hold us prisoner, while our unforgiving hearts act like vigilant prison guards whose job is to prevent soul-satisfying conversations. The guards of our hearts whisper to us that we can never forgive those who hurt us. These guards diligently search for ways to link our PPIFSt and PPIFEx to our present relationships, making it even harder to forgive. They cleverly match up our past relational pain to the present relational struggles. The weight of past unforgiveness sinks our attempts at current forgiveness. Not forgiving past and present offenses adds one more ingredient to the communication mess in which we find ourselves.

Constantly searching for links between unaddressed past and present offenses leaves us riddled with panic, anxiety, and fear. These past and present experiences team up and harden our hearts to prevent us from forgiving ourselves, others, and even God. It is our own hardened hearts which refuse to forgive others, that sabotage the words we say and hear. Additionally, how do we ever trust the person who has sought forgiveness from us and continues to sin against us? The thought of trusting that person yet again is almost beyond our comprehension.

Describe how the vigilant guard and watchman of your heart prevents you from forgiving someone deeply and from your heart.

Whom have you not been able to forgive, and why? Write it out.

CONSEQUENCES OF NOT FORGIVING

Many of us reading these words right now are living out the consequences of not forgiving that person who has done us great harm. We may trick ourselves into thinking we can ignore, forget, deny, or minimize the offense. The person owns us when his very existence is caught up in our self-talk. We deliberately tell ourselves to stop thinking about him or we will obsess over the situation. Our self-talk influences the CODE we speak, which affects the words we choose in our conversations.

Additionally, our unforgiving heart will turn our impeccable theology on forgiveness upside-down. We may tell ourselves that because this person did us great harm, we do not have any obligation to interact with him. But he is an image bearer. Anytime we deny a person his humanness because of his actions, we make up our own theology that governs our behavior.

It is exhausting to hold onto an offense. The Bible tells us that our physical wellness could be compromised if we do not become confessing and forgiving people. Not forgiving holds immense power over us. Read the Word of the Lord in Psalm 32:1–7:

Blessed is the one whose transgression is forgiven,
whose sin is covered.
Blessed is the man against whom the Lord counts no iniquity,
and in whose spirit there is no deceit.
For when I kept silent, my bones wasted away
through my groaning all day long.
For day and night your hand was heavy upon me;
my strength was dried up as by the heat of summer. *Selah*
I acknowledged my sin to you,

> and I did not cover my iniquity;
> I said, "I will confess my transgressions to the Lord,"
> and you forgave the iniquity of my sin. *Selah*
> Therefore, let everyone who is godly
> offer prayer to you at a time when you may be found;
> surely in the rush of great waters,
> they shall not reach him.
> You are a hiding place for me;
> you preserve me from trouble;
> you surround me with shouts of deliverance. *Selah*

You may be wondering to yourself: "Diana, aren't these verses referring to us not asking God to forgive the sins we have committed against Him?" Good question! We must first be forgiven by God before we can address our need to forgive others. As we read the Psalm, we should note the impact a lack of forgiveness has on our bodies. When we are unforgiven our very bodies feel as though they are wasting away and have no strength.

Jesus addresses the topic of forgiveness. Read the Word of the Lord from Matthew 6:9–15:

> Pray then like this: "Our Father in heaven, hallowed be your name. Your kingdom come, your will be done, on earth as it is in heaven. Give us this day our daily bread, and forgive us our debts, as we also have forgiven our debtors. And lead us not into temptation but deliver us from evil." For if you forgive others their trespasses, your heavenly Father will also forgive you, but if you do not forgive others their trespasses, neither will your Father forgive your trespasses.

The clear teaching of these verses is that we must forgive. If we do not forgive others, we ourselves will not be forgiven by God. If we do not confess and repent of the sin of unforgiveness, we can experience the effects of unconfessed sin described in Psalm 32. Thus, if we believe the Bible is truly all we need for life and godliness, we have no other choice but to forgive deeply and from the heart.

Write out who it is you need to forgive, and why.

List the reasons that you have not forgiven that person.

Write out how your self-talk has been affected by not forgiving that person.

Write out how you have Spoken CODE to this person because you have not forgiven him.

List how your communication with that person has been affected.

Write out how not forgiving this person has affected your other relationships, especially in the area of communication.

FORGIVENESS AS A COMMAND

It might be tempting to think of forgiveness as just a recommendation and not an explicit command. However, if we set aside the command to forgive, we are left with our Two Influential Forces, self-talk, and Speaking CODE, which we already know sabotage our interactions. Let's not fool ourselves. Not forgiving will damage our relationships. That is a path away from soul-satisfying communication.

If, however, our sweet Jesus has lived a sinless life, died a wrath-bearing death, and crushed death itself for our justification, then our response is to believe. We must obey all that He commands, including forgiving those who have harmed us. God will give us His grace so that we can be people who forgive. Jesus tells us in John 14:15, "If you love me, you will keep my commandments." Since He commands us to forgive others, we must forgive.

Lesser Offenses

If we do not forgive those who have committed greater offenses, we slowly lose the ability to forgive others for lesser offenses. We transfer past emotions to current situations, which makes it difficult to forgive other people. This transfer feels bewildering to others because it makes them feel like they are walking on eggshells.

Failing to forgive past terrible offenses affects us so that any hint that our friends or acquaintances are like our abusers causes us to relive our past. Unforgiveness toward those past offenses makes us view lesser offenses as though they were the same.

Those who suffer from complex trauma have greater difficulty in forgiving lesser offenses. For example, a survivor of sexual abuse may find it difficult to forgive someone who slights him in social settings. This slighting enhances pre-existing feelings of being rejected, unloved, used, or ignored. It becomes difficult to interact comfortably in social gatherings.

The Unforgiving Servant

In Matthew 18, Jesus tells us a parable about an unforgiving servant. Read the conversations between all the players in this parable. Jesus compares this parable with the Kingdom of Heaven. To summarize, a servant owed the king a huge sum of money (v. 24). The man could not possibly pay that amount, so he and his family were sold to settle the debt (v. 25). The servant begged the king for patience and promised to repay the debt in full (v. 26). The king took pity on the servant, released him, and forgave his debt (v. 27).

Soon thereafter, this servant found a fellow servant who owed him a small amount compared to the great debt this servant owed the king. This forgiven servant choked the man demanding payment and was unmoved by his friend's plea for patience. Additionally, this servant refused to extend mercy for the same crime he himself had committed (vv. 28–30). Upon witnessing this distressing situation, the onlookers reported the incident to the king (v. 31). The king rebuked the servant. Read the Word of the Lord in Matthew 18:32–35:

> Then his master summoned him and said to him, "You wicked servant! I forgave you all that debt because you pleaded with me. And should not you have had mercy on your fellow servant, as I had mercy on you?" And in anger his master delivered him to the jailers, until he should pay all his debt. So also my heavenly Father will do to every one of you, if you do not forgive your brother from your heart.

This parable teaches us invaluable information on forgiveness. Forgiveness affects community. The Bible says the onlookers were distressed over the forgiven servant's behavior toward his fellow servant. When we do not forgive deeply and from the heart, our community will suffer. For example, if we do not forgive the family member who hurt us, our relatives will suffer. They may feel forced to take sides. Gossip will flourish. The same is true for our church family. If we do not forgive a member of our church, the congregation will suffer. Suffering may put undue stress or pressure on those in our community who watch the ramifications of our unforgiving heart play out. In fact, our unforgiving attitude will cause anger within our community. The writer to the Hebrews tells us to strive for peace with everyone. He writes that the failure to obtain grace will allow a "root of bitterness" to spring up, causing trouble and defiling many (Hebrews 12:14–15). A bitter root can take hold in a heart that cannot forgive.

How has your community suffered because you have not practiced forgiveness? Please think of your community as your family, circle of friends, church, acquaintances, or workplace.

This parable also teaches us to pity those who fall onto hard times, whether by stupid decisions, sinful actions, or unfortunate circumstances. That means we must consider the circumstances surrounding issues that necessitate forgiveness. Forgiveness shows us that mercy triumphs over truth. This is especially hard if we need to forgive someone who abused us or did us great harm.

Write out the surrounding circumstances that make it hard for you to forgive the person in question. The surrounding circumstances may include the person's death or his refusal to engage you in any meaningful dialogue. The surrounding circumstances may involve past sexual or physical abuse, which can make it seem nearly impossible to forgive.

This parable teaches us that there are hard consequences waiting for us if we do not forgive others as we have been forgiven. The king threw the servant into jail, which was consistent with the king's original judgment. If we do not forgive, the judgment we receive will take away our freedom and hold us hostage to the person who needs our forgiveness. And our King will not forgive us.

List ways in which the person you cannot forgive holds you prisoner. For example, does fear of seeing this person keep you from attending events where he may be present that can affect your quality of life.

How often does this person occupy both your external and internal conversations which prevents you from living your life well?

This parable teaches us that we need to live our lives based on God's law rather than what seems best for our broken hearts. Our broken hearts tell us not to forgive. But God says otherwise. We can either please ourselves or please God.

Write out how you follow your own heart rather than God's Word when it comes to forgiving. Please note that anytime you behave differently than what the Bible says, you are following your own heart.

KNOWING GOD WELL

Maybe we need to look at the problem of forgiving a difficult person in a different way. Perhaps there is a separate issue here. Let's look deeper into what prevents us from forgiving that harmful person. The deeper issue involves not knowing God as well as we should. We need to confess to God that we do not know Him well enough. If we knew Him well, we would believe He put this person in our lives so we can have a deeper relationship with Him. Knowing God well enables us to see that He has the power to help us forgive others.

The inability to forgive is a gospel issue, and thank God it is! It is theological and it is personal. We are grateful this is a gospel issue because gospel issues are always addressed in the Bible. All of us find the remedy for our inabilities in God alone through the Scriptures alone. Sola Deo! Sola Scriptura! We need to confess that we do not know God well enough to see He is able to do more than we can imagine. I know that I do not know God well enough to trust Him fully when dealing with issues of forgiveness. Hear my confession:

Oh Lord, I confess I cannot forgive this person on my own. I also confess that my understanding of Your ability to help me forgive is weak and pathetic. If I knew You well, I would trust that You put me in this situation where someone I love has hurt me deeply. Even through this pain You are working out Your good pleasure in my life for Your glory and my good. Forgive me for not knowing You deeply enough to see that the Cross stands as a powerful signpost pointing me to Your power to forgive. Forgive me for satisfying myself by preferring a god of my imagination. In my inability to forgive, help me to learn that at the foot of the Cross, You forgave me so I am free to forgive others. ***Amen.***

Read the word of the Lord in 1 John 1:9:

> If we confess our sins, he is faithful and just to forgive us our sins and to cleanse us from all unrighteousness.

Write out your confession of not knowing God well enough to trust Him.

The inability to forgive is a form of unrighteousness. In Psalm 103, the psalmist lays out a blueprint and a reasonable explanation for us to follow as we forgive. Read the Word of the Lord in Psalm 103:8–14:

> The Lord is merciful and gracious,
> slow to anger and abounding in steadfast love.
> He will not always chide,
> nor will he keep his anger forever.
> He does not deal with us according to our sins,
> nor repay us according to our iniquities.
> For as high as the heavens are above the earth,
> so great is his steadfast love toward those who fear him;
> as far as the east is from the west,
> so far does he remove our transgressions from us.
> As a father shows compassion to his children,
> the Lord shows compassion to those who fear him.
> For he knows our frame;
> he remembers that we are dust.

List the attributes we share with God that allow us to forgive deeply and from the heart (e.g., mercy).

What does God do with our transgressions?

How can you follow God's example in how He handles sin?

Write out a strategy you can follow to forgive difficult people based on God's character.

FORGIVENESS: A NEW WAY TO LOVE

God begins Scripture with conversations He has with His creation. Jesus ends His earthly ministry with conversations with those He dearly loves. We explored Genesis 1–3 extensively. Let us now look at Jesus's last will and testament, as seen in the essential conversations Jesus has with His disciples in the book of John. Our goal is to see how forgiveness is not only essential but also possible. Read the Word of the Lord in John 13:34–35:

> A new commandment I give to you, that you love one another: just as I have loved you, you also are to love one another. By this all people will know that you are my disciples, if you have love for one another.

Earlier in His ministry, Jesus reminded His followers about the two greatest commandments offered in the Law: fully love God, love others, and love self. At the culmination of His ministry, Jesus gives His followers a new commandment: love each other as Jesus loved them. That's odd. Why does Jesus give a new commandment on love that sounds very similar to the two greatest commandments already contained in the Law? What does this have to do with forgiveness? I incorporated many of the following thoughts based on sermons preached by my pastors.

Jesus becomes the actual embodiment of love. Recall the Predicate Nominative game: Jesus is love. Jesus and love are the same. Love becomes all that Jesus is. Jesus is all that love is. Jesus then challenges His disciples to be marked as His own by loving as He loves. How is that a new commandment? It is a new commandment because Jesus gave us a blueprint on loving. This did not exist before His incarnation. Jesus lived out forgiveness in His flesh, in front of His creation.

We now have the life and work of Jesus, the only true Lover of our souls, to show us how to live out His new commandment. God gives us the Holy Spirit so that we are able to love as Jesus loves. Our goal is to see how this new commandment helps us forgive one another deeply and from the heart so that our conversations can be righteous and fruitful.

Continuing with the ideas presented from John 13 to the end of the Gospel of John, let's look at ways we can love like Jesus that can help us become forgiving people:

- Knowing His end was near, Jesus loved His own to the end. To the end! Let that sink in. Loving like Jesus means we love to the end. That means we find ways to talk instead of remaining silent.
- Knowing His end was near, Jesus washed the feet of His disciples. Loving like Jesus means we immerse ourselves in acts of sacrificial love akin to washing the feet of others. If that means forbearing through difficult conversations, so be it.

- Knowing His end was near, Jesus focused on the glory both He and God would receive through His death and resurrection. Loving like Jesus means we decide to focus on glorifying God in this world and the next, despite the problems we face because of difficult conversations.
- Knowing His end was near, Jesus talked extensively with those whom He loved. Loving like Jesus means we make it a point to continue talking to one another even though we can think of many good reasons why we should not.
- Knowing His end was near, Jesus restrained Himself from calling down legions of angels during His trial to stop the evil perpetrated on Him. Loving like Jesus means we can remain present in our difficult relationships even if we believe all hope is lost. Sometimes we must bear the effects of painful conversations on our own rather than stirring up trouble.
- Knowing His end was near, Jesus asked God to forgive all those who bore responsibility for His death as He hung on the Cross. That includes you and me. Loving like Jesus means we can forgive deeply and from the heart those who have violated our body and soul. Jesus provides a path toward healing.

Believers have a new commandment: love like Jesus. This new love marks us, as surely as Jesus still bears the marks in His hands, side, and feet. We are marked to carry on the work Jesus has for us to do, including the hard work of forgiveness which opens up new ways for us to communicate. This new commandment to love like Jesus makes forgiveness possible. Linger at the Cross for just a bit longer. Listen to Jesus forgive people who had no idea what they were doing. Read the Word of the Lord in Luke 23:34:

> And Jesus said, "Father, forgive them, for they know not what they do." And they cast lots to divide his garments.

How could Jesus forgive us as He hung on the cross?

◀ ... .– –. . .– –.– .. –. – –.   –.–. – – – –.. .

As you love like Jesus loves you, what truths can you tell yourself when it comes to forgiving someone deeply and from the heart so that you can be free to talk again?

◀ ... .– –. . .– –.– .. –. – –.   –.–. – – – –.. .

Now, let us go practice that kind of forgiveness as we love like Jesus.

FORGIVENESS: EASY AS 1-2-3

Now that God has given us a blueprint on how we are able to forgive, let's look at a three-step process. The first step is non-negotiable. The second step is transactional and may or may not be possible. The third step is sacrificial.

STEP ONE: Non-Negotiable

The first step in forgiveness is forgiving the person to God, regardless if the situation has been worked out or not. If we do not forgive, our own prayers will go unheard and our own sins will not be forgiven. Forgiveness lies at the very heart of the Gospel. Read the Word of the Lord from Matthew 6:14–15:

> For if you forgive others their trespasses, your heavenly Father will also forgive you, but if you do not forgive others their trespasses, neither will your Father forgive your trespasses.

God demonstrates what it looks like for us to forgive, when He took our dead hearts and made them alive. Now, He who forgave us sets the example for us to follow. Read the Word of the Lord from Ephesians 2:1 and 2:4–5:

> And you were dead in the trespasses and sins . . . But God, being rich in mercy, because of the great love with which he loved us, even when we were dead in our trespasses, made us alive together with Christ—by grace you have been saved."

God put us in a right relationship with Jesus even when we were a rotting corpse in a suffocating casket. When I first saw my mom laid out in her coffin, I wished with all my heart that she could just put her hand on mine and say one last time, "Diana, don't let this trouble your heart." My mom said those very words to me in the middle of a mad woman's rant when she was committed to a psychiatric hospital.

However, my mom could not comfort me as I stood beside her body laying in that claustrophobic coffin. Neither of us could seek or grant forgiveness because she was dead. Neither of us could console each other over so many sad experiences because she was dead. We could not experience joy together because she was dead.

God's great love for us and His infinite power over life and death called us from death to life in Him. He forgave us while we were still dead and, therefore, unable to even raise our putrid hand to receive salvation. God's great love, and the new life He gave us, allows us to forgive people who may be dead to us in this very moment. These people may be dead in the grave or they may be alive, but deathly silent. Deathly silence can feel the same as dead in the grave. In these cases, there is no hope for soul-satisfying communication. What do we do? How do we forgive people who are dead to us?

We must forgive that person to God without prefacing our words with statements like, "*if* only he had not said that," or "*and* he needs to ask forgiveness, too," or "*but* he really must see his part in this." Peacemakers Ministries says that *ifs, ands,* or *buts* put qualifications on forgiveness and makes it no forgiveness at all![17] Rest assured, this is not forgiving that person deeply and from the heart. I would encourage you to wait until all your *ifs, ands,* or *buts* are satisfied. Then ask for and receive forgiveness.

That means if, in this present moment, we are unable to forgive that person face to face, we must whisper prayers of forgiveness to our God who hears us. We can say, "Lord, it is not possible for me to talk to this person now. Will You accept my desire to forgive this person until the time comes for us to be reconciled? Help me take no revenge by my actions, my thoughts, or my words. Amen."

Forgiving this person to God allows our prayers to be heard and our sins forgiven. We cannot re-negotiate Matthew 6:14–15 with God. Jesus's words are non-negotiable. As impossible as this sounds, we are required to forgive others based on the grace poured out to us through the life, death, and resurrection of Jesus Christ. His yoke is easy and His burden is light, even when it comes to forgiving what seems to us to be unforgivable. God give us grace to trust Him who is able to do more than we could possibly imagine.

> Write out your prayer of forgiveness to God for that person who has harmed you. Look at Stephen's prayer of forgiveness in Acts 7:54-60, as he was being stoned by haters of Christ. If you need more help, read Jesus's words of forgiveness while He hung on that cursed cross in Luke 23:26–49.

STEP TWO: Transactional

Forgiveness is transactional. It is something we do together. We talk over the offense that has separated us. In some cases, only one person is the offender and the other is the offended. In other cases, both people offended each other. They could be divided by misunderstandings or by blatant sin. In any case, the ensuing conversations are brave, life-giving, and unifying! Read the Word of the Lord from Psalm 133:1–3.

> Behold, how good and pleasant it is
> when brothers dwell in unity!
> It is like the precious oil on the head,
> running down on the beard,
> on the beard of Aaron,
> running down on the collar of his robes!
> It is like the dew of Hermon,

which falls on the mountains of Zion!
For there the Lord has commanded the blessing,
life forevermore.

Unity can only happen when nothing stands between us except the love that binds us together. Because we are sinners, our offenses against each other must be forgiven for unity to be complete! Unity is the fruit of reconciliation. Reconciliation is the process where all offenses are removed through mutual forgiveness and perhaps restitution. Offenses are remembered no more. Our Two Influential Forces, self-talk, and Speaking CODE lessen as we practice transactional forgiveness.

List some actions you can take to invite someone into a transactional forgiveness.

However, transactional forgiveness may not be possible. The other person may be dead. Or they may be unwilling to enter a transactional dialogue, even after we pursue a conversation designed to lead us to forgiveness. What happens if this is the case? Are we unable to live in the benefits of forgiveness? In such cases we can forebear with them, as seen in Section Two. Forbearance is also transactional. We will discuss this more in a later chapter.

God is ever gracious. He allows us to enjoy the benefits of forgiveness even if the other person will not enter that transaction with us. We can still forgive and beg our Heavenly Father to heal our wounded hearts. We have confidence that God will take our hurt and pain and exchange it for Jesus's peace.

We can still speak redemptively to one who refuses transactional forgiveness. Our conversations may be few and far between, and they may feel forced or awkward. However, we can still use words that are soul-satisfying rather than soul-crushing.

We must believe that only God can change the human heart. At some point, we may stop pressing into that person and embrace the reality that our lives are hidden in Christ. We press into Jesus who sets our hearts on heavenly joys rather than on earthly sorrows. Who knows? That person may someday do the seemingly impossible and enter that forgiveness transaction, where the payoff is reconciliation and peace.

Describe a situation where the other person refused to enter a transactional forgiveness with you.

In this situation, list the benefits you enjoy as you are hidden in Christ.

If a relationship is so broken that our conversations are bruising and filled with assumptions, we may need a skilled mediator. A mediator will help us hear one another well and assist us in choosing the words that make our meaning most clear. It is wise to seek out a mediator if the words we speak make matters worse.

If we have been invited to enter into transactional forgiveness and refuse, we are not following what the Scriptures teach. We have looked at this passage already, but now we are looking for how Jesus addresses two different categories. This category addresses a situation where a brother has something against us. Read the Word of the Lord in Matthew 5:23–24:

> So if you are offering your gift at the altar and there remember that your brother has something against you, leave your gift there before the altar and go. First be reconciled to your brother, and then come and offer your gift.

This next passage addresses the category where we have been offended by a brother. Read the Word of the Lord in Matthew 18:15:

> If your brother sins against you, go and tell him his fault, between you and him alone. If he listens to you, you have gained your brother.

In these passages, we see both sides of conflict. Either our brother has something against us (Matthew 5:23) or we have something against him (Matthew 18:15). Regardless of who sinned against whom, we must be reconciled one to another, particularly as we come to worship God in the giving of our gifts.

How do we accomplish reconciliation? When we approach God in formal worship or even in ordinary life, we need to begin the process of forgiveness leading to restoration. We may have thought that we were only obligated to seek reconciliation if we held something against others. Clearly that view is woefully incomplete. God tells us to examine ourselves before we offer ourselves. Our gift has no value if we are not reconciled. Therefore, ask God to check our hearts and make us bold to either tell our brother his sin or humble us to confess our own sin toward our brother.

We are to be initiators. The Bible says that, if it is at all possible, we are to be at peace with everyone. We initiate conversations in order to love God, love our neighbor, and love ourselves. This fulfills the Law and the Prophets. We are free to leave our gifts after we begin the process of reconciliation. How our brother responds to us is between him and God.

These passages challenge our desire for comfort above all else. We ignore the command to go and tell or be humble and confess because we do not want the intrusion in our life. We replace it with our own idea that nothing is more important than the gifts we give to God. While this idea sounds very spiritual, it is anemic and pitiful. In contrast, transactional forgiveness makes our hearts right and our gifts worthy.

What prevents us from pursuing transactional forgiveness in light of Jesus's commands? We must examine our self-talk. Self-talk provides the cover we need to ignore the discord between ourselves and our brother as we present our gifts. This cover may be controlled by our Two Influential Forces that lead to the CODE we speak. Speaking CODE puts us and our brother in situations where we both make assumptions because we only say a snippet of our thoughts. It is far wiser to start the process of going and telling or humbly confessing before we worship God.

Write about a time when someone told you he had something against you and you refused to be reconciled.

Write about a time when you told someone you had something against him and he refused to be reconciled.

Write out how Speaking CODE prevents you from addressing the offense your brother has against you.

Always remember, if transactional forgiveness is not possible, forgiving the person to God is always available. Take advantage of this life-giving forgiveness, as it lessens the effects of our Two Influential Forces, self-talk, and Speaking CODE.

STEP THREE: Sacrificial

Sacrifice is a word that we often confuse with acting like a doormat. Read the Word of the Lord from Proverbs 19:11:

> Good sense makes one slow to anger,
> and it is his glory to overlook an offense.

Read the Word of the Lord from Proverbs 12:16:

The vexation of a fool is known at once,
but the prudent ignores an insult.

God provides a righteous path forward in a broken relationship which enables us to choose not to be offended. We are free to act sacrificially and to give up our right of self-satisfaction. We can ignore insults from foolish people. This is a hallmark of the new commandment to love like Jesus loved us. Who receives the benefit of covering an offense? According to the proverb, the person who covers it!

Write out how you could use good sense to cover an offense.

What would you gain if you covered the offense?

Peter also addresses how we are to act sacrificially by allowing love to cover many offenses. Read the Word of the Lord from 1 Peter 4:8 (NLT):

Most important of all, continue to show deep love for each other,
for love covers a multitude of sins.

The entire chapter of 1 Peter 4 is worth reading so that we can get the context for this verse. Peter exhorts us to love deeply, because loving well makes it possible for us to remain in difficult relationships. The near context is about what happens as we approach the end of human history, where Jesus says in Matthew 24 that the love of most will grow cold. It is hard to imagine that the love of most Believers would grow cold. The larger context, in Peter, concerns suffering. Peter says showing deep love for one another is of utmost importance. That means loving deeply is more important than being told we are right. Sacrificing our sense of rightness allows us to cover the insults we hear from people who are absorbed in their own ideology.

Peter would know what a multitude of sins looked like based on his own experiences in life. All four Gospels record Peter's denial of Jesus after Peter proclaimed that he would never do such a thing! Peter took Jesus aside and rebuked Him when Jesus began to speak plainly about His upcoming death (Matthew 16:21–23). Peter's rebuke prompted Jesus to tell Satan to take his rightful place behind Jesus.

Describe what you have had to sacrifice because you chose to let love cover a multitude of sins from a difficult person in your life.

How has your sacrifice impacted the way you speak to that person?

Describe your feelings when you realized that your only choice was to let your love cover a multitude of sins, ignore the insult, or pass over the offense.

Are there ways in which you are that difficult person, and you will not enter a conversation that will lead to forgiveness? Write out how that other person acted sacrificially toward you.

This third step is difficult but should not be an excessive burden. If it is, the offense may rise to a level that it cannot be covered by love. Some offenses are serious and require transactional forgiveness. There is a difference between forgiving sacrificially or appeasing someone by allowing him to harm us or others. Should we sacrificially forgive him? Perhaps not, but how do we know the difference between the two?

It is hard to distinguish between sacrificial forgiveness based on loving like Jesus and sacrificial forgiveness based on appeasing out of fear. One way we could discern between the two is to examine our self-talk, which fuels the CODE we speak. In our self-talk, we may think of ways to appease the person who has harmed us. We may be afraid that we will lose something very dear to us. In that case, covering an offense may not be the righteous path to take. If our self-talk leads us to seek revenge, overlooking the offense is not godly. Our self-talk may cause anxiety from excessive or intrusive thoughts regarding the offense. If this is the case, sacrificial forgiveness is not the righteous path for us. The results of these types of self-talk will show up in the CODE we speak. If we edit what we think, then use words that appease the person, sacrificial forgiveness is not what we need to offer in this moment.

However, our self-talk may create empathy and understanding toward the person with whom we are involved. Covering or ignoring the offense may then be the path of righteousness upon which God has placed us.

What do we do when we want to sacrifice and bear with that person, but our self-talk will not stop replaying the offense in our head? Without having a meaningful conversation over this, it would be unwise for me to direct you either way. But we must look for what is true in this confusing situation and consider our reaction to the offense. If we replay the wrongdoing and have accusatory thoughts about the event, it may indicate that the other person's words were severe enough to lead us to Speak CODE. This could be a reason we are not ready to sacrificially forgive.

Perhaps our self-talk leads us to say true things in our hearts about our problematic situations. We feel mercy, empathy, and kindness toward the person with whom we are speaking. These internal thoughts are ways that we tell ourselves the truth about our circumstances. When we love God, others, and ourselves, we live out the truth of the Gospel. Preaching the gospel to ourselves, this way, is a form of soul-care. This may lead us to remain in the conversation as we sacrifice our own emotions to maintain the relationship.

Love is able to cover lesser offenses that fall more in the area of hurt feelings, accidental wounding, or perhaps thoughtless actions or words. It may be appropriate to talk to the person so that we can help them understand their thoughtlessness. To sacrificially cover the offense, our mind must be at rest over their words or deeds.

Write out what is true in your specific situation when it comes to sacrificially forgiving or forgiving based on appeasement. This could be as simple as saying that the offence was so severe it can be forgiven to God but not overlooked.

WHAT IS LEFT

Forgiveness is at the heart of the Gospel. Therefore, we need to forgive the other person to God, or our own sins will be unforgiven and our prayers unanswered. Thankfully, the heart of the Gospel is that God forgives our sins through the atoning work of Jesus Christ. Our ability to forgive is based on the truth that God forgave us. Therefore, we must be forgiving people. Never forget, Jesus tells us we must forgive from our heart. Thanks be to God, Jesus owns our heart, giving us His ability to forgive the seemingly unforgivable!

First, forgive that person to God; this is non-negotiable. Second, let us seek to enter a transaction of forgiveness with that person. Third, let us forgive sacrificially as we overlook, ignore, or cover the offenses of others when appropriate. These steps will move us closer to soul-satisfying conversations for our good and God's glory.

But what if these steps fail and our conversations remain soul-crushing? We still need relief from the burden that unforgiveness lays on our hearts. We still long for soul-satisfying conversations. We want to use the three steps to help get us there. But we are stuck. What do we have left?

If all else fails, we pray. We pray for the person without an agenda and confess our own sin of not knowing God well enough to trust Him. We pray for the person when none of the steps related to forgiveness seem to work. Pray that we will not give into retaliation by speaking hurtful words or settling into deadly silence. With the Lord's Prayer, we should pray that God's will would be done on Earth as it is in Heaven. Pray that God would help us see that He is specifically good to us. Believe me when I write this: we have nothing else but prayer to heal our broken conversations.

Write out your prayer for that specific person when all else fails. What is your role in this prayer?

ONE LAST REMINDER

Here is one last reminder when our hearts are in deep despair: do not seek revenge. Read the Word of the Lord in Deuteronomy 32:35–36:

> "Vengeance is mine, and recompense, for the time when their foot shall slip; for the day of their calamity is at hand, and their doom comes swiftly." For the Lord will vindicate his people and have compassion on his servants, when he sees that their power is gone and there is none remaining, bond or free.

One of the simplest but deadliest ways we seek revenge is through gossip. Read the Word of the Lord from Proverbs 17:9:

> Whoever covers an offense seeks love,
> but he who repeats a matter separates close friends.

I confess that this is hard; it is my struggle. Gossip separates us from each other, but confession, which leads to forgiveness, unites us as one. In the meantime, when we are desperate for truly redemptive conversations and are tempted to draw others to our side, do not seek revenge by gossiping. It is deadly. Do not gossip! Instead, let us forgive one another deeply and from the heart.

MOVING AWAY: NOT SEPARATING PAST FROM PRESENT

We have examined how we move away from each other by making assumptions rather than asking good questions and by not forgiving one another, deeply and from the heart. Let's look at the third relationship killer that also moves us away from each other: how our past and present link up to disrupt our communication.

ROSSI AND HIS PPIFST/PPIFEX

Rossi grew up in a family where nothing he did was good enough for his parents. He frequently heard statements like, "You got a B on your test? Why didn't you get an A? Didn't you study hard enough? Getting a B is fine, but I am sure you want to be the very best and get an A. Try a little harder next time. You will make us so proud of you and that will make you happy, too!"

Rossi wanted to be the best. In fact, Rossi knew his deficiencies all too well and felt that being known as a brainiac would mitigate the emotions he experienced when his failures in other areas surfaced. Receiving a B irritated Rossi because the B revealed that there was an area in his life where he wasn't perfect. Perfection was Rossi's ultimate goal, because perfection gave him control over how people viewed him. Therefore, the powerful statements made by his parents became both a challenge to his success and a confirmation that pursuing his goal would help him become perfect. His parents loved him and surely would only suggest what was good for him. They must be right, and Rossi certainly wanted to make them proud! Rossi set his heart on getting A's to please his wise parents and mitigate his own perceived deficiencies, which kept any feelings of inadequacy at bay.

Years later, Rossi and his business partner, John, were in a tense conversation after a business meeting went terribly wrong. John wondered out loud if they had prepared well enough to answer specific questions in that crucial meeting. When John expressed his concerns, Rossi experienced a familiar sense of inadequacy in the pit of his stomach, brought about by his desire to be perfect. Plus, he still sought to make his parents proud of him.

Rossi felt John attacked him for his lack of preparedness. Rossi wanted to dig a hole and crawl into it so that John could not see Rossi's embarrassment over his imperfections. The shame of inadequacy overwhelmed him. He could not control his flushing face or the numbness in his limbs. Rossi believed that all eyes were focused on his lack of preparedness. The sick feeling in the pit of his stomach almost led him to vomit. Rossi's inner thoughts began to race uncontrollably. His self-talk secretly condemned him as a failure and he assumed that everyone involved knew it. He began to write his inner script. He felt sure that he was about to lose his job. The chapter headings in Rossi's imaginary book included "Embracing Embarrassment," "Falling into Financial Ruin," "Second Rate Service," "Short Selling Your Home," and "What to Do When Your Family Abandons You." In Rossi's mind, his book was ready for publication.

For a brief moment, Rossi's deepest thoughts left his inner script and went back to his childhood days where the only way to satisfy his parents was to get A's. *You only got a B and not an A?* Rossi remembered how important it was to be successful in his parents' eyes. Their approval mitigated his perceived inadequacies, which seemed out of his control. He fought valiantly to dismiss the flashback, because he could not confront both his childhood memories and the prospect of losing the life he had worked so hard to build. Rossi felt physically paralyzed. But still his mind raced back and forth from one extreme thought to another. "How dare they doubt my abilities? But maybe I did not do my best, like Mom and Dad used to say. I am not good enough. Now everyone will see I am a screwup."

Maybe he was fully conscious of the reason for his shame cycle, or maybe not. In either case, Rossi felt a sense of hopelessness welling up deep within him. Rather than asking John a good question, Rossi exploded: "I can't believe you are accusing me of not being prepared! What did *you* do to prepare for the meeting?"

You see, Rossi's PPIFSt and PPIFEx defined his current situation, which condemned him for not achieving his standard of perfection. The possibility of being unprepared reminded him of a long-ago conversation in which his parents encouraged him not to settle for a B but to try harder to get that A. His parents' words and Rossi's own standards had been hidden in his heart. The combination of the real-life events plus his PPIFSt prevented Rossi from wise thinking. Rossi remembered past fears and shame. As a result of his self-talk, Rossi Spoke CODE and shared only a snippet of his thoughts. This combination, past and present, caused Rossi to make accusations that reflected his heart. Rossi's heart spoke louder than John's actual question. John hadn't blamed Rossi. John just wondered about their preparedness. Rossi heard John's remarks with ears tuned into what he had heard in the past.

The ensuing conversation confused both Rossi and John, but for different reasons. Rossi felt fearful when he realized he could not control the situation. John struggled to understand what he had said that caused Rossi to attack him. To be sure, John's own PPIFSt and PPIFEx may have guided him toward blame shifting. Sadly, neither Rossi nor John understood that God had them in intersecting holy sanctuaries, designed to make them both His own as they honored God as holy.

FUSING PAST TO PRESENT

We all fuse our past with our present. Some of us are aware of how our PPIFSt and PPIFEx affect us. Others have no clue how controlling these statements and experiences can be or how they lead us to Speak CODE. In either case, we are crushed by the painful conversations we have based on the power of our past statements and experiences. Without intervention, we live in a world of anxiety, hatred, walking on eggshells, hopelessness, control, and despair as we try to mend conversations that cannot be fixed. These conversations cannot be fixed unless we invest the time to know the back stories of both ourselves and the person with whom we are speaking.

Rossi and John's PPIFSt and PPIFEx informed their present circumstance which set off feelings of self-condemnation, self-aggrandizement, arrogance, defensiveness, abusiveness, isolation, control, and silence. These feelings were paralyzing to them and caused them both to Speak CODE disguised in a rant, filled with defensive and accusatory words. Finally, Rossi stormed out of the office, leaving John bewildered.

Rossi Spoke CODE and only told John a snippet of his self-talk. Had Rossi confessed that John's words reminded Rossi of past words his parents had said to him and exposed his need to control his failures, a more understanding conversation might have taken place. The power of the past fusing to the present resides in unspoken memories and experiences. If John knew from where Rossi's anxiety originated, John might have more easily defused the situation by answering the unspoken accusations that hid in Rossi's heart.

Here is where we can apply the idea of asking good questions in the moment, rather than making assumptions. Rossi could also have responded to John's confusion by asking John a good question. Had Rossi asked a good question, he may have moved closer to John by gaining a better understanding of John's statement. Instead, Rossi made an assumption which pushed them farther away. My Italian mother used to say, "In order to know a person, Diana, you must first eat a pound of dirt with him." In other words, get to know the person's PPIFSt/PPIFEx by asking good questions rather than making assumptions. There always is a compelling backstory, but it is dirtier than dirt!

One good question Rossi could have asked might go like this, "John, help me out here because I am confused. I felt attacked when you said that we may not have prepared as well as we could for this meeting. Are you blaming me? It sure feels like it. What did I miss?" John also had an opportunity to ask Rossi good questions even if Rossi was escalating.

Think of a crushing conversation in which you were involved. Describe how your PPIFSt and PPIFEx informed your conversation.

Write out the direct links between what the other person said and things you heard long ago.

What did your self-talk and CODE Speaking sound like?

Ezekiel 37 talks about dry dead bones into which God needs to breathe new life. What are your most important dry bones that need the breath of God to revive in present conversations?

Think back to the earlier chapter on assumptions. Which good question could you have asked in this conversation, instead of hearing with ears locked onto your past?

What do you get out of fusing your past with your present?

Rossi might have been correct—perhaps John *was* pointing his finger at Rossi's lack of preparedness. However, without asking good questions or confessing the whole of their self-talk, neither one would experience a soul-satisfying conversation over the outcome of the business meeting. Our PPIFSt and PPIFEx hide truth and cloud the meaning of our present conversations. But how do we separate our past from our present so that we can move toward each other?

THE PAINFUL BUT NECESSARY SEPARATION

If we are to communicate well with each other, we must separate what we heard in the past from what we hear in the present. Unfortunately, most of us cannot separate our past powerful statements and experiences from what we hear in real time because our memories have become a part of who we are. Powerful statements are hard to let go. Past experiences still hurt. Perhaps we have tried to separate the past from our present, but we have been unsuccessful. This separation requires humility. It requires honesty. It requires confrontation. It shakes up our status quo. It makes us question our own belief systems, including what role God played in our past. It might make us grieve the loss of something we love.

Unfortunately, we allow our Two Influential Forces, self-talk, and CODE Speaking to sabotage our communication because our past is very familiar to us. Our familiar is powerful, overtakes our inward narrative, and provides us with cover to justify our behavior. Dr. Ed Welch writes the following about our familiar:

> Bad consequences are not sufficient in themselves to change us, insight alone is not able to change us, the offer of heaven itself is not sufficient to change us. We instinctively regress to the familiar. Only the Spirit can revive our moribund souls.[18]

Dr. Welch speaks truth about the nature of our familiar . . . Only the Spirit can intervene.

List how your familiar affects your present conversations.

FIRST STEP: Recognition

If we are to separate our past from our present, we must take three necessary steps. First, we need to identify our PPIFSt and PPIFEx. Whatever our past powerful statements and experiences happen to be, if we do not recognize them and the power they have over us, they will sabotage our conversations, and those experiences will drive us away from ourselves and others. The effects are like a tsunami that sweeps everything out of its path. If we recognize how our past disrupts our present conversations, we despair that communications will ever be free from what happened to us in the past.

We are tempted to try anything to shut out past voices. We try to get into people's good graces, even if that means we capitulate to their horrid demands. As an alternative, we may bulldoze them into submission. We throw up our hands in despair and grieve that past statements/experiences will always find their way into our everyday lives. We lose hope that we will ever be truly known or valued. Worse, we feel confused as to how our past is affecting our present, and we do not know how to stop it.

We can also see the troubled legacy from our PPIFSt/PPIFEx in our harsh tones or shaming gestures. We might say the right words, but we may have a hidden agenda. Our harsh tones may be tantamount to a slap in the face, no matter which words we speak. Our carefully crafted words can be deceptive, especially if we only promote our side of the issue (which, of course, is always the correct side). When we do not recognize the hold our past has on us, we are usually unable to value the listener's side of the conversations. Knowingly or unknowingly, we will Speak CODE that makes it hard to experience soul-satisfying interactions.

In your conversations where you are tied to your past, what cues you that your PPIFSt/PPIFEx are surfacing in your present conversations?

◀ ... .--. . .- -.- .. -. --. -.-. --- -.. .

To shut out the voices from your past, which tactics do you use to control the conversation?

◀ ... .--. . .- -.- .. -. --. -.-. --- -.. .

Which words do you use to confront people about their tone/gestures? Which words do others use to confront you regarding your tone/gestures?

◀ ... .--. . .- -.- .. -. --. -.-. --- -.. .

It is our responsibility to recognize what motivates us to link our past to our present. This is a heart issue. What do we do? Read the Word of the Lord in Psalm 51:10:

> Create in me a clean heart, O God,
> and renew a right spirit within me.

What we treasure resides in our hearts. Our treasure may include holding onto our past because it is our familiar—it is all we know. But David points us to a path of righteousness where we beg God clean out the dirt from our past and renew a right spirit within us. Oh, that God would sanctify our past so that we can live well in the everyday moments of our lives. Only then can we recognize that our past need not interfere with our present.

THE SECOND STEP: Acknowledgement

We need to acknowledge that our PPIFSt and PPIFEx affect our ability to communicate with integrity. This is harder than it sounds because the statements made to us and the experiences we have had, make up who we are. We may feel lost without the comfort our past provides. By clinging to our familiar and succumbing to the power of our past, we avoid digging deep and taking responsibility for the chaos of our present life. Sad to say, well-meaning and good people often encourage us to follow secular proverbs that ignore the power our past has on us. To control the effects of our past, we say:

- "It's water under the bridge."
- "Why cry over spilled milk?"
- "What's done is done."
- "Sweep it under the rug."
- "Forget-about-it!"
- "You can't go back."
- "Let bygones be bygones."

While this advice may sound wise, following it may be what prevents us from soul-satisfying conversations. Sweeping unresolved issues under the rug will result in a pile so high that eventually we will trip over it. We will never be able to go back and undo our past. But we can begin to seek meaning and purpose in the pain brought to us from our past. Merely letting go of our PPIFSt and PPIFEx promotes poverty-stricken relationships filled with uncertainty that leads to soul-crushing conversations. Also, what is to say these statements and experiences will not surface again if we just let them go? Words and deeds always take us somewhere, which is why ignoring our past can be ruinous.

How have you employed secular proverbs when it comes to confronting your past?

When you find it too difficult to let go of past pain, how are your conversations affected?

It is important that we do not confuse the choice to forbear with letting go. As mentioned in earlier, forbearance is a means by which we can stay present in difficult relationships even as our past resurfaces. Our Two Influential Forces make it more difficult to forbear because our past screams loudly at us. Forbearance means we take no revenge while we let love cover the offense.

We simply cannot adhere to secular proverbs and believe that God is working out the details of our lives for His good pleasure. We are not created to let it go. We cannot accomplish this type of emotional brain or heart surgery because we are helpless to do so. That is why we must find God in our Two Influential Forces, self-talk, and CODE Speaking.

But God comes to us at just the right time. He enters our hearts and helps us acknowledge the hold our past has on our present. The Spirit encourages our hearts to be brave and courageous. Jesus takes our yoke in exchange for His.

Write about a time when God gave you insight into a memory that prevented you from entering a painful conversation. How did that insight help you?

THE THIRD STEP: Confession

We must separate our present conversations from the ghosts of our past. Our Two Influential Forces that lead to our self-talk which fuel the CODE we speak, will sabotage nearly every aspect of our present life. Once we acknowledge how we are tied to our past we can begin the process of exposing and loosening their hold on us.

We start with confession. We can confess to Jesus how we have allowed these powerful statements and experiences to dominate our lives. They move us away from ourselves and others. We may even confess that we secretly blame God for allowing these past circumstances that caused these memories in the first place. Blaming God always separates us from our humanness.

What do we confess? We confess that we have allowed the *power* of our past to have a *hold* on our hearts. What we need is the *power* of God to *hold* us tight. Notice, I did not say we need to confess our past powerful statements and experiences themselves—unless, of course, we were the perpetrators. Do you see the difference between the two? The *hold* our past has on our hearts is the culprit because it promotes Speaking CODE. In fact, this hold denies God's specific goodness to us. God always delights in hearing our confession.

Describe the hold your PPIFSt and PPIFEx have had on your ability to communicate redemptively.

Write a prayer of confession to God that states how you have allowed your PPIFSt/PPIFEx to have a powerful hold on you. Include how that hold kept you from knowing God well.

Never forget that our ECMs, PPIFSt, and PPIFEx are a means by which God brings us to Himself. Our past is unique to us because God uniquely knit us together in our mother's womb and directs our path until He calls us home. These powerful statements and experiences are necessary because without them our cries to Jesus would lack urgency, authenticity, and passion. Without our past, we would not see how desperately we need God's mercy and hope. We need to confess to Jesus that we do not see what He sees.

A sure way to keep our PPIFSt/PPIFEx from exerting power in our present conversations is to increase our understanding of Jesus, who gives purpose and meaning to our past, present, and future. Jesus is our High Priest who has never taken His eyes off us. His duties remain the same; He is not bound by space or time. That means every moment of our lives has dignity. Dig deep, and find meaning and purpose in Jesus. Later we will deal specifically with finding meaning and purpose in our suffering.

How can Jesus help you make sense out of your past?

ARABELLA'S EXPERIENCE AND *ANOMIE*

Please do not think these three steps neatly solve our problem with separating our past from our present. Read the following profound story to see how challenging it can be to untie the bonds that confine us.

Arabella had been molested multiple times in her life. Among other things, the PPIFSt and PPIFEx associated with these events prevent her from speaking fearlessly in the present because she cannot separate her past from her present. For Arabella, the abuse is always present with her. The abuse is the monster that haunts every corner. The abuse is the mistrust behind nearly every smile. The abuse is the image reflected to her when she looks into her mirror.

Her life has been sabotaged by the people responsible for the sexual abuse. Her body had been raped, but so had every aspect of her identity—her soul, senses, spirituality, confidence, and dreams. Who she was, right down to the words she uses in conversations, had been violated by her abusers. It left her with a crippling desire to control every aspect of her life. The joyous life lived in freedom gives way to the slavery that comes with managing her everyday existence. It is almost impossible for Arabella to separate her past from her present.

We can never fully understand how past sexual abuse forms and shapes our experiences unless we have lived through it. Even then, it is inexplicable. These PPIFSt and PPIFEx are deeply destructive to those who have suffered at the hands of an abuser. Words fail to fully describe these evils. Dr. Paul Tripp has addressed the inexpressible damage done by evil using the concept of *anomie* in an article entitled, "Living in Job's House". He writes:

> There is a Latin word that says it all. *Anomie.* This word captures those moments in life where you feel detached from meaning, detached from purpose, detached from your identity, detached from your values. Literally, if you translate this word, it means this: "There's no name for this."[19]

The suffering imposed by sexual abuse is profound in its effect. As a result of such anomie, Arabella's communication is not soul-satisfying or authentic. She either carefully crafts her words for safety or spews them out angrily like shrapnel. Arabella's words can damage others just as she was damaged by her abuser. In addition to the trauma already suffered from the abuse, survivors travel a dark downward pathway in order to grab hold of some control. This dark path normally is filled with self-abuse. Job's House has many dark rooms where suffering reoccurs.

Anomie is not, however, just for those who have suffered sexual trauma, although they experience it most profoundly. It can describe the feelings of any of us who have endured PPIFSt/PPIFEx that seek to disrupt and take ownership of our lives, including how we talk to each other. Our self-talk deafens us and causes us to Speak CODE that obscures who we are.

If you are able, write about your anomie and what you would like to do with these experiences.

◀ ... .— —. . .— —.— .. —. — —. —.—. — — — —.. .

In summary, we are most comfortable living in the familiar. We need to accept that our past has a strong hold on our present conversations. Therefore, we need to recognize, acknowledge, and confess how this hold can move us away from ourselves and others. Let us ask God to renew our hearts so that we can separate our past from our present for His glory and our good.

MOVING AWAY: IDENTITY IN ANYTHING EXCEPT CHRIST

The fourth way we sabotage communication is by not having our identity in Christ alone. When we rely on anything to give our lives meaning and purpose, we move away from ourselves, contributing to soul-crushing communication. I define moving away from ourselves as a process whereby we tightly grasp created things, tangible or intangible, making it harder to hear the desperate cries of our hearts. This definition also equates created things with idols, since we substitute both for God. Somewhere in this process we lose sight of Jesus, in whom our true identity rests. We build ritualistic worship systems around created things that we believe will protect and defend our ever-wandering hearts.

Grasping created things or idols fits into the world's narrative that says we are free to find our identity in whatever gives our lives meaning and purpose. These things fool us into thinking we are acceptable to ourselves, others, and God. Created things can be good, such as when we are motivated by God to participate in acts of service that He has given us to do. But acts of service are not always noble and good. Our motivations could be selfish, intended to cause others to admire us, praise us, or promote us. Such works have an appearance of goodness but are focused on ourselves rather than God.

To identify the idols we grasp, we must begin the process of naming those fears which cause us to seek created things in the first place. Identifying with created things often leads us to feel acceptable, powerful, or worthy. The idols we worship quiet our fears.

List those created things you grasp that help you placate or appease your fears.

SHADOWS AND CHEATS

Created things become shadows and cheats when we use them to give meaning and purpose to our existence. They loom large and cast shadows over God's work in our lives. Created things cheat us out of finding our identity hidden in Jesus alone. By nature, created things are insufficient—they cannot define us. They are merely subjects in God's kingdom that the Creator of Heaven and Earth uses to bring Him glory as He works for our good.

What are those created things with which we self-identify? A complete list would be endless. But know this: we move away from ourselves when we grasp anything that keeps us from our true identity hidden in Jesus, for "in Him we live and move and have our being" (Acts 17:28). When created things become our identity, our conversations are at risk, especially if our created thing conflicts with someone else's.

Below is a partial list of created things we may grasp to give our lives meaning, purpose, and identity:

- Gender
- Race/Skin Color
- Family
- Titles
- Poverty
- Talents
- Position
- Class
- Sexual, Physical, or Emotional Suffering
- Property
- Belongings
- Intellect
- Deficiencies
- Vocation
- National Heritage
- Appearance
- Shared Interests
- Money/Resources
- Fame
- Notoriety

We can take any one of these categories and use them to define how we self-identify. These categories influence how we think and speak about God, others, and ourselves.

SELF-IDENTITY, COMMUNICATION, AND JONAH

The biblical narratives provide deeper understanding of how we grasp created things use them to supplant God in our lives. Let's consider the life of Jonah and the conversations he had with God and his shipmates. His life will help us see how self-identification moves us away from ourselves and God, affecting our thoughts, words, and deeds.

The Lure of Created Things

The Word of the Lord came to Jonah, telling him to go to the great city of Nineveh and preach against its wickedness. Jonah's actions suggest that he identified with something more compelling than God's direct command. Perhaps his hatred of a nation that dominated his homeland spoke louder than his duty as a prophet of God. Whatever the reason, Jonah refused to obey God's authority and booked passage to Tarshish. In doing so, he revealed those created things which formed and shaped his identity. Jonah moved away from himself the moment he elevated his heart's desires above God's directives. We see how Jonah's disobedience communicated his heart's intentions.

> Write out how your desires overrule your call to obedience. In other words, what created thing or idol keeps you from obeying God?

But God was about to astonish Jonah. Read the Word of the Lord in Jonah 1:1–3:

> Now the word of the Lord came to Jonah the son of Amittai, saying, "Arise, go to Nineveh, that great city, and call out against it, for their evil has come up before me." But Jonah rose to flee to Tarshish from the presence of the Lord. He went down to Joppa and found a ship going to Tarshish. So he paid the fare and went down into it, to go with them to Tarshish, away from the presence of the Lord.

When we, like Jonah, self-identify with created things we lose our good sense. Jonah deluded himself into thinking that he could run away from the presence of the Lord. But David had already pointed out the folly of such a thought. Read the Word of the Lord in Psalm 139:7–10:

> Where shall I go from your Spirit?
> Or where shall I flee from your presence?
> If I ascend to heaven, you are there!
> If I make my bed in Sheol, you are there!
> If I take the wings of the morning
> and dwell in the uttermost parts of the sea,
> even there your hand shall lead me,
> and your right hand shall hold me.

We cannot flee from God's presence, no matter which idols we chase. Our idols will only complicate our lives and make our conversations inauthentic. The closer we get to our idols the farther we move away from ourselves and God.

Which created things do you grasp to enable you to flee from the presence of God?

God at His Best

When we begin to think that those things by which we self-identify frustrate God's plan for us, we should remember Jonah. This is where we see God at His best. God uses the very vehicle by which Jonah planned his escape, the sea, to catch him. Read the Word of the Lord in Jonah 1:4–6:

> But the Lord hurled a great wind upon the sea, and there was a mighty tempest on the sea, so that the ship threatened to break up. Then the mariners were afraid, and each cried out to his god. And they hurled the cargo that was in the ship into the sea to lighten it for them. But Jonah had gone down into the inner part of the ship and had lain down and was fast asleep. So the captain came and said to him, "What do you mean, you sleeper? Arise, call out to your god! Perhaps the god will give a thought to us, that we may not perish."

Do not be surprised if God uses the very thing by which we self-identify to catch us. God emphatically states He will have no other gods before Him. Created things are idols even if they seem good, noble, or righteous. Be warned. It is risky business to move away from ourselves by grasping created things. God pursues us unrelentingly and will use those very things with which we self-identify to catch us

Tell about a time when God drew you back to Himself using the very thing you used to escape Him.

We have all witnessed people in our lives who made idols of created things. We have seen how God used these very idols to bring them to their knees before Him. Whether we worship our money, family, addictions, sufferings, health, or reputation, God often gives us enough rope to hang ourselves, which causes us to hate our idols.

When you are in a conversation, which words do you use to reflect the things you worship?

Jonah's Death Wish by Assisted Suicide

In the chaos, Jonah went below deck and fell asleep while his shipmates cried out to their gods, hurling their cargo overboard. We wonder if the prophet Jonah knew that when he went below deck to fall asleep, he could die when the ship broke apart. It was as if Jonah laid himself down in his own coffin. We may ask ourselves why Jonah seemed to welcome death. The biblical evidence suggests that Jonah had several suicidal ideations as seen in Jonah 1:12, 4:3, 4:8–9. If we, like Jonah, self-identify with created things and attach strong emotions to them, what we feel often separates us from our ability to reason. This is especially true when we experience overwhelming sorrow, suffering, and pain.

How do we avoid traveling this dark path? The answer is complex, because we are complex people. Maybe we will not choose suicide, but our hearts certainly cry out that we see no way of escape from our pit of despair. Maybe the despair of our Two Influential Forces causes us to grasp at created things that become our identity. Our self-talk may sound uncertain, fueling the CODE we speak. We can become lost in this process, causing us to throw up our hands, pull the covers over our heads, and shelter in the safety of our cloistered world. Authentic conversations shut down because Speaking CODE hides the hopeless thoughts we entertain.

Write out how Speaking CODE hid the cry of your heart from those closest to you.

To find a way out of our despair, we must look for a starting point. We start by uncovering and naming those created things into which we have placed our identity. If we do not name them, our conversations will be inauthentic. As God hounds us, He will reveal those created things that moved us away from His heart and from ours as well. In response, we simply repent with thanksgiving as we call out to Jesus.

How have you prayed to God and asked Him to show you those created things that drive you from the heart of God and away from your reason?

What if our idols are never revealed and our path gets darker and darker until we are utterly hopeless? Will our pathway look like Jonah's? Perhaps. But rest assured, as we run from Jesus and identify with created things as Jonah did, God will pursue us all the way to the gates of hell itself.

Write out your self-talk that says everyone, including yourself, will be better off if you are not around.

How do your Two Influential Forces prompt you to identify with created things? For example, if you were abused sexually, physically, or emotionally, you may identify yourself by your abuse rather than identifying as a child of God who was abused.

Write out how identifying with created things makes it harder for you to engage in soul-satisfying conversations.

Our Raging Storm

As Jonah moved away from himself and his Creator, we wonder if he knew that he was putting others in great danger. Think of this. The path that leads us away from ourselves and God is never traveled alone. Willingly or unwillingly, the gods we choose to serve pull everyone into our ritualistic worship systems, just as Jonah's shipmates were pulled into his. Because of Jonah, the crewmen were forced to take a financial loss as they threw their cargo overboard. People drawn into our raging storm will suffer loss as well. Conversations around financial loss are filled with greed, ingratitude, squandered resources, dashed expectations, pointed fingers, and unmet obligations. All this because we, like Jonah, move away from ourselves when we grasp at created things to identify us rather than Jesus.

How have you put people in danger because you identified in created things? How has this affected your conversations?

We see the captain, risking his own life, calling Jonah to join the crew in battling the raging storm. We, too, have Captains in our lives that invest in us at their peril. They feel trapped when we drag them into the results of our idol worship. These Captains can be our parents, grandparents, relatives, friends, church leaders, or siblings. As with Jonah, our Captains hopelessly try to arouse us from our deep sleep as they question our choices. They may call us out of our lethargy and demand we man up. Our Captains may even ask us to help in the chaos we have created just as the Captain and crewmen asked Jonah to help fight against the raging storm. Jonah teaches us that as we move away from ourselves by grasping at created things, we pull others into our turmoil.

Who are your Captains, and which words have they used to point you toward solutions that would have enabled you to rid yourself of the idols you served?

Captains and Conversations

Conversations with our Captains can be quite brutal. They may be characterized by assumptions, name-calling, accusations, demands, selfish motives, gossip, denial, and denigration. In fact, our Captains' idols may surface, adding another layer to our painful conversations. We can almost hear our believing mother scream at our rebellion, "What have I done that this is happening to us? You are breaking this family apart because of your behavior. You better pray to God because only He can help you." She does this knowing that her idol of a Norman Rockwell family is going up in smoke! And still, in the fury, we cling white-knuckle-tight to those created things that move us away from ourselves and God.

Our Crowded Path

We are never alone on our path of darkness even though we believe that we alone carry the burden of our chosen idol. We demand that those who love us accept how we self-identify, regardless of their thoughts and concerns. Our idols are so firmly entrenched that subsequent interactions with our Captains endanger our conversations and taint our relationships. Our Captains may take matters into their own hands. Unwittingly, they may seek answers to the wrong questions, offering damaging solutions.

In the process, our Captains' own lives are dismantled just like the crew members dismantled their ship to save everyone on board. Our Captains press in hard in a desperate attempt to formulate a rescue plan. As we draw people into our ritualistic idol worship, our conversations will not sound righteous because only we are privy to our secret words said to appease our idols. We resort to Speaking CODE fueled by our self-talk, making conversations soul-crushing.

Write about a conversation between you and your Captain where neither of you felt heard or understood because of the underlying idols that have captured your heart.

Self-Identity and Rational Thinking

Pause here and ask if Jonah's behavior was rational. Jonah was a prophet of God whose duty was to proclaim God's word as God directed. A rational prophet would do the work of a prophet. Jonah acted irrationally when he chased after whatever created thing took him away from God and his own humanity. Grasping at created things is irrational.

As God's children, it is our duty to obey His commands. Like Jonah, when we disobey God's commands and seek after created things, we act irrationally. God commands us to love Him, others, and ourselves. We act irrationally when we do otherwise. We would be wise to look at the outcome of Jonah's irrational decisions and apply it to our own choices regarding how we self-identify. This lesson will help us see how we move away from ourselves when we find our identity in anything except Christ alone.

> Explain ways that your decision to self-identify in your chosen idols is irrational.

Collateral Damage

Our devotion to created things, whether physical or conceptual, moves us away from ourselves and God. The resulting folly from our idol worship creates a vortex which draws others into our chaos, disrupting everyone's daily lives. They become collateral damage. Read the Word of the Lord in Jonah 1:7:

> And they said to one another, "Come, let us cast lots, that we may know on whose account this evil has come upon us." So they cast lots, and the lot fell on Jonah.

When was the last time our family members had to cast lots to see who would take care of us when we were actively participating in ritualistic worship of our idols? Perhaps our idol was drugs or alcohol, and someone had to put their life on hold because our addiction was out of control. Perhaps our idol was gambling, overspending, overworking, overeating, or any indulging behaviors that had consequences either visible or invisible.

Our Captains had to make the agonizing decision to cut ties with us because of the behavior stemming from the created things we served. Maybe we implored a friend or family member to fetch our drugs or alcohol to temporarily stop our cravings. Maybe we pressured family members to support causes with which they disagreed. In pursuit of idols that move us away from ourselves and God, we forget that those around us are humans made in God's image. Idols make us unaware of others, because they tempt us to focus mainly on ourselves.

Jonah's shipmates were collateral damage. They were exhausted, confused and exasperated. The storm in which these men found themselves seemed like no other. Perhaps, when our loved ones are caught in our fierce storm, they experience what Jonah's shipmates did. Additionally, these men were forced to casts lots to uncover who had brought this evil upon them. Imagine the guilt these men must have felt when they threw him into the raging sea.

But, like Jonah, we do not care who gets damaged when people must draw straws to see who will intervene in our ritualistic idol worship. The impact of our behavior terrifies those who are forced to be around us. Family and friends must make choices that are heartbreaking. They often feel as though there is no escape except by enacting dire measures. They may be forced to cast lots, but the answer always belongs to God. Read the Word of the Lord in Jonah 1:8–10:

> Then they said to him, "Tell us on whose account this evil has come upon us. What is your occupation? And where do you come from? What is your country? And of what people are you?" And he said to them, "I am a Hebrew, and I fear the Lord, the God of heaven, who made the sea and the dry land." Then the men were exceedingly afraid and said to him, "What is this that you have done!" For the men knew that he was fleeing from the presence of the Lord, because he had told them.

Facing Idols, Facing Truth

Eventually, we will be confronted with the consequences of serving our idols. We may feel abandoned as our Captains pursue other means to survive in the storm. We may feel guilt or shame when we see the carnage around us. We may feel completely justified because, after all, it is our life anyway. Or we may be delusional as we blame our Captains for our own choices without a single fact to prove our case. Worse, we blame God or deny that He is specifically good to us, as we move away from our own humanity in pursuit of created things. Jonah had no choice but to face God's truth when he admitted he ran from the presence of the Lord. We, too, will face God's truth either in this life or the next. What we do with that truth will make all the difference.

When others force you to confront your idols, how do you react?

How does grasping at created things affect your conversations in necessary relationships?

When Jonah faced his idol, he admitted he was a God-fearing Hebrew, fleeing from God's presence. Jonah acknowledged that he ran away from God. That gives us hope that we may eventually acknowledge our idols which affect our conversations. Initially we may resist this, and our speech may be characterized by angry rants and ugly accusations because our idols are pitiless and unyielding. But there is hope we can repent from our idol worship and begin having redemptive conversations. Be warned: even as Jonah acknowledged that God caught him and confronted his idol, he still challenged God's guidance—and so may we.

Once we acknowledge the existence of our idols, we now face new questions. There is more at stake than merely identifying our idol of choice. We must uncover the heart issues that led us to choose our idols in the first place. If we do not deal with heart issues, our life becomes an endless carnival game of whack-a-mole. We smack that pesky mole when it pops out of its hole only to see it reappear in a different location. Our idols are like that. If we do not get to the underlying issues that cause our idol worship, we may whack one idol out of our heart only to find a similar idol pop up somewhere else in our lives.

List the underlying heart issues that set you up to serve your idol.

How have you observed the replacement of one idol with another?

Conversations that get at truth can be some of the most painful discussions into which we will ever enter. As we press into the discussion, the process is challenging. We state our thoughts, and then reframe what we stated. Next, we retell what we reframed and get exasperated over the unwelcome questions about our original statement. All this is necessary, because it leads us to ask good questions and to form fewer assumptions. A peace treaty, albeit tenuous, could cautiously be on the table.

Captured

What happens when God captures us? We see accountability, truth-telling, grace in action, and a tremendous price to be paid. Read the Word of the Lord in Jonah 1:11–12:

> Then they said to him, "What shall we do to you, that the sea may quiet down for us?" For the sea grew more and more tempestuous. He said to them, "Pick me up and hurl me into the sea; then the sea will quiet down for you, for I know it is because of me that this great tempest has come upon you."

When our idol worship swirls into a tempest, as it did for Jonah and his shipmates, finding a solution will always come at a great price. God often gives us no choice but to obey and give the idol worshiper over to Him. Jonah's solution was to be picked up and hurled into the sea. For us caught up in the worship of created things, others may need to throw us into our raging sea. In essence, our Captains and crewmen are giving us over to God, hoping we will find our true identity.

Everyone shares emotions like those who were onboard that ship to Tarshish. Captains and crewmen, mothers and fathers, siblings and friends feel a sickening remorse as they contemplate the thought of abandoning us by giving us over to our idols! Such an idea appears senseless, but it does reflect reality when we move away from ourselves and God by grasping created things rather than the Creator. Read the Word of the Lord in Jonah 1:13–16:

> Nevertheless, the men rowed hard to get back to dry land, but they could not, for the sea grew more and more tempestuous against them. Therefore they called out to the Lord, "O Lord, let us not perish for this man's life, and lay not on us innocent blood, for you, O Lord, have done as it pleased you." So they picked up Jonah and hurled him into the sea, and the sea ceased from its raging. Then the men feared the Lord exceedingly, and they offered a sacrifice to the Lord and made vows.

When we grasp created things as a form of self-identity, we face unintended consequences. Those who love us will row as hard as they can to figure out a way to help us disavow our idols and survive. Our Captains may cry out to God for absolution as they let us live out the natural consequences of our idol worship. We might fight against it, but in the end, God will always be feared and glorified, both in this life and the next. Our Captains may make appropriate sacrifices and vows to the Lord. Those vows may include sacrificing our relationship as they separate themselves from us, entrusting us into

God's capable hands. In fact, those watching our descent into idol worship may find themselves turning toward God in repentance and acceptance. As for our vows, the more we move away from ourselves and tighten our hold on our idols, the harder it will be to offer true sacrifices to God.

What would you need to do to leave your idols and come back to your senses?

If you are a Captain (authority figure) or a Helper (a counselor), how can the account of Jonah help you interact with your loved one who moved away from himself and God, sabotaging his relationships as seen in soul-crushing conversations?

Jonah in Free Fall

We also see how God, that Great Hound of Heaven, redeemed Jonah as he was in free fall. Read the Word of the Lord in Jonah 2:1–2, 7–9:

> Then Jonah prayed to the Lord his God from the belly of the fish, saying . . . "When my life was fainting away, I remembered the Lord, and my prayer came to you, into your holy temple. Those who pay regard to vain idols forsake their hope of steadfast love. But I with the voice of thanksgiving will sacrifice to you; what I have vowed I will pay. Salvation belongs to the Lord!" And the Lord spoke to the fish, and it vomited Jonah out upon the dry land.

Jonah realized he was losing his life as he sunk deeper into the sea. He prayed. He recognized that his identity as an opponent of Nineveh ended all hope for God's steadfast love and grace. In the belly of that great fish, Jonah became thankful and sacrificed his own self-identity to fulfill the vow he made to God. Finally, in that murky sea, where Jonah cried out to the Lord, he saw that his identity was rooted in the salvation that came only from the Lord. What a moment of clarity! Unfortunately, this confession was not the end of Jonah's narrative.

Have you experienced a belly-of-a-fish story where God showed you your idol and brought you back to Him? Explain.

A FAILED LESSON LEARNED

God is a God of many chances. So God called Jonah a second time to go to Nineveh. This time, Jonah set aside his idolatry and obeyed God. Jonah prophesied that Nineveh would be overthrown in forty days if they did not repent. God used Jonah's words to bring conviction on the people. Jonah's words reached the King. The king published a proclamation calling on all his subjects to repent by fasting, wearing sackcloth, and sitting in ashes. Perhaps, the king hoped, God would relent and turn away His fierce anger. The king was right. God had compassion on the Ninevites, relented of the threatened disaster, and spared them (Jonah 3:1–10).

Suicidal Ideations Revisited

Earlier we read how Jonah flirted with what Prince Hamlet called "that sleep of death,"[20] as Jonah descended into the inner parts of the ship. Several times Jonah asked God to take his life because Jonah believed death was better than life. Listen to how Jonah invited the Almighty into a conversation after Nineveh repented. Do we hear ourselves in this conversation? Read the Word of the Lord in Jonah 4:1–3:

> But it displeased Jonah exceedingly, and he was angry. And he prayed to the Lord and said, "O Lord, is not this what I said when I was yet in my country? That is why I made haste to flee to Tarshish; for I knew that you are a gracious God and merciful, slow to anger and abounding in steadfast love, and relenting from disaster. Therefore now, O Lord, please take my life from me, for it is better for me to die than to live." But the Lord replied, "Do you do well to be angry?"

Rather than inexpressible joy at the salvation of many Ninevites, Jonah expressed anger and frustration with God. Jonah believed he had to flee from God's presence because he knew that God was gracious, compassionate, slow to anger, abounding in love, and that He hated to bring calamity upon His creation. Jonah justified his disobedience by pointing out God's attributes of mercy and grace. Jonah wanted no part in bringing Nineveh to repentance. His old identity resurfaced. Can we see ourselves in Jonah's position if a gracious outcome in a terrible situation surprises us?

Jonah's anger over the Ninevites' repentance shows us why idols are dangerous. Grasping at created things moves us away from God even as we acknowledge His glorious character. We then use our blindness to point our finger at God and blame Him for the wreck we have made of our lives. Worse still, we may reimagine God, making Him into our idea of what we want Him to be. Our imagined god comes with all the benefits of satisfying our most longed for desires.

The created things we grasp have such a hold on us that they will resurface throughout our lives. This was true for Jonah and it is equally true for us as well. The way Jonah viewed himself caused him to be so angry that he desired a whole city of human image bearers be destroyed. God caught Jonah again. But this time God used Jonah's very own emotional state of anger to do so. Read the Word of the Lord in Jonah 4:4:

> And the Lord said, "Do you do well to be angry?"

Jonah was angry even as he recited a blessed list of God's attributes. We cannot hide our emotional state from God. Do not even try. Look at Cain: Cain became so angry, because his offering was not acceptable to the Lord as his brother's had been, that he killed his brother Abel. God confronted Cain's anger. Read the Word of the Lord in Genesis 4:6–7:

> The Lord said to Cain, "Why are you angry, and why has your face fallen? If you do well, will you not be accepted? And if you do not do well, sin is crouching at the door. Its desire is contrary to you, but you must rule over it."

In what ways do you try to hide your true emotions from God and why?

◀ ... .– –. . .– –.– .. –. – –. –.–. – – – –.. .

Jonah went out of the city and found an eastern location where he made a shade booth. He sat under its shade to see what would happen to Nineveh. The shade booth Jonah built was not adequate for the job. God appointed a plant to grow up over Jonah that provided sufficient shade to comfort him. In the worst of our idol worship and running from God, God is always at His best, even if we think He is not! Read the Word of the Lord in Jonah 4:7–8:

> So Jonah was exceedingly glad because of the plant. But when dawn came up the next day, God appointed a worm that attacked the plant, so that it withered. When the sun rose, God appointed a scorching east wind, and the sun beat down on the head of Jonah so that he was faint." And he asked that he might die and said, "It is better for me to die than to live."

Let's look at what God does to Jonah in this passage. Underline the sentences that show how God's actions seem harsh and lacking goodness. We must remember that our definition of goodness is not like God's. God's goodness is life-sustaining and always works for our specific good just as that plant, worm, scorching east wind, and blazing hot sun was for Jonah's good.

But God does for man what man cannot do for himself. In His goodness, God appointed a lowly plant to protect Jonah. Jonah drew comfort from the plant, which in and of itself was not wrong. It appears Jonah believed the plant would provide daily shade, and he expected God would not take away his source of comfort.

Once again, Jonah grasped at a created thing (comfort) rather than the Creator. None of us would welcome the exhausting effects of a scorching east wind or a blazing sun beating down on us without the benefit of shade. In this way, we can be kindred spirits with Jonah. But what if Jonah's and our adversities were designed for good? Perhaps we, like Jonah, must learn that when our desires are thwarted, our anger comes out in our conversations and behaviors. We question God's intentions; we may freely share our doubts with others or secretly complain in our hearts. The consequences of ignoring or refusing to accept what God gives us are much worse than any discomfort we experience. God gives us difficult circumstances that are hard for us to accept, but they are for our good.

When we ponder our sad lives, it is hard to see that God is good. Perhaps we become angry when the only comfort we experienced is taken away from us. However, what brings us comfort may not necessarily be good for us. In that case, we must find our identity in God rather than the created things we grasp.

Jonah invested his identity in a plant that made him glad, as well as his prized hostility toward Nineveh. God used the worm to take away Jonah's comfort, forcing him to see that he pitied a plant more than thousands of image-bearing humans. Jonah's heart led to attitudes and behaviors that were rebellious, apathetic, uncaring, selfish, reckless, stubborn, self-absorbed, ungrateful, angry, and unafraid to contend with God.

A Good Question Answered

Read the Word of the Lord in Jonah 4:9:

> But God said to Jonah, "Do you do well to be angry for the plant?" And he said, "Yes, I do well to be angry, angry enough to die."

God comes to us with good questions. He asks not because He needs clarity but because we need to hear the silly things we say to ourselves. God wanted to know how Jonah reacted to the destruction of the plant. We may ask, what is it about this plant's life cycle that made Jonah angry enough to want to die? He went from being exceedingly glad to bitterly angry.

Jonah's reply showed a lack of intellectual commitment: "Yes, I do well to be angry, angry enough to die." We can almost hear Dr. Phil, the popular television psychologist, say, "Hey Jonah, how's that anger working out for you?" When the idols Jonah served failed to satisfy or save him, Jonah's ritualistic idol worship allowed him to experience anger unto death. All he had left was anger strong enough to overshadow the gift of life.

> Imagine that the plant represents an idol you grasped that took you away from yourself and God. Write out what happened when that idol was taken away and could no longer satisfy you. How did your conversation make you angry to the point of death?

Did Jonah really care about the plant? Perhaps, or perhaps not. But we do know he absolutely cared about the comfort the plant provided. It is similar to how we feel when our drug of choice satisfies our anguish. Idolatry takes root when we self-soothe our pain by serving that illusory alternative to reality. Before long, our identity fuses with the created things we grasp. Sometimes God puts us in holy sanctuaries that we would have avoided except for the devotion to the idols we serve. He does this for our good even though it is hard for us to see His purpose. We cannot see that what we think needs to be soothed in our broken hearts is actually God making us His own in our holy sanctuaries. Unfortunately, sin blinds us to God's work in our lives. Like Jonah, we do not do well when we console ourselves with created things rather than clinging to God, who is our Consolation.

God Meets Us

But God pointed out Jonah's misplaced identity. Read the Word of the Lord in Jonah 4:10–11:

> And the Lord said, "You pity the plant, for which you did not labor, nor did you make it grow, which came into being in a night and perished in a night. And should not I pity Nineveh, that great city, in which there are more than 120,000 persons who do not know their right hand from their left, and also much cattle?"

Let's explore how God loved Jonah in the specifics of his life. God could have given Jonah no explanation of why He acted as He did and left Jonah to wallow in his intense anger. Instead, God communicated with Jonah and met him where he was. God pointed out to Jonah that he emotionally involved himself in a plant he did not sow, tend, or control. Removing the plant frustrated Jonah's expectations and led him to become angry unto death. Idols are like that. If our idols fail to meet our expectations, our ritualistic worship becomes utterly pointless. Rather than abandoning our idols, we try even harder to appease them, just as Jonah did. When we appease our idols during difficult conversations, the words we speak will not esteem the listener.

Also, God demonstrates His love for Jonah by pointing out the difference between Jonah worshiping God and Jonah worshiping his idol. He does this by making a comparison between Jonah pitying a lowly plant to his lack of pity for an entire nation. It is for us to see how our idols expand what is grand in our eyes but is minuscule compared to God's grandeur. In fact, what we idolize is infinitesimal when compared to God Almighty.

Unlike Jonah, we must root our identity in God and trust that He will sustain us as we do the work He has called us to do. Instead of moving away from ourselves by searching for something with which we can self-identify, we affirm that we are children of God whose identity is hidden in Christ. With this hidden identity, we live as people of God who identify in Jesus and not in the created things we grasp.

In all the ways we relate to others—whether as spouses, parents, grandparents, siblings, relatives, friends, employees, employers, sinners, saints, sufferers, citizens, rich, poor, male, female, gay, straight, transgender, or by our skin color, nationality, political affiliation, or religious affiliation—our identity is in Christ. We identify as people in one human race, all to the glory of God.

In the End

The book of Jonah ends abruptly, leaving us to draw some conclusions as we tie up loose ends. On this side of eternity, we will never know if Jonah ultimately rooted his identity in God rather than in created things. We will never know how the people of Nineveh lived differently after they repented from their great evil.

In our struggle to find identity in the created objects we grasp, let us trust that God will use these very things to draw us back to Him and show us how desperately we need Him. In rooting out our idols, God shows us that there is meaning and purpose as we struggle through the pain idols cause. This struggle is our path of righteousness that brings us closer to God. Just as it was for Jonah, God has 120,000 people, plus cattle, that need our attention. Our conversations will reflect where we find our identity. The idols we serve lead to soul-crushing words, while our identity in Christ leads to more soul-satisfying speech.

What can we learn from Jonah?

- We learn that it is disastrous when we move away from ourselves and God by identifying with anything other than Jesus.
- We learn that our idols' voice can speak louder than God's voice.
- We learn that God will use any means to dislodge our grasp on created things.
- We learn that in the end, our identity outside of Christ could lead to suicidal thoughts or behaviors.
- We learn that how we self-identify is often deeply rooted in created things rather than in the Creator Himself.
- We learn that God is gracious, compassionate, slow to anger, abounding in love, and hates to bring calamity upon His creation.

- We learn that we get angry when what we grasp does not fulfill our expectations.
- We learn that God is concerned about 120,000 people who do not know their right hand from their left, He is concerned about their cattle, and He is concerned about us.
- We learn that God has work for us to do.
- We learn that fifth century BC Nineveh had the same needs as twenty-first century Earth.

We read how disastrous it was for Jonah to identify with created things. Jonah struggled as he moved away from God and foolishly ran after idols that he hoped would satisfy him. His conversations were selfish and showed little regard for lost people or God's commands. Jonah's true identity was based in his comfort and the hostility he felt.

ABIDE

Now, we will look at John 15 to find our path of righteousness that moves us ever closer to our Savior as we *abide, believe,* and *commune* with Him. Understanding these concepts helps us shift our paradigm when our Two Influential Forces, self-talk, and CODE Speaking interfere with our ability to enjoy soul-satisfying communication.

John 15 is part of Jesus's final discourse before His crucifixion. We would be wise to read John 13–18 to understand the context in which Jesus discusses abiding. As you read these chapters take special note of our three themes that help us with true identification: abide, believe, and commune. Let's begin by considering what it means to abide.

Unlike Jonah, where we read several conversations with God, John 15 is an uninterrupted monologue where Jesus introduces a Gardening Analogy that describes the functions and benefits of each participant. We are looking to see how this analogy points us to our true identity as we abide, believe, and commune with Jesus. Ultimately, the fruit of this relationship will be reflected in every area of our lives: past, present, and future. The fruit of our relationships will affect our conversations.

The Gardening Analogy

Read the Word of the Lord in John 15:1–3, 26:

> I am the true vine, and my Father is the vinedresser. Every branch in me that does not bear fruit he takes away, and every branch that does bear fruit he prunes, that it may bear more fruit. Already you are clean because of the word that I have spoken to you. . . . But

> when the Helper comes, whom I will send to you from the Father, the Spirit of truth, who proceeds from the Father, he will bear witness about me.

The Players

In the Gardening Analogy, Jesus identifies the participants, which allows us to move toward true identity in Christ.

- Jesus identifies Himself as the True Vine. He is the giver and sustainer of life. The True Vine is the Connector between the Vinedresser and the Branches.
- Jesus identifies God as the Vinedresser. The Vinedresser takes away every Branch on the True Vine that does not bear fruit and prunes those Branches that already produce fruit. The pruning process allows these connected Branches to produce fruit in a greater abundance.
- Jesus identifies Branches as humans who are connected to and live under the authority of the True Vine and Vinedresser. Branches are designed to be fruit bearers under the watchful eye of the Vinedresser. Branches are made clean by the spoken word of the True Vine.
- Jesus identifies the Helper as the Holy Spirit that He sends to the Branches. The Helper is the Spirit of Truth who proceeds from the Vinedresser and will bear witness to the True Vine.

Now that we understand the participants in the Gardening Analogy, we can see how Jesus has the authority to call us into a deeply connected and identifying relationship with Him, the Vinedresser, and the Helper. Read the Word of the Lord in John 15:4–6:

> Abide in me, and I in you. As the branch cannot bear fruit by itself, unless it abides in the vine, neither can you, unless you abide in me. I am the vine; you are the branches. Whoever abides in me and I in him, he it is that bears much fruit, for apart from me you can do nothing. If anyone does not abide in me he is thrown away like a branch and withers; and the branches are gathered, thrown into the fire, and burned.

In the eighty-seven words of these two verses, Jesus uses *abide* five times. The frequent use of abide makes this word crucial in understanding this text. Notice the three interrelated parts in Jesus's invitation.

- First, we are invited to abide in Jesus.
- Second, Jesus declares He will abide in us.
- Third, fruit production is the evidence proving the abiding relationship exists.

We cannot separate any three of these distinguishing parts in this abiding relationship. The decision to sever this relationship rests on the work of the True Vine and Vinedresser. The concept of fruit-bearing is also integral in this analogy.

As Jesus calls us into an abiding relationship, our identity is secure because of our communion with Him. Jesus abides in us and we in Him so that we will bear much fruit, proving we are His disciples. If we do not abide in Him, we will not produce fruit, because without Jesus we can do nothing. In fact, we will wither up and burn just like those Branches who produce no fruit. We Branches bring God glory, share in His love, and enjoy communion with the Vinedresser and the True Vine. Our identity is tied to keeping His commandments and producing an abundance of fruit. Our conversations are guided by our identity in the True Vine, not by our Two Influential Forces, self-talk, and Speaking CODE.

What does it mean to abide in Jesus and He in you?

How does abiding affect your true identity?

Consider how your conversations are part of the fruit you bear. How does abiding in Jesus affect the way you enter difficult conversations?

When your conversations were guided by your Two Influential Forces, self-talk, and CODE Speaking, rather than by the True Vine, how did the Vinedresser prune you?

Moving Toward Jesus and Bearing Fruit

We move toward Jesus when we abide in Him. As Jesus abides in us, He produces fruit that bears evidence we are His disciples. Fruit produced in this abiding, Christ-identifying relationship brings glory to God. The Vinedresser makes the fruit more abundant through the pruning process. Just as any pruning process strains the Branches, so does this process put a strain on us. Pruning is similar to the discipline seen in the book of Hebrews. Read the Word of the Lord in Hebrews 12:11–13:

> For the moment all discipline seems painful rather than pleasant, but later it yields the peaceful fruit of righteousness to those who have been trained by it.
>
> Therefore lift your drooping hands and strengthen your weak knees, and make straight paths for your feet, so that what is lame may not be put out of joint but rather be healed.

It makes sense that the Vinedresser prunes the Branches to yield the peaceful fruit of righteousness. We have discussed the theme of having our powers of discernment trained by constant practice to distinguish good from evil. Pruning is the vehicle by which the Vinedresser sets this practice into motion. Pruning seems painful at the time, but through it, God cultivates strength and endurance in us. He sets us on straight paths so that we may share in His holiness.

Many times, we feel the Vinedresser's pruning start in our hearts, move to our self-talk, and bear fruit in our conversations, where He replaces Speaking CODE with speaking truth in love.

How can your conversations bear the peaceful fruit of righteousness as you abide in Jesus?

It is almost incomprehensible that this abiding relationship makes our jars of clay into holy vessels. God in flesh abides in us and produces fruit that identifies us as His disciples. Even as we foolishly grasp for created things, Jesus abides in us. In our striving or stillness, we are His and He is ours. Our conversations need no longer be guided by our Two Influential Forces, self-talk, and Speaking CODE.

Write out how your powers of discernment are being trained by constant practice to distinguish good from evil.

"If" Statements of Christ

Jesus gives us a series of "If" statements in John 15 to help us abide when we are tempted to flee. Abiding is not a blind relationship, although sometimes it feels that way. Abiding is a faith relationship that, because of who Jesus is and the work He has done, can never be severed. We would be wise to remember that when we are dealing with frustrating conversations.

Jesus offers "If" statements to keep our identity steadfast in Him. Our self-talk convinces us that as the Vinedresser prunes us, we feel cut off from the True Vine. Pruning is painful, but it is not nearly as painful as when we feel alone, disconnected, or abandoned by Jesus. When we experience these emotions, our tendency is to move away from Jesus and seek our identity where we can control the outcome. "If" statements help us to abide when the pressures of life appear to be unmanageable. Let's look at Jesus's statements and see how they affect our Two Influential Forces, self-talk, and Speaking CODE:

- If anyone does not abide in me he is thrown away like a branch and withers; and the branches are gathered, thrown into the fire, and burned (John 15:6).
- If you abide in me, and my words abide in you, ask whatever you wish, and it will be done for you (John 15:7).

These "If" statements offered by Jesus are precious to us because our Two Influential Forces, self-talk, and CODE Speaking can make things muddy, especially in our conversations. No matter what has happened in our past, what is going on in our present, or what will happen in our future, Jesus abides in us and we in Him.

Additionally, look at the tiny phrase Jesus inserts, "and My words in you." Remember, it is Jesus's words that make us clean. The only way to know Jesus's words is to read the Bible. Knowing His words is integral to abiding. Therefore, read the Bible!

Considering the "If" statements above, tell about a time when you felt cut off from the True Vine when it was actually God pruning you.

How do you understand God giving you whatever you wish? Does that mean you can ask and receive riches and power?

Let's continue our consideration of Jesus's "If" statements.

- If the world hates you, know that it has hated me before it hated you (John 15:18).
- If you were of the world, the world would love you as its own; but because you are not of the world, but I chose you out of the world, therefore the world hates you (John 15:19).
- If they persecuted me, they will also persecute you (John 15:20).
- If they kept my word, they will also keep yours (John 15:20).
- If I had not come and spoken to them, they would not have been guilty of sin, but now they have no excuse for their sin (John 15:22).
- If I had not done among them the works that no one else did, they would not be guilty of sin, but now they have seen and hated both me and my Father (John 15:24).

Let's be honest. Believers will face persecution. Jesus's "If" statements prepare us for the pain we can expect when we experience opposition to the gospel. Notice how this group of "If" statements reflect an almost us-against-them mentality.

We need to be careful to distinguish between situations where we create conflict by our own regrettable language and those that come from people who hate Jesus. We would be incorrect to say people who hated Jesus now hate us when the real problem is that our words cause our conversations to sound offensive. That being said, these "If" statements help us abide when the CODE we speak, fueled by our self-talk, allows worldly pressures to guide our conversations and not the sustaining words of Jesus. This is especially true with those of us who are people-pleasers.

These "If" statements are part of our path of righteousness because they lead us to abide even more deeply in Jesus. We find relief from His explanation of why we encounter such opposition in our conversations. These "If" statements serve as cushions designed to prevent our hearts from breaking due to the ravages of the soul-crushing words said to us. Take heart. Jesus heard the same kind of words we may hear. Just imagine how it affected Him knowing He did not deserve it. May we use these "If" statements as reminders that Jesus understands the necessary challenges we face on our path of righteousness as we find our identity in Him.

Which of these "If" statements most helps you when you hear hurtful words in an important conversation with necessary people in your life?

How do these statements deepen your identity in Jesus?

◀ ... .— —. . .— —.— .. —. — —. —.—. — — — —.. .

Let us become Abiders in Christ and find our identity in Him!

BELIEVE

It is difficult to talk about belief when we live between the complexities of obedience or disobedience and clarity or doubt. Disobedience pierces our conscience and produces agonizing questions about our identity in Christ. Sometimes even Abiders have reservations about God's presence in our lives. If He is present, are we disqualified as Abiders if we doubt our identity in Jesus? Belief is integral to our identity in Christ. But how can we live in the tension between our belief and unbelief?

Write out your struggle with unbelief and how it has affected your self-talk, people-talk, and God-talk.

◀ ... .— —. . .— —.— .. —. — —. —.—. — — — —.. .

How do your PPIFSt and PPIFEx affect your ability to believe others and God?

◀ ... .— —. . .— —.— .. —. — —. —.—. — — — —.. .

What CODE do you speak because your self-talk questions your very belief in God?

◀ ... .— —. . .— —.— .. —. — —. —.—. — — — —.. .

Thankfully, the burden to believe does not rest on our shoulders alone. Here is where we must live out our theology personally, because how we self-identify is at stake. God has not left us alone in our unbelief. We know this to be true because God has given us His word, confirmed by His Spirit. Before Jesus was taken up into the clouds, His last promise to us makes us cry out, "Yes and amen!" Read the Word of the Lord in Matthew 28:20:

> And behold, I am with you always, to the end of the age.

The question is, do we believe Him?

What keeps you from believing Jesus's last words to us?

There are no shortcuts or alternatives to believing Jesus's words found in Scripture. We must not make up our own stories as to why we struggle with belief. Read the Word of the Lord in John 20:30–31:

> Now Jesus did many other signs in the presence of the disciples, which are not written in this book; but these are written so that you may believe that Jesus is the Christ, the Son of God, and that by believing you may have life in his name.

We may wonder what other signs Jesus did in the presence of His disciples that John did not include in his Gospel. We fool ourselves if we believe those excluded things would be exactly what we need to believe. John says that what has been written is enough for us to believe that Jesus is the Son of God and, by believing, to have life in His name. Unbelief moves us away from ourselves and from Jesus. Belief moves us toward Jesus, where we find our true identity.

Cosmic Conversation and Unbelief

In John 12:27–29, we read a prayer Jesus offered to His Father in front of the assembled crowd. Jesus lamented that His soul was deeply troubled and perplexed. We listen to a heart-wrenching conversation between Jesus and His Father, where Jesus agonized over the type of death He was about to experience. Read the Word of the Lord in John 12:27–28:

> Now is my soul troubled. And what shall I say? "Father, save me from this hour? But for this purpose I have come to this hour. Father, glorify your name." Then a voice came from heaven: "I have glorified it, and I will glorify it again."

What must Jesus have felt when he said that His soul was troubled? Asking God to save Him from that hour seemed like a legitimate prayer, considering the horrific carnage that was about to unfold. However, Jesus was not willing to simply save Himself, because the purpose of His life was to bring glory to His Father.

The crowds clearly heard God's proclamation but had trouble making sense out of it. They began to ask questions that revealed their hearts. Jesus tried to explain the kind of death He was about to experience, until He finally withdrew and hid Himself from them. Read the Word of the Lord in John 12:36–40:

> When Jesus had said these things, he departed and hid himself from them. Though he had done so many signs before them, they still did not believe in him, so that the word spoken by the prophet Isaiah might be fulfilled: "Lord, who has believed what he heard from us, and to whom has the arm of the Lord been revealed?" Therefore they could not believe. For again Isaiah said, "He has blinded their eyes and hardened their heart, lest they see with their eyes, and understand with their heart, and turn, and I would heal them.

We should weep over these verses. We have had conversations that laid us low for days, perhaps weeks. Take heart. Our High Priest hears our desperate cries of forsakenness. Jesus's words as He faced the horror of the Cross shows us the alternative to unbelief. As Jesus bravely accepted what His Father set before Him, He acknowledged that the Father's plan was glorious despite the pain it would cause Him. As we abide in Jesus, we face difficulties that, mercifully, are so much less horrific than the Cross. Can we emulate Jesus and believe that whatever our Father sets before us is for our good? By believing and abiding, we move toward Jesus and find our identity securely hidden in Him. Knowing this helps us talk to the people in our necessary relationships. We can speak righteous words in difficult conversations we thought we would never have.

I am not saying we do not face profound sadness in our lives. Our struggles may tempt us to journey down a path away from Jesus as we seek our identity elsewhere. What I am saying is that Jesus—in whom we abide, believe, and find true identity—has already cleared this path before we ever walked it. In our text, those who heard Jesus's explanation never believed Him. But maybe for us . . . maybe we will apply these Scripture to our hearts and abide and believe in Jesus to the glory of God!

As you read the conversations between Jesus, God, and the crowds, how can they help you deal more affectively with your unbelief?

◀ ... .— —. . .— —.— .. —. — —. —.—. — — — —.. .

Write a prayer asking God to help you understand His Word that you may believe.

◀ ... .— —. . .— —.— .. —. — —. —.—. — — — —.. .

John 11:21–27, John 14:6–14, John 20:24–29, 39–40, and Mark 9:14–29 are but a few precious examples in passages about belief. These passages teach us that the burden of belief does not rest on us alone. Choose one of these passages and answer this question. How does Jesus help us believe in Him, and how does belief help you in difficult conversations?

Let us become Believers in Christ and find our identity in Him!

COMMUNE

We have seen how our true identity is found in abiding and believing in Jesus. Abiding and believing help our conversations become more soul-satisfying. Actively participating in Holy Communion shows everyone that we are Abiders and Believers. Partaking in the bread and wine tells the world that we move toward Jesus where we identify in Him. Read the Word of the Lord in John 6:52–56:

> The Jews then disputed among themselves, saying, "How can this man give us his flesh to eat?" So Jesus said to them, "Truly, truly, I say to you, unless you eat the flesh of the Son of Man and drink his blood, you have no life in you. Whoever feeds on my flesh and drinks my blood has eternal life, and I will raise him up on the last day. For my flesh is true food, and my blood is true drink. Whoever feeds on my flesh and drinks my blood abides in me, and I in him."

According to Jesus, to prove that we abide in Him and He in us, we must eat His flesh and drink His blood. The outward demonstration of our abiding happens every time we celebrate Holy Communion. Notice also that Communion is a life-or-death observance. Unless we eat and drink, Jesus says we have no life in us even though we go about our daily activities. When we lay dead in our coffin, Jesus will raise us up on that Last Day because we are Abiders and Believers. Partaking in true food and drink is a provocative idea, isn't it? In fact, Jesus's invitation to eat His flesh and drink His blood caused many of His disciples to abandon Him.

We must not diminish what is required of us to have our identity in Jesus. Holy Communion compels us to a deep commitment that surpasses anything we have ever known. Whatever our theological view is on Holy Communion, let it not separate us from the personal fellowship we enjoy when we outwardly show how we inwardly abide and believe.

If Holy Communion outwardly demonstrates your inward abiding and believing, how will this reality be reflected in your conversations that have been controlled by your Two Influential Forces, self-talk, and Speaking CODE?

Passover and Communion

In ancient Israel, the Jews found their identity and distinctiveness by participating in specific holy days. These holy days commemorated God's faithfulness in their lives. Passover was a required observance rooted in an historical event that the Jewish people were commanded to keep. Observing Passover memorialized this event which became an outward sign of an inward reality.

Exodus records that Moses instructed God's people to put the blood of a lamb on the lintels around the doors of their homes. That night the Angel of Death, upon seeing the blood-stained door, would pass over that home and spare those inside. Faithfully observing God's command saved every person living in houses marked with blood. This ultimately led to God delivering Israel from their bondage to Egypt.

The night before His crucifixion, Jesus observed Passover with His disciples. However, Jesus changed the significance of this Passover by instituting the first Holy Communion. During the ceremony, Jesus took the well-known elements of bread and wine and redefined them as His body and blood. Jesus fulfilled the prophetic significance of Passover when the blood of the Lamb of God, poured out on that terrible Cross, delivered His people from the bondage of sin.

The Jews commemorated their shared identity in the Passover ceremony. Similarly, Abiders and Believers in Jesus express their identity as Communicants by partaking in Holy Communion. Holy Communion allows us to participate with Jesus's sacrifice, love, and devotion to God making it possible for us to sacrifice, serve others, and love even our enemies, all to the glory of God.

Because of this, our conversations can be different. We are no longer chained to our Two Influential Forces, self-talk, and Speaking CODE. Our new identity promotes conversations where we do not make assumptions or talk to past ghosts that harmed us. Instead, we look at biblical language to guide our words. Read the Word of the Lord in Colossians 3:16–17:

> Let the word of Christ dwell in you richly, teaching and admonishing one another in all wisdom, singing psalms and hymns and spiritual songs, with thankfulness in your hearts to God. And whatever you do, in word or deed, do everything in the name of the Lord Jesus, giving thanks to God the Father through him.

Write out how communing with Jesus allows you to choose words in keeping with this passage and not with your Two Influential Forces, self-talk, and Speaking CODE.

Holy Communion inspires our hearts to feed on Jesus in faith with thanksgiving. Let us abide in Jesus, believe He is the Son of God, and commune with Him at His table. In doing so we demonstrate an outward sign of our inward identity in Him. Finally, let us be active participants, rather than mere observers, in this heavenly feast until the Lord comes again.

Here is a list of verses that help our conversations reflect our true identity:

- Ephesians 4:29
- James 1:19
- Proverbs 15:1
- Psalm 141:3
- Colossians 4:6
- Proverbs 12:18
- Proverbs 18:12
- Proverbs 25:11
- Proverbs 10:19
- Proverbs 16:23
- Colossians 3:8
- Ephesians 4:15
- Matthew 15:18–19

Identify which Scripture most helps you and why. Make sure you read the verse in context!

Let us commune with Christ as we find our identity in Him!

CHRIST, WHO IS OUR LIFE

How do we stop identifying with our old self and start identifying with our new self? Changing positions is radical and cannot be achieved by human effort. Read the Word of the Lord from Colossians 3:1–4:

> If then you have been raised with Christ, seek the things that are above, where Christ is, seated at the right hand of God. Set your minds on things that are above, not on things that are on earth. For you have died, and your life is hidden with Christ in God.

When Christ who is your life appears, then you also will appear with him in glory.

The switch happens when Christ, who is our life, raises us up from a position of spiritual death to a position of new life where we will appear with Him in glory. We can now set our minds on things that are above (eternal) rather than things that are on earth (temporal). Hence, the difference between these two positions pivots on Christ.

Look at Christ seated at the right hand of God. Imagine the bliss as we hide ourselves (or identity) in Him. Then envision Christ, who is our life, appearing. Who appears with Jesus? We do, and that will be glorious. Until then we identify with this all-encompassing statement: Christ, who is our life. Nothing we lost, or have, or will ever possess is our life—only Christ!

Let's not misunderstand each other. If we were sitting together sipping hot tea, we would be asking some probing questions. We would ask, "If Christ is really my life, then why the abuse, death, loneliness, disappointments, anxiety, shunning, hard conversations, brokenness, self-loathing, etc.?" Yes. And when Christ who is your life appears, then you also will appear with Him in glory. Hang on, Dear Friend, He will come!

What does the statement "Christ, who is your life" mean to you when it comes to the words you choose in your difficult conversations?

Name what prevents you from identifying with Christ in whom you have been hidden.

If Christ is really your life, how does He affect your self-talk?

The more we understand that we are hidden in Christ, who is our life, the more our hearts will be at rest. Saint Augustine of Hippo said, "Thou hast made us for thyself, O Lord, and our heart is restless until it finds its rest in thee."[21] A rested heart loses its desire to wound others with its words.

Often, we hurt one another because we want people to acknowledge the depth of our wounds. We are broken, and our soul-crushing conversations reflect that brokenness. In Isaiah 53:3-5, Jesus is described as despised and rejected, a Man of Sorrows, and acquainted with grief. He hears our confessions and with His wounds He heals us. We typically think of Jesus's work as healing our sinfulness. But the cure for sin can also heal wounded communication. Let us confess our own brokenness that leads us to use words that wound.

Describe a time when your wounds were so painful that you wounded someone with your words. What made you use the words you used?

In this chapter, we dug deep into how we move away from ourselves and God when we find our identity in anything but Christ alone. Moving away from ourselves and God stresses our conversations to a breaking point. However, Christ, who is our life, hides us in Him. Jesus bids us to become Abiders, Believers, and Communicants in Him so that our true identity can help make our soul-crushing conversations soul-satisfying.

MOVING AWAY: A THEOLOGY OF SUFFERING

Another way we move away from ourselves is by not finding meaning and purpose in suffering. Instead of seeking understanding we deny, exaggerate, or minimize our pain. This prevents us from working out the consequences of suffering and makes it difficult for us to move to a place of acceptance and wholeness. This will influence our self-talk, people-talk, and God-talk and drain our conversations of substance.

For example, denying or minimizing our own suffering makes it hard to enter conversations with others who express their pain. When we exaggerate our suffering, we may not be able to see the pain of others. We use words that may be disingenuous or brutally honest. Sustaining authentic conversations becomes problematic. Without sharing our sufferings (but not as hijackers or scene-stealing thieves), we can feel detached from others or numb toward our own heartaches. We need to move toward each other by sharing our woes so that we can begin to find meaning in purpose in our profound sadness. Sharing our burdens moves us toward each other and our own humanity where we can begin the journey to healing and wholeness.

Sometimes it takes what seems like an eternity to find purpose and meaning in our suffering—if we ever find it at all. The process of finding meaning and purpose takes time. We cannot rush to find answers. But when we begin to have the mind of Christ, we will gratefully sing the hymn "It Is Well with My Soul," written by Horatio G. Spafford in 1873. Here is just one verse of that well-loved hymn:

> When peace, like a river, attendeth my way;
> When sorrows like sea billows roll;
> Whatever my lot, Thou has taught me to say,
> "It is well, it is well with my soul."[22]

Learning this quietness of a settled spirit during our suffering is a lifelong quest. If we were sharing a pot of hot tea, we would wait for just the right time before we sing this hymn together. Understanding our suffering takes us down a dimly lit path with many twists and turns. All the detours need to be explored. Finding purpose in our suffering should not be rushed; nevertheless, the journey toward understanding it must begin.

THE SUFFERING WE ENDURE

Our spouse confesses to living a double life, including acting on same-sex attractions. Our friend tells us her daughter had an abortion. Our best friend expresses bitterness, over something we did years ago. Our friend admits to a porn addiction over which he has no control. A dear friend tells us that our behavior in group settings is obnoxious at best and abusive at worst. We are told to butt out of a loved one's life, even though we believe they are headed for a train wreck. Our doctor tells us we have a terminal illness. We are told that we are unwanted because our presence causes pain. In conversations, we say and hear words said to us in soul-crushing tones of rejection, harshness, apathy, and carelessness. The list of suffering is endless.

If we do not find purpose and meaning in the suffering we experience in conversations, we move away from ourselves as we disengage from Jesus Christ. In disbelief, we tell ourselves that Jesus would never ask us to endure the abuse we hear and experience. Sure, He suffered while on this earth. But does that mean we have to suffer as well? Aren't we more than conquerors in Jesus?

There are many ways we can react when we fail to find purpose and meaning in our soul-crushing conversations. We may go into denial over the words or tones we just heard. We may lash out and speak words meant to eviscerate the listener. Perhaps we confidently say God is on our side, which makes us right and him wrong. We should weep over the fact that we just denied the power of the Gospel in our conversations.

Renewed Theology on Suffering

We need a renewed theology of suffering that is robust, biblical, and focused on how we interact with each other. Without a vigorous biblical theology of suffering, our personal interactions will be ruled by our own interpretation of it. This leaves our self-talk, people-talk, and God-talk vulnerable to bitterness and despair. Our lives will be fractured because, when we don't trust God to give meaning to our pain, we are left to concoct our own personal version of why we suffer. Remember, we live out our theology for good or for ill, and our theology is always deeply personal.

How do you understand a biblical theology of suffering?

How do you make this theology personal?

When suffering does not have purpose and meaning, the hard work of achieving soul-satisfying communication is pointless. We deny our humanity when we fail to search for purpose in our suffering. As a result, we run from ourselves and toward alluring idols which promise us relief, but inevitably disappoint us .

Consider this: we have inflicted suffering on others and others have inflicted suffering on us. Suffering may have caused us to lie and be lied to. We have unfairly accused others and others have unfairly accused us. Unrelenting pain from our brokenness leaves us with little patience for the feelings of others.

As a result of our suffering, our words are not loving toward others, or theirs to us. We may bring suffering upon ourselves when we assume the worst of others because we have not asked good questions. The suffering brought on by our PPIFSt and our PPIFEx seeps into our conversations and hurts both us and others. Our souls' pain fuels our self-talk resulting in Speaking CODE. We act on assumptions that hurt both ourselves and the hearer. All of this separates us from God, others, and ourselves.

We experience distress when we cannot see God's purpose in our painful conversations, the inexplicable behaviors/interactions of others, or the deadly silence that often follows. Our blindness causes us to move away from ourselves as we refuse to look deeply at the core of our pain. We struggle to integrate or connect our feelings with God's purposes. Somehow, we believe that if we got to the core of the grief, we would be so shattered we might never be whole again. That fear separates us from ourselves and keeps us from being whole.

We might find ourselves becoming numb. The verbal assaults we hear shut us down. We check out of conversations, even though our bodies are still present. The force of another's words might revive a past memory, in which misery was all we knew. We split off. We fracture. We hide. We retaliate. We deny. We stare. We cry. We rage. We do anything to stop the senselessness of our pain. We question God as we run and hide from the circumstance in which we find ourselves. We search for self-soothing idols to provide comfort in a world that is comfortless. We hope our idols can make us feel like we are in the land of the living rather than some shadowland. We build internal and external walls to keep intruders out who may try to force us to address our pain.

Jane was young when she was physically and verbally abused by her parents. As a young adult, Jane had a confrontation with her employer, who screamed and cursed at her for failing to meet a deadline. A coworker asked how Jane put up with her boss's cursing tirade. In her surprise she said, "Oh, did he curse?" Jane had completely blocked out the abusive outburst, just as she had during her parents' mistreatment of her. Jane now realizes that this is symptomatic of her personal life, where she finds it hard to be fully engaged in family problems.

Write out how suffering, devoid of meaning and purpose, has moved you away from yourself. How have you detached from your pain to avoid reliving it?

Write out your chosen self-soothing idol that helps you feel like you are in the land of the living.

We move away from ourselves when we deny the anguish that actually happened. Our suffering may be shrouded by the-never-to-be-answered questions which force us to disengage with life. Questions about our acceptability (such as, are we worthy, loved, treasured, or valued) keep us in a fog that makes it hard for us to breathe. Our conversations reflect our fractured souls as we inwardly wrestle with the ultimate question: "Can my suffering ever be understood by me or anyone else, or am I doomed to live alone in this pain forever? Is there anyone on my side?"

List ways in which you have been misunderstood in your suffering.

Think about your suffering. Write out what would you like me to know about your pain that would help me understand how your suffering has affected you.

What do you want Jesus to know about your suffering that will help you connect to Him?

ETERNAL WEIGHT OF GLORY

Where do we start? Let's approach suffering from the presupposition that suffering has meaning and is a huge part of the human experience. Let's look at what Paul has to say about suffering. Read the Word of the Lord from 2 Corinthians 4:17:

> For this light and momentary affliction is preparing for us an eternal weight of glory beyond all comparison.

Paul does not expound on the nature of this light and momentary affliction. He certainly experienced many forms of suffering recorded in the epistles. Suffering can mean anything from bodily suffering to emotional distress. This book is about communication, so it is wise to stay close to this topic. During those moments when our conversations cause great division leading to heartache, what do we see? Do we see light and momentary affliction? Or do we see the eternal weight of glory?

You might think this sounds like that trite old adage, "Sticks and stones will break my bones but words will never harm me." This is a fair concern. But it does not make 2 Corinthians 4:17 any less true, does it? It just makes this passage harder to understand considering our experiences. Again, there is no rush for us to find meaning in our suffering. However, we must start the process, so why not take a step forward now?

Look at the most difficult situation you are in right now that involves conversation (or the lack thereof). Consider your experiences. I will tell you mine. In my most recent difficult conversation, I felt profound sadness and confusion. I felt ignored, shamed at being exposed, unloved, angry, rejected, alone, judged, and marginalized. I felt a sense of injustice and an impending doom, as if the other shoe was about to drop. And, in the name of Jesus, I wanted to punch somone in the face.

Describe your experiences in a conversation that left you bewildered.

Explain how this situation could be viewed as light and momentary. Perhaps you do not see your suffering as light and momentary. That is okay. In that case, write how you do not see that your suffering is light and momentary, and explain what you do see.

In your current situation, write out how God might be orchestrating your suffering to prepare you for an eternal weight of glory—one beyond all human comparison.

◀ ... .— —. . .— —.— .. —. — —. —.—. — — — —.. .

THE SUFFERING AND TRIUMPHANT LIFE OF JOSEPH

Joseph's life presents us with two themes that almost seem contradictory. The first theme demonstrates the powerful command our Two Influential Forces have over our present conversations. The second theme demonstrates God's power as He allows us to see specific good even in our suffering. The account of Joseph's life shows us several personal conversations between real people where we see these two themes play out. These conversations are as instructive today as they were to the people who engaged in them so long ago.

In Genesis 37, we read that Israel sent Joseph to check up on his brothers, who were pasturing the sheep (v. 12). Let's imagine ourselves perched above the unfolding drama as we eavesdrop on the conversations below. As we see Joseph approaching his brothers in Dothan, we listen to them devise a murderous plot against him (v. 18). We hear the brothers discuss their Two Influential Forces with their spoiled brat of a brother. To them, Joseph was self-centered, the favorite son of their father, and a grandiose dreamer whom they hated. They conspired against Joseph to kill him. As the conversation continues, we hear words of jealousy, revenge, intrigue, deception, and selfish ambition based on their PPIFSt and PPIFEx (vv. 1–11).

Reuben, however, wanted to rescue Joseph out of his brother's hands (v. 21). He convinced his siblings not to kill Joseph but rather to throw him into a pit (v. 22). Reuben's self-talk led him to plan to rescue Joseph from the pit and return him to his father (v. 22). Reuben Spoke CODE to his brothers and chose not to share all his self-talk regarding the rescue. The brothers listened to Reuben and threw Joseph into the pit to die (vv. 23–24).

But God had a plan where Joseph's suffering would have heroic repercussions. Judah decided it would be better to profit from Joseph's life rather than leaving him in the pit to die (v. 26). He convinced his brothers to sell Joseph for twenty shekels of silver to a caravan of Ishmaelites on their way to Egypt (v. 27). After all, Joseph was their own flesh and blood, so why should his blood be on their hands (v. 27)? The charmed life Joseph once led came to an end, and his life of intense suffering began. In Genesis 39, God demonstrates how He was ever near Joseph who suffered greatly at the hands of his brothers and others. The whole time Joseph was imprisoned, God was present amid his suffering.

God orchestrated a series of events that caused Joseph to flourish despite his brothers' evil plan (Genesis 39–41).

God used the vile actions of those jealous brothers to set a greater plan into action. His plan would demonstrate meaning and purpose in Joseph's torment. The entire account of Joseph's life should be read for the good of our soul. For now, read the Word of the Lord in Genesis 50:15–21:

> When Joseph's brothers saw that their father was dead, they said, "It may be that Joseph will hate us and pay us back for all the evil that we did to him." So they sent a message to Joseph, saying, "Your father gave this command before he died: 'Say to Joseph, "Please forgive the transgression of your brothers and their sin, because they did evil to you."' And now, please forgive the transgression of the servants of the God of your father." Joseph wept when they spoke to him. His brothers also came and fell down before him and said, "Behold, we are your servants." But Joseph said to them, "Do not fear, for am I in the place of God? As for you, you meant evil against me, but God meant it for good, to bring it about that many people should be kept alive, as they are today. So do not fear; I will provide for you and your little ones." Thus he comforted them and spoke kindly to them.

The And/And of the Bible

A wise pastor once told me about the *And/And* of the Bible, where we see two conflicting things happening at the same time. Throughout this account, we see the And/And of Joseph's life. We see Suffering Joseph and Triumphant Joseph. The brothers meant evil for Joseph and God meant good. The brothers conceived a treacherous plan and they eventually recognized their guilt when they remembered how desperately Joseph pleaded for his life (Genesis 42:21–22). In Genesis 39, God prospered Joseph in Potiphar's house and Joseph was thrown into prison based on a false accusation of sexual assault. In Genesis 40, God gave Joseph the ability to interpret dreams and God prevented Joseph from being released from prison. Suffering and triumph!

We may wonder if Joseph would say that his sufferings were light and momentary. Joseph suffered in an ancient prison for years. How could years be seen as momentary? How could treachery from your own flesh and blood seem light? They are not! But these sufferings prepared Joseph for an eternal weight of glory beyond all comprehension in both his earthly and his heavenly life. Eventually, Joseph's conversations reflected the road of suffering that led to triumph.

We may ask ourselves how Joseph's life relates to ours? We have conversations today that are like those that Joseph and his brothers had long ago. Our conversations are traceable to our ECMs, PPIFSt, and PPIFEx, just as these brother's conversations could be traced back to theirs. Our conversations are often fueled by jealousy, revenge, intrigue, deception, and selfish ambition that cause us great suffering, just as his brothers' conversation did to Joseph. And God does not change. God promises He will be ever near to our suffering hearts, just as He was ever near to Joseph. The two themes in Joseph's life show that while PPIFSt and PPIFEx powerfully impact our conversations, good comes from personal suffering as God directs our path of righteousness.

How can you use the account of Joseph to help you understand your personal suffering and the weight of glory?

Perhaps painful conversations point out a character flaw in us. Once addressed, we may love God and others more wisely and less selfishly. Maybe our conversational partner needs to see how his words are painful. Perhaps the full measure of our sin must be revealed in both of us before we see meaning and purpose in our problematic conversations.

Describe how you can see both themes (suffering and triumph) in your painful conversations.

Difficult Questions

A biblical theology of suffering informs us that painful conversations eventually lead us to an incomparable and eternal weight of glory. How can affliction bring an eternal weight of glory? Honestly, I do not know. What I do know is that both statements are true simultaneously: light and momentary affliction prepares us for an eternal weight of glory. Both truths are inextricably tied together, and both truths are equally important as we center ourselves in the one who is Truth. This is an example of the And/And of the Scriptures. Remember, God knows all that we do not.

What is an eternal weight of glory? I do not know that, either. But Jesus does, as He sits in glory at the right hand of His Father. All I know is that our "light and momentary" afflictions prepare us for whatever weight of glory means. This eternal weight of glory must be so fantastical and incomprehensible that God sends us affliction so that we can increase our understanding of it. My view is that this glory is too other for us. Because suffering is light and momentary in comparison to glory, the more we understand suffering the more we understand its enormity. It makes sense that we need lots of practice in suffering in order for our dull minds to catch a glimpse of glory.

Write out what suffering God gives you to practice so that you will have a better understanding of glory.

Therefore, we need to practice suffering well, so that we will not move away from ourselves as we search for meaning and purpose in it. Suffering keeps us centered in the One who works all things together for our specific good, because we are specifically called by Jesus to suffer.

LIVING WELL IN SUFFERING

The question then becomes, how do we live well in our suffering? In the circumstances of our unfruitful conversations or deadly silence, how can we live well in that present moment? Jesus tells us that thinking of the future makes us anxious. Living in the past denies the truth of where we are in the present. Therefore, how do we live well right where God has placed us? Read the Word of the Lord in Matthew 6:34:

> Therefore do not be anxious about tomorrow, for tomorrow will be anxious for itself. Sufficient for the day is its own trouble.

Jesus says that each day will have sufficient troubles for us. That means the troubles we experience today are sufficient—not too much and not too little. It is now out there for all of us to read: we will have daily troubles. If you think tomorrow will be free of anxiety, you are denying the truth of this passage.

If we know this ahead of time, it makes no sense for us to be anxious about tomorrow's troubles. Let tomorrow take care of itself. Right now, we need to have our head in today's game, where Jesus says our troubles are sufficient and He is with us. We would be wise to look for meaning and purpose in today's troubles and let tomorrow's anxiety be only for tomorrow. Besides, if we live today with the thought of tomorrow's anxieties, our present conversations will overwhelm us.

List ways you have focused on tomorrow's anxieties. How has that affected your present conversations?

Affliction and the Weight of Glory

Paul knew suffering, and he learned contentment from it. But he did not minimize his experiences. Neither should we. Rather, Paul gives us hope that our affliction has purpose and connects us to an unfathomable and everlasting weight of glory. This hope is reflected in our conversations. If our affliction is not linked to it, then suffering seems cruel, capricious, wicked, and meaningless. That view will influence the words we say to ourselves, to our God, and to those around us.

If we do not tie God's purpose in our affliction to the weight of glory, we make up our own tragic stories. Not only are our personal conversations compromised, but any dialogues between opposing parties—whether they take place on Wall Street, Main Street, or our street—will be impaired. Across the globe, people justify hostility and claim victimization when they fail to link God's purpose in suffering to His eternal weight of glory.

Write out how your conversations reflect Paul's description of the eternal weight of glory that gives meaning to your suffering.

Before you linked your suffering to Paul's concept of eternal weight of glory, what stories did you make up to explain why you suffer?

How do your made-up stories affect the words you use in your conversations?

Write out what it looks like for you to move away from your own humanity by not seeing the meaning and purpose in your suffering. If you find this hard or confusing, try starting like this: "I move away from myself when I deny the suffering caused by this specific painful conversation. This denial makes me . . .".

How do you see God's goodness to you specifically in these bruising conversations that are preparing you for an eternal weight of glory?

Let your imagination run wild as you describe how an eternal weight of glory is so much greater than the suffering you experience.

Paul's Dilemma

How do we find God's meaning and purpose in the suffering when our past pain seems to present itself in our daily lives? Paul faced this dilemma. Read the Word of the Lord from 2 Corinthians 12:7–10:

> So to keep me from becoming conceited because of the surpassing greatness of the revelations, a thorn was given me in the flesh, a messenger of Satan to harass me, to keep me from becoming conceited. Three times I pleaded with the Lord about this, that it should leave me. But he said to me, "My grace is sufficient for you, for my power is made perfect in weakness." Therefore I will boast all the more gladly of my weaknesses, so that the power of Christ may rest upon me. For the sake of Christ, then, I am content with weaknesses, insults, hardships, persecutions, and calamities. For when I am weak, then I am strong.

When we read this passage, we see that at some point in Paul's past, he was given unspeakable visions and fantastical revelations from the Lord. God gave Paul a thorn in the flesh to keep him from becoming conceited due to these amazing experiences. After asking God three times to take the thorn away, Paul learned that God's grace was exactly enough to sustain him in the effects brought about by his thorn. From this, Paul changed his attitude. He found contentment in his weakness, insults, hardships, persecutions, and calamities. Without that specific thorn in his flesh, Paul would never have truly seen the power of Jesus resting on him.

While our past may not have the same harassing thorns that Paul's did, we can still learn important lessons from him. Sometimes we miss the ability to experience contentment if we live without these thorns. We may not understand the true meaning of humility when we resist the effects of our thorns.

We may find it interesting that Paul did not choose to be caught up in a paradise with visions and revelations too wonderful for words. Nor did he choose the specific thorn in his flesh. These were God's goodness and mercy following Paul all the days of his life.

Similarly, we do not choose our blessings or our thorns. That means the same sustaining God who showed Paul meaning and purpose is the same sustaining God who shows us purpose as He guides and directs us. The question is, do we pray that our thorn be removed, or do we pray for understanding if it remains? In either case, the thorns from our past will affect how we live in the present moments of our lives, including how we speak to one another.

Write out what your thorn in the flesh is and how it affects your ability to communicate.

Typically, we pray that God will take away the thorns in our flesh because they disrupt our lives. That makes sense. We pray over our needs. Jesus prayed three times that the cup He was about to drink would be taken away from Him. But what if our thorns scratched off the scales from our eyes so we could see God's work more clearly? Would we still pray them away?

What are the criteria you use to evaluate the nature of your thorn that you want taken away?

We may also negotiate with God regarding the nature of the thorn He sends us. Maybe we ask God to give us a thorn of our liking that is easier to endure than the one He chose for us.

What suffering would you negotiate with God for one that is acceptable to you?

Which of your thorny past experiences do you wish had never happened to you and why?

Have you ever begged God to send you a thorn in your flesh and why?

Oh, snap! That was a trick question. For God ordains even our thorns for His glory and our good. Our most deeply embedded thorn has purpose in our lives. Paul specifically says that when he is weak, then he is strong. That holds true for us well. Therefore, we need to rethink how we pray or negotiate them away. Like Paul, we can certainly ask the Lord to remove them. But if they are not removed, we need to beg God for grace as we look for meaning and purpose in the suffering they produce, including how they affect our ability to communicate righteously.

Explain how your Two Influential Forces form the basis for how you interpret your thorns and give meaning and purpose to your conversations.

Is this hard for you to do? I get that. Explain why.

Suffering is designed to drive us to our knees before Jesus, leaving us unable to negotiate which sufferings we want God to give us. But God is specifically good. He designs our path of righteousness with thorny and smooth walkways that lead us to Him. God's grace is sufficient for us, for His power is made perfect in our weakness. And at our weakest, Jesus's power rests upon us. Praise God for His mercy and grace!

Write out how the thorn in your flesh drives you to your knees.

Let me wonder out loud for a bit. I wonder what kind of people we would be without our thorns. How could our holy sanctuaries intersect with others if we did not understand suffering? Our suffering equips us to be burden bearers. We would be blind to the redeeming work of God if we had no thorns. Our thorns lead to contentment, so we would be much wiser to embrace them than reject them.

Prayer in the Moment

What happens if the thorn in our flesh does not drive us to our knees in prayer? Maybe we cannot pray because our wounds stop our words. Inability to pray simply means we are human. Let us not be so self-important that we believe our inability to pray somehow stops the Spirit of God from His work on our behalf. So, what do we do when our thorns are deeply embedded in our souls and silence our lips?

We can ask someone to pray intercessory prayers on our behalf. We can find comfort in reading the Scriptures. We can go to a good hymnal, such as the Trinity Hymnal, and read the words written by men and women who wrote songs and lyrics about God dealing with His creation. Hymns act as prayers. We can also find help in *The Book of Common Prayer.* Liturgical prayers guide our hearts toward God when our own words fail. *The Valley of Vision* (Arthur Bennett), *Every Moment Holy: Volumes I & II* (Douglas Kaine McKelvey), or *Revealed: A Storybook Bible for Grown-Ups* (edited by Ned Bustard) are good books to read if our words are all dried up because of our pain. These resources can help us experience God our Father, through Jesus our Brother, led by the Spirit our Comforter.

Stephen's Suffering

Let's read the conversation between Stephen and the crowd in Acts 6–8. In the middle of intense persecution, the severity of which we probably will never understand, Stephen preaches a sermon. At the end of the sermon, Stephen has an incredible soul-satisfying vision that he communicates to the crowd. Read the Word of the Lord from Acts 7:54–60:

> Now when they heard these things they were enraged, and they ground their teeth at him. But he, full of the Holy Spirit, gazed into heaven and saw the glory of God, and Jesus standing at the right hand of God. And he said, "Behold, I see the heavens opened, and the Son of Man standing at the right hand of God." But they cried out with a loud voice and stopped their ears and rushed together at him. Then they cast him out of the city and stoned him. And the witnesses laid down their garments at the feet of a young man named Saul. And as they were stoning Stephen, he called out, "Lord Jesus, receive my spirit." And falling to his knees he cried out with a loud voice, "Lord, do not hold this sin against them." And when he had said this, he fell asleep.

Let this conversation sink into our hearts. Upon hearing Stephen's words, the people experienced rage and reacted physically by stoning him. This example shows us the truth that our words have power. Stephen's words took us to heaven itself. Even though Stephen's body was battered beyond recognition, he died a whole man. He integrated God's meaning and purpose into his suffering. His momentary affliction became an incomparable weight of glory. Additionally, we see the nearness of God during Stephen's suffering as Jesus stands to receive him into glory.

Saul, who later became the apostle Paul, heard Stephen's incredible words. One must wonder how Stephen's words of absolution affected Saul. Read the Word of the Lord in 1 Corinthians 15:9–11:

> For I am the least of the apostles, unworthy to be called an apostle, because I persecuted the church of God. But by the grace of God I am what I am, and his grace toward me was not in vain. On the contrary, I worked harder than any of them, though it was not I, but the grace of God that is with me. Whether then it was I or they, so we preach and so you believed.

Because Stephen and Saul experienced intersecting holy sanctuaries, we can see the suffering Paul and the triumphant Paul. The words spoken by Stephen as he was stoned to death stuck with Paul throughout his life. Paul understood and accepted his PPIFSt/PPIFEx and used them to the glory of God. Our words are powerful and have great influence. We need to remember this as we enter our conversations. Here we can apply the And/And of our own lives. We are what we are because our Two Influential Forces and God's grace to us will never be in vain.

To this very day, the account of Stephen's death is an encouragement to us amidst our suffering. Our conversations can look like Stephen's as we search for meaning and purpose. Pray that God will help us to unite our suffering with His tender leading. May we pray forgiving prayers like Stephen: "Lord, do not hold this sin against them." And may our words have profound effects on people who hear them.

GOD'S INTENTIONS FOR OUR BROKEN HEARTS

There are many verses in the Bible that speak about our suffering and God's intentions. Theologians have written volumes on this subject. Musicians have sung songs and hymns about suffering. Artists have conceived, created, and performed art—in all mediums—meant to express the depths of our affliction. In the everyday moments of our lives, we experience pain in various ways. It may be an annoying paper cut, an open-heart surgical incision, or a crushing conversation that reminds us of the suffering we endure in this world. In our anguish we fall to our knees in despair.

Suffering is everywhere, and it seeks to separate us from ourselves by forcing us to put our distress into a compartment which we tuck away in our hearts. This anguish contributes to our PPIFSt and PPIFEx, which shape how we interpret our lives. Without the belief that God is up to something in our suffering, that compartment can do massive damage to our hearts, words, and behaviors.

Suffering is inescapable. Indeed, nature itself suffers and groans in anticipation of redemption. Affliction comes to all people. If we seek to escape it, we lose our connectedness to ourselves, others, and Jesus. Without connectedness, suffering becomes a burden too heavy for us to carry. We need help from others and especially from God. Read the word of the Lord from Isaiah 53:10–12:

> Yet it was the will of the Lord to crush him; he has put him to grief; when his soul makes an offering for guilt, he shall see his offspring; he shall prolong his days; the will of the Lord shall prosper in his hand. Out of the anguish of his soul he shall see and be satisfied; by his knowledge shall the righteous one, my servant, make many to be accounted righteous, and he shall bear their iniquities. Therefore I will divide him a portion with the many, and he shall divide the spoil with the strong, because he poured out his soul to death and was numbered with the transgressors; yet he bore the sin of many, and makes intercession for the transgressors.

This passage points out that one place where we are most connected with Jesus is in our suffering. God caused Jesus to suffer with a specific purpose in mind. In His suffering, Jesus was numbered among the transgressors, making Him able to bear our sins. In some ways, we are like Jesus, because God brings about our suffering and gives it meaning. We, too, become burden bearers as we participate in Jesus's suffering.

Write about a conversation where you were able to bear the burden of another because of your suffering. How did your words help him in his pain?

We cannot separate God's purpose from the torment He imposed upon the Suffering Servant, and we cannot separate God's purpose from our suffering either. As Christ was made to suffer, we also will suffer as "Little Christs." Therefore, we should not attempt to separate ourselves from our suffering.

In the Isaiah passage above, circle the words that show God's hand in His Son's suffering. Underline all the words that show how Jesus's suffering had meaning and purpose.

And Then There Is Job

The book of Job records a series of conversations between Job, his friends, and God about suffering. Job never understood why God afflicted him with so many thorns. His worthless friends raised equally worthless ideas as to why Job suffered so greatly. Job rejected all of them and maintained his integrity. God finally spoke to Job out of the whirlwind. He told Job to dress for action like a man because God was about to question him! Job's response was singular. Read the Word of the Lord in Job 42:1–6:

> Then Job answered the Lord and said: "I know that you can do all things, and that no purpose of yours can be thwarted. 'Who is this that hides counsel without knowledge?' Therefore I have uttered what I did not understand, things too wonderful for me, which I did not know. 'Hear, and I will speak; I will question you, and you make it known to me.' I had heard of you by the hearing of the ear, but now my eye sees you; therefore I despise myself, and repent in dust and ashes."

If we were sipping hot tea together, we would discuss how our thorns affect our conversations and lead us to Speak CODE. We might consider how we could be like Job and confess that we speak of things too wonderful for us to understand (like the eternal weight of glory). Like Job, we may have heard of God, but is our connection such that it is almost as though we (like Job) can really see Him with our own eyes? Let us earnestly repent for not knowing God well enough to trust Him in the sufferings He sends us.

Cocooning Sufferers

Just a word of encouragement to some of us who are in the middle of intense suffering brought about by unwanted separation, life-altering illness, or tragedy. Many times, we find ourselves cocooning or turning inward because that is about all we can do to survive. We simply cannot help others bear their burdens. Am I saying that cocooning denies God's purpose in our suffering? Maybe this is not the right question. Maybe the better question is to ask if cocooning is necessary for a while. If we cocoon, we must not forget that even in our deep pain, our grief has meaning and purpose as we search for God.

PERCEIVED OVERSHADOWING EMOTIONAL/ PHYSICAL SUFFERING (POEPS)

What I am about to say is based on meaningful conversations I have had over my many years as a biblical counselor and my personal experiences. We must note that the *Diagnostic and Statistical Manual of Mental Disorders,* 5th edition (DSM-5), describes variations on what we will discuss in this section. The DSM-5 classifies how we see confusing symptoms in our physical bodies as Anxiety Disorder, Somatic Symptom Disorder, or any number of other related symptoms. I invite you to read the more technical aspects of this in the DSM-5 if you are so inclined.

For our purpose, I will group my observations under the heading I call Perceived Overshadowing Emotional/Physical Suffering (POEPS). Not everyone experiences POEPS but it is a real issue for some people. I use POEPS to describe the connection we make between physical health difficulties (real or perceived) and how we live life, including our conversations. Because our bodies and souls are linked, there are many different expressions of POEPS. Our emotional and physical reactions can make us an anxious bystander in our lives rather than a joyful participant.

For some of us, a legitimate health issue can dominate our lives, coloring how we view our world. For example, our sickness may be used to justify conversations that run the gamut from complaints about specific symptoms, to justifying self-centered behavior. We may find that even though we receive a clean bill of health, fear of a specific illness may continue to overshadow our lives. Even after our health crisis has passed, our PPIFEx still echoes with reminders of the suffering we endured. Any ache or pain may trigger the trauma associated with our former infirmity.

Some of us may not have experienced serious illnesses. However, we may feel undifferentiated anxiety when we confront stressful situations, leading to symptoms that either mimic or produce panic attacks.

In Romans 12:4f and I Corinthians 12:12–14, Paul describes us as individuals who are part of one body. Our individuality accounts for how differently we experience the effects of suffering, whether it is physical or emotional, perceived or real. That means traumatic events (physical ailments or emotional wounds) will affect our conversations differently.

Emotional Symptoms Tied to POEPS

If we had cancer and its complications still haunt us today, we may be cautious with our bodies even after our doctor gave us a clean bill of health. We may feel emotions such as nervousness or apprehension, fearing that a new pain may signal the return of our old illness. The last self-talk we recite before falling asleep wonders if tomorrow is the day the illness returns. We awake only to fixate on what new symptoms will greet us. This thinking has a disastrous effect on how we talk to others as we go about our daily lives.

We experience a range of dreadful feelings imagining the return of our illness. We make endless doctor's appointments, anticipating that an expert will explain why our body feels broken or sick, and hope it is not the same illness we thought we beat. We feel heard when our doctor takes our symptoms seriously. We may experience emotional relief when he sends us for additional tests or reassures us that he will keep an eye on the situation.

In our mind, we speculate that we may face the return of that devastating illness, or perhaps it is some new undetected cancer that escaped routine tests. We have certainly heard our share of horror stories. The not-knowing leaves us anxious, fear driven, emotional wrecks and causes us to re-evaluate where we spend our resources. Our conversations may suffer because we either do not have the emotional reserves to speak or we cannot moderate our words.

Write out how POEPS kept you from engaging in important conversations or attending social gatherings.

Physical Pain Tied to POEPS

Perhaps we have not had a life-threatening illness. But maybe we experience unusual symp-toms, such as pain in our arm or a suspicious mole that we choose to ignore. We find that dismissing these symptoms makes us anxious, which causes us to be grumpy, dogmatic, aloof, detached, or preoccupied. We believe that something is not quite right, and that belief may be enough to have a profound effect on our conversations with others.

The bodily symptoms of POEPS can be complicated as well. The physical warning signs our body sends us are authentic, even though we try to ignore their consequences. It is hard to enjoy life when we encounter nagging physical symptoms that can produce heightened anxiety and overshadow how we experience our work, recreation, family, hobbies, and even our unpredictable conversations.

Imagine anticipating a distressing conversation while in the throes of physical pain that we are trying to ignore because we are fearful of the diagnosis. Whether we are physically ill or not, that conversation seems to add more stress to an already stressful time in our lives. We experienced difficult conversations in the past and we did not like the physical symptoms associated with them. Why add feelings of lightheadedness, increased sweating, heart palpitations, or gastrointestinal symptoms to what we are already experiencing? We may tell ourselves that we do not have the resources to fight two battles: our physical discomfort and an anxiety-producing discussion.

Write out how POEPS impacts you during important conversations by creating physical symptoms reflective of panic or stress.

Describe how the warning signs your body sends you, leaves you with few if any resources to fight a battle.

How does POEPS affect your conversations?

Behavior and POEPS

People react to POEPS in different ways. In some cases, we search the internet for any information that might shed light on our symptoms. We emphatically tell those who dare confront us to mind their own business when they point out something that needs attention. Fear, rather than wisdom, drives our decisions when it comes to our bodies. If we continue to allow our emotional/physical concerns to keep us from the necessary work of building or maintaining relationships, we will sit on the side-lines as observers. When we allow our suffering to define us rather than finding meaning and purpose for it, we detach ourselves from ourselves and move away from God.

Our conversations lack authenticity when our suffering overshadows our lives. We may shut down. We may lash out. We may believe we are too sick to exert ourselves. We may use words that manipulate others to get the response we desire. We may vociferously deny our pain, perhaps making matters worse. Our suffering may make us susceptible to being bullied or tricked into substituting someone else's truth in place of our own reality.

We find it hard to see Jesus in POEPS. We may believe that God has not been gracious to us in our suffering. We wonder why we find ourselves in this situation. David's words in Psalm 31 resonate with us. Read the Word of the Lord in Psalm 31:9f:

> Be gracious to me, O Lord, for I am in distress;
> my eye is wasted from grief, my soul and my body also.
> For my life is spent with sorrow,
> and my years with sighing;
> my strength fails because of my misery,
> and my bones waste away.

We hear David's words and our hearts stay in Psalm 31 rather than seeing that David balanced that sorrow with other Psalms that expressed the joy and comfort he found in God. In POEPS, we linger in the pain and grief that David knew. The difference is that David visited this place of lament as expressed in the Psalm, but he did not remain there.

When we are afraid to understand our suffering, our ability to have genuine conversations deteriorates. We feel as though we are left in the dark when it comes to our own bodies. The suffering itself—or the thought of it—overwhelms us, which sometimes causes us to live our lives inwardly. To keep people away, we mimic words that satisfy them in the short term or demand that they understand the emotional component of our real pain. We use barbed words toward those we feel don't take our suffering seriously or who urge us to push past it. Sadly, we feel inadequate to seek the meaning and purpose of our suffering.

We blame others for not seeing what we see when it comes to our illness. We refuse to hear when people implore us to get a professional opinion for our physical symptoms. In our emotional suffering, we challenge those around us to show concern that our devastating illness may return or perhaps a new disease will take its place.

We may say, "You know I am dealing with past health issues that may return so why are you pushing me to move on? I would think you would be more sympathetic because of what I have been through, especially knowing I experience panic attacks that make me feel like I am about to die! No one understands my fear and anxiety. I do not want to talk about this or anything else." Or we say, "Get off my back. This is my body and I make the decision to see the doctor or not. Besides, neither you nor the doctor know what you are talking about. For the last time, there is nothing wrong with me. I do not want to talk to you about this or anything else. You are just trying to make me afraid."

Write out how you talk to someone who tries to give you advice regarding your pain. Start with a past experience that affects your self-talk and leads to Speaking CODE.

BIBLICAL COMFORT

However, God gives us His Word for our comfort. In the Scriptures, God shows us the purpose in the suffering that great men and women of faith have endured. Hebrews 11 is one example. The human suffering of those saints is beyond our comprehension. Even though we do not have details of specific conversations, the writer of the Hebrews draws us into the human drama. Read the Word of the Lord in Hebrews 11:32–38:

> And what more shall I say? For time would fail me to tell of Gideon, Barak, Samson, Jephthah, of David and Samuel and the prophets— who through faith conquered kingdoms, enforced justice, obtained promises, stopped the mouths of lions, quenched the power of fire, escaped the edge of the sword, were made strong out of weakness, became mighty in war, put foreign armies to flight. Women received back their dead by resurrection. Some were tortured, refusing to accept release, so that they might rise again to a better life. Others suffered mocking and flogging, and even chains and imprisonment. They were stoned, they were sawn in two, they were killed with the sword. They went about in skins of sheep and goats, destitute, afflicted, mistreated—of whom the world was not worthy—wandering about in deserts and mountains, and in dens and caves of the earth.

There is real purpose found in the suffering of these great heroes. In some cases, these men and women suffered unto death and we do not even know their names! However, their suffering did not define them because they found their identity in God alone.

For some of us, our suffering makes us feel unknown or unseen, as though no one knows our name. Maybe our parents abandoned us. Maybe the color of our skin or the lifestyle we choose to live marginalizes us. Just like those unnamed saints in this chapter are given a place in biblical history, God gives us place as well.

How does your suffering make you feel unknown or unseen?

◀ ··· ·— —· · ·— —·— ·· —· — —·   —·—· — — — —·· ·

Notice the sentence, "Some were tortured, refusing to accept release, so that they might rise again to a better life." While our suffering is nothing like that of these martyrs, our purpose in suffering is the same: so that we may rise again to a better life.

List ways in which these verses can help you see that our suffering may allow us to rise to a better life.

◀ ··· ·— —· · ·— —·— ·· —· — —·   —·—· — — — —·· ·

One last observation about the nature of suffering. Paul tells us that we are united to Jesus in a very unusual way. This connection prevents us from separating ourselves from ourselves during suffering. Read the Word of the Lord in Colossians 1:24:

> Now I rejoice in my sufferings for your sake, and in my flesh I am filling up what is lacking in Christ's afflictions for the sake of his body, that is, the church.

Filling up what was lacking in Christ's affliction refers to the ongoing suffering of the Church after the death of Christ. The Church is Christ's body, of which we are members. When Christ died on the Cross, His work was complete. However, as sufferers our work continues when we incarnate Jesus to those around us.

Throughout history, each individual sufferer participates in Christ's death and resurrection. Not only are we joined to Christ in our suffering, but we are also linked together as one Body, one Baptism, and one Church. Therefore, our sufferings unite us to ourselves, to one another, and to Jesus. Let us find meaning and purpose in our suffering rather than separating ourselves from it. Let us rejoice as we continue Christ's earthly ministry as we participate in filling up Jesus's sufferings.

IS THERE HOPE?

Will we ever enjoy consistent soul-satisfying conversations? In the moment, will we be able to identify how our Two Influential Forces, self-talk, and Speaking CODE sabotage our conversations? Or will these issues prevent us from speaking redemptively with one another? Are we doomed to soul-crushing speech because we make assumptions, fail to ask good questions, refuse to forgive, fuse our past to our present, identify in anything but Jesus, and misunderstand our suffering?

In all honesty, I must confess that it is hard to get soul-satisfying communication right. We cannot achieve these kinds of conversations on our own. To this very day, I engage in conversations where I neglect to ask good questions, am unforgiving, hold onto my past, don't look to Jesus, and fail to find meaning in my suffering. Just ask my family. They would probably say, "Mom, when have you practiced the things written in your book?" And I would say, "You are right. I have failed. Forgive me. Let's start now."

BUT GOD!

But God, through the blood of Christ and the indwelling of the Holy Spirit, can make our ravaged conversations righteous. Our hope for redeemed speech is in God who, Michael Crawford, says "camps out" with broken-hearted people. God's Word is a lamp to our feet and a light to our path. Substituting heroic efforts or self-awareness in place of God's Word in our conversations is just as effective as a hamster running on an exercise wheel. It is a lot of running, but it takes that hamster nowhere.

But God sent Jesus, who forgives us so that we have hope. Call out to Him and ask Him to enter our broken conversations. God inspired Saint Paul to write about the desperate condition in which we find ourselves. After Paul describes our hopelessness, he uses two words that are some of the most hopeful words in recorded literature. These two words are *But God,* often followed by a declaration of God's work and character. The words connect our inability with God's ability.

Paul's writings are not the only time we see these words in the Bible. There are numerous scriptural uses of *But God* in both the Old and New Testaments, which give us hope for redemptive conversations despite the despair in which we find ourselves. The following is a lengthy list:

In Genesis 8:1, Moses tells us that the waters prevailed on the earth for 150 days:
But God remembered Noah and all the beasts
and all the livestock that were in the ark.

Joseph said to his brothers in Genesis 45:8:
It was not you who sent me here, *but God.*

In Genesis 50:20, Joseph said again:
As for you, you meant evil against me, *but God* meant it for good, to bring it about that many people should be kept alive as they are today.

Saul sought David's life in 1 Samuel 23:14:
But God did not give him up into his hands.

In Psalm 49:15, fearing Sheol, David says:
But God will ransom my soul from the power of Sheol,
for he will receive me.

In Psalm 73:25–26, David declares:
Whom have I in heaven but you?
And there is nothing on earth that I desire besides you.
My flesh and my heart fail,
but God is the strength of my heart and my portion forever.

In Matthew 19:26, Jesus saw how confused his disciples were about who could be saved. Jesus looked at them and said:
With man this is impossible, *but* with *God* all things are possible.

In Acts 13:30, Paul preached that great sermon in Antioch about Christ being crucified. Paul exclaimed:
But God raised him from the dead.

In Romans 5:6–8, Paul discusses God's everlasting love for us:
For while we were still weak, at the right time Christ died for the ungodly. For one would scarcely die for a righteous person—though perhaps for a good person one would dare even to die—*but God* shows his love for us that while we were still sinners, Christ died for us.

In 1 Corinthians 1:27, Paul says:

But God chose what is foolish in the world to shame the wise."

In 1 Corinthians 3:6, Paul talks about the different roles there are in ministry and says:

I planted, Apollos watered, *but God* gave the growth.

In Ephesians 2:4, Paul describes the hopeless condition we are in and says:

But God, being rich in mercy, because of the great love with which he loved us, even when we were dead in our trespasses, made us alive together with Christ—by grace you have been saved.

In Philippians 2:27, Paul recounts how his beloved Christian brother Epaphroditus fell ill. Paul says:

Indeed he was ill, near to death. *But God* had mercy on him, and not only on him, but on me also, lest I should have sorrow upon sorrow.

Do you grasp the power behind the reality of *But God?* We cannot ever hope to achieve soul-satisfying communication under our own power. We are sinners and the people with whom we talk are sinners as well. But God, by His power, is at work in us, and He is able to do far more than we can ask or imagine.

I ask again: Is there hope that we can ever achieve soul-satisfying communication? No. On our own we are unable. But God is at work and He is able. God designed our Two Influential Forces, self-talk, and Speaking CODE to show us how much we need Him. God offers Himself to us in all the fullness of the Trinity where He works for our good and His Glory.

GOD'S POWER

As we mature into a greater understanding of our own helplessness, the Bible teaches us how to trust Him. God gives us the power of His indwelling Spirit to move beyond the frustrating conversations in which we are engaged. God then shows us His steadfast, unending, and everlasting love, which gives us hope that our past no longer dictates our present or future. Our response is to become abiders, Believers, and communers to the glory of God.

The question is, and always will be, what stops us from believing God? We can no longer offer up our Two Influential Forces, self-talk, and Speaking CODE as the reason we do not believe God works for our specific good. God is more powerful than any sadness and trauma brought about by the misery from our past.

JESUS BIDS US COME

Jesus bids us to bring Him our heavy burdens that sabotage our present life, and He promises to give us rest. Read the Word of the Lord from Matthew 11:28–30:

> Come to me, all who labor and are heavy laden, and I will give you rest. Take my yoke upon you, and learn from me, for I am gentle and lowly in heart, and you will find rest for your souls. For my yoke is easy, and my burden is light.

Rest includes making a way for us to redeem our wearying conversations. Rest includes finding meaning and purpose in what we have suffered. Rest includes stopping our persistent, debilitating self-talk so it no longer adds fuel to our Speaking CODE. Rest includes putting an end to our attempts to be loved and accepted, as evidenced by the words we choose in our conversations. Rest includes rejecting the hold our past has over us. Rest includes not chasing after the gods of our imagination in order to gain a modicum of relief from our distress.

Describe your heavy burden from which you need rest.

Be warned. There is always a yoke we must bear. However, whatever heavy burdens we carry, Jesus calls us to exchange them for His easy and light yoke. Why would we not take Jesus up on that offer? Jesus says His yoke is easier and lighter for us to carry than our own back-breaking load. Jesus invites us to learn from Him. Imagine that!

Write out what makes it hard for you to exchange your heavy burden for Jesus's lighter yoke.

How will this exchange of burdens affect your conversations?

Jesus invites us into a burden-bearing relationship. He asks us to carry His light burden as He carries our heavy ones. It seems to be an unfair swap. But so does that great exchange at the Cross where our sins were substituted for Jesus's righteousness. Every single thing that causes us to use soul-crushing words in our conversations is a burden Jesus wants to bear. When we come to Jesus, we have hope to find soul-satisfying rest so that our conversations can be righteous.

TWO WAYS OF VIEWING GOD'S POWER

The way we view God's power to accomplish soul-satisfying speech places us in one of two categories. First, there are those of us who, publicly or secretly, believe God's power is non-existent because God Himself is not real.

To those of you who do not believe in the reality of God's power because you doubt that God Himself is real, I understand. But our disbelief, by itself, does not make God's existence or His power unreal, does it? Perhaps something in our hearts leads us to affirm that God does not exist. I would like to challenge you to think about whether you are prepared to live life where there is no God.

C. S. Lewis deals with this issue very well. In his book, *The Silver Chair,* the evil Queen attempts to erase the memory of Aslan and his Overland from Puddleglum and the children, thinking this tactic will make the children's floundering memories disappear. Here is Puddleglum's response:

> "One word, Ma'am," he said, coming back from the fire; limping, because of the pain. "One word. All you've been saying is quite right, I shouldn't wonder. I'm a chap who always liked to know the worst and then put the best face I can on it. So I won't deny any of what you said. But there's one more thing to be said, even so. Suppose we have only dreamed, or made up, all those things—trees and grass and sun and moon and stars and Aslan himself. Suppose we have. Then all I can say is that, in that case, the made-up things seem a good deal more important than the real ones. Suppose this black pit of a kingdom of yours is the only world. Well, it strikes me as a pretty poor one. And that's a funny thing, when you come to think of it. We're just babies making up a game, if you're right. But four babies playing a game can make a play-world which licks your real world hollow. That's why I'm going to stand by the play-world. I'm on Aslan's side even if there isn't any Aslan to lead it. I'm going to live as like a Narnian as I can even if there isn't any Narnia. So, thanking you kindly for our supper, if these two gentlemen and the young lady are ready, we're leaving your court at once and setting out in the dark to spend our lives looking for Overland. Not that our lives will be very long, I should think; but that's a small loss if the world's as dull a place as you say."[23]

Puddleglum got this right. His faith in the Overland was fading because of the evil Queen's tactics. But Puddleglum chose to believe in Aslan regardless of his circumstances. Therefore, even in our direst of circumstances, the reality of God's power remains true.

If we do not believe in the existence of God or His power to change even our broken conversations, then the only hope we have is in ourselves. Every conversation that has gone bad is on us to redeem since, in our reality, we are our own god. Untangling bewildering conversations will be like spending our lives in a "black pit of a kingdom" of our own making.

Second, some believe God does exist, and His power is real. However, God seems too distant to help or care about the likes of us. Perhaps He is preoccupied with the business of being God. Meanwhile, we are left facing devastating conversations about rejection, lovelessness, infidelity, poverty, injustice, deception, death, or abandonment. The specific details of our problematic conversations seem to lack significance when we measure them up to the daily duties of God, who created and sustains all things.

How is that belief working out for us? More to the point, what evidence do we have that God is unconcerned, distracted, uncaring, uninvolved, busy, or preoccupied and doesn't care about our conversations?

If our evidence is that God has taken too long to answer, then we may want to revisit God's view on time. It is quite unlike our view. Peter tells us in 2 Peter 3 that the Lord is not slow in keeping His promises as we understand slowness. Instead, God is patient with us—and thank God He is because our salvation depends on His timing! We are far better off taking the psalmist's approach and ask God to teach us how to number our days so that we might gain a heart of wisdom. Read the word of the Lord in Psalm 90:9–12:

For all our days pass away under your wrath;
 we bring our years to an end like a sigh.
The years of our life are seventy,
 or even by reason of strength eighty;
yet their span is but toil and trouble;
 they are soon gone, and we fly away.
Who considers the power of your anger,
 and your wrath according to the fear of you?
So teach us to number our days
 that we may get a heart of wisdom.

If our evidence is that God said "no" to our specific and repeated requests, then we are serving a god of our imagination and not the God of the Bible. I do not know that god simply because that god works as you alone imagine him to work; in this I am of little help to you. We imagine things quite differently. I can only suggest that you sincerely ask yourself how the details of your life are working out. And I mean every single detail.

Whether we believe that there is no God or that the god who does exist is the god of our imagination, our life will not be satisfying. Our conversations will not be redemptive or fulfilling. Why? As I said before, without the God of the Bible, our words and our outcomes depend solely on us. That is dangerous, because we are all sinners. We all have gone astray as we carry on with the fallible gods of our own making.

Describe the God who you believe guides your conversations. How does your view of God affect the words you choose in difficult discussions?

What I say next may sound redundant. But it is important. Let us stay encouraged and faithful in our Bible reading. If there are those of us who do not read the Bible but go to study aids or commentaries, consider going back to reading the books in the Bible. All of us need to let the Bible speak to us as we ask the text good questions. Look for surprising things from the text itself rather than our preconceived ideas. Read the accounts where we see God acting on behalf of His creation. Read the great conversations people had with each other. Let us not be afraid of theology but rather look at how biblical theology personally affects us.

For those of us who faithfully read the Bible, the same exhortation applies as well. Stay away from commentaries or books about the Scriptures until you know God's Word well. Read the Bible in context. Seasoned Believers will find that the more we read the less impressed we are with our own ideas. We are still but babies in our biblical knowledge, so read on!

We know very well the god of our imagination. Now we can compare our imagined god to the God of the Bible. Let's look at the two verses from Isaiah 49 that paint a tender portrait of God's attentiveness toward us so we can see that the God of the Bible licks any other god hollow. Read the Word of the Lord from Isaiah 49:14–16:

> But Zion said, "The Lord has forsaken me; my Lord has forgotten me." "Can a woman forget the nursing child, that she should have no compassion on the son of her womb? Even these may forget, yet I will not forget. Behold, I have engraved you on the palms of my hand; your walls are continually before me."

God answers the question about Zion being forsaken. Silly us for thinking God can forsake us or not care about the tiniest details of our lives, like the words we say to one another. He starts by describing His unending concern with the analogy of a nursing mother. God will not forget us, just as a nursing mother cannot forget her nursing child or the son of her womb.

We sometimes marvel over the psychological attachment mothers have to their nursing babies. But there is also a physiological reason that a nursing mother cannot forget her child. Even if a mom chooses not to nurse her child, she will still deal with sore breasts as her milk diminishes. In either case, if her baby does not nurse, the mom's milk will so engorge her breasts that it causes tooth-aching pain and could even cause an infection! This throbbing makes it impossible for a mother to forget her nursing child. Therefore, according to this passage, it is physically, emotionally, and psychologically impossible for God to be so distracted that He forgets His children.

We are babies engraved on the very palm of God's hand. Here is an interesting thought: our hands keep our treasures safe. I have often said that if I wanted anyone to carry my grandbabies to safety, it would be an NFL quarterback or wide receiver. Why? His palms know how to protect a football and keep it safe when a 300-pound defensive lineman tries to flatten him like a pancake.

Finally, God puts an end to any thought that He can forsake His own. He says our walls are continually before Him, even those of us whose walls are frail! Walls provide safety and protection. Walls keep us safe by monitoring what passes to us from the outside or comes out of us from the inside. We have an unshakeable hope, knowing that the God of the Bible has our walls always before Him. Nothing that happens to us catches God off guard. Our imagined gods cannot hold a candle to the power of God Almighty.

REDEMPTIVE WORDS

Without God's redeeming work in our lives to show us purpose in suffering, our ECMs, PPIFSt, PPIFEx, and Speaking CODE will hinder our ability to talk graciously, or perhaps tempt us not to speak at all. Believing in the revealed God of the Bible is our only hope to speak redemptively despite the powerful past forces we encounter. This revealed (not imagined) God cares about us, right down to the number of hairs on our head and the very words we speak.

Speaking redemptively is rooted in God's transformational power in our lives. Where is my proof that this is true for you? Without hearing your story, I cannot answer you specifically. I will say this: if we are estranged from a necessary relationship in our lives, the only means by which reconciliation can happen is through the transforming power of God. If not, our Two Influential Forces, self-talk, and Speaking CODE will strangle our attempts to enter into soul-satisfying conversations. The best we can hope for is inauthentic and poverty-stricken exchanges, angry rants, obligatory niceties, or total silence. Please be aware that those of us who have suffered from sexual and physical abuse will find soul-satisfying conversations even more difficult. However, the same gracious God gives the same grace to all His children regardless of the circumstances. Even in the worst abuse, but God!

What if only one participant in the dialogue believes in the reality of God and His transformational power to heal? Good question. If you are the only person in the relationship who believes in the God of the Bible, start by approaching the conversation using the tools already offered in this book.

What is my goal for the conversation?

What do I want from this person and what am I willing to give up to get it?

How can the outcome allow both of us to live well?

If our goal is to use the right words in order to get the hearer to implement our good ideas, then the motive behind our goal could be manipulative. Do we believe that if we can just find the right words, said in the right order, with the right tone, we will convince the other person we are right? Is it our job to convince him and win? What about the hearer's desire to be right? Suppose the other person is more right than we are?

Worse still, suppose we are interacting with a non-Believer? It is wrong if we, as Believers, suggest to the non-Believer that if only he turns to God and believes, he will see how right we really are. This approach does not lead to redemptive conversations. Whoever God sends our way—saved or unsaved—let's commit to know him well as we eat a pound of dirt together.

As Believers, we are obligated to choose words that are consistent with biblical instruction regarding how we talk to one another. We must check our heart motives before entering conversations. We need to carefully guard against selfish motives. Speaking the truth in love is always a good place to start. Truth without love is harsh and judgmental. Love without truth is meaningless. To know how we are to talk to one another means we must read the Bible. As my dear friend Alice would say, "Look it up, honey!" There are no shortcuts here.

Our job is to present our case righteously and let God's Spirit work in the heart of the person to whom we speak. This takes the pressure off us, as we submit to the fact that God alone changes the human heart. After all, He created that heart in the first place. Never forget that our conversations happen in our intersecting holy sanctuaries, where God is making us His own as we honor Him as holy.

Our job is not to convince others that our ideas are better than theirs. I am not saying that our ideas are not good. They may very well be the best ideas on the table. Their ideas may be just plain stupid. I am not saying the other person's soul-killing words or deadly silence are not punishing. I believe you when you say they are.

What I am saying is, we who love Jesus must present our case in a soul-satisfying way. Words matter, or why else would God speak creation into being in the first place? Why would God even speak to Adam and the Woman, especially after they sinned? Why are there so many recorded conversations in the Bible? In fact, why even have God's Word at all? Presenting our case means that no Speaking CODE, assumption making, or PPIFSt/PPIFEx influences the words we choose.

Instead, let us ask good, clarifying questions rather than making assumptions or defending ourselves. Esteem the human in front of us, who has his own Two Influential Forces that fuels his Speaking CODE. Forgive one another deeply and from the heart. Trust the outcome to Jesus, the only true Lover of our soul. Only He has the power to penetrate and change hearts.

Pie vs. Cake

Let me give you a little autobiographical analogy here that will help us recognize the importance of knowing the other person well in order to have soul-satisfying conversations. Alan Dean and I love dessert after our dinner meal. After more than thirty-nine years of marriage, I know that Alan Dean prefers pie over nearly all baked goods. He especially loves black bottom pie, apple crumb pie, or strawberry pie. Did I mention blueberry pie? If not, add that to his list.

I, on the other hand, love cake. I love rich, dark, chocolate cakes with buttercream icing—and hold the cream, if you get my meaning. That is it. Just cake and butter with a little bit of cream to make the butter easier to spread. Well, maybe my good pound cake with whipped cream and strawberries would do. Or Bellissimo—how could I forget Bellissimo?

If I wanted to love my husband sweetly, I would make a nice dessert for dinner. If I wanted to love him wisely, I would make him pie for dessert and forgo my favorite cake. Both of us love desserts, but Alan Dean prefers pie. All this to say, when we enter a conversation with someone, we should make the effort to know if he likes pie or cake. This allows us to use words that make sense to him and demonstrates that we are interested in loving him well.

List ways in which you can speak to someone using words that show you understand him.

MISGUIDED CHRISTIAN ENTITLEMENTS

Before we discuss this topic, let me tell you what I do not mean. Christians are entitled to emulate men and women in the Bible who pleaded, begged, or cried out to God for help. Sometimes crying out, "Lord, have mercy on me a sinner," is our only hope. It is important to express our heart to God no matter how raw our emotions sound. Every heart is laid bare before God, so why not be truthful? There is no place to hide from Him. Therefore, we grab hold of God and pour out our hearts as a baby cries out to his parents. It is not a Misguided Christian Entitlement to throw ourselves before the throne of grace to beg our Father for help. Now that we understand what "Misguided Christian Entitlements" does not mean, let's look at what it does mean.

"Misguided Christian Entitlements" means that we, as Christians, cling to our belief that God should behave as we think best. This is certainly misguided and borders on lunacy. But how did we get to the place where we claim a right to have God behave as seems best to us? We may unwisely tell ourselves that we have decided to follow Jesus; therefore, we are entitled to get a say in how this decision turns out. We are too sophisticated to suggest that God owes us. But we do utter words that sound like this: "God, where is the abundant life You promised me? How come You allowed me to go through this? Can't I just catch a break? I think You are not seeing the big picture here."

Perhaps you would argue, "Diana, I would never ever entertain the thought that I am entitled to have God give me what I want because I am a Christian! That sense of entitlement is certainly misguided, as well as sinful, arrogant, dangerous, and crazy."

Maybe you do feel entitled or maybe you don't. I am just saying that if we listen closely to our conversations, via our self-talk, people-talk, and even our God-talk, we may just begin to see that I have a point. Our Misguided Christian Entitlements show up in the dark places of our hearts but become cleverly disguised by the words that come out of our mouths. Maybe we express our entitlements when we view ourselves as better than another image bearer. Maybe our entitlements seep out in our body language or our attitude toward difficult people in our lives. Maybe we do not accept rebukes from others because we have abandoned God's precepts. Maybe these entitlements come out in our secret or blatant self-soothing behaviors. Maybe we stop going to church or fellowshipping with other Believers. Maybe we secretly tell ourselves to just curse God and die.

The exchanges between Jesus and the ruling party in Israel are instructive to us. These men considered themselves true Believers. In Matthew, we see Jesus on blast, especially when Jesus associated the leaders with the Seven Woes found in Chapter 23. But the Seven Woes have context. Beginning in Matthew 21:23 and continuing through the end of Chapter 23, we observe a series of teachings and parables that address people who feel entitled based on their religiosity. They ask questions to trap Jesus by presenting problems too difficult to solve. Here are a few examples of those difficult questions. Read the word of the Lord in Matthew 22:15-17:

> Then the Pharisees went and plotted how to entangle him in his words. And they sent their disciples to him, along with the Herodians, saying, "Teacher, we know that you are true and teach the way of God truthfully, and you do not care about anyone's opinion, for you are not swayed by appearances. Tell us, then, what you think. Is it lawful to pay taxes to Caesar, or not?"

Also, in Matthew 22:23-28:

> The same day Sadducees came to him, who say that there is no resurrection, and they asked him a question, saying, "Teacher, Moses said, 'If a man dies having no children, his brother must marry the widow and raise up offspring for his brother.' Now there were seven brothers among us. The first married and died, and having no offspring left his wife to his brother. So too the second and third, down to the seventh. After them all, the woman died. In the resurrection, therefore, of the seven, whose wife will she be? For they all had her."

However, Jesus points out that it is not their position that entitles them to God's kingdom. Rather it is God's invitation to unworthy outsiders, good and bad. For us today, we question how God works in our lives and think we are entitled to so much better. We wonder why things are not working out the way we expected them to.

If we are able, do we see any Misguided Christian Entitlements we may be holding in our heart that show up in our life? We may tell ourselves that because we suffer like this, we deserve to get what we want or think what we think. Eventually, our behavior will reflect what is in our heart. For help, look for overindulging or excessive behaviors in our lives, like sex, food, gambling, working, drinking, spending, etc.

> Which Misguided Christian Entitlements do you hold on to? How do you see them expressed in your life?

◀ ··· ·— —· · ·— —·— ·· —· — —·   —·—· — — — —·· ·

Our Misguided Christian Entitlements give us cover to reject the hard work needed to enjoy soul-satisfying conversations. We complain that we are misunderstood rather than asking good questions to seek clarity. When those estranged from us ask to work out the key issues that keep us apart, we either reject their requests or deny their observations. We would rather wait until the

Spirit moves us before we jump into the mess. Perhaps God will wave His God wand, and all will be well, so we do not need to do the hard work necessary to mend our broken relationships or have soul-satisfying conversations. Or we consider ourselves the victim in our dialogues, and our questionable behavior is never our fault. It is always their fault. Our conversations reflect these truths as we cling to our Misguided Christian Entitlements.

List your sufferings that you believe entitle you to speak in ways that are not redemptive.

Write out what it feels like when others act out of their Misguided Christian Entitlements on you.

We also believe that our Misguided Christian Entitlements give us cover to speak however we wish to others. If someone courageously calls us out, we crush them. We believe that we have been hurt so badly by that person that we deserve to be suspicious, ruthless, or controlling toward him—but in the name of Jesus. We may use words that are controlling, bitter, cutting, deadly, full of assumptions, and unrighteous. Our Misguided Christian Entitlements tell us that we can take matters into our own hands. And so we do.

In conversations, list how your Misguided Christian Entitlements give you cover to take matters into your own hands.

Our Misguided Christian Entitlements wrongly use God's Word to defend our unrighteous behavior. We blame our unkind words and sinful assumptions on the Holy Spirit. We let it be known that we are not there yet, indicating that the Spirit has not convicted us of the sin that someone has brought to our attention. To us, that sin does not exist. The god of our imagination now has his very own theological playbook, which we ourselves have authored.

Sadly, our Misguided Christian Entitlements often make our conversations with God sound like the conversations we have with others. Some of us may even dare to accuse God of evil or doubt His existence because we do not get what we think we are entitled to receive. By creating a god of our imagination, whom we can control, we make our imagined god a substitute for Almighty God.

Entitlement and autonomy (self-rule) affect our corporate worship with other image-bearing Believers and may ultimately lead us to withdraw from public worship. Other Worshipers simply cannot understand the level of our pain, and therefore cannot minister to us the way they should. And the pastor? Well, he just does not get us or our situation at all. Our Misguided Christian Entitlements tell us we deserve specific attention to our needs because our pain is overwhelming.

May I lay out a challenge here? Look at your Misguided Christian Entitlements and ask what you believe they authorize you to say, think, or do. Do not be afraid. We all have our Misguided Christian Entitlements. But here is a warning: sometimes it is difficult to distinguish between our Misguided Christian Entitlements and the necessary work of the Spirit in our lives to make us holy.

Write out how you confuse the work of the Holy Spirit with your Misguided Christian Entitlements.

Maybe our entitlements give us reasons not to confront that bully in our lives. We say we are entitled to hold onto the pain the bully caused us. Instead of confronting the real bully or abuser in our lives, we redirect our words to others who may be safer to bully or control. These substitutes act as our scapegoats. Scapegoats are often innocent bystanders who happen to be in our line of fire when we exercise our Misguided Christian Entitlements. Many times they are our children, our spouse, our friends, our parents, or strangers on the phone that happen to call us at a bad time.

We may also raise our entitled fists toward the face of God and ask, "How dare you allow this happen to me?" Raising our fist to God's face is easier than examining the nature of our entitlements. But, be warned, raising our fist to God is not as safe as we may think. Our heart will be exposed as well as who or what we serve.

Like any other gods we make up, our Misguided Christian Entitlements will make unrelenting demands on us. We find ourselves bouncing from church to church or relationship to relationship because no one can satisfy our entitled expectations. In following the god of our imagination, our conversations become soul-crushing rather than soul-satisfying. We become insatiable. But God's sacrifice is sufficient and serving Him only can satisfy our hearts completely. Therefore, we must confess the sin of Misguided Christian Entitlements.

THE GREAT I AM

Here is the truth that counters our Misguided Christian Entitlements: God is not a man like us, nor is He a superhero like Batman. He is not a father like our earthly father, who may have been good or bad. We should not be fooled into thinking He is just a bit better than a Jedi Master. Our imaginary god is like the Queen's black pit of a world in *The Silver Chair.* Imaginary gods may offer us what we think we want, but imaginary gods can never satisfy us.

You and I need to lay down our Misguided Christian Entitlements and raise up our banner to El-Elyon, meaning God Most High. In doing so, our conversations will not be based on the effects of our PPIFSt and PPIFEx. Instead, our conversations will be rooted in the God who is like no other. We are not entitled to know God as we wish. Rather we are invited to know God as revealed in His Word. The revealed God vanquishes our imaginary gods.

In Isaiah, we see how God summons us by name and gives us titles of honor, even though we do not acknowledge Him. In His care for us, He goes before us to level mountains, break down gates, and give hidden treasure stored in secret places. God does this for His name sake and for His glory. Read the Word of the Lord in Isaiah 45:5–9 and 11b–12 (NIV):

> I am the Lord, and there is no other; apart from me there is no God. I will strengthen you, though you have not acknowledged me, so that from the rising of the sun to the place of its setting people may know there is none besides me. I am the Lord, and there is no other. I form the light and create darkness, I bring prosperity and create disaster; I, the Lord, do all these things.
>
> You heavens above, rain down my righteousness; let the clouds shower it down. Let the earth open wide, let salvation spring up, let righteousness flourish with it; I, the Lord, have created it.
>
> Woe to those who quarrel with their Maker, those who are nothing but potsherds among the potsherds on the ground. Does the clay say to the potter, "What are you making?" Does your work say, "The potter has no hands"? . . . Concerning things to come, do you question me about my children, or give me orders about the work of my hands? It is I who made the earth and created mankind on it. My own hands stretched out the heavens; I marshaled their starry hosts.

In summary, let us find meaning and purpose in our suffering while considering the weight of glory we are called to practice. Our POEPS try to persuade us to self-identify with our suffering but let us remember: But God. Rather let us take Jesus's yoke upon us. As we consider Isaiah's declaration, let us dispel the god of our imagination and stop raising our misguided entitled fists against the true God.

THE GOSPEL OF THE CROSS

As we approach the end of this book, what last thoughts should we consider regarding soul-satisfying conversations. What truths does the Gospel of the Cross teach us in how to speak redemptively? The Cross speaks louder than we can ever imagine. Let's consider some truths the Cross tells us.

THE GOOD CROSS

God's definition of good is nothing like ours. His definition of goodness includes perfect wrath, perfect anger, perfect sacrifice, perfect obedience, perfect torture, perfect justice, perfect punishment, and perfect love. This list could go on and on!

We struggle with the idea of associating "perfect" with these words and rightly so. We struggle because we have been sinful since our mother's womb, and that blinds us to the perfection of Jesus's sacrifice. I believe that is why we, even as Believers, wonder why inexplicable things happen to us or to those we love. We desperately try to make sense of our soul-killing conversations, while paying lip service to serving God. We need to relinquish our definition of goodness and replace it with God's definition. Read the word of the Lord in Psalm 23:6:

> Surely goodness and mercy shall follow me
> all the days of my life,
> and I shall dwell in the house of the Lord
> forever.

Considering God's definition of good, Psalm 23:6 makes perfect sense to skeptics like me. David assures us that goodness and mercy follow us every day of our lives and then we die. That means we can find goodness and mercy in our challenging and painful conversations when we begin to see them through God's definition.

David also says, in Psalm 27:13, that we will see God's goodness in the land of the living. The Cross of Christ expresses God's perfection of goodness. Understanding this perfection leads us to confess that our knowledge of His goodness is limited by our own sinfulness. All that follows us and all that we experience in the land of the living is good.

We may rightly say, "Diana, I believe you when you suggest that our view of God's specific goodness toward us is woefully inadequate when compared to the kind of goodness displayed on the Cross. But I still feel as though God is not paying attention to me or listening to the cry of my heart." How could a good God allow me to go through the things I experienced?"

In all honesty, I agree that we experience feelings that God has turned away His gaze and His arrows appear to be headed directly at us. Many of David's Psalms, speak to our incredulousness. Read the Word of the Lord in Psalm 38:1-3:

> Lord, do not rebuke me in your anger or discipline me in your wrath. Your arrows have pierced me, and your hand has come down on me. Because of your wrath there is no health in my body; there is no soundness in my bones because of my sin. My guilt has overwhelmed me like a burden too heavy to bear.

You may say, but Diana, the context of David's Psalm is about how our sinfulness plays itself out in our life. True but that is not the only thing Scripture says on the subject. Read the righteous Job's sadness in Job 3:23–26:

> Why is life given to a man whose way is hidden, whom God has hedged in? For sighing has become my daily food; my groans pour out like water. What I feared has come upon me; what I dreaded has happened to me. I have no peace, no quietness; I have no rest, but only turmoil.

Dear Friend, if we were sitting together sharing a cup of hot tea, we would weep over the fact that our circumstances do not look like a good God sent them to us, no matter how they came into our lives. But then we go to the Scriptures. Read the Word of the Lord in Psalm 30:4–5:

> Sing praises to the Lord, O you his saints, and give thanks to his holy name. For his anger is but for a moment, and his favor is for a lifetime. Weeping may tarry for the night, but joy comes with the morning.

This Psalm is a fuller picture and helps us acknowledge what is true. For but a moment, we feel the effects of what we may conclude is God's anger. In response, we say God has forsaken us. But then, if we move beyond the pain and sorrow, we discover that His favor is for a lifetime. This is part of God's specific goodness and mercy following us until we go into His outstretched arms.

THE CROSS IS CURSED, BUT GOOD

How can something cursed be good? Because of our sin, we could never hang on the cursed Cross to make peace with a righteously angry God. For us, bearing the Cross could never fully atone for our sins because we are sinful. Sin blinds us from soul-satisfying conversations and guides us toward soul-crushing speech. Even if our words sound redemptive, the motivations of our sinful hearts will eventually play out in our interactions with each other.

But Jesus earned the right to hang on the cursed Cross because He is good. In doing so, He made that cursed Cross good for us. God's righteous wrath was satisfied when Christ bore the curse of our sin. Even though we are still corrupted by sin, our souls have an unshakable hope that our conversations can be righteous.

The power and the grace of the indwelling Holy Spirit enables us to speak redemptively. Unfortunately, indwelling sin mutes the voice of the Holy Spirit, which leads us to make assumptions, practice unforgiveness, and Speak CODE. We use harsh, judgmental, or accusatory words filled with critical tones, shaming gestures, or unrelenting silence.

As the Holy Spirit guides us through our sanctification as it relates to our ability to communicate, we would be wise to realize that we are at different check points along this path. When it comes to understanding conversations, some of us are at the beginning of the process, while others have progressed further. Wherever we are on this path, we are still responsible for the words we use in difficult conversations.

You may rightly ask, can those whose sin has not been covered by the blood of Christ have soul-satisfying conversations? That is a good question. Let me make two relevant points. First, God's common grace is for all His creation. The sun shines and the rain falls on both the just and the unjust (Matthew 5:45). It would make sense that a non-Believer could communicate well depending on how he understands his Two Influential Forces, self-talk, or Speaking CODE.

Second, we should not act as if we know the intentions of a non-Believer's heart. That is up to God. Instead, let's presume on God's mercy when we are in tough conversations with non-Believers. God calls us to love everyone. He desires that no one should perish. He will not break a bruised reed or quench a smoldering wick until He brings justice to victory (Matthew 12:20). So why shouldn't we act the same way? We must follow God as we speak graciously to those who do not believe in Jesus's atoning work and leave the rest to Him.

The Foundation, the House, and the Materials

Many of us who are in difficult relationships experience soul-crushing conversations with a necessary person in our life. Based on the words he says, we wonder if the other person, who professes Jesus, is truly born again. We wonder how a Believer can talk to us as he does. In 1 Corinthians 3, Paul addresses this issue. In the context of this passage, Paul warns the Corinthians not to judge between him and Apollos based on the execution of their different offices. Paul goes on to say that the essential issue is not how we *express* our faith but rather the *foundation* upon which our faith is built. That foundation is Jesus Christ. Read the Word of the Lord from 1 Corinthians 3:10–15:

> According to the grace of God given to me, like a skilled master builder I laid a foundation, and someone else is building upon it. Let each one take care how he builds upon it. For no one can lay a foundation other than that which is laid, which is Jesus Christ. Now if anyone builds on the foundation with gold, silver, precious stones, wood, hay, straw—each one's work will become manifest, for the Day will disclose it, because it will be revealed by fire, and the fire will test what sort of work each one has done.
> If the work that anyone has built on the foundation survives, he will receive a reward. If anyone's work is burned up, he will suffer loss, though he himself will be saved, but only as through fire.

This passage is interesting because Paul may be describing how pastors build the foundation of Jesus Christ through their ministry. Or it may describe individuals who build their foundations on Jesus. In either case, Jesus is the foundation for the local church and for each Believer. Let's apply this illustration to how we personally build our lives on the True Foundation.

Paul says that we may build our faith with either worthy or worthless materials. Whichever materials we use, we must build our faith on the only sure foundation, Jesus Christ. We are not able to assess the other person's foundation. Only God can do that. Unless a person denies having faith in Christ, we cannot comment on that difficult person's salvation based on their words or behaviors. The poor expression of their faith (or building materials), as seen in their conversations, will burn up. However, if they have Christ as the sure foundation upon which they built their faith, they will be saved, but only as through a fire. Ultimately, the day of Christ's return will reveal how well or how poorly everyone's house is built.

Since a Believer's foundation is built on Jesus Christ, we have hope that the works built upon that foundation will be redemptive, particularly in our conversations. Less mature Believers may not yet be building with what Paul would describe as costly materials. Less costly materials, in our conversations, could mean words based on assumptions, unforgiveness, or reactions to our past painful experiences. Less costly materials will affect what we say and do.

Non-Believers build on a different foundation. Because of common grace, they still may use gracious language. It is not our place to judge someone else's intentions and actions. Asking good questions in an argument is far more gracious than using language that diminishes our fellow human.

Pretense and Our Words

Sometimes, we hide behind our own pretense of goodness. We can reek of false nobility as we cut each other to pieces with our words or our silence. We may use clever sentences to shift blame, so that we can become the hero of our own story, and they the villain. Perhaps we try to control conversations, believing that we are entitled to deferential words from others. However, we no longer need to fall into these traps, because on that cursed Cross, Jesus brought goodness to us.

Therefore, the next time we feel like climbing up on that cursed Cross to humble our neighbor with our words, stop and repent. We must climb back down our ladder of perceived goodness. We are not the savior in our own story—Jesus is.

THE CROSS IS BRUTAL, BUT GOOD

Only God can design such a horrific death for His beloved Son and make the outcome good! The brutality displayed during the crucifixion is beyond human comprehension. But the brutality of that good Cross gives us peace, because through it the wrath of God was satisfied. Every brutal wound Jesus endured brought us healing. The outcome of such brutality shows us how far God would go to redeem us.

We may still bear the brutality of our Two Influential Forces. While these forces are fierce, they are ultimately for our good and God's glory. It is through our path of righteousness that we learn humility in our words, compassion in our tone, and strength in our resolve. We learn that we are equal with each other in our humanity as we stand beneath that brutal but good Cross of Jesus. Beneath that Cross we learn that there is forgiveness for our sins. We learn that we can speak redemptively because we have been redeemed by that brutal but good Cross. Consequently, we have renewed hope in every area of our lives, including how we talk to each other.

THE CROSS IS SHAMEFUL, BUT GOOD

It was on that shameful Cross, alongside Jesus, that a thief-of-a-man passed from death into life as he was being crucified. This thief-of-a-man confessed his own shame as he accepted his fate. The words he spoke came from observing Jesus and using Jesus as an example to follow. This thief-of-a-man spoke deep truths about himself and his fellow criminal. That shameful Cross where the thief-of-a-man hung ultimately became his passage into glory. Read the Word of the Lord from Luke 23:39–43:

> One of the criminals who were hanged railed at him, saying, "Are you not the Christ? Save yourself and us!" But the other rebuked him saying, "Do you not fear God, since you are under the same sentence of condemnation? And we indeed justly, for we are receiving the due reward of our deeds; but this man has done nothing wrong." And he said, "Jesus, remember me when you come into your kingdom." And he said to him, "Truly, I say to you, today you will be with me in paradise."

This ought to bring us to tears! Can we not be as tenderhearted in our rebukes, accepting of our consequences, and humble in our confessions as was this thief-of-a-man? This thief's last recorded words were redemptive despite his own past. Look at his words. He rebuked his fellow criminal, not as one who stands over his fellow lawbreaker but as an equal. The only thing that stood between this thief-of-a-man and his fellow criminal was Jesus. Sometimes, the only thing that stands between us and our conversational opponent is Jesus, the only true Lover of our souls.

He asked his fellow criminal one of life's most important questions in the context of deep suffering: "Do you not fear God?" In our intense suffering, do we not fear God? The Bible says fearing Him is where understanding begins (Proverbs 1:7). Let us begin to fear our Holy God and believe He works for our good in every way we suffer, including in our death-like relationships.

We can follow the example of this thief-of-a-man and stop blaming Jesus for our broken lives that seem unrecognizable. Even as he was dying, this thief-of-a-man was not afraid to speak up against his own sin and the injustice Jesus suffered. We can honor this man's death by fearlessly speaking truth in love even in conversations where we stand to lose what is precious. The truth is, we might lose it even if we speak fearlessly.

The Scriptures record the last moments of this dying man so that we can live better. This thief-of-a-man literally had Jesus on his side! We do not know if that gave him courage to confront his fellow criminal. But we have something that thief-of-a-man never had. We live our lives under the constant watchful eye of the Holy Spirit. The thief-of-a-man experienced the work of the Spirit when he encountered Jesus on that fateful day. The Spirit's work is masterful. Read the Word of the Lord from Romans 8:26–30:

> Likewise the Spirit helps us in our weakness. For we do not know what to pray for as we ought, but the Spirit himself intercedes for us with groanings too deep for words. And he who searches hearts knows what is the mind of the Spirit, because the Spirit intercedes for the saints according to the will of God. And we know that for those who love God all things work together for good, for those who are called according to his purpose. For those whom he foreknew he also predestined to be conformed to the

> image of his Son, in order that he might be the firstborn among many brothers. And those whom he predestined he also called, and those whom he called he also justified, and those whom he justified he also glorified.

In our broken or nonexistent conversations, we must be brave and not give up as the Holy Spirit intercedes for us in accordance with the will of God. Just as that thief-of-a-man had Jesus by his side we, too, have the very Spirit of God living within us. Be brave at the foot of that shameful-but-good Cross!

THE CROSS IS HUMILIATING, BUT GOOD

God offers a way to move toward soul-satisfying communication with those who may want to do us harm. Christ's humiliation on the Cross gives us a pathway to be humble with one another, especially in our conversations. A professor at CCEF called this going low. I first heard this concept during one of his convicting lectures at CCEF in Glenside, Pennsylvania.

He describes this humbling process of going low as taking up our cross and following Jesus. What does that mean if our cross is bearing the load of soul-crushing communication (or deathly silence)? This communication hurts too much. We can't even think about these people without a tremendous sense of loss, let alone have a conversation with them. The anxiety level is so overwhelming that we shut down or live in denial. We fear that we will be devastated by what they will say to us or us to them. The rejection of who we are as humans leaves us wondering if we are too broken to be loved by anyone. In order to counteract what the other person says, we consider using defensive words that sound almost murderous. Going low can be uncomfortable because it requires a Christ-like humility.

And yet, Christ often requires us to humbly go low and find something for which we can confess and seek forgiveness. We may need to go low even if the blame rests mainly on the other person. By going low, we recognize that deeper issues exist that we cannot fix. It is more loving to cover the offense, to be willing to be wronged, and to not take offense. Humility can accept that we may not gain the satisfaction of knowing that the other person recognizes that they were wrong as well.

I am not saying that we make up something for which we can confess. It is not a question of compromising our integrity. I am saying that if we move closer to those who grieve our hearts, we might better see how, in truth, we may have used words that hurt them, just as they used words to hurt us. It is hard to swallow a pound of dirt, as my mom encouraged me to do. Prayer for wisdom is essential. David's prayer for wisdom is instructive. Read the word of the Lord in Psalm 139:23–24:

> Search me, O God, and know my heart!
> Try me and know my thoughts!
> And see if there be any grievous way in me,
> and lead me in the way everlasting!

We can pray that prayer. It is possible to call out to Jesus and ask Him to show us how we have hurt others with our words. We can go low and ask how our words affected them. Perhaps we have done nothing wrong. If so, can we pray a prayer for humility in the moment when we want justice? Can we pray a prayer for humility to love that person where they are and not lash out or seek personal gratification? It is to our credit to go low and humbly love others in their weakness. Our only alternative is to isolate ourselves and become prisoners of our own selfish echo chambers. Read the Word of the Lord from Proverbs 18:1:

> Whoever isolates himself seeks his own desire;
> he breaks out against all sound judgment.

Jesus humbled Himself by taking on a human form and, through obedience, hung on a humiliating Cross. Let us follow Jesus, humbling our hearts as we speak words that reflect graciousness. Let us draw near to God as we resist the urge to use words based on our self-talk. Let us reject the desire to Speak CODE so that our words are clear and there is no need for assumptions. Additionally, we can go low by turning our assumptions into good questions and our self-righteousness into wisdom. In our humility, Jesus will exalt us.

JESUS HIGH AND LIFTED UP

Jesus was high and lifted up for all mankind to see as He hung on the Cross. What do we see as we gaze upon Jesus lifted up before us? Let us linger here just briefly, as we witness the unfolding drama before us.

What do we see? Among other things, mankind saw the humility of obedience, a mutilated body, an unprecedented vulnerability never seen before, the sinless made sinful, a once-for-all-time sacrifice for an undeserving race, a task finished, and, finally, God's wrath satisfied.

Mankind saw a defenseless Savior as He was high and lifted up. Jesus was extraordinarily helpless, subject to every insult or sneer by anyone who played a part in His death sentence—and that includes us. Jesus did not retaliate, nor did He keep completely silent. Jesus was verbally and physically assaulted to the point of utter exhaustion. We know this because He could not carry His own cross to Golgotha.

Mankind saw Jesus's nakedness, both body and soul, as He was high and lifted up. We know that Jesus's body was nearly naked because people cast lots for his clothes. We know His soul was naked because we read the words of scorn, accusation, and contempt hurled at Jesus even though no one gave evidence that He did anything wrong. Because of this, Jesus sympathizes with us and understands our sorrow when we are falsely accused in soul-crushing conversations.

Mankind saw Jesus forsaken by His Father as He was high and lifted up. As Believers, we will never understand the true meaning of being forsaken by God. Jesus willingly took this separation onto Himself so that we would never experience what forsakenness truly means. Let us rejoice in the fact that on the high and lifted-up Cross, Jesus took our place. If you have not called out to Jesus as your Savior, I invite you to ask Jesus to show Himself to you. Accept Jesus as the One who was forsaken by His Father so that you will never be forsaken in this life or the next.

What were the results as Jesus was high and lifted up on the Cross? Where once we were alienated from God, we are now His sons and daughters. Jesus is our Brother. The Holy Spirit is our Comforter. This new relationship gives us courage to engage in soul-satisfying conversations.

What did mankind hear when Jesus was high and lifted up? We heard insults, cries of incomprehensible agony, the last request of a dying Son, a sinner's confession, and the best benediction ever composed: "It is finished." Our cries of incomprehensible agony will not go unnoticed, because Jesus completely understands such cries. We can utter words of confession or hear someone else's confession, even under the most difficult circumstances. We can forgive as Jesus forgave us while He hung on that Cross. Such confessions and forgiveness will change the trajectory of our relationships and our conversations.

Mankind also heard how important family relationships are in the eyes of Jesus. While dying, Jesus provided for the care of His mother. That tells us we need to care for our families and seek reconciliation whenever possible. This will affect the words we use in our conversations, even when our ECMs, PPIFSt, and PPIFEx would drive us apart. We can keep our self-talk from fueling the CODE we speak. If we cannot achieve reconciliation, we must remain present in the relationship while we actively forebear.

What did mankind learn as we saw our Savior high and lifted up on that Cross? We learned that even in the worst situations, we can stop using beastly language or resorting to deadly silence in our conversations. As we enter Christ's agony, we can learn to use life-giving words of hope instead of words of death. We can choose words that are not driven by assumptions but are guided by good questions. We can use words that cover sin because our love is stronger than hate. We can be willing to speak the truth in love, based on understanding and not on self-talk driven by our past. We can forgive both those in the grave and those still breathing God's air.

What can mankind do as we see Him high and lifted up? We can join Jesus in His vulnerability in how we talk to each other. Jesus spoke truth in love throughout the entire process of His crucifixion. We know this by the words Jesus uttered as He was crucified. He spoke words of care, hope for future glory, and forgiveness.

We can model vulnerability with our words as we see Jesus high and lifted up. We can show willingness to investigate past statements and experiences said and done to us. This investigation will help us stop hiding who we are in the middle of our pain. We no longer live in the fear that makes us want to control conversations. We have a great High Priest who understands our vulnerability and nakedness. Pray for our hearts to be like Jesus's heart, even when talking is excruciating.

WORDS FROM THE CROSS

Let us listen to our Jesus as He spoke to us from His cursed, brutal, shameful, humiliating-but-good Cross. Let us hear His words speak into our lives. Let Him guide how we talk to one another. Jesus asks us to learn from Him, for He is gentle and lowly in heart. Even though these words were spoken over two thousand years ago, they are for us today.

THE FIRST SAYING: "Father, forgive them, for they know not what they do."(Luke 23:34)

It is never too late to forgive the people who have wounded us to the point of emotional death. We must do this without reservation or excuse. Jesus is our High Priest and has shown us the way of forgiveness. Jesus never sinned against anyone, and yet He forgave. Remember, forgiving the person to God is non-negotiable. Because of this, we have hope in Jesus for soul-satisfying conversations rather than soul-crushing speech.

THE SECOND SAYING: "Truly, I say to you, today you will be with me in paradise." (Luke 23:43)

It is never too late to repent of our sins and seek the saving power of Jesus, who promises to "remember us in Paradise." Jesus promises not only to welcome us into Paradise but also to be with us every day of our life here on Earth. During those countless moments of joy and sadness, Jesus tenderly guides and directs us until He calls us home. He redeems our souls to glory as surely as He redeems our broken lives on this earth. Because of this, we have hope in Jesus for soul-satisfying conversations rather than soul-crushing speech.

THE THIRD SAYING: "Woman, behold your son! . . . Son, behold your mother!" (John 19:26–27)

In the last moments of His life, Jesus recognized His mother, which tells us that He honors necessary relationships. Jesus took care of His mother by providing protection for her. What do we know about this parent-child relationship? We know that Jesus never sinned against His mother. But Mary was sinful. We do not know how her sinfulness played itself out in how she raised Jesus, but we know her sinfulness was present.

For my dear Roman Catholic friends who read this, I am more than willing to accept your disagreement with me about Mary's sinless state. Let me point out that Joseph was the man who stepped in as Jesus's earthly father. He was a sinner. As a sinner, at least Joseph would have sinned against Jesus. Nevertheless, Jesus displayed a high regard for His mother and sought to care for her throughout the remainder of her life.

Let's consider Jesus's love for His mother and how it speaks to us today. Many of us suffer because of the neglect, abuse, and selfishness of our earthly parents or caretakers. There is no excuse for what was done to us by those in authority over us. Either in this life or the next, they will be required to give an account. Hopefully, they will confront their own story which gave them cover to behave badly toward those of us who suffered the effects of their sin while we were under their care.

And yet, the brokenness in our family relationships is God's goodness and mercy following us. It is hard to see how this dysfunction is good, but that does not mean we must remain blind to hope. We can see Jesus as He cared for His mother under horrific circumstances and at least consider what it would take to reconcile our necessary relationships even in our pain. The burden of the damaging memories our parents bore were placed on us, and they still with our present relationships, including our conversations. The sins of the father become the sins of the children. It is no wonder our relationships are characterized by brokenness and unforgiveness.

Are our harmful words to the people in our lives really about what our parents did or did not do to us? They may well be! Let us decide here and now that our past will no longer have the power to direct what we say or hear in the present. The relationship we have with our parents is important. Let us ask God to help us heal from the pain inflicted by our selfish, neglectful, or abusive parents and caretakers. Ask Jesus to keep us from retaliation. Ask Jesus to help us identify how their bad behavior sabotages our ability to speak redemptively with others. Ask Jesus to give us wisdom to recognize the soul-crushing words we use in present conversations and see how these words link to our past. We need insight to see that we may be addressing our abusers and not the person to whom we are speaking. Ask Jesus to free us from the hold our past has on us.

I am not advocating open rebellion against our parents for their failures. I am challenging us to actively engage our thoughts and ensure that it is God who directs our path. It is God who gives meaning and purpose to our earliest suffering. I am also asking that we seek to engage our parents in conversations, if possible. We may need the help of a biblical counselor for this.

When all else fails, we should not throw up our hands in despair and give up. Our last resort in unsatisfying conversations is to raise up our broken hands and hearts to God in active prayer and beg Him for mercy and grace. His mercy and grace are there in abundance for us.

For those caregivers who perpetrated evil or did damage to their children, what stops you from seeking reconciliation? Are you too proud? Do you say you did the best you could do given your limitations? Do you cast off your children's request to have that painful conversation that might help them discover truth?

Taking responsibility for harming someone in our care is very difficult. Perpetrators feel shame and wish to hide their sin for fear of exposure or condemnation. There is too much to lose—especially one's reputation. However, the perpetrator must humbly repent and be gracious when confronted by the victim, even if that victim is his child. Repentance involves vulnerability as the once-powerful perpetrator follows the now-powerful victim's lead.

One more thought about our parents. God specifically picked our parents for us (and our siblings for that matter). We generally pick our friends, but we do not pick our biological parents. God does. There is no rationality to the progressive concept that we pick the family we choose. If we had abusive parents—physically, emotionally, or sexually—we may rightly ask, "God, what made you give me these people that I am forced to call parents?"

I believe God gives us our parents because only these particular parents can teach us a side of God's character that He specifically wants us to know. If our parents were absent, God is ever present. If our parents were neglectful, God is generous toward us. If our parents were abusive, God carries us like little lost sheep and speaks tenderly to us. No one else could teach us about God's everlasting love as well as our specific parents. Our earthly parents' poverty toward us is a perfect contrast to God's riches for us.

God's plan for our good is purposeful, not evil or capricious. The challenge is to ask God to reveal His character to us through our earthly parents. The relationship we have with our parents is vital. It is a necessary relationship into which God has placed us so we can see Him better. As we understand the purposefulness of God's plan, we can overcome the Two Influential Forces that tend to obscure God's providential care. If not, our self-talk will lead to Speaking CODE and soul-crushing speech. We will mistrust God just as we mistrust our parents. Instead, the imperfect parents whom God has chosen for us will show us how He parents us with perfection. But we must search for God's purpose behind our parents' imperfection and that is very hard. Finding

God's purpose will help us untie our past from our present so that we can work toward enjoying soul-satisfying conversations.

If we were sipping hot tea together, I would confess that I have no idea why you and I have the parents we have. I would also confess that I am clueless as to why God would refer to Himself as Father when many of us have terrible fathers. In all my years, the only answer that makes any sense is that by giving us earthly parents who fail us, we are driven to God who never fails. Whatever they lack, God has in perfect abundance.

THE FOURTH SAYING: "My God, my God, why have you forsaken me?" (Matthew 27:46)

As Believers, we will never experience the kind of forsakenness that Jesus experienced while He hung on that sin-cursed Tree. Jesus is the perfect Lamb of God who did what no one else could do. Jesus still bears the brutal marks in His resurrected body. God now sees us through His Son's righteousness and not through our sin. If you do not believe in the atoning work of Jesus, you will experience forsakenness. Do not doubt the Scriptures because your immortal soul depends upon it.

Believers will never be forsaken by God. Ever. We may be tempted to ask God why He has forsaken us. But we misunderstand God if we don't know that He watches over us and treasures us. Read the Word of the Lord from Isaiah 62:3–4:

> You shall be a crown of beauty in the hand of the Lord, and a royal diadem in the hand of your God. You shall no more be termed Forsaken, and your land shall no more be termed Desolate.

Jesus alone was forsaken as He willingly bore what, for us, would have been absolutely unbearable. Please do not get me wrong. We can tell God that we cannot see Him in the middle of the storm. We can cry out with a bitter heart that we feel alone. We can ask Him if He hears us. But we can never, ever say that He has forsaken us. Why? Because God needed perfection to forsake and that we are not! As those who will never be forsaken, we can rest in God's grace to speak redemptively.

THE FIFTH SAYING: "I thirst." (John 19:28)

Satisfying thirst is a primal need. It is a live or die need. While dying on the Cross, Jesus remarked about His thirst to fulfill biblical prophecy. While I do not want to over-spiritualize this, I do want to acknowledge something Jesus said about the ultimate thirst-quenching experience. After He and the woman at the well exchanged comments about cultural differences, historical events, and the importance of the well, Jesus made her an unusual offer of tasting living water. Read the Word of the Lord from John 4:13–15:

> Jesus said to her, "Everyone who drinks of this water will be thirsty again, but whoever drinks of the water that I will give him will never be thirsty again. The water that I will give him will become in him a spring of water welling up to eternal life." The woman said to him, "Sir, give me this water, so that I will not be thirsty or have to come here to draw water."

This living water welling up to eternal life goes even deeper than the primal thirst Jesus experienced on the Cross. We need that living water to live, just as Jesus needed water in that very moment to survive a bit longer. That same living water offered to the Samaritan woman rains down like righteousness on us. Jesus's living water cleanses our hearts from the ravages of our past. This frees us from the need to Speak CODE so that we can begin to enjoy satisfying conversations.

Jesus taught about hungering and thirsting after righteousness. But what does that mean? I believe there is a sense in which we can hunger for righteous conversations and thirst for understanding as we taste and see that the Lord is good. Read the Word of the Lord in Matthew 5:6:

> Blessed are those who hunger and thirst for righteousness,
> for they shall be satisfied.

We long for lives that are fulfilling, including conversations that are soul-satisfying. What if we took Jesus up on the promises found in His word that He alone provides life-giving waters that will deeply satisfy our insatiable souls? While we may still wrap ourselves in past despairs, Jesus's righteousness will clothe us anew as we hunger and thirst after Him.

THE SIXTH SAYING: "It is finished." (John 19:30)

"It is finished" is our Savior's benediction. Jesus obediently completed the work He was sent to do by His Heavenly Father. We cannot say "it is finished" the way Jesus said it, because we have no idea when God will call us home or meet us in the clouds. But we can use this text to talk about how well we finish the race God has set before us.

As I write these words, one dearest to my heart is dying. She may not read this manuscript or see it in print. I get to witness how she finishes her race while giving glory to God in the middle of relentless suffering. When her life is finished, her family, especially her granddaughters, will know how intensely she loved them. Who knows when she or any of us will finish our race? The question is what our race looks like until it is finished. One day, Jesus will call the one I love to a banquet that will satisfy her like nothing else ever has.

What about us? We can think about how soul-satisfying words in a conversation are more like Jesus than soul-crushing words. Let that be part of our race, as we use Jesus's life as an example to finish the course set before us. If we could look down the tunnel of time and know when God will say, "It is finished for you. Come home now," how would that knowledge change the everyday conversations we have with each other? This is worth considering.

How do we live well under the circumstances in which we find ourselves until we are finished? How does the one I dearly love live well, knowing that tomorrow may never come? How does one live well in the middle of intense loss? How does one live well in the elation of unexpected joy or the calmness of the ordinary? Without knowing your circumstances, I cannot tell you how to live well in the particulars of your experience. I can say that our walk is by faith and not by sight. Jesus specifically authored the circumstances under which He calls us to live well. He promises never to leave us as we abide, believe, and commune in Him. We may struggle to live well as we suffer in this world. But in the world to come, the struggle will be over; we will live in the presence of Jesus forever. Because Jesus pronounced this benediction on the Cross, we have hope in Jesus for soul-satisfying conversations rather than soul-crushing speech.

THE SEVENTH SAYING: "Father, into your hands I commit my spirit!" (Luke 23:46)

There will come a day when every knee will bow and every tongue confess that Jesus is Lord to the glory of God. But what about now? Is there a sense in which we can commit our spirit into the Father's hands while still on this earth? I think so. By committing our thoughts, words, and deeds to God we lessen the effects our Two Influential Forces have on our conversations. Our lives are safer when we give them into the hands of our God, who will help us in the in-between time (the time between birth and death) as we engage in our everyday dialogues.

During this in-between time, suppose we said to God, "Father, into Your hands I commit my attitude, my sinful speech, my anguish, my sorrow, my loneliness, my rejection, my failures, my fears, my pride, my arrogance, my self-righteousness, or my unbelief," and we never picked it back up again?

We can commit these things to Jesus. I say this knowing full well that it is nearly impossible for us to do this consistently. We will take it back up because we are still in this body. But we can return it to Jesus with greater haste and a stronger resolve. Giving our pain back to Jesus more hastily gives Jesus a longer time to keep us safe from our pain. We can give Jesus our tendencies to sin against each other which affect our speech. This gives us hope for soul-satisfying conversations rather than soul-crushing speech.

Considering the Cross where Jesus uttered His last words, our hearts can meditate on and appropriate their significance for how we conduct our conversations. As we meditate on the Cross as an historic and cosmic event, we participate in His broken body and His shed blood for us. We feed on Jesus by faith with thanksgiving and commit our lives to Him.

THE CRY OF THAT BLOOD-STAINED CROSS

But then there is that blood-stained Cross. The soul-crushing communication between us and the people in our lives reflects the horrible goodness of that blood-stained Cross. Here is how this works:

- The Cross speaks louder than those Two Influential Forces that affect our words. These forces may inform us, but they no longer determine our path. Follow the Cross!
- The Cross speaks louder than our self-talk which fuels our Speaking CODE. Our self-talk can easily condemn or confirm our thoughts and give us cover to say only snippets of our thinking, which leads to the CODE we speak. Speaking CODE hides who we really are and forces the hearer to make assumptions. The power of the Cross frees us so that we can be truly known. Listen to the Cross!
- The Cross speaks louder than our humiliation, pain, loneliness, frustration, self-righteousness, anger, and disappointments. All of these are displayed in our sad conversations with our spouses, children, friends, family members, and God. Heed the Cross!

Through this blood-stained Cross, God designs and uses our failures to bring us to Himself. Read the Word of the Lord from Psalm 23:

The Lord is my shepherd; I shall not want.
He makes me lie down in green pastures.
He leads me beside still waters.
He restores my soul.
He leads me in paths of righteousness
for his name's sake.
Even though I walk through
the valley of the shadow of death,
I will fear no evil,
for you are with me;
your rod and your staff,
they comfort me.
You prepare a table before me
in the presence of my enemies;
you anoint my head with oil;
my cup overflows.
Surely goodness and mercy
shall follow me all the days of my life,
and I shall dwell in the
house of the Lord forever.

Look at the purposefulness of our Shepherd. It is this Good Shepherd who does the hard work. It is He who leads, directs, restores, prepares, and anoints us. It is His rod and staff that comfort us, so that we can walk fearlessly with Him through the darkest valley.

This psalm concludes with one of the most startling verses in all of Scripture which I have used throughout this book: "Surely goodness and mercy shall follow me all the days of my life, and I shall dwell in the house of the Lord forever."

Somehow, all the soul-crushing conversations we have are actually God's goodness and mercy following us all the days of our lives. While we are responsible for the sinful words we say and think, whatever befalls us is God's goodness and mercy to us. The final good will come when we enter the house of the Lord and live with Him forever.

Soul-crushing speech does not look good or merciful to us, especially when we are in the middle of it. True, but that blood-stained Cross does not look good either. Yet it is God's it is on the Cross where we see God's glory. By now, we know that our problem is that we do not fully understand the goodness and mercy of that blood-stained Cross. Who would have thought to have the Holy One die for unholy humanity? Only God, who is good, can plan the utter goodness and mercy of that blood-stained Cross.

God designed that blood-stained Cross to demonstrate how His goodness and mercy follows us. Therefore, His goodness and mercy will be evident in those soul-crushing conversations and the affect they have on us. Look for it. God will lead us through the hurt that stings with every word spoken or heard. God is always up to something that is for our specific good and His glory, even in our most despairing times.

By now, you should not be surprised by what I say. Do we think that God, who did not spare His one and only Son from death by crucifixion, would spare us from heart-wrenching conversations? We should not flatter ourselves in such a manner. Does this statement deny the pain we experience? Of course not. What we do deny is the thought that this pain is worthless and useless. We affirm that our circumstances in life are God's goodness and mercy following us until we die. In our holy sanctuaries, God is weaving the details of our sweeping narrative into His grand, historic, and redemptive tapestry.

Therefore, all that we experience as Believers is a means by which God accomplishes His two-part goal for us. He ensures that goodness and mercy follow us and then He provides us a place to dwell in His house forever. This confirms the Lord's Prayer where, just as we pray, "Your will be done on earth as it is in heaven." Every hateful word said to us, every experience we have, all the confusion when we Speak CODE, every Earliest Childhood Memory is for our specific good. We may never see the reason for it, and we may never stop grieving over it; nevertheless, it is for our good and God's glory. There is no better end to the matter.

Do we believe this? Maybe we believe it a little. Can we cry to Jesus with the same desperation as the father in Mark 9:24, whose son had an evil spirit since childhood? He exclaimed, "I believe; help my unbelief!" *Jesus, help our unbelief, too.*

WHERE DO WE GO FROM HERE

Where do we go from here? Is there hope that our conversations will ever be soul-satisfying? As I have written, no—not completely in this life. But this we know: we can be free from our Two Influential Forces, self-talk, and Speaking CODE and be assured our lives have meaning and purpose at the foot of that blood-stained Good Cross!

God is our Heavenly Father and has chosen us to be His beloved children. The path of righteousness He designs leads us to Him. There is no need for Speaking CODE as we live out our freedom in Him.

Jesus is our Brother and we inherit all He has. Because Jesus knows us intimately, we abide, believe, and commune in Him, removing our need for Speaking CODE.

The Holy Spirit lives in us and gives us words full of truth and love. We have no need for Speaking CODE.

We hide our identity in Christ alone, on the Cross alone, revealed in the Bible alone, through the help of the Holy Spirit alone, to the glory of God alone!

Amen.

APPENDIX

The following accounts were written by my brave and beloved clients. While I did not ask them to use the terminology I have outlined in Speaking CODE, *see if you can identify these concepts and apply them to your own story. I offer the following with deepest gratidude.*

S's STORY

At various times during my childhood, my mother worked the night shift. She also had bouts of depression. I do not recall many interactions with my mother, mostly errands or housework. She did teach me to knit and sew. My siblings and I never had set chores, but we were often told to do household chores. I am not sure we were taught how the chores should be done, we were just expected to get the work completed. There were many times when my lack of focus inspired first frustration, then exasperated words from my mother. Whether she was tired or depressed, or just had other children to attend to, I perceived her as unavailable. I perceived myself as unworthy of her attention.

My father was more fun than he was an authority figure. He willingly participated in our games and would include us in his interests of hunting and fishing. Crowds or long lines of people made him anxious or impatient. I remember times when we arrived at a fair or picnic only to turn around and go home because the line was too long. Once we drove to a city many hours away to visit a tourist site. Six children aged one to fourteen do not sit in a car for half of a day without some irritation. Upon arriving, we were told to take a good look because we were going home. He had had enough. We had not been trained to respect his word and obey. I learned to attach no permanence to promises.

My father's control of money helped to define my value as a person. I have always known that I should never ask for my dad to pay for anything. I cannot recall a single instance when I was personally yelled at or made to feel I had overstepped because of something I had requested. But I know there were arguments between my parents when my mother spent too many pennies on some unapproved item. My brother shared with me that he had asked for a couple of dollars for admission to a school event and was denied, only to watch another brother be given the money and told he was a football player and needed to attend. I observed all this. No doubt my child's mind believed that I was not important enough or deserving enough to receive help from my father. Not a dollar for a dance. Not a new pair of shoes. Not a ride home so I could participate in an after-school activity. I learned to avoid situations rather than ask for anything. Asking runs the risk of being told no, of being rejected. I still believe I am not worthy of receiving what I want or need. There is a constant mulling in my head: do I want something enough to risk asking for it and being denied? I usually do not ask. I did not and do not feel valuable.

Children at school teased me, because I was chubby, I thought, or maybe because I was quiet. Rather than stand up for myself, I retreated from my classmates. I played alone. I do not remember sharing this with my parents. I did not ask for consolation or help. I often said, "If I don't get along with one sibling, I can just go play with another." These are the roots of a pattern of running away from difficult situations. I struggle with conflict resolution to this day.

My second-grade teacher sticks out in my mind as someone I feared. I was singled out and embarrassed at the front of the class. A triangular ruler whacked my knuckles as payment for inattention. Everyone saw. Everyone knew. I did not seek help, but instead coped in the best way I could. Hiding, if not already part of my personality, became routine that year. At recess I played by myself. There was a large tree just off the school grounds that lent itself to imaginative play. I felt invisible. I did not ask for, and so did not obtain, help or attention when I needed it at home, and I did not know how to attain it anywhere else. (Note: I could not describe myself as a hider until I was in my fifties.) My childhood taught me that I was on my own. I believed that no help was available to me in any situation.

As a teen I never dreamed of my wedding day. I would not have one. My life would be a solitary one. I would be happy that way. More accurately, I would survive. I had no dreams of the future. Just get by. I met and married a man who made me believe that I was loved. He told me he loved me and even convinced me I was beautiful. His past held secrets of being molested, which caused him to believe no one could love him. (Here I will note that we each needed counseling as individuals before we added the complexity of a relationship, but one of us did not know we needed it, and the other could not bear to deal with the past. We kept our pasts to ourselves because we could not articulate them to each other.) Most often we hung out with his friends or did what he wanted. Looking back, I had already learned that merely identifying what I wanted opened me up to rejection not just of my desire, but of me. He was dismissive of my contrasting opinions and rarely heard what others said. I could not insist that he hear me. I was not entitled to be heard. I could articulate as fact that he never lost an argument. I could not recognize his focus on himself or his inability to empathize with other people. I would accept the love he professed, and life would be better than I had ever dreamed.

As time passed, I inwardly knew I was being stifled by my husband. I deferred to how he wanted to spend time together, and now I was giving in to his perception of me. He defined who I was to me and seldom got it right. He assigned motives for everything I did that he did not like and despised me for those motives. Standing up for myself was a skill I did not possess. There were a handful of instances that resulted in physical harm to me. Each was preceded by my attempt to stand up for myself. Once I had missed a direction and could not read the map quickly enough to make an exit. He yelled and I yelled back. He punched me in the arm. Silence. When he calmed down, he requested that I wear shirts that would cover up the darkening bruise. He could see it, and so would his family, since we were en route to vacation with them. Nothing in my suitcase for this July beach vacation would cover the evidence of his aggression. I sat there and thought about how very badly I did not want to do this anymore. The car crossed a body of water. Jump, and it would be over. I had no fear of the fall. What held me in the car was the knowledge that this would be the final memory my three babies would have of their mother. I could endure being invisible and silent. I could survive.

Verbal attacks from my husband affected not only me but our children. When I called my husband out for what he was doing, he accused me of always taking up for others and never being on his side. I felt trapped. My kids were trapped, but they would someday get out of the house. They would leave. I developed strategies for drawing his attention away from the children, so they would not feel the full effects of his irrational behavior. I could shift his focus away from them, but not in a way that was healthy for any of us.

My husband was controlling and manipulative and deeply in need of God's love. I did not recognize any signs of dysfunction in him when I married him. I now believe and accept that my exact childhood prepared me to marry this person who would eventually hurt me. I believe God has given me the drive to do for others what I cannot ask for myself, and so I could stay with this man. God gave his precious child, my husband, to me to love here on Earth and to shine light in his life whether he saw it or not. I am not perfect by any means. I retreated from him and "hid" when he lashed out with words or looks of displeasure over who I was.

When going through a very dark time, we were counseled to ask God to show us His good. I was privileged to then remind my husband of what God was showing us while he lay in hospice care. I was entrusted to hold his hand when he passed away. I can praise God for all the ways He protected me, one being that I could not grasp how abusive it was to be molded into what my husband wanted me to be instead of the person God designed me to be. God has given me strength when I had none of my own. I am now free to begin to discover who I am, redeeming the misconceptions I have of myself. "Be transformed by the renewing of your mind, that you may prove what is that good and acceptable and perfect will of God" (Romans12:2 NKJV). When my husband passed, I was on a mission to root out every thought held captive by lies. The urgency was fueled by the need to be able to help my children recover from their childhood. My focus is shifting to the understanding that perhaps I am supposed to thrive. It is still scary to make a decision based on what I want to do, or to give myself permission to want anything at all.

A few years before the death of my husband, I began participating in a Bible study with other women in the church. I became a Christian when I was young, but studying and discussing Scripture in the safety of this small group increased my understanding of who God truly is and what He has done throughout history. God has distinct purposes for each of us. We are to live in community with fellow Believers and to live boldly among those around us. We are not to live in fear of this world. God's glory shines brightly in our weakness. These are truths that echo in my mind as I try to live courageously and overcome my perception of worthlessness. I am learning to not only accept help, but to ask for it. Communicating with people can trigger intense fear in me. There is no reason to expect rejection except that I have attached feelings of rejection to interactions with people for as long as I can remember. But we are called to communicate the Gospel. To people. I am confident that God will continue to equip me to overcome the many fears that fight for control of my life.

LIZZIE ROSE's STORY

My house wasn't big. It was a pretty, two-level rancher with a massive yard, in a wonderful neighborhood with a pool out back. If someone were to visit and, instead of stepping onto the porch, had gone around the side, they'd find the bathroom window. I used to climb out that window in order to escape the house without my brother seeing me. I got decently good at popping out that screen, perching on the four-inch ledge while I replaced it, and then softly jumping to the flower bed ten feet below. Someone visiting that house when I was twelve might have seen me make that jump. Then I'd run across the yard, airsoft pistol in hand, to visit the cows in the field below.

Looking back, I wonder why I didn't find more healing from being with those cows. Animals often have a way of protecting or healing souls. But not in my case. To me they were just another big terrifying animal that could hurt me anytime they felt inclined, and then not care. Perhaps I could have found a feeling of safety behind the butt of my Berretta airsoft pistol. I could've shot my brothers if they got too close. But there again I would reason with myself that the anger I'd cause them would be more of a motivation than the slight pain a plastic BB induces. Making them angry was something I always avoided.

I couldn't turn to my parents for help. Looking back now, I see that perhaps they would have listened. Perhaps they would've stopped those countless afternoons that my brother would call me into his room and lock the door. I want to think that, had I said something, they'd have told him he couldn't follow me around, and boss me until I went back to his room. However, at that time I knew I couldn't trust them. They had taught me not to trust a soul. So I didn't. Not even them.

How could I have trusted someone who taught me to never disobey my abusers? The boys in my family were always in charge. We served them. We learned early on that they were more useful and, therefore, more valuable than the girls. So I knew for a fact that, had I brought up my fears, I would have been the one to blame for all of it. Thus I lived in fear of becoming pregnant and having to tell my mother that it was her son who did it. I wanted to die. I wanted to run away. I wished and imagined that my parents would tell me they hated me so I could stop feeling crazy for thinking I was worthless.

I never truly trusted anyone but God until I was sixteen and my sister asked me if I had been sexually abused by my brothers. I lied. I told her no. I had already discussed it in my head, and I had decided to never tell anyone. Not ever. But God had different plans for me. He didn't want me hiding. He didn't want lies to rule my life anymore. The first step He had for me was to just say yes. That's all I could say. Actually, my exact words were, "Well, yes. I guess they did." And then she cried. I had never seen someone emote on my behalf. Of course I'd had people mad at me before, but never had someone cared enough to ask what my poems meant, or to show they cared by weeping on my behalf. I saw Jesus that night. He was dressed in jeans and a t-shirt with the face of my sister, and He wept over me.

There are two or three sentences that have followed me all my life. One of them was, "Don't make them mad." Then, as I became autonomous, the sentence changed to, "They are mad at you." The other most prevalent ones were: "You're not worth it," and "Don't trust anyone." Every person I've ever come to trust has one of those sentences hung above their head, in bold lettering visible only to me. As soon as that person shows the smallest amount of discomfort, confusion, or—heaven forbid—frustration, those letters flash red.

The first sentence God taught me to fight was, "Don't feel." This was a follow up statement to every thought I had. The idea of not feeling ruled me for ages. I remember waking up many a morning and pep-talking myself into not showing any emotion that day: "Don't let Mom see you laugh." "Don't get annoyed." I believed that if I didn't show my emotions, my mother couldn't use them against me. Having big eyes and feeling everything very deeply made this my constant struggle. If I have a thought, you can see it on my face. It really doesn't bode well for playing poker. It bodes even worse for living with a manipulative mother.

It's hard to look back and remember how it truly was. I can see God in retrospect far better than I could feel Him at the time. I can see God there, as I watch my twelve-year-old self climb out the second-story window and crawl along the two-foot roof ledge under my brother's window, praying that he wouldn't see me trying to get away. At the time however, I felt completely alone. God has allowed memory to be fluid. The human mind cannot remember in perfect detail, and I thank Him for it. God is not confined by the timeline we live in. He can actively reveal Himself to us in the past if we will recall the days of old as He tells us to. He is merciful to reveal Himself in our memories when we cannot see Him in the present.

Perhaps I heard someone else say it, or maybe a friend told me, but somehow God taught me that blanket statements were lies. If the correct path of life is narrow, then so is the brush that paints the way. He showed me that painting every human with the same broad brush was going to lead me to a lonely, but more importantly, unfruitful life. Not every man wants to hurt me. Not every father screams at his children. Not every family pretends things didn't happen. Of all the things I fear, a wasted life is by far the most frightening. I'd rather fight my own mind every day then live in the fear that Christ's death freed me from.

I've learned that the words which shaped my life then do not have to shape it now. I can exit out of our timeline, move back into my memories, and address the lies with truth. Lies don't rule me anymore.

K's STORY

Sitting across from my in-laws in our living room my anger boiled to the surface. "You don't know where I am from? Vancouver is on the West Coast and they don't speak French there. My mom is from Quebec, but I am from Vancouver. You can just look it up on the map!"My mother-in-law, confounded, tried to explain that she isn't in the habit of looking at maps and doesn't understand why I am making a big deal of something so insignificant. She suggested that the family doesn't really need to know a lot about where I came from. They love me, so isn't that all that matters?

No, this was anathema. How could someone possibly say they loved me and not be willing to ask questions and get to know even the most basic facts about my life story? It reinforced what I had already been thinking: that she wanted to fashion me into the daughter-in-law she wished me to be rather than get to know the messy and interesting life I had really lived.

What followed was a heated interaction that went nowhere good. Both sides said things that weren't helpful. In the end, I was hurt and shocked at their indifference about something I thought was self-evident. They were lost and confused as to why I cared so much about something so seemingly trivial. From their perspective, they were loving people, and that's all that mattered.

It wasn't until years later that I recognized that my near obsession with being known was connected to one of my first Early Childhood Memories. I grew up in a home where, for the first ten years of my life, my father was an alcoholic. It was still a relatively happy home, because he wasn't an angry drunk and my mom was skilled enough on her own to care well for our basic needs. But still, being the oldest and my personality such as it was, I was very aware of his drinking habits. Not only that, but after I became a Christian, somewhere between the ages five and seven, I was convinced that it was my job to help him become sober through my prayers and by passing him relevant Bible verses written on scraps of paper. This was particularly important for me to do because my mom was not a Christian. I felt a special sense of responsibility in moving him toward sobriety, because we were on the same team.

One of my most vivid childhood memories dates back to third grade and starts with me sitting on the floor, in a circle, with my classmates. We were all tasked with sharing something about our lives with the group. I spoke about my dad's drinking habits. I have no recollection of the details of what I said, but it was enough to prompt the concern of my third grade teacher, who then called my mom in for a meeting. When my mom got home, it was clear I had done something wrong. I was sent straight to my room. She then told me not to talk about his drinking anymore and that she had told my teacher he only drank socially. I was mistaken. And that was it.

Early on it was made clear to me that you don't talk about your life with other people. Privacy was paramount. But at the same time, I desperately wanted to talk about what was going on in our home. I hoped that people would ask, but usually they didn't.

So when confronted with my mother-in-law, who seemed uninterested in my backstory and didn't see any reason for asking even basic questions about my past, I felt I couldn't let it go. Here was another adult who seemed to have little interest in the truth but wanted me to play a role in maintaining an image for her benefit. My messy story, including the fairly recent suicide of my sister, didn't fit in again with the nice tale that my in-laws wanted to present as part of their big family story. From my perspective, I saw another set of parents leaving me on my own again to deal with a painful reality, telling me to just "hush up" and pretend it didn't happen.

But when I was having the conversation with my in-laws, I had no idea why I was feeling so strongly about their not knowing where I was from. However, I did know I had a deeply developed conviction that people should be interested in getting to know others, and they should do so by asking questions. In the moment, I couldn't have explained to you the rationale and the thought process behind my conviction. It just blew up in our faces.

E's STORY

As a small child I didn't wonder where hell was. I knew right where it was. It was under my bed.

I'm not sure what all the contributing factors were. There are the obvious ones: growing up in a very fundamentalist church, being in a religious family, and the formative years of behavior-learning and you-better-nots.

I'm sure these played a roll. But a lot of times I think it's just how I'm wired: the hyper-sensitivity.

Whatever the cause, I was sure of one thing: unlike the monsters of most kids' fears, it was hell that was under my bed, its flames licking up the sides at me, the devil's arms reaching up to pull me down and under into the pit.

Then there were the faces. This was even worse, and more real to me. Faces floating in the air in my room, genderless and foreboding. Looking.

Lying in my bed, gripped by terror, I could see the enemy arms reaching up and searching, seeking to find me. Nearly paralyzed by fear, I'd center myself in my bed as perfectly as possible and do the one thing that brought me comfort and perceived safety.

I'd line up my stuffed animals around me, as a barrier that for some reason was strong enough to keep away the supernatural. One by one, I'd set them around me until I was surrounded, encircled with protection and provided some semblance of peace.

It's been almost three decades since those bedtime struggles. And almost three since my first freeing encounter with Christ.

But the same fears and struggles still leak through.

I've been no stranger to the hard side of life. Before leaving for college, I had lost two grandparents, been betrayed by my best friend, watched my mom battle mental health struggles in deep waters, and walked alongside my dad as he fought cancer.

I'm not sure when it started feeling like hell flames were licking against my life again, but once my thirties hit I started feeling scalded.

We had our first miscarriage, then another the next year, and with that one a storm of complications. A rare type of ectopic pregnancy meant two rounds of chemo to get rid of the lingering gestational sac. I still ended up with sudden life-threatening hemorrhaging at home, with only my two small boys with me. An ambulance ride and emergency hysterectomy later, I found myself burning in suffering, and in all of this same storm surge, my dear mother-in-law was almost lost as well. She then received the heart-wrenching diagnosis of ALS.

Two babies gone, barren and mourning for my mother-in-law, I found myself also strapped with a catheter due to a bladder injury I suffered during the surgery. At some point during all of this, my brain took a new stance with PTSD.

What do you do when it seems the devil wins? When you can't see God tying the bow of the happy ending? Rescuing you from the flames?

I've found as an adult that I still reach for those same young coping skills, only now instead of stuffed bears and dolls, I reach for new pieces of protection to try to surround myself with. And these look like good things.

Rigid Bible reading, faithful prayer lists, specific devotionals, adamant church attendance. The right steps, proper motions, followed rules. Obsessive protocols and principles.

Returning to a place of effort and legalism and works to try to keep the enemy at bay. I'm that little girl under a steepled roof singing, "Don't let Satan blow it out, I'm gonna let it shine," and "Read your Bible, pray every day, or you'll shrink, shrink, shrink."

But I was shrinking, and I was forgetting that the only One who can keep my light from being blown out is God Himself.

This hyper awareness of the enemy—but where has my awareness of my Rescuer been? This knowledge of dark forces, but do I know I don't battle alone? Do I think I'm battling alone, or is it that my view of God is itself tainted, and left hollow of His love and control?

Do I flinch at the enemy or at my God?

Who do I think is actually hurting me?

I've found myself tearing down the walls of bad theology and practices, and, in this new place of rebuilding, laying out a healthy theology of suffering. I am learning to see His sovereign hand over these events, but learning to rest in His hand being full of love. And I'm finding peace in recognition that the enemy has been crushed.

I need to recognize the importance of the spiritual armor, yes, but not at the cost of viewing my check list as the captain of the army.

I want to rest in abiding in my Father God, the true and victorious Captain, in a way of relationship and joy, not of ritual. I am safe under His wings. Even when it seems the flames are licking.

ENDNOTES

1 Curt Thompson, MD, *The Soul of Shame: Retelling the Stories We Believe About Ourselves* (Downers Grove, IL: InterVarsity Press, 2015), 50.
2 Robert Lowry, "Nothing But the Blood," *Trinity Hymnal: Revised Edition* (Suwanee, GA: Great Commission Publications, 2008), 307.
3 Westminster Confession of Faith, 1648, Larger Catechism, Question 1
4 Pagliacci by Ruggero Leoncavallo, aria Vesti la Giubba
5 A. D. Bauer, *The Beginning: A Second Look at the First Sin* (Baltimore, MD: Square Halo Books, 2004).
6 A litany is a series of petitions used in church services, usually recited by the pastor and responded to by the people in a prescribed format. Litanies are found mainly in liturgical worship services, but other churches incorporate prescribed prayers in their services.
7 There's Only One Messiah, video at www.paultripp.com
8 Roger E. Olson, "Did Karl Barth Really Say . . . 'Jesus Loves Me, This I Know?'" *My Evangelical Arminian Musings,* January 24, 2013, https://www.patheos.com/blogs/rogereolson/2013/01/did-karl-barth-really-say-jesus-loves-me-this-i-know/.
9 https://www.stuarttownend.co.uk/song/in-christ-alone/.
10 C.S. Lewis, *The Weight of Glory and Other Addresses* (New York: Harper Collins, 1949), 46.
11 Michael Crawford, "Let's Talk About It—Part 3: Racism," Freedom Church, August 20, 2017, https://www.freedomchurchbaltimore.org/sermons.
12 Ken Sande, *Peacefakers, Peacebreakers, and Peacemakers Parables,* (Hannibal Books, 2005).
13 For more information on this topic, I highly recommend Ed Welch's article, "They Call it Narcissism" (*CCEF,* April 27, 2018, https://www.ccef.org/they-call-it-narcissism/).
14 www.paultripp.com/bible-study/posts/ecclesiastes-summary
15 *The Hiding Place,* Corrie Ten Boom, John L. Sherrill, Elizabeth Sherrill, Old Tappan, NJ 1971
16 https://www.thegospelcoalition.org/article/desire-friend-of-the-devil-grace-from-god/ https://assets.speakcdn.com/assets/1804/rhrn_transcript_survival_skill_5.pdf
17 *Peacefakers, Peacebreakers, and Peacemakers Parables*
I highly recommend reading the *Seven A's of Confession* from Peacemaker Ministries. This explains how to achieve true and lasting forgiveness that leads to unity. It is one of the best guides on how people can biblically enter into painful discussions—despite their CODE Speaking, ECMs, PPIFSt and PPIFEx—and find forgiveness leading to reconciliation.
18 Ed Welch, "When Familiar Beats Good," *CCEF,* February 21, 2017, https://www.ccef.org/familiar-beats-good/.
19 Paul David Tripp, "Living in Job's House," *The Journal of Biblical Counseling,* Vol. 22:4 (2004).
20 William Shakespeare, *Hamlet* (New York: Washington Square Library, 1992), 127.
21 St. Augustine's *Confessions* (Lib 1,1-2,2.5,5: CSEL 33, 1-5)
22 Horatio G. Spafford, "It Is Well with My Soul," *Trinity Hymnal: Revised Edition* (Suwanee, GA: Great Commission Publications, 2008), 691.
23 C.S. Lewis, *The Silver Chair* (New York: HarperCollins Publishers, 1953), 196–197.

ABOUT THE AUTHOR

DIANA DI PASQUALE

Diana Di Pasquale writes this book to connect our broken conversations to Jesus, the only true Lover of our souls. She has over 20 years experience as a counselor and writes as a friend talking to another over a cup of hot tea. Diana and her Alan Dean live in Baltimore, Maryland. They love on their four independent-thinking children, two talented sons-in-law, six marvelous grandchildren, one darling great-granddaughter, and incredibly happy grandpuppies. Diana and Alan love competition in marriage, cooking, woods-walking, and especially café sitting in Europe. Diana is president of Square Halo Books and runs Third Way Counseling. *thirdwaycounseling@gmail.com*

ACKNOWLEDGEMENTS

To Lou Catelli for staying out of the disagreements
and providing the extraordinary view.
To my long suffering kids Maya, Ryan, William,
Suzannah, Brad, and Chara. You know my failures.
To my very heart Lyric, Lexei, Isabella, Isaac, Gideon, Silas, and Solis.
To Dear My Ned and his one and only Leslie. Who would have guessed?
To Alice, Kim, and the tearful road from Baltimore to Glenside.
To my Lunch Bunch.
To John, GM Extraordinair.
To Pastors like Mike and Jeremy who know how to "shut up and preach!"
To CCEF and the School of Biblical Counseling.
To every client-friend who shared their lives with me.
To Amazing Grace that saved a wretch like me.

Grace and peace from God our Father and the Lord Jesus Christ. I thank my God always when I remember you in my prayers (Philemon 1:3–4)

KEY TERMS

And/And

The multidimensional approach we see in Scripture where two apparent contradictions can be true at the same time. For example, in this body we are both Saints and Sinners.

Communication Hijackers

A communication approach where someone shares his heart and we turn his thoughts around so that the conversation is about us.

Communication Hitchhikers

Those people who speak words of empathy as they encourage others in their expressed pain.

Earliest Childhood Memory

The earliest memory we can recall. ECMs influence how we take in and give out information.

The Five Sabateurs

Five components that sabotage communication. These are making assumptions, not forgiving, not separating our past from our present, not finding our identity in Christ alone and failing to find meaning and purpose in our suffering.

Flip side of the same coin

A technique we use to prevent us from repeating a detrimental behavior done to us by determining we will behave the opposite. This is unwise thinking. What we need is a new coin altogether.

God's specific goodness

A sure belief that goes beyond the acknowledgement that God is good. God's specific goodness debunks our idea that God is good to us most of the time based on what we think we need. God's specific goodness is precisely what God knows we need all the time. This includes the suffering we endure. Ruth and Lazarus are examples of God's specific goodness in the details of their lives.

Holy Sanctuaries

The workroom in which God places us so that we can be still and learn His goodness. For example, Jonah's holy sanctuary was in the belly of a great fish. Our holy sanctuaries often intersect with others like Daniel and Darius.

Misguided Christian Entitlements

A belief we Christians hold, either secretly or openly, that God must behave in the way we think best for all concerned, particularly us.

Necessary Relationships

Connections which we cannot sever. These include parent to child, husband to wife, and sibling to sibling. Other relationships are necessary but can be severed. Legal or court mandated decrees can become necessary relationships such as adoption or court appointed guardianship.

One-Fleshing

The relationship between one man (husband) and one woman (wife) that God joins together so that the two become one flesh.

Paradigm Shift

A total directional change in your thinking. For example, before your paradigm shift you believed one thing. However, upon further investigation you changed your thinking and now believe the exact opposite.

Past Powerful Identity Forming Experiences (PPIFEx)

Physical events in our lives that leave a deep and lasting impression on us and form our identity.

Past Powerful Identity Forming Statements (PPIFSt)

Statements (verbal or non-verbal) we have heard that leaves a deep and lasting impression on us and form our identity.

Path of Righteousness

The totality of God's sovereign circumstances He directs in our lives that bring Him glory and provides for our good.

Perceived Overshadowing Emotional/Physical Suffering (POEPS)

A range of feelings associated with physical or emotional illness from our past, real or perceived that produces fear. This fear causes us to think and behave in ways that lead us to be either an observer or participant in our lives.

Personal Communication Objectives

The approach we use in conversations to achieve our goals. The methodology can be on a broad spectrum from aggressive to passive language. We can gravitate toward ***Animators, Wallflowers,*** or ***Provocateurs***, as each type is defined in this book.

Scene Stealing Thieves

A communication approach where we steel another's "thunder" which minimizes or exaggerates the speakers' pain.

Speaking CODE

A type of communication when we first have an internal conversation (self-talk), but only tell the listener snippets of our thoughts. The listener now has the difficult task of interpreting our meaning without access to all our thoughts.

Two Influential Forces

Our ***Earliest Childhood Memory*** plus the combination of our *Past Powerful Identity Forming Statements* and *Past Powerful Identity Forming Experiences*.

LET'S TALK ABOUT SOME GOOD BOOKS

THE BEGINNING: A SECOND LOOK AT THE FIRST SIN

"... a very readable and engaging discussion on the nature and consequences of the original sin using the biblical accounts as his primary authority ... A sound background in scripture, a solid presentation of his positions, and generous application make this book a very good reference on the subject."
—*The American Journal of Biblical Theology*

GODLY CHARACTER(S): INSIGHTS FOR SPIRITUAL PASSION FROM THE LIVES OF 8 WOMEN IN THE BIBLE

"... these 'great eight' propel you towards habits of godliness—putting you in a place to receive grace and fall more deeply in love with your savior—and that in His love you might be re-shaped and re-formed."
—ROBERT WILLIAM ALEXANDER, author of *The Gospel-Centered Life at Work*

REVEALED: A STORYBOOK BIBLE FOR GROWN-UPS

"*Revealed* sets out to crush any notion that the Bible is a safe, inspirational read. Instead the artwork here, historic and contemporary, takes a warts-and-all approach to even the most troubling passages, trading well-meaning elision for unvarnished truth."
—J. MARK BERTRAND—novelist, speaker, and founder of the Bible Design Blog

NAILED IT: 365 READINGS FOR ANGRY OR WORN-OUT PEOPLE

"... if you, like me, long for a devotional that is sharpening, witty, and downright real, well then, you simply must read this book."
—KAREN SWALLOW PRIOR, author of *On Reading Well: Finding the Good Life Through Great Books*

GOOD POSTURE: ENGAGING CURRENT CULTURE WITH ANCIENT FAITH

"I couldn't recommend this book more highly. Please read it cover to cover. Please share it. And please, for the love of God, start living it."
—SCOTT SAULS, pastor and author of *Jesus Outside the Lines*

SQUAREHALOBOOKS.COM